Histories of Tax Evasion, Avoidance and Resistance

Tax evasion, tax avoidance and tax resistance are widespread phenomena in political, economic, social and fiscal history from antiquity through to medieval, early modern and modern times. This book shows how different groups and individuals around the globe have succeeded or failed in not paying their due taxes, whether in kind or in cash, on their properties, or on their crops.

It analyses how, throughout history, wealthy and poor taxpayers have tried to avoid or reduce their tax burden by negotiating with tax authorities, through practices of legal tax avoidance or illegal tax evasion, by filing lawsuits, seeking armed resistance or by migration, and how state authorities have dealt with such acts of claim making, defiance, open resistance or elusion. It fills an important research gap in tax history, addressing questions of tax morale and fairness, and how social and political inequality was negotiated through taxation. It gives rich insights into the development of citizen-state relationships throughout the course of history. The book comprises case studies from Ancient Athens, Roman Egypt, Medieval Europe, Early Modern Mexico, the Ottoman Empire, Nigeria under British colonial rule, the United Kingdom of the early 20th century, Greece during the Second World War, as well as West Germany, Switzerland, Sweden and the US in the 20th century, including transnational entanglements in the world of late-modern offshore finance and taxation. The authors are experts in fiscal, economic, financial, legal, social and/or cultural history.

The book is intended for students, researchers and scholars of economic and financial history, social and world history and political economy.

Korinna Schönhärl is the Heisenberg-Professor for Modern History at Paderborn University.

Gisela Hürlimann is Professor of History of Technology and Economic History at the Technical University (TU) Dresden.

Dorothea Rohde is Lecturer of Ancient History at the University of Bielefeld.

Financial History
Edited by Farley Grubb and Anne L. Murphy

Money, Politics and Power
Banking and Public Finance in Wartime England, 1694-96
Richard A. Kleer

Regulation of the London Stock Exchange
Share Trading, Fraud and Reform 1914–1945
Chris Swinson

Monetary Plurality in Local, Regional and Global Economies
Edited by Georgina M. Gómez

Share Trading, Fraud and the Crash of 1929
A Biography of Clarence Hatry
Chris Swinson

The Origins of Modern Banking in Spain
Monetary Plurality and Local Monopolies
Edited by Carles Sudrià and Yolanda Blasco-Martel

European Investment in Greece in the Nineteenth Century
A Behavioural Approach to Financial History
Korinna Schönhärl

A History of Public Banking in Portugal in the 19th and 20th Centuries
The Caixa Geral de Depósitos
Pedro Lains

Histories of Tax Evasion, Avoidance and Resistance
Edited by Korinna Schönhärl, Gisela Hürlimann and Dorothea Rohde

For more information about this series, please visit: www.routledge.com/series/FINHIS

Histories of Tax Evasion, Avoidance and Resistance

Edited by Korinna Schönhärl, Gisela Hürlimann and Dorothea Rohde

We acknowledge support for the Open Access publication by the Saxon State Digitization Program for Science and Culture.

Routledge
Taylor & Francis Group
LONDON AND NEW YORK

First published 2023
by Routledge
4 Park Square, Milton Park, Abingdon, Oxon OX14 4RN

and by Routledge
605 Third Avenue, New York, NY 10158

Routledge is an imprint of the Taylor & Francis Group, an informa business

British Library Cataloguing-in-Publication Data
A catalogue record for this book is available from the British Library

Library of Congress Cataloging-in-Publication Data
Names: Schönhärl, Korinna, editor. | Hürlimann, Gisela, editor. | Rohde, Dorothea, editor.
Title: Histories of tax evasion, avoidance and resistance / edited by Korinna Schönhärl, Gisela Hürlimann and Dorothea Rohde.
Description: 1 Edition. | New York, NY : Routledge, 2023. | Series: Financial history | Includes bibliographical references and index.
Identifiers: LCCN 2022035182 (print) | LCCN 2022035183 (ebook) | ISBN 9781032366739 (hardback) | ISBN 9781032366746 (paperback) | ISBN 9781003333197 (ebook)
Subjects: LCSH: Tax evasion.
Classification: LCC HV6341 .H67 2023 (print) | LCC HV6341 (ebook) | DDC 364.1/338--dc23/eng/20221020
LC record available at https://lccn.loc.gov/2022035182
LC ebook record available at https://lccn.loc.gov/2022035183

ISBN: 978-1-032-36673-9 (hbk)
ISBN: 978-1-032-36674-6 (pbk)
ISBN: 978-1-003-33319-7 (ebk)

DOI: 10.4324/9781003333197

Typeset in Bembo
by KnowledgeWorks Global Ltd.

Contents

Tables and Figures

Tables

Figures

Contributors

Prof. Dr Steven A. Bank is the Paul Hastings Professor of Business Law at **UCLA School of Law**. He has taught Federal Income Taxation, Business Associations, and a variety of related courses. Professor Bank's primary area of research generally explores the taxation of business entities through the lens of legal and business history. He has published numerous articles and chapters in the fields of business taxation, tax policy and tax history and has authored or co-authored several books, including *Anglo-American Corporate Taxation* (Cambridge University Press, 2011), *From Sword to Shield: The Transformation of the Corporate Income Tax, 1861 to Present* (Oxford University Press, 2010), and *War and Taxes* (Urban Institute Press, 2008) (with Kirk Stark and Joseph Thorndike).

Christina Bröker is a Research Assistant at **Paderborn University**. She studied history at RWTH Aachen University and graduated with a master's degree in 2017. Her master's thesis examined the relationship between King John (1199–1216) and his half-brother William of Salisbury. Her PhD thesis focuses once again on English history with the working title "Grim Look and Teeth-Gnashing. Conditions of Constructing John and Henry III's (emotional) Behaviour in Chronicles and Letters (1199–1272)". The thesis combines her general research interests in English history, royal history and the history of emotions. Since 2017, she has been working on her PhD at the University of Regensburg where she was a Research Assistant. To further develop this research, she received a PhD scholarship from the German Historical Institute in London in 2021.

Dr Lucia Cecchet is Assistant Professor in Greek History at the Department of Historical Studies of the **University of Milan**, which she joined in 2021 after working at the Universities of Mainz, Zurich, Trento and Heidelberg. She is interested in the social and cultural history of the Greek world from the classical to the imperial period, with a focus on poverty and citizenship. Her most recent publications include the books *Poverty in Athenian Public Discourse* (Steiner 2015), *Citizens in the Graeco-Roman World* (with A. Busetto, Brill 2017), *The Ancient War's Impact on the Home Front* (with Ch. Degelmann and M. Patzelt, Cambridge Scholars

2019) and *Poverty in the Graeco-Roman World: Discourses and Realities* (with F. Carlà-Uhink and C. Machado, Routledge 2022). She is a member of the international research group *Twisted-Transfer: Discursive Constructions of Corruption in Ancient Greece and Rome.*

PD Dr Kerstin Droß-Krüpe is a Senior Researcher at **Ruhr-Universität Bochum**. She previously held positions at Philipps-University Marburg, Kassel University and Leopold-Franzens-Universität Innsbruck. She studied ancient history, classical archaeology and business administration at Philipps-University Marburg and gained her PhD with a thesis about textile economics in the Roman province of Egypt, which was published as a monograph in 2011. Her postdoctoral thesis dealt with the reception of the Babylonian Queen Semiramis from antiquity to Baroque opera and was published as her second monograph in 2020. Her main research interests are ancient economic history, ancient textiles studies, the reception of antiquity and gender studies.

Aniko Fehr is a Graduate Assistant in Financial History at the **University of Lausanne.** After studying social sciences and history in Lausanne (Faculty of Social and Political Sciences), she obtained her master's degree in social and cultural anthropology in 2010. For two years she worked as a project manager in a non-profit association, and in 2013 resumed her studies at the Faculty of Letters of the University of Lausanne. She obtained a master's degree in history in 2015 and in the same year she began her PhD on the financial policy of the Swiss Confederation between 1958 and 1977.

Prof. Dr Boris Gehlen has been Professor of Business History at **Stuttgart University** since 2021. He has previously worked at the Universities of Bonn (History Department), Cologne, Bochum and Vienna as well as at the Leibniz Institute for Contemporary History Munich. He holds a PhD (*Paul Silverberg (1876 bis 1959). Ein Unternehmer*, Stuttgart: Steiner 2007) and postdoctoral thesis (*Der Deutsche Handelstag und die Regulierung der deutschen Wirtschaft 1861–1914*, manuscript 2014, under contract with Mohr Siebeck, Tübingen) from the University of Bonn. Gehlen's main research fields are business history, corporate governance, history of regulation and financial history. He has recently published a book on *Die Thyssen-Bornemisza-Gruppe: Eine transnationale business group in Zeiten des Wirtschaftsnationalismus (1932–1955)*, Paderborn: Ferdinand Schöningh 2021. He also co-edited a special issue "Economic Nationalism and the Nationality of the Company" which appeared in the *Journal of Modern European History* (18 (2020) 1).

Dr Thibaud Giddey is a Lecturer (maître-assistant) at the **University of Lausanne** and an Associated Researcher at the **University of Oxford.** He obtained his PhD in arts (history) at the University of Lausanne in 2017. He was a visiting Research Fellow at KU Leuven (2013), City University London (2014) and Uppsala University (2019). His research interests include the history of banking supervision, financial scandals, the development of political and financial elites, the history of white-collar crime and of lawyers as business professionals and, finally, the development of taxation and tax-induced mobility. His book *Histoire de la régulation des banques en Suisse (1914–1972)* (Librairie Droz 2019) deals with the evolution of banking supervision in Switzerland during the twentieth century and draws on numerous unpublished archival documents.

Rodrigo Gordoa de la Huerta is a historian at the **Instituto de Investigaciones Dr. José María Luis Mora, Mexico City**. He specialises in the fiscal and social history of Colonial Mexico, particularly in the tax farming system established in New Spain between the seventeenth and eighteenth centuries, and its relation with the institutional design of the Spanish Royal Treasury in the Indies. He is currently working on a PhD project regarding the administrative and judicial institutions of the Royal Treasury of New Spain and the distribution of quicksilver for mining production in the seventeenth century. He also collaborates in different history divulgation publications and radio programmes. He studied history at Instituto Mora and holds a postgraduate diploma in economic history from the National Autonomous University of Mexico (UNAM) and a master's degree in modern and contemporary history (Instituto Mora). His most recent book is *La Contaduría General de Alcabalas. Una oficina y tribunal del real erario novohispano (1677-1756).*

Anna Grotegut most recently worked as a Research Assistant at the Department of Economic History at **Bielefeld University**. From 2018 to 2021, she was a member of the Collaborative Research Centre (SFB) 1288 "Practices of Comparing". She is working on her PhD project focusing on the taxation of real estate. The project rests on the assumption that the economic valuation of real estate for taxation purposes was directly linked to explicit practices of comparison. It concentrates on German and British examples between 1870 and 1939. Grotegut wrote her master's thesis about practices of comparison during the Boxer War in China and graduated from Bielefeld University with a master's degree in history in 2017. She is a participant in the PhD programme of the Bielefeld Graduate School in history and sociology.

Prof. Dr Gisela Hürlimann is Professor of History of Technology and Economic History at the **Technical University (TU) Dresden**. She graduated and earned her PhD at the University of Zurich, was an Assistant Professor (*Oberassistentin*) at ETH Zurich, and wrote her postdoctoral thesis on Swiss tax history in the twentieth century. Her works on taxation also include international workshops (organised during her fellowship at the GHI Washington and as a guest scholar in Kyoto) and international volumes on the *Worlds of Taxation: The Political Economy of Taxing, Spending, and Redistribution Since 1945* (with W. Elliot Brownlee and Eisaku Ide, Palgrave

MacMillan 2018) and on taxation and inequality (*Fiscalité et inégalités*, with Sébastien Guex and Matthieu Leimgruber, Chronos 2021). Currently, she is co-authoring a DFG-research group proposal on tax reforms in Germany and other European countries between the 1850s and the 2000s. Other research interests refer to the history of mobility, network infrastructure, gender and technology, environmental humanities, commodities, and farm animals and their "production cycle".

Dr Daniel Olisa Iweze is a Senior Lecturer with the Department of History and International Studies, **University of Benin, Nigeria**. He holds a doctorate degree in social history from the University of Nigeria, Nsukka. He also holds a bachelor's and a master's in history from Bayero University, Kano. His research interests are in economic and social history. Dr Iweze has won several fellowships, research grants and awards including a fellowship at the French Institute for Research in Africa (IFRA 2013), an Individual Research Grant (IRG 2017) from the African Peacebuilding Network (APN) of the Social Science Research Council (SSRC) of the Carnegie Corporation, New York, USA and a scholarship from the Carnegie Corporation of New York (CCNY 2019). He has participated in many workshops including the African Peacebuilding Network (APN), Methods Training Workshop, Legon, Accra; African Peacebuilding Network (APN), Training Workshop on Writing and Dissemination, Rabat, Morocco, 2017; African Studies Association's Pipeline for Emerging African Studies Scholar Workshop, Boston, USA, 2019 among others. He has published a number of articles in reputable scholarly international and local journals and contributed chapters to edited book volumes.

Dr Yener Koç holds a master's and a doctorate degree from the History Department of **Boğaziçi University**. In his PhD dissertation titled *Nomadic Pastoral Tribes at the Intersection of the Ottoman, Persian, and Russian Empires (1820s–1890s)*, he examines the social, political and economic relations between nomadic tribes and imperial states during the nineteenth century. His main research areas are the social and economic history of the Ottoman Empire and the Middle East, pastoral economy, environmental history and digital humanities.

Dr Vasilis G. Manousakis teaches at the Political Sciences Department of **Aristotle University of Thessaloniki**. He studied international and European studies at Panteion University in Athens (B.A. and master's) and War Studies at King's College London (MA). His PhD from Aristotle University of Thessaloniki (Political Sciences Department) is entitled: "Economy and Politics in Wartime Greece, 1940-1944" and won the first prize from the Vasiliki and Olga Stavropoulou Foundation in 2015. His main research foci are the economic and social history of Greece during the 1940s, war economies, intelligence and the history of military technology. His book *Στο νότιο προπύργιο του Ράιχ* (*In the southern bastion of the Reich*) was recently published by Crete University Press. His postdoctoral project (University of Crete) deals with the black market in Occupied Greece (1941–1944).

PD Dr Christian Marx is a Senior Researcher at the **Leibniz Institute for Contemporary History in Munich** and currently working on a collective biography of the leading figures at the Bank deutscher Länder and the Bundesbank during the first two decades of West Germany. After studying mathematics, history and political science he worked at the research cluster "Societal Dependencies and Social Networks" at the Universities of Trier and Mainz and on a project on corporate networks in Germany, France and the United States (1896–1938). In 2011, he finished his PhD with a study of the corporate governance of the German iron and steel company Gutehoffnungshütte (Walstein 2013), and in 2020 he completed his postdoctoral thesis on European multinational companies of the chemical industry in the last third of the twentieth century. His main fields of research are contemporary European history, business history, economic and financial history and corporate networks.

Sylvain Praz is a PhD student at the **University of Lausanne**. He studied humanities at the same university (2010–2016), graduating with a master's specialised in history. His master's thesis was on the tax law of 1917 in the Canton of Zurich (*Plus d'argent avec moins d'impôts? La révision de la loi fiscale du canton de Zurich de 1917*, 2016). He is currently writing a thesis on the history of taxes in the cantons of Zurich and Sankt-Gallen, from the mid-nineteenth to the mid-twentieth century. This research is part of a project of the Swiss National Science Foundation, under the direction of Professor Sébastien Guex, which aims to study cantonal taxation in Switzerland.

Dr Rachel Renault is Maîtresse de conférences (Associate Professor) at **Le Mans Université** and Junior Member of the Institut Universitaire de France. She holds a PhD from Université Paris 1-Panthéon-Sorbonne and Westphälische Universität Münster (2014) and was a Postdoctoral Researcher at the École des Hautes Études en Sciences Sociales (Paris). She was also a Lecturer at the Centre for French Studies at Leipzig University and studied at École Normale Supérieure de la Rue d'Ulm (Paris). Her main research interests are the history of taxation, financial history; popular politics and politicisation; social conflict and social strategies; state and territory building, non-state powers and the Holy Roman Empire. She is now investigating conflicts about food supply in the Thuringian area (1648–1848) and their inscription in the different public spheres.

Prof. Dr Dorothea Rohde is a Lecturer of Ancient History at the **University of Bielefeld**. She studied Ancient History, Philosophy and Classical Philology in Bonn, Münster and Rome, and did her PhD in Ancient History at Münster, Rome, London and Kassel. She has also held teaching appointments at Kassel, Münster, Oldenburg and Hamburg.

Her research focuses on the social, political and economic history of the ancient world, particularly the impact of economic factors on social life and politics. She is, inter alia, author of *Zwischen Individuum und Stadtgemeinde. Die Integration von collegia in Hafenstädten* (Vandenhoeck & Ruprecht 2012) and editor (with Michael Sommer) of a sourcebook on ancient economy (WBG 2016). Another monograph focuses on the correlation between public finances and changes in the socio-political elite of Athens in the fourth century BC (*Von der Deliberationsdemokratie zur Zustimmungsdemokratie*, J.B. Metzler 2019), and will be published in 2023 in English translation at Palgrave MacMillan. Her publications also include studies on taxation and tax mentality in classical Greece, especially in Athens and Sparta. In her new project she turns to the social structures of resilience against impoverishment in the ancient world.

Prof. Dr Korinna Schönhärl is a Heisenberg-Professor for Modern History at **Paderborn University**. She holds a PhD from Goethe-University Frankfurt about the economists in the circle around the poet Stefan George (De Gruyter 2008). Her postdoctoral thesis (University Duisburg-Essen) was on European investment in Greece in the nineteenth century (Routledge 2021). Her current research project is entitled "International cultural history of tax morale" and compares discourses on tax paying behaviour in Western Germany, Spain and the USA between the 1940s and 1980s. In 2016/17 Schönhärl was a Research Fellow at the Centre for Advanced Studies in History in Munich. In 2018/19 and 2019/20 she was a guest professor at University Lumière Lyon II and in 2020/21 a substitute professor at the KIT Karlsruhe. Further research foci are moral economics and historiographic methodology.

Dr Mikael Wendschlag, PhD, is a researcher at the Department of Economic History at **Uppsala University, Sweden**. His main research interests are financial supervision, central bank history, financial crisis management and white-collar crime in a historical perspective.

Acknowledgments

This volume is the result of the workshop "Not paying taxes. Tax evasion, tax avoidance and tax resistance in historical perspective", which was organised by the three editors of this publication in March 2020, shortly after widespread pandemic-related lockdown situations came into force in Western Europe. For this reason, we held the workshop digitally on 26 and 27 March 2020. We thank the German Research Foundation (DFG), which funded the workshop as part of the Heisenberg Program. We would also like to thank the Association of Friends and Sponsors of the Goethe University Frankfurt a.M., the Department for Third Mission and the Foundation for the Promotion of International Academic Relations of the Johann Wolfgang Goethe University as well as the Institute for Banking History Research for their support. The Saxon State and University Library (SLUB) Dresden made the Open Access publication of the volume possible through its generous sponsorship. Our special thanks go to Katharine Thomas for the linguistic revision of the manuscript and to Aminah Schneider for standardising the layout and citations.

*Korinna Schönhärl, Gisela Hürlimann
and Dorothea Rohde*

The Ability and Intention of Not Paying Taxes in History

Some Introductory Observations

Korinna Schönhärl, Gisela Hürlimann and Dorothea Rohde

No matter whether the focus is on the Panama, the Paradise or the Pandora Papers[1] or, as in Germany and other European countries, the CumEx-Files[2], revelations of practices to avoid, evade or dodge taxes and to defraud state tax authorities abound. So too do attempts, by governments, the media or organised civil society,[3] to stop, convict or prevent such procedures.[4] Late twentieth and early twenty-first centuries spotlights on tax avoidance mostly illuminate transnational or even global scale practices of so-called ultra-high-net-worth individuals (UHNWI) and their businesses, or the profit-shifting strategies of multinational corporations. In some cases, such individuals or firms pay much reduced taxes offshore, while in other cases, their tax liabilities seem to evaporate on the sinuous paths of shifting and transferring assets, establishing charitable trusts, writing off investments and the like. Yet, the global scope of organised avoidance and evasion schemes is recent, and the attempt to instigate coordinated government action against it by establishing international "fiscal governance" is a novelty.[5] Our volume transcends the scope of present by focusing on the historical dimensions of not paying (due) taxes or not paying taxes at all.

1 The so called "Panama Papers" were first published by newspaper journalists of the International Consortium of Investigative Journalists (ICIJ) in April 2016; the Paradise Papers followed in November 2017 and the online-publishing of the "Pandora Papers" began in October 2021, see ICIJ 2021.

2 Correctiv (2021).

3 We here refer to NGOs such as the internationally organised Tax Justice Network, Oxfam or Attac, some with national platforms, but also to smaller and more regional NGOs like the French *Plate-forme paradis fiscaux et judiciaires* or the German *Netzwerk Steuergerechtigkeit Deutschland.*

4 For the "disclosure work" of the ICJI-media network see above; on government action see for the case of Germany: Federal Ministry of Finance 2021. For the United Kingdom see Seely 2021; for Paraguay see Pierri et al. (2021).

5 On recent measures addressed by the EU Parliament see EU Parliament 2021; on the OECD endeavours to combat international tax avoidance and profit shifting, see OECD (2021); OECD attempts to convince member countries to analyse and fight international tax evasion go back to the 1970s, but have only gained strength since the late 1990s and the 2000s, paralleling processes of second-wave globalisation and financialisation and also reflecting the time when these issues entered the agenda of the G7 and G20 meetings, see e.g. Hürlimann (2019, 2020).

DOI: 10.4324/9781003333197-1

Taxation and Not Paying Taxes as an Object of Trans-Epochal Historical Research

Jean Bodin's list on how the absolutist monarchical state could raise its revenue ranked (direct) taxation only in seventh place.[6] Other sources of income were historically more important, e.g. access to domestic resources such as precious metal deposits (like silver in Classical Athens, see the chapter by Lucia Cecchet in this volume) or state entrepreneurship. However, complex political entities, whether centralised or with a federal structure, have long since relied on regular incomes to fund all kind of expenditures related to common responsibilities ranging from basic government functions such as the military and police force to more elaborate public needs. The majority relied on taxes for law-making and governing activities, food supply, public infrastructures and buildings, and also for education, social welfare and sometimes religious activities. Thus, states usually depended on the "power to tax"[7] those individuals – subjects and citizens – who lived in their territory and under their jurisdiction. Paying taxes or tax-like levies – on a myriad of tax bases, in kind or in cash – has therefore been a general characteristic of every complex political entity. Twentieth-century scholars sometimes tended to compress Bodin's elaborate distinctions by claiming that there was "no state" where there was "no taxation"[8], or they viewed "war making and state making as organized crime", for both of which raising taxes proved pivotal.[9] Such a ubiquity of taxation makes the obligation to pay taxes an extraordinarily suitable phenomenon for a comparative historical analysis between state entities that criss-crosses historical epochs.

From a modern legal perspective, taxes are compulsory transfers of resources that households and enterprises pay to one or several government bodies without receiving an individual, specific benefit in return.[10] In the twentieth and twenty-first centuries, this is what distinguishes taxes from fees or from social contributions, a distinction that was unknown or at least less clear before the nineteenth century. But even in times without such

6 The other six modalities were: income from royal / state domain economy, war booty, gifts and inheritances, pensions and tributes paid by allies, income from commerce and customs revenue, see Bodin (1993 [1583]), livre 6ème, chapitre II.

7 Brennan/Buchanan (1980).

8 Schwennicke (1996).

9 A notion famously defended by sociologist and historian Charles Tilly, see Tilly (1985); this "militarist theory" strand (categorisation by Martin, Mehrotra and Prasad (2009b, 10f.)) was renewed in: Tilly (1990). Whether historical developments in approximately the last 150 years have seen an ongoing transition from raising taxes for "warfare" to doing so for "welfare", or whether the relationship between the two "-fares" is more complex, is a topic of academic controversy, see Obinger et al. (2018).

10 Brockhaus Enzyklopädie (2006, 309). The definition refers to the German Tax Code § 3 Abs. 1 Satz 1 AO. The onset of the modern (tax) state was, fiscally, marked by dissolving the medieval connection between service and reward which characterised the feudal system, see Reimer (2013, 119).

differentiations, taxation was always perceived as interfering with property rights – invoking Charles Tilly's coercive power of state bodies to extract a share of people's income, profit or wealth. Throughout history, the levy and payment of taxes have led to scrutiny of the relationship between social and professional groups as well as, under more participatory conditions, between households/individual taxpayers and state authorities. In their call for a New Fiscal Sociology, Isaac Martin, Ajay Mehrotra and Monica Prasad claimed that taxation was the epitomisation of the "social contract" in the modern world,[11] offering a starting point for international historical tax research.[12] Even if democratic consent, tacit or explicit, seems to be a relative historical novelty for most parts of the world, the question of how the ruling class managed to make their subjects or citizens pay, and why and how the latter tried to avoid or evade tax liability or to fundamentally question such an obligation is paramount for understanding the state- and society-making qualities of taxation. The negotiation processes surrounding the legitimacy and power to tax can be observed best where taxation was the object of conflicts between government and taxpayers and where taxpayers openly or covertly refused to pay the imposed tax sum or indeed opposed paying taxes at all. In the phenomenon of *not* paying taxes throughout history we can, therefore, observe the subject/citizen – state relationship from antiquity to modern times in a condensed form. Thus, our international comparative approach across epochs informs about the traditions, prerequisites and meanings of not paying taxes, also when considering questions of group identity, solidarity, bargaining power and sheer necessity. The historical analysis of tax evasion and avoidance also helps us to contextualise the contemporary normative question concerning the amount of power wielded by state authorities to siphon off private and business money with the aim of financing public infrastructures and services and redistributing wealth within society.

Tax Evasion and Tax Avoidance: A Challenge to Historiography

Historians have dealt with not paying taxes in various contexts, such as analysing tax resistance and tax resistance movements in history.[13] Well-known cases stretch from the so-called Boston Tea party in 1773 up to French Poujadism in the 1950s or the protest against property taxation in California in the late 1970s.[14] Such cases of organised tax revolt and anti-tax resistance are normally highly publicised and can be well-examined, which makes it

11 Martin, Mehrotra and Prasad (2009b, 1).

12 Huerlimann, Brownlee and Ide (2018).

13 Beito (1989); Wong (2001); Redding (2006); Delalande (2011); Delande (2012); Sánchez Román (2013); Spire (2018).

14 Hoffmann (1956); Lo (1990); Souillac (2007); Martin (2008); Carp (2011); Delalande/Huret 2013.

easier for historians to access suitable sources.[15] Black markets have also been the subject of historical research.[16] Tax havens as a transnational institution for profit shifting and tax avoidance are another field that has attracted considerable historiographical attention.[17] Other "silent" forms of tax evasion and avoidance have, however, seldom been subject to historical research.[18] One reason for this research gap might be that tax evasion and avoidance from the perspective of the "offenders" – or, simply, of those who are liable to paying taxes – is naturally underrepresented in sources, in terms of both the practices, procedures and techniques and of the underlying motives. It is not often that we meet frank and explicit evaders (such as in the case studied by Boris Gehlen and Christian Marx in this volume), or find, typically in the twentieth and twenty-first centuries, scientific examinations of tax evasion motives which can be used as sources.[19] The sources that originate from "deceived" government and public administration bodies tend to criminalise and condemn tax evaders, without further examination of their motivation or reasons.

Not Paying Taxes – Acting Inside or Outside the Legal or Legitimate Space?

If we dare to take up this slack, many forms of not paying taxes can be the object of historical research. The scope ranges from legal forms of tax avoidance – the lawful use of privileges, abatements and loopholes – to illegal modes of tax evasion in the sense of an unlawful refusal to pay taxes and to initiate tax protest and resistance with political or even military means.[20] What was and is considered to be legal tax avoidance, illegal tax evasion or tax fraud varies and changes over time as societies determine a legal frame by enforcing legal constraints and thus also define what can be understood as tax compliance.[21] However, a differentiation between tax evasion and tax avoidance only makes sense where two initial requirements are met: first, the compulsory character of taxation and, second, the existence of a generally binding definition of legal and illegal practices. In Classical Athens, conditions were different, and no sharp line can be drawn between avoidance and evasion (as is shown in the chapter authored by Lucia Cecchet). The performers of the so-called *liturgies* (essentially a "voluntary" contribution which was expected only from the wealthy and was used to finance and perform

15 Spoerer and Schönhärl (2021).
16 Kersting (2006); Zierenberg (2015); Potamianos (2022); Barciela López (2003).
17 Palan (2010); Zucman (2013); Farquet (2017); Ogle (2017); Boon and Wubs (2018); Guex (2021) Guex and Buclin (2023).
18 Schönhärl (2019a; 2019b).
19 Groves (1958); Beichelt et al. (1969); Schönhärl (2021).
20 Slemrod (2008).
21 Torgler (2004).

essential state services) were, in practice, free to fix the size of their financial and personal contributions.[22] The question in this case and in similar ones was much more the legitimate or illegitimate limits of avoiding or evading such forms of taxation, and the social acceptability of such practices, which were fundamental for the integration of the wealthy into the socio-political system of direct democracy. Furthermore, in every period, there is a range of practices which are not considered legal but remain nevertheless unpenalised; in modern times, tax amnesties were sometimes used to render illegal behaviour scot-free in hindsight.

However, also in the nineteenth and twentieth centuries, where the compulsory character of taxation is beyond doubt, avoidance and evasion often appeared in combination and simultaneously. Taxpayers tried to extend their tax savings in a fluent process and thereby tested, transcended and ignored the line between legal and illegal behaviour or used legal loopholes, whether unintentionally or intentionally.[23] Sometimes, even the borders between tax avoidance and tax resistance became blurred, for example, when taxpayers used both bargaining power and violence to reduce their tax burden (as with the Kurdish frontier tribes in the late Ottoman period described by Yener Koç in this volume). In certain cases, state authorities and courts referred to other legal offenses that went along with tax evasion in order to get hold of suspected tax dodgers. Such was the case with the Swiss banker Jacques Hentsch who in 1972 was arrested by the Swedish authorities not for facilitating or inciting the tax evasion of Swedish citizens but for exporting an illegal amount of cash and thus for a violation of currency acts (as is shown in the chapter authored by Thibaud Giddey and Mikael Wendschlag). Combining tax evasion with other crimes was (and is) a well-known phenomenon in the realm of international tax evasion, where international (private or corporate) taxpayers actively use the scope that emerges from differences in national tax legislation systems, double taxation conventions or complicated tax collection systems to minimise their tax duties.[24] Tax competition between nations and their attempts to undercut one another in advertising tax conditions has made this even easier.

Tax Law as a Site of Political and Economic Powerplay

What is the role of law in these demarcation processes? Tax law is best understood as an outcome of long-term, often conflictual, negotiations and as an expression of specific political mentalities and ideologies, as the historical analysis in the chapters of this volume shows. As a consequence, tax law and

22 Rohde (2012); Franzen (2019).
23 Torgler (2007).
24 Izawa (2020).

sometimes even the tax juridical system have a strongly politicised character.[25] Loopholes in tax legislation that enable or facilitate avoidance or evasion can thus be regarded as a result of the interest-driven politics of parliamentary majorities, as the success of concerted lobby pressure (see the case of the Land Union's fight to abolish land taxes in Great Britain after the Great War in Anna Grotegut's chapter). Sometimes, lobby groups were able to capture a wider public and win them over for their specific aims, even by using false information (as in the case of the fierce 1962 campaign against the Kennedy administration's project to introduce a withholding tax on dividends and interests, analysed by Steven A. Bank in this volume). In Switzerland, tax amnesties were repeatedly granted to sweeten tax reforms that had to undergo popular referendum. The amnesties benefited tax dodgers – and wealthy ones to a higher degree, but would generally also be accepted by the other political camps as part of the deal (see here the examples discussed by Sylvan Praz and Aniko Fehr).

Debates about tax law and its reform were the battleground for negotiating not only the socially and politically accepted line between legal and illegal behaviour, but also the tax burden that the different social groups had to shoulder or were allowed to avoid. Or, using and adapting political scientist Harold D. Lasswell´s simple and famous title: Tax Law: Who Pays What, When, How?[26] The seemingly modern concept that each individual or group should "pay their fair share" can already be found in pre-modern debates and court speeches, whether they referred to (neo-)Aristotelian ideas of distributive justice or not. Which tax bases were best suited to generate fiscal revenue was an object of fervid negotiations as well. Real estate was the main basis for calculating the state's tax demands in the Roman Empire, even if other forms of taxes and income also existed (as is shown in the contribution by Kerstin Droß-Krüpe). We see this overwhelming importance of real estate in most pre-modern societies and well into the nineteenth century. In the industrialising nations of the nineteenth century, industrial enterprise became an ever more effective source of capital accumulation. In political power struggles, tax law was adapted to changing economic and societal circumstances,[27] and the expansion or contraction of tax loopholes was one important battlefield.

Conflicts About Paying Taxes as Proxies for the Big Questions

Thus, conflicts about (not) paying taxes can be considered as proxies for the (self-)conception of a political entity, as they entail class struggle, tensions and allocation battles between different social and power groups, be these

25 Scott and Walker (2020).

26 Original title: Harold D. Lasswell, Politics: Who Pays What, When, How?, Cleveland/New York 1936.

27 For the US, see Brownlee (2020); for Germany Buggeln (2022).

the monarch vs. the aristocrats, the ruler vis à vis his or her subjects, the emperor vs. the lords, dukes or kings of the empire's different estates, old vs. new elites, and elite vs. non-elite. In modern and contemporary societies, such distributional and socially constitutional questions also arise when debating taxation according to gender, marital and family status, household type and the old (and retired) vs. the young (and gainfully employed). This symptomatic or proxy character of taxation conflicts corresponds precisely with the dimension that classical fiscal sociology, as represented by Amilcare Puviani[28], Rudolf Goldscheid[29] and Joseph Schumpeter[30], amongst others, awarded the study of public finance. More recently, the proponents of a "New Fiscal Sociology" advocated for a similar interest in taxation in terms of both its symptomatic and its causal relation to questions of state (trans-)formation, economic and social structures and power relations.[31] This younger research strand particularly claimed to have revitalised philosophical and sociological contract and conflict theories surrounding the legitimacy of tax levying and the conditions under which negotiation will result in obedience/compliance, or usher in political change.

The avowal and defence of or the blame for (not) paying taxes offered opportunities for the respective counterparts to negotiate their relationship and to clarify their standing towards each other, as several chapters of this volume show. Refusing, delaying or obstructing tax demands often indicated a questioning of hierarchical relations or a testing of limits and conditions, be this in thirteenth-century England (as in the chapter authored by Christina Bröker), in eighteenth-century Germany (as revealed to us by Rachel Renault) or in the already mentioned case of the tribes in the Ottoman empire (Yener Koç). Not paying taxes was then a symptom (and cause) of the demand to (re) negotiate or redistribute politic power. In these cases, taxes were usually not clandestinely evaded. Instead, they were openly resisted and highly symbolically refused – in certain cases even by using physical violence.

Legitimisation of Tax Demands: Pay for What and How?

Alongside the question of who had to pay how much (to whom) and whether this was legitimate and fair, another field of dispute might arise from the complex why, upon what, and for what purposes taxes were to be levied. The pressure on state authorities to legitimise their financial demands, be they for regular taxes or for extra or irregular levies for special purposes, existed in different contexts, even in non-democratic and pre-modern times. How rulers, princes or democracies would discuss, argue and license their tax

28 Puviani (1903).

29 Goldscheid (1976), first ed. 1917.

30 Schumpeter (1918).

31 Martin, Mehrotra and Prasad (2009).

demands is of central importance for understanding tax compliance. There were different legitimation strategies, amongst them transparency (or the lack of it) of the purpose for the tax levy: Was the tax money invested for the benefit of the very subjects or citizens who paid it, was it raised in one area and spent in another (e.g. in the periphery and the centre of an imperium) or was it used for purposes that were not in the strict interest of a tax-paying majority (such as for conspicuous consumption by the ruling class, or for "unnecessary" wars)? Did the taxpayers have any political influence in such decision processes and were they represented in the bodies where the decisions were taken? Could they find ways to influence a) which kind of taxes, fees or remittances were raised, b) the way in which taxes were collected, e.g. by intermediary institutions such as tax farmers or by a more disinterested tax administration and c) the amount of taxes levied and the basis of calculation on which taxes were to be paid?[32]

Governmental tax administrations that implement bureaucratic procedures have often been regarded by historiographical research as proof of "modernity", whereas tax farming by self-interested third persons is described as "antiquated".[33] From a modern point of view, the difference between a disinterested administration and profit-maximising individuals might be fundamental. But such a dichotomy is far from expedient, historically, as it, first, ignores state and fiscal organisation in pre-modern periods and, second, overlooks that both systems could co-exist in societies like the Roman Empire or Colonial Mexico or even in Russia prior to 1862.[34] Third, and in order to understand the dynamics of not paying taxes, it is not only essential to identify *who* levies taxes (foreign occupiers, monarchs or democratically organised governments), but also *how* tax collection was structured. Especially in remote areas, it was decisive for tax authorities to gain acceptance and compliance by organising tax collection locally and integrating the local elite into the administrative system. Both in the Roman and in the Eastern Ottoman Empire, systems were developed in which distinct members of a community were intensively involved in the collection of taxes (see Droß-Krüpe and Koç).[35] The challenge was therefore to find ways of raising and collecting taxes that accorded with the taxpayers' own identity,[36] be it as a ward, a subordinate in a colony, a peer (with the emperor being only the first amongst equals), a citizen of a nation state or even a multinational world citizen like Hans Heinrich Thyssen-Bornemisza (Gehlen/Marx).

32 Sociological research on present tax morale judges taxpayers' influence as an important variable of tax morale, see e.g. Feld and Kirchgässner (2000).

33 Cuno (1992). Korchmina (2018). A similar understanding in Frankema and Buelens (2013), 109–129.

34 Korchima (2019).

35 A similar idea was applied in Spain under Franco's dictatorship, but turned out to enforce tax evasion massively, see Comín Comín (2003); Comín Comín (1994).

36 For this multi-layered term, see e.g. Brendecke/Regazzoni 2021.

"Foreign" Rule and the Power(lessness) to Tax

The balance between the principals and techniques of taxation on the one hand and the identity of the taxpayers on the other hand, which has to be adjusted in negotiations again and again throughout all time periods, proved extraordinarily unstable in the context of the "inner" or "borrowed" colonialism[37] exerted by the Roman Empire in Egypt (see Droß-Krüpe), in the eastern regions of the Ottoman empire (Koç), under Spanish rule in eighteenth-century Mexico (Gordoa de la Huerta), in British imperialism and colonialism in early twentieth-century Nigeria (Daniel Olisa Iweze), and in the case of Greece under Nazi occupation (Vasilis Manousakis). The contributions that deal with such contexts examine practices which range from clandestine evasion and the use of loopholes to violent and armed resistance. Tax extraction and the attitudes of the "subjects" to tax demands by (distant) emperors, colonisers and invaders serve as a magnifying glass for understanding deeper socio-economic conditions and power relations.

The attempts by colonial and other rulers to legitimise tax collection or tax reform as an essential part of "modernisation" and "civilisation"[38] were often met by resistance and failed, while the prospects for success grew when and where pre-existing local elites who had profited from pre-colonial tax systems could be integrated into the new system of taxation. Notwithstanding the differences between the case studies in terms of time, players and actors, a cross-reading of the chapters reveals the fecundity of a historical comparison that is interested in the taxed subjects' agency, in their ability to resist taxation fully or partly. Practices may be similar across time and space. First, emigration, flight or temporary migration and hiding was used as a strategy to avoid taxes by the Igbo people in the south-east of British-ruled Nigeria (Olisa Izewe), by provincials in Roman Egypt (Droß-Krüpe), and by the Hill people in north-eastern India.[39] Second, in the eastern regions of the Ottoman Empire in the nineteenth century, violent resistance was practised by the Kurdish "Aghas" against the modernisation programme of Ottoman reformers, which endangered the tribal chiefs' power and economic position (Koç). In the case of occupied Greece during the 1940s, resistance to Axis taxation was epitomised as resistance against Italian and German foreign rule in general, and tax evasion was thus ennobled as a symbol of national action against fascist occupation (Manousakis). Third, unwilling taxpayers proved highly skilful in finding loopholes or in circumventing taxation as the case of eighteenth-century "New Spain" (Mexico) and Peru show. Here colonial merchants either shifted the tax burden by becoming tax farmers themselves or employed indigenous intermediaries who were legally exempt from certain taxes (Gordoa de la Huerta).

37 Gardner (2012); Frankema and Booth (2020); Albiez-Wieck and Marx (2020).

38 See for the role of science in the "civilizing missions" Neill (2014).

39 (Muivah 2020).

Not Paying Taxes – A Phenomenon Reflecting a Lack of Consensus Within Society?

Especially in times of economic crises, the tax burden simply outstripped the economic capabilities of the average taxpayer, and tax compliance was no longer a question of choice. However, when tax avoidance was not a necessity for physical survival, it was often motivated by a lack of political consensus. This sometimes was caused by the inability of the taxing entity to construct a commonly shared feeling of identity amongst the taxpayers, be it during a critical phase of competing state powers or due to foreign rule. Sometimes, however, when missing feelings of belonging were not the key issue, the nucleus of open or hidden resistance could be taxpayers' impression that the tax burden was unevenly distributed. A perception that tax revenues were not being spent in a meaningful way could also be relevant in explaining taxpayers' disagreement and denial. In this regard, our historiographical examination supports the results of social scientific research on tax morale, which vehemently underlines the significance of the right to be informed and have a say for taxpayers' willingness to contribute voluntarily.[40] Because they understood this context, democratic twentieth-century governments tended to educate or convince taxpayers to accept and support changes to the tax systems, especially in unstable political situations, in times of war and crisis or in order to cope with (post-war or other) political ruptures and transformations.[41] They did so by explaining the (democratic) processes of public budgeting and the spending purposes of tax monies to win taxpayers' compliance, thus appealing to rationality and a sense of community. This was, e.g., the case in the USA during the Second World War or in the Federal Republic of Germany after Nazism and the lost war (Korinna Schönhärl´s chapter in this volume). The ways in which and modes of how governments communicated to and with taxpayers are often well documented and meaningful objects for historical research. The frequency of government attempts to advertise a consensus amongst taxpayers tended to increase the more endangered this consensus seemed to be.

Outlook

Notwithstanding all kinds of historical and geographical peculiarities, tax avoiders in completely different historical periods, tax systems and cultural contexts used legal loopholes to reduce taxes that they did not consent to, or at least tried to negotiate the legitimacy and/or burden of taxes they were supposed to pay with the help of political or judicial power. Ruling elites and governments around the globe and across eras have applied a comparable variety of countermeasures, ranging from tax education to negotiation

40 Steinmo (2018); OECD (2019); Steinmo and D'Attoma (2022).
41 Likhovski (2007).

to enforcement with the help of tax collectors and the use of police and/or military force to break down tax resistance. This observation of similarities and resemblances but also clear differences through time and space makes the discourses and practices of not paying taxes a perfect research object for a comparative approach across epochs, considering the multifaceted relations between different social and economic groups and political rulers, governments and state administrations. The analysis of processes of not paying taxes opens up deeper understandings of the community/state – member/citizen/subject relationship and its transformation in the course of history. Even if a blanket transfer to present days is certainly neither possible nor desirable, we nonetheless hope to add new insights for interdisciplinary tax morale and tax policy research.

References

Albiez-Wieck, Sarah and Christoph Marx (eds.). 2020. *Taxing Difference: Empires as Spaces of Ordered Inequality*. Dhau 5. St. Ingbert: Röhrig Universitätsverlag.

Barciela López, Carlos (ed.). 2003. *Autarquía y mercado negro: El fracaso económico del primer franquismo, 1939 - 1959*. Historia del mundo moderno. Barcelona: Crítica.

Beichelt, Bernd, Bernd Biervert, Jürgen Daviter, Günter Schmölders, and Burkhard Strümpel (eds.). 1969. *Steuernorm und Steuerwirklichkeit. Steuermentalität und Steuermoral in Großbritannien, Frankreich, Italien und Spanien*. Forschungsberichte des Landes Nordrhein-Westfalen II. Köln: Westdt. Verl.

Beito, David T. 1989. *Taxpayers in Revolt: Tax Resistance during the Great Depression*. Chapel Hill, NC: University of North Carolina Press.

Bodin, Jean. 1993 [1583]. *Les six livres de la République*. Paris: LGF/Le Livre de Poche.

Boon, Marten, and Ben Wubs. 2018. "'Safe Haven Curacao': The Origins of an Offshore Centre, 1940-1960." Paper presented at the WEHC Boston, August 2nd. http://wehc2018.org/passage-to-panama-nation-states-taxation-and-multinational-enterprise-in-the-twentieth-century/. Accessed Dec. 6th 2021.

Brendecke, Arndt and Lisa Regazzoni. 2021. Das umstrittene Wir: Auf der Suche nach neuen Wegen zur historischen Erforschung von Kollektiven, Section at the 53th German Historikertag, Oct. 6th. https://www.historikertag.de/Muenchen2021/sektionen/das-umstrittene-wir-auf-der-suche-nach-neuen-wegen-zur-historischen-erforschung-von-kollektiven/. Accessed Nov. 29th 2021.

Brockhaus (ed.). 2006. *Brockhaus Enzyklopädie: In 30 Bänden*. 21st online, ed. Brockhaus NE GmbH, Leipzig: F.A. Brockhaus.

Brownlee, Wilson E. 2020. "Tax and Fiscal Regimes in the United States." In *The Oxford Handbook of American Political History*, eds. Paula Baker and Donald T. Critchlow, 311–338. New York, NY: Oxford University Press.

Buggeln, Marc. 2022. Das Versprechen der Gleichheit. Steuern und soziale Ungleichheit in Deutschland von 1871 bis heute, Berlin: Suhrkamp.

Carp, Benjamin L. 2011. *Defiance of the Patriots: The Boston Tea Party and the Making of America*. New Haven: Yale University Press.

Comín Comín, Francisco. 1994. El fraude fiscal en la Historia de España. In *El fraude fiscal en la historia de España*, ed. Instituto de Estudios Fiscales, 5–21. Hacienda pública española Monografias 1. Madrid: Instituto de Estudios Fiscales.

Comín Comín, Francisco. 2003. "La Hacienda pública en el Franquismo autárquico, 1940-1959." In *Autarquía y mercado negro: El fracaso económico del primer franquismo, 1939 – 1959*, ed. Carlos Barciela López, 247–72. Historia del mundo moderno. Barcelona: Crítica.

Correctiv. 2021. Cum Ex Files. https://correctiv.org/en/latest-stories/2021/10/21/cumex-files-2/. Accessed Nov. 29th 2021.

Cuno, Kenneth. 1992. *The Pasha's Peasants: Land, Society, and Economy in Lower Egypt, 1740-1858*. ACLS Humanities E-Book edition. Cambridge UK, New York: Cambridge University Press. http://hdl.handle.net/2027/heb.00228.0001.001.

Delalande, Nicolas. 2011. *Les Batailles de l'impôt: Consentement et résistances de 1789 à nos jours*. L'univers historique. Paris: Seuil.

Delande, Nicolas. 2012. Reforming the Tax State: Taxation and Democracy in a Transatlantic Perspective. *The Tocqueville review = La revenue Tocqueville* 33(2): 71–85.

Delalande, Nicolas/Huret, Romain (2013). Tax Resistance: A Global History? *Journal of Policy History* 25(03): 301–307.

EU Parliament. March 24th 2021. Tax policy: EU solutions to prevent tax fraud and avoidance. https://www.europarl.europa.eu/news/en/headlines/economy/20210415STO02118/tax-policy-eu-solutions-to-prevent-tax-fraud-and-avoidance. Accessed Nov. 29th 2021.

Farquet, Christophe. 2017. The Swiss Tax Haven, the Bretton Woods System Crisis and the Globalisation of Offshore Finance. In *The Political Economy of Public Finance: Taxation, State Spending and Debt since the 1970s*, eds. Alexander Nützenadel, Marc Buggeln, and Martin J. Daunton, 126–48. Cambridge: Cambridge University Press.

Farquet, Christophe. 2017. *La défense du paradis fiscal suisse avant la Seconde Guerre mondiale: une histoire internationale: analyse de la politique helvétique dans les négociations sur la double imposition et l'évasion fiscale durant l'entre-deux-guerre*. Neuchâtel: Éditions Alphil - Presse Universitaires Suisse.

Federal Ministry of Finance. March 31st 2021. Scholz: "We're taking action to eliminate tax havens". Defence against Tax Havens Act adopted. https://www.bundesfinanzministerium.de/Content/EN/Pressemitteilungen/2021/2021-03-31-defence-against-tax-havens-act.html. Accessed Nov. 29th 2021.

Feld, Lars P. and Gebhard Kirchgässner. 2000. "Direct Democracy, Political Culture, and Theoutcome of Economic Policy: A Report on the Swiss Experience." *European Journal of Political Economy* 16: 287–306.

Frankema, Ewout and Anne Booth (eds.). 2020. *Fiscal Capacity and the Colonial State in Asia and Africa, C. 1850-1960*. Cambridge: Cambridge University Press.

Frankema, Ewout and Frans Buelens. 2013. *Colonial Exploitation and Economic Development: The Belgian Congo and the Netherlands Indies Compared*. Routledge Explorations in Economic History. Hoboken: Taylor and Francis.

Franzen, Wolfgang. 2019. "Tax Culture in Classical Athens." *Journal of Ancient Civilizations (JAC)* 34(2): 273–288.

Gardner, Leigh A. 2012. *Taxing Colonial Africa: The Political Economy of British Imperialism*. Oxford: Oxford University Press.

Goldscheid, Rudolf. 1976. "Staatssozialismus oder Staatskapitalismus. Ein finanzsoziologischer Beitrag zur Lösung des Staatsschulden-Problems." In *Die Finanzkrise des Steuerstaats: Beiträge zur politischen Ökonomie der Staatsfinanzen*, eds. Rudolf Goldscheid, Joseph Schumpeter, and Rudolf Hickel, 40–252. Edition Suhrkamp 698. Frankfurt am Main: Suhrkamp.

Groves, Harold M. 1958. "Empirical Studies of Income Tax Compliance." *National Tax Journal* 11(4): 291–301.

Guex, Sébastien. 2021. The Emergence of the Swiss Tax Haven, 1816–1914. *Business History Review*: 1–20.

Guex, Sébastien, and Hadrien Buclin. 2023. *Tax Evasion and Tax Havens since the Nineteenth Century*. Cham: Springer International Publishing.

Hoffmann, Stanley. 1956. *Le mouvement poujade*. Paris: Colin.

Huerlimann, Gisela, W. E. Brownlee, and Eisaku Ide (eds.). 2018. *Worlds of Taxation: The Political Economy of Taxing, Spending, and Redistribution Since 1945*. Palgrave Studies in the History of Finance. Cham: Palgrave Macmillan.

Hürlimann, Gisela. 2019: Marktgerechtigkeit und Steuer(un)gerechtigkeit. Internationale Ordnungsvorstellungen und die schweizerischen Steuerwelten. In *Ordnung und Chaos – Trends und Brüche*, ed. Günther Schulz, 187–205. Stuttgart: Franz Steiner Verlag.

Hürlimann, Gisela. 2020. Switzerland as a Laboratory for Fiscal Federalism and Global Fiscal Governance. *Economic Sociology – The European Electronic Newsletter* 21: 15–25.

ICIJ (International Consortium of Investigative Journalists). 2021. Investigations. https://www.icij.org/investigations/. Accessed Nov. 29th 2021.

Izawa, Ryo. 2022. Corporate Structural Change for Tax Avoidance: British Multinational Enterprises and International Double Taxation between the First and Second World Wars. *Business History* 64(4): 1–23.

Kersting, Gabriele. 2006. *Steuerwiderstand und Steuerkultur: Der Kampf gegen das Umgeld im Königreich Württemberg (1819 - 1871)*. Stuttgart: Kohlhammer.

Korchmina, Elena. 2018. Peer Pressure: The Puzzle of Tax Compliance in the Early Nineteenth-Century Russia. *The Economic History Review* 75(3): 779–800.

Likhovski, Assaf. 2007. "Training in Citizenship": Tax Compliance and Modernity. *Law & Social Inquiry* 32(3): 665–700.

Lo, Clarence Y. H. 1990. *Small Property versus Big Government: Social Origins of the Property Tax Revolt*. Berkeley, CA: University of California Press.

Martin, Isaac W. 2008. *The Permanent Tax Revolt: How the Property Tax Transformed American Politics*. Stanford, CA: Stanford University Press.

Martin, Isaac W., Ajay K. Mehrotra, and Monica Prasad. 2009. The Thunder of History. The Origins and Development of the New Fiscal Sociology. In *The New Fiscal Sociology: Taxation in Comparative and Historical Perspective*, eds. Isaac W. Martin, Ajay K. Mehrotra, and Monica Prasad, 1–27. Cambridge, New York: Cambridge University Press.

Muivah, Yaruipam. 2020. "Tax Evasion and Avoidance by the Hill People in the North-East Frontier of India in the Early Colonial Period, C. 1880-1913." In *Taxing Difference: Empires as Spaces of Ordered Inequality*, eds. Sarah Albiez-Wieck, 135–156. Dhau 5. St. Ingbert: Röhrig Universitätsverlag.

Neill, Deborah J. 2014. "Science and Civilizing Missions. Germans and the Transnational Community of Tropical Medicine." In *German Colonialism in a Global Age*, eds. Bradley Naranch and Geoff Eley, 74–92. Politics, history, and culture. Durham: Duke University Press.

Obinger, Herbert, Klaus Petersen, and Peter Starke (eds.). 2018. *Warfare and Welfare: Military Conflict and Welfare State Development in Western Countries*. Oxford: Oxford University Press.

Ogle, Vanessa. 2017. Archipelago Capitalism: Tax Havens, Offshore Money, and the State, 1950s-1970s. *American Historical Review* 122(5): 1431–1458.

OECD. 2019. *Tax Morale. What Drives People and Businesses to Pay Taxes?*. Paris: OECD Publishing. https://doi.org/10.1787/f3d8ea10-en. Accessed Nov. 29th 2021.

OECD. 2021. Ending offshore profit shifting. https://www.oecd.org/about/impact/combatinginternationaltaxavoidance.htm. Accessed Nov. 29th 2021.

Palan, Ronen. 2010. *Tax Havens. How Globalization Really Works*. Ithaca, NY: Cornell University Press.
Pierri, Gastón et al. 2021. Combatting Tax Evasion and Increasing Financial Transparency in the Time of COVID19: The Case of Paraguay. IDB. https://publications.iadb.org/publications/english/document/Combatting-Tax-Evasion-and-Increasing-Financial-Transparency-in-the-Time-of-COVID19-The-Case-of-Paraguay.pdf. Accessed Nov. 20th 2021.
Potamianos, Nikos. 2022. Do Shopkeepers Have Their Own Moral Economy? Profiteering, Unfair Competition and the Black Market in Greece, 1916-1945. *Social History* 47(1): 35–59.
Puviani, Amilcare. 1903. *Teoria Della Illusione Finanziaria*. Biblioteca di scienze sociali e politiche 46. Milano u.a.: Sandron.
Redding, Sean. 2006. *Sorcery and Sovereignty: Taxation, Power, and Rebellion in South Africa, 1880-1963*. Athens: Ohio University Press. http://site.ebrary.com/lib/academiccompletetitles/home.action.
Reimer, Ekkehard. 2013. Die Sieben Stufen der Steuerrechtfertigung. In *Demokratie und Wirtschaft. Eine interdisziplinäre Herausforderung*,eds. Boris Gehlen und Frank Schorkopf, 113–141. Tübingen: Mohr Siebeck.
Rohde, Dorothea. 2012. "Bürgerpflicht und Gleichheitsideal. „Besteuerung "und Ihre Diskursiven Grundlagen in Sparta und Athen." In *Ordnungsrahmen antiker Ökonomien: Ordnungskonzepte und Steuerungsmechanismen antiker Wirtschaftssysteme im Vergleich*, ed. Sven Günther, 23–40. Philippika 53. Wiesbaden: Harrassowitz.
Sánchez Román, José Antonio. 2013. Resistance without Revolt: Shaping a Tax Culture in Modern Argentina, 1930–1955. *Journal of Policy History* 35(3): 422–443.
Schönhärl, Korinna. 2019a. Steuermoral in Westdeutschland nach dem Zweiten Weltkrieg. Eine Diskursanalytische Rekonstruktion. *Leviathan* 47: 169–191.
Schönhärl, Korinna. 2019b. "Der Imperativ des Nassauerns, Durchmogelns und Absahnens". Debatten um Steuermoral in der Bundesrepublik Deutschland Anfang der 1980er Jahre. *GWU* 70(11/12): 678–694.
Schönhärl, Korinna. 2021. "Steuerzahlverhalten quantifizieren. Die Entwicklung von Messmethoden und ihre politische Dimension am Beispiel von Günter Schmölders´ Erfassung der Steuermoral." *Economic History Yearbook* 62(2): 473–503.
Schumpeter, Joseph.1918. *Die Krise des Steuerstaats*. Zeitfragen aus dem Gebiete der Soziologie. Reihe 1 H. 4. Graz, Leipzig: Leuschner Lubensky.
Scott, Peter, and James T. Walker. 2020. "The Comfortable, the Rich, and the Super-Rich. What Really Happened to Top British Incomes During the First Half of the Twentieth Century?" *The Journal of Economic History* 80(1): 38–68.
Seely, Antony. 2021. Tax Avoidance and Tax Evasion. House of Commons Library. https://commonslibrary.parliament.uk/research-briefings/cbp-7948/ Accessed Nov. 29th 2021.
Slemrod, Joel. 2008. Tax Compliance and Tax Evasion. In *The New Palgrave Dictionary of Economics Online*, 8th ed., ed. Steven N. Durlauf, 167–71. New York, NY [u.a.]: Palgrave Macmillan.
Souillac, Romain. 2007. *Le mouvement Poujade. De la défense professionnelle au populisme nationaliste (1953 - 1962)*. Paris: Sciences Po Histoire.
Spire, Alexis. 2018. *Résistances à l'impôt, attachement à l'État: Enquête sur les contribuables français*. Paris: Éditions du Seuil.
Spoerer, Mark and Korinna Schönhärl (eds.). 2021. State Finances and Conflict: Special Issue Economic History Yearbook 62(2): 291–302.

Steinmo, Sven (ed.). 2018. *The Leap of Faith. The Fiscal Foundations of Successful Government in Europe and America*. Oxford: Oxford University Press.

Steinmo, Sven, and John D'Attoma (eds.). 2022. *Willing to Pay? A Reasonable Choice Approach*. Oxford: Oxford University Press.

Schwennicke, Andreas. 1996. "Ohne Steuer kein Staat": Zur Entwicklung und politischen Funktion des Steuerrechts in den Territorien des Heiligen Römischen Reichs (1500-1800). *Studien zur europäischen Rechtsgeschichte* 90. Frankfurt/Main: Klostermann.

Tilly, Charles. 1985. War Making and State Making as Organized Crime. In *Bringing the State Back In*, eds. Peter Evans, Dietrich Rueschemeyer, and Theda Skocpol, 169–191, Cambridge: Cambridge University Press.

Tilly, Charles. 1990. *Coercion, Capital, and European States, AD 990-1990*. Cambridge MA: Basil Blackwell Ltd

Torgler, Benno. 2004. Cross-Culture Comparison of Tax Morale and Tax Compliance: Evidence from Costa Rica and Switzerland. *International Journal of Comparative Sociology* 45(1–2): 17–43.

Torgler, Benno. 2007. *Tax Compliance and Tax Morale: A Theoretical and Empirical Analysis*. Cheltenham, UK, Northampton, MA: Edward Elgar.

Wong, Roy B. 2001. Tax Resistance, Economy, and State Transformation in China and Europe. *Economics of Governance* 2: 69–83.

Zierenberg, Malte. 2015. *Berlin's Black Market. 1939-1950*. Basingstoke, New York: Palgrave Macmillan.

Zucman, Gabriel. 2013. *La richesse cachée des nations. Enquête sur les paradis fiscaux*. Paris: Seuil et al.

Part I

Negotiating Lower Taxes, or No Taxes at All

1 Tax Evaders in Classical Athens?

Attacks and Strategies of Defence in Attic Oratory[1]

Lucia Cecchet

1.1 Introduction

Tax evasion is not a phenomenon peculiar only to the modern and contemporary world. It also existed in ancient societies. In two important works, M. Christ explored the practice of tax evasion in classical Athens based, mainly, on orators' speeches. He shed light on a large number of passages in which orators refer to citizens evading (or attempting to evade) fiscal duties.[2] However, while we have many attestations of attacks and arguments targeting supposed tax evaders, there is only scanty evidence concerning the point of view of these people. What were the arguments and the rhetoric strategies that the presumed tax evaders used in order to defend themselves or even legitimise their position? In this chapter, I argue that we can attempt to answer this question by looking, on the one hand, at the way references to tax evasion were framed in court speeches and, on the other, at the widespread attestations of discontent concerning the distribution of financial duties among the wealthy of Athens in the fourth century BC. This discontent is probably at the root of several attempts made by the Athenians to reform their tax system in the period between 378 and 340 BC. In order to understand Athenian taxation, a broad tax conception is required that not only includes financial obligations pertaining to the Athenian elites, but also the "financial performances" that the elites were required to conduct.[3]

One caveat for the reader: this chapter does not investigate the historical practice of tax evasion in terms of its extent, frequency and impact, but rather its discursive presentation in court speeches. In many cases, tax evasion is not the central topic of these speeches, nor is it the charge at issue; rather it is usually one of the facts speakers refer to in order to discredit their opponents.

1 My special thanks go to the organisers of the Frankfurt Conference "Not Paying Taxes!" in March 2020 and to the other participants, both for their useful comments on the drafts of this paper and their successful work in making a digital event possible during the Covid-19 pandemic.

2 Christ (1990, 2006). The pioneering study on rhetoric *topoi* in Attic oratory and strategies of communication between the elites and their audiences is Ober (1989).

3 On the applicability of the modern concept of "tax" to the ancient Greek world, see Rohde (2019, 6–7). Cf. Rohde (2012, 23–40).

DOI: 10.4324/9781003333197-3

This does not mean that facts concerning dodging taxes were always just invented as part of rhetoric strategies (though some probably were). Tax evasion did indeed exist and it was perceived as negative behaviour, violating the ethics of civic generosity and the regulations of the *polis*.

Two other preliminary clarifications are necessary. First, the public speeches discussed in this chapter, as the major part of Athenian orations, were written for (and by) members of the Athenian elites and mostly concerned the actions of these elites, but they were delivered to large audiences, such as the assembly or the courts. Thus, they addressed not only the elites but also ordinary citizens. The fact that tax evasion is a recurring topic in these orations suggests that this phenomenon was well-known to Athenian society at large.

Second, in classical Athens, there was no system of *pro capite* taxation applied to all citizens, while indirect taxes were levied on several kinds of goods and commercial activities. Only resident aliens (*metics)* were required to pay a direct *pro capite* tax, the *metoikion*. However, wealthy Athenians (and wealthy resident aliens) were expected to financially support the city by means of liturgies and *eisphorai*. These two kinds of contributions, which were, as we shall see below, different in terms of both their nature and appointment procedures, were fundamental for providing the city with the financial resources it needed in many fields, from sport and theatre competitions to infrastructure and war equipment.[4]

1.2 Liturgies, *Eisphorai* and their Performance

When we look at the fiscal system of Classical Athens, it is the *eisphora* that more closely resembles a direct wealth tax. This was, originally, a special contribution, based on income and property assessments, which was levied ad hoc for military purposes. In the course of the fourth century BC, the *eisphora* became a regular requirement falling on the elites and on the upper middle classes. Decisions about levying an *eisphora* were based on the decrees of the assemblies, the execution of which was mandatory.[5] Liturgies, by contrast, were a different form of institution. They did not entail the direct levy of money, but rather the organisation and performance of a task or service for the community. These kinds of private expenses for the public good can further be subdivided into festival liturgies (such as the *choregia*, i.e. bearing the costs for equipping and training a chorus for a play or funding a *lampadarchia*, a torchlight procession) and war liturgies (such as the *trierarchia*, i.e. bearing the costs for equipping a warship). Some of the liturgies were cyclical institutions, which were regularly performed (generally on an annual basis); others, by contrast, were occasional services.[6]

4 For detailed discussions, see Liddel (2007) and Rohde (2019) (see also footnotes 4 and 5 below).

5 For the first attested *eisphora* in 428/7 BC, during the Peloponnesian War, see Thuc. 3.19.1. On *eisphora* in general, see Thomsen (1964); Christ (2007, 53–69); Rohde (2019, 189–197); Lyttkens (1992).

6 For a discussion of the different types of liturgies and the procedural aspects of these institutions, see Liddel (2007, 109–209); Rohde (2019, 198–215).

But who were the people required to perform and pay liturgies and *eisphorai* in Athens? In his seminal work on wealth in classical Athens, J. K. Davies argued that citizens became liable to perform liturgies at an individual wealth threshold of at least three talents.[7] The threshold for *eisphora* is judged to have been lower by most scholars, possibly between 2,500 drachmae and 1 talent.[8] Following the work of Davies, there has lately been renewed discussion of the financial criteria for performing liturgies in favour of a less rigid threshold,[9] but it remains a fact that liturgists were among the wealthy, usually described as *plousioi* in the literary record. Their number varied over time but is estimated to be in the range of 1,200–1,500 individuals from an overall male citizen population of approximately 30,000 in the fourth century BC.[10] The group of individuals liable to pay the *eisphora*, by contrast, was more heterogeneous, ranging from the very rich to those whose fortune was close to the threshold. There is no consensus on their number, with estimations between 1,200 and 6,000 individuals.[11] Resident aliens (*metics*) were also liable to perform liturgies and pay the *eisphora*-tax.[12]

According to the Aristotelian *Constitution of the Athenians*, a document written in the fourth century BC, which is our best source of information on the institutional organisation of Athens, liturgies were appointed by the city officials.[13] This fact is at odds with the picture of liturgists as generous benefactors, which is strongly promoted by court speakers. Scholars generally

7 Davies (1971, xxiii–xxiv) and (1981, 30–31).

8 On the 2,500 drachmae threshold, see Jones (1957, 23–29; 83–84). For the one-talent threshold, Davies (1981, 34), followed by many; among them, recently, Van Wees (2011, 111).

9 Gabrielsen (1994, 45–53). For a new discussion of Davies' criteria, see Kierstead and Klapaukh (2018, 376–401).

10 Davies (1981, 19–20, 34) argued for a low figure of 200–400 liturgists, whose number increased to 1,200 in the fourth century after Periander's reform (357 BC, see footnote 27 below). Already Rhodes (1982, 1–19) noted that the figure 200–400 was too low, arguing in favour of a figure of 1,200 liturgists even before 357 BC. For objections to Davies' theory, see also Gabrielsen (1994, 45–53). A figure of 1,200–1,500 liturgists is generally accepted among scholars. On Athenian demography, see Akrigg (2011, 37–59) and (2019) with discussion of earlier scholarship.

11 On 6,000 as the total number of *eisphora*-payers, see Jones (1957, 56, 83–84); more cautious is Osborne (2010, 130): "at least 1,200 and perhaps rather more". The reform in 378 BC (see footnote 25 below) comprised a pool of 1,200 *eisphora*-payers; this pool, however, might not refer to all of the individuals liable to pay *eisphora*, but rather to those liable to pay in a given year, in order to raise the necessary sum of money. The majority of scholars believe a plausible figure for *eisphora*-payers is in the range of 1,200–2,000 contributors.

12 On *metics* performing liturgies, see Whitehead (1977, 77–82); on *metics* as *eisphora*-payers see Isoc. 17.41. Cf. Van Wees (2011, 105).

13 The *choregoi* of the City Dionysia and the Thargelians were appointed by the eponymous archon ([Arist.] *Ath. Pol.* 56.3); trierarchs by a *strategos* ([Arist.] *Ath. Pol.* 61.1). In other cases, liturgies were assigned by lot (for example, the *athlothetai*; [Arist.] *Ath. Pol.* 60.1). For commentary on these passages, see Rhodes (1981, 623–624, 669, 677). On the possibility that the *choregoi* at the Lenaia Festival were chosen by the *archon basileus*, see Rhodes (1981, 624). On assignment of liturgies by public officers, see Christ (2006, 194–198); Liddel (2007, 265) (*choregia*) and 270 (*trierarchia*); Kremmydas (2012, 18–19).

consider liturgies as semi-voluntary practices, i.e. contributions in which personal initiative often intermingled with social pressure and formal procedure (appointment by the city's magistrates).[14] The fact that magistrates appointed liturgists also raises questions regarding possible registers for the liturgies. While official lists of *eisphora*-payers are documented, the existence of such lists for the liturgies is subject to discussion among scholars.[15] However, whether recorded in official lists or not, the identity of the rich and their liability to act as potential liturgists must have been well-known at least within the restricted territorial and administrative unit of the deme.[16]

Presenting liturgies as voluntary donations in court speeches indeed contributed to the self-portrayal of the wealthy as generous citizens, but was not just a rhetorical strategy. The performance of liturgies did in fact contain some elements of voluntarism, an aspect which was prompted by intra-elite competition and the desire of the liturgists to acquire public visibility. This mechanism is not per se surprising in light of the competitive character of Athenian public life.[17] In *Lysias 21*, for example, a court speech presumably delivered in 403/2 BC, the speaker made a detailed list of the liturgies and *eisphorai* he had undertaken for the city, and he concluded:[18]

> Of these sums that I have enumerated, had I chosen to limit my public services to the letter of the law, I should not have spent one quarter.

The element of private initiative, in this case, is the fact that the speaker claims to have spent a considerably larger sum than required.[19] Nonetheless,

14 Cf. Whitehead (1977, 88) spoke of a "paradoxical conjuction of burden and honour"; cf. Fawcett (2016, 156): "[liturgies] held a position in the 'gray area' between compulsory taxes, like *eisphora*, and *epidoseis* [i.e. voluntary contributions, my addition]".

15 See, for example, the debate on the existence of registers for the *trierarchia*: Davies (1971) and (1981) believes they existed and were stored in central archives; Stanley (1993, 29–30) argues in favour of their preservation in deme's archives. Gabrielsen (1994, 182–199, 221) believes no such registers existed. Rohde (2019, 198–199) maintains that liturgical lists existed (not only for the trierarchy) and that they were drawn up with the same procedure as cavalry lists, as described in [Arist.] *Ath. Pol.* 49.2.

16 Finley (1973a, 1973b) believed that Athens was a "face-to-face society", a definition challenged first by Osborne (1985, 64–65). Although Athens was too vast a community to be defined overall as a "face-to-face society", the deme was indeed a more restricted community, in which the identity of "big men" was likely to be well known. On the people's knowledge (including non-elites) of financial matters concerning the city, see Pritchard (2019, 229–243).

17 For a case study on public competition for offices (*gymnasiarchia*), see Günther and Weiße (2014, 59–97). On the aristocratic tradition of displaying wealth in the archaic period, see Duplouy (2006).

18 Lys. 21.1–5. Citation is from Lys. 21.5: καὶ τούτων ὧνκατέλεξα, εἰ ἐβουλόμην κατὰ τὰ γεγραμμένα ἐν τῷ νόμῳ λητουργεῖν, οὐδ'ἂν τὸ τέταρτον μέρος ἀνήλωσα. This and the following translations of classical texts are based upon those of the Loeb Classical Library, unless otherwise noted. The emphasis added to each translated text is mine.

19 Liddel (2007, 267) notes that this is not a reference to a specific law but rather to statutory requirements.

the degree of voluntarism was fairly limited. In addition to appointments for liturgies by city officials, public pressure could lead the wealthy to take them up. Attic orations, for example, attest to a recurring rhetoric of public praise surrounding performers of liturgies. This kind of rhetoric, which finds an echo in the enumeration of liturgies in public dedications, was itself a powerful tool in the hands of the community to persuade rich citizens to bear these financial burdens.[20] But there were other, more direct instruments such as the *antidosis* procedure. Someone who was appointed to perform a liturgy (or perhaps just pointed out as a potential liturgist) could refuse by indicating a fellow citizen liable to perform the liturgy. In the event of this fellow citizen refusing, the individual originally appointed to the task could challenge him to an exchange of property.[21]

Thus, if a liturgy was not directly assigned by a magistrate, the decision to perform a liturgy was fostered by various motives, such as a sense of civic duty, honour and pride, the drive to acquire prestige and visibility and also by the fear of being involved in the *antidosis* procedure and the public shame evoked by a refusal. Undertaking a liturgy therefore often had little to do with choice and generosity. The mixed nature of this institution, which was halfway between donation and taxation, was often exploited by court speakers in their rhetorical strategies when they accused somebody of dodging such duties or defended themselves against such claims. In the next section, we will see some examples of this rhetoric.

1.3 *Topoi* and Rhetoric Strategies Concerning Tax Evasion

In Isocrates' speech *Against Callimachus*,[22] the speaker describes the behaviour of the Athenian trierarchs after the lost battle at Aegospotamoi in 405 BC – one of the decisive Athenian defeats during the Peloponnesian War:

> Now when the city had lost its ships in the Hellespont and it was short of its power, I so far surpassed the majority of the trierarchs that I was one of the few who saved their ships: and of these few I alone brought back my

20 See Liddel (2007, 196–209) for discussion of public dedications as instruments of collective coercion and pressure on liturgists; for competitive outlay, see ibid., 273–274.

21 [Dem.] 42 provides useful information. On *antidosis*, see Gabrielsen (1987, 7–38); Christ (1990, 161–164).

22 Isoc. 18.59-60: [59] ὅτε γὰρ ἡ πόλις ἀπώλεσε τὰς ναῦς τὰς ἐν Ἑλλησπόντῳ καὶ τῆςδυνάμεως ἐστερήθη, τῶν μὲν πλείστων τριηράρχων τοσοῦτον διήνεγκον, ὅτι μετ' ὀλίγων ἔσωσα τὴν ναῦν, αὐτῶν δὲ τούτων, ὅτι καταπλεύσας εἰςτὸν Πειραιᾶ μόνος οὐ κατέλυσα τὴν τριηραρχίαν, [60] ἀλλὰ τῶν ἄλλων ἀσμένως ἀπαλλαττομένων τῶν λῃτουργιῶν καὶπρὸς τὰ παρόντ' ἀθύμως διακειμένων, καὶ τῶν μὲν ἀνηλωμένων αὐτοῖςμεταμέλον, τὰ δὲ λοιπὰ ἀποκρυπτομένων, καὶ νομιζόντων τὰ μὲν κοινὰδιεφθάρθαι, τὰ δ' ἴδια σκοπουμένων, οὐ τὴν αὐτὴν ἐκείνοις γνώμηνἔσχον, ἀλλὰ πείσας τὸν ἀδελφὸν συντριηραρχεῖν, παρ' ἡμῶν αὐτῶνμισθὸν διδόντες τοῖς ναύταις κακῶς ἐποιοῦμεν τοὺς πολεμίους.

> ship to the Piraeus and I did not resign my duties as a trierarch; but when the other trierarchs were glad to be relieved of their duties and were discouraged over the situation, and not only regretted the loss of what they had already spent, but were trying to conceal the remainder and judging that the city was completely ruined, were looking out for their private interests, my decision was not the same as theirs; but after persuading my brother to be joint-trierarch with me, we paid the crew out of our means and proceeded to harass the enemy.

The speaker was an anonymous Athenian trierarch who was proud not to have interrupted his service of equipping warships for the city after the defeat of 405 BC, unlike many other trierarchs who "were glad to be relieved of their duties", as he claimed. The orator further notes that these people tried to conceal the remainder of their wealth, which seemed to be an attempt to avoid future liturgical appointments. The exact significance of the description (or reproach) that fellow trierarchs had concealed their wealth is not entirely clear, but other orations give some clues about similar practices, as we shall see further on.

In the comedy *The Frogs*, authored by Aristophanes in 405 BC,[23] we read the following fictional conversation between the two tragedians Aeschylus and Euripides upon their encounter in the underworld:

> AESCHYLUS: First you dressed the kingly types in rags, so they'd look pitiful to the audience.
> EURIPIDES: And what harm did I do by that?
> AESCHYLUS: Because of that, no wealthy man was willing to fund the navy, but wrapped in rags he weeps and claims that he's poor.

Aeschylus refers here to a typical feature of Euripides' dramas, namely, the display of rags to enhance the pathetic character of the scene and the protagonists involved.[24] The idea that these dramatic performances contributed to the fact that, at the end of the fifth century, no one was willing to undertake a trierarchy is an obvious exaggeration. But Aristophanes might here well refer to the widespread discontent among trierarchs who were bearing the costs of war operations in good part. This discontent intensified in the period following the end of the war. After 404 BC, following Athens' defeat in the Peloponnesian War, the loss of the tribute paid by its allies and the loss of Athenian land overseas, Athens entered a period of financial hardship. One of

23 Ar. *Ran*. 1063–65: Αἰσχύλος. πρῶτον μὲν τοὺς βασιλεύοντας ῥάκι' ἀμπισχών, ἵν' ἐλεινοὶ / τοῖς ἀνθρώποις φαίνοιντ' εἶναι./ Εὐριπίδης. τοῦτ' οὖν ἔβλαψά τι δράσας;/ Αἰσχύλος. οὔκουν ἐθέλει γε τριηραρχεῖν πλουτῶν οὐδεὶς διὰ ταῦτα, /ἀλλὰ ῥακίοις περιειλάμενος κλάει καὶ φησὶ πένεσθαι./

24 On this, Cecchet (2015, 67–88).

the many consequences of the war was the necessity to internally restructure the economy, rebuild the fleet and, from the mid-390s onward, supply money for the costs of new military operations during the Corinthian War. All of these operations entailed intensified fiscal pressure, requiring the more efficient organisation of taxes and liturgies. In the 370s, Athens introduced some important reforms pertaining to the liturgical system and the levying of the *eisphora*, presumably in order to achieve a better and fairer distribution of the financial burden and at the same time a more efficient system of raising money. With the *eisphora* reform of 378 BC, payers were grouped into 100 taxation units (the *symmoriai*).[25] From 362 BC, the entire amount of money in each taxation unit had to be paid in advance by the three richest members of each tax unit, the so-called *proeispherontes*, who thereafter had to collect the rest of the tax debt from their fellow members.[26] The total of 300 *proeispherontes* belonged to the richest stratum of the Athenian society. With the law proposed by Periander in 357 BC, the *symmory* system was also extended to the trierarchy: 20 tax categories were introduced consisting of 60 liturgy payers each.[27] In the year 354, Demosthenes proposed another reform of the trierarchy, namely, to increase the number of contributors from 1,200 to 2,000 in order to compensate for the high number of exemptions. The proposal was probably rejected.[28] In 340, however, the orator succeeded in having another law passed, which restricted the number of contributors to the trierarchy to the 300 wealthiest.[29]

How should we interpret these different reforms and attempts to reform the *eisphora* and the trierarchy system over a time span of almost 40 years? It is conceivable that they were a way to cope with the problem of equity which is intrinsic to the question of who must carry the fiscal burden. In fact, in parallel with growing financial pressure on the wealthy since the last period of the Peloponnesian War, the problem of adopting reasonable criteria for a fair distribution of the fiscal burden arose as a topic of public debate, at least among the well-to-do class. As shall be shown, echoes of this debate are attested in several expressions of discontent regarding the performance of liturgies contained in court speeches. This discontent focused on two key aspects. Firstly, the presumably unfair distribution of the fiscal burden among the wealthy was discussed by orators such as Demosthenes who claimed that the "less wealthy" among the *plousioi* were carrying too large a share of this

25 On 378 BC as the date of the reform of the collection of the *eisphora*: Phil. FrgrHist 328 F 41; on the new number of *symmoriai*: Cleid. FrgrHist 323 F 8.

26 Is. 6.60. On the *proeispherontes*, see Wallace (1989, 473–490); cf. MacDowell (1990, 368–369).

27 On Periander's law of 357 BC, see [Dem.] 47.21; Rhodes (1982, 5–11); MacDowell (1986, 438–449; 1990, 372); Gabrielsen (1994, 182–193); Liddel (2007, 271).

28 Dem. 14.16. For discussion, see Canevaro (2018, 459–460). For an earlier discussion, see also Rhodes (1981, 680).

29 Dem. 18.102–109; Aeschin. 3.222; Din. 1.42; Hyp. Fr. 134 Jensen. However, Gabrielsen (1994, 153–158) maintains that this group of 300 was in charge of bearing most but not the entire cost of trierarchy. Cf. Hansen (1999, 172–173).

burden. Secondly, court speeches can be read as a source for cases where fiscal duties were evaded or attempts were made to evade such duties.

When we look at orations, we see that they show two different rhetoric narratives concerning liturgies and taxes, which were, nonetheless, related. Along with the narrative that denounces the dishonest rich man who tries to escape his duties, there is also the narrative of the honourable rich man who spends large sums of money on the city, performing his liturgies even more generously than he is supposed to do. The second *topos* often served the purpose of enhancing the contrast between one's virtuous behaviour and the behaviour of tax evaders. It presumably also served as protection against prospective accusations of tax evasion and, in general, was a way to gain the favour of the audience in case of future law-suits. The speaker in Lysias 25, for example, says that he undertook the trierarchy five times as well as several other liturgies in order to win the people's favour in case he should have trouble in future.[30]

A very clear example of these two narratives – the rich tax dodger and the rich honest citizen – can be found in Demosthenes' speech *Against Meidias*, presumably written in the early 340s. The speech contains an interesting portrayal of Meidias, a liturgist and *eisphora* leader or *hegemon*, responsible for the collection of contributions from the members of his tax bracket.[31] Demosthenes attacks Meidias largely by highlighting that the hegemon had avoided liturgies on many occasions, and in several ways.[32] The orator delivers a long list of all the retraction strategies Meidias applied in order to avoid taxation, starting with the fact that he performed the trierarchy only after reform of the system following Periander's law, i.e. after the introduction of the *symmoriai* and the board of 1,200 contributors (*synteleis*).[33] According to Demosthenes, Meidias collected one talent from all of the other contributors and in this way managed to avoid paying his own contribution.[34] Other tricks involved the use of the trireme, an oar-propelled warship, which Meidias had equipped in the trierarchic service as his private cargo vessel, and riding a friend's horse instead of buying one when he was cavalry leader.[35] To this description of Meidias's ill behaviour, Demosthenes juxtaposed his self-portrayal as an honest and generous liturgist: despite being younger than Meidias, Demosthenes claimed that his own liturgies were equal in number

30 Lys. 25.12–13.

31 It is unclear whether this oration was actually delivered in a trial. Aischines 3.52 claims it was not, but not all historians agree, see Harris (1989, 117–136). Be that as it may, the orator's intention in the oration is to discredit his rival Meidias, and we cannot take every accusation at face value. But, as mentioned at the beginning of this chapter, we are interested here in the rhetoric concerning tax evasion and this oration offers a good example.

32 Dem. 21.152–174.

33 See n. 27 above.

34 Dem. 21.155.

35 Dem. 21.167 and 174. On the rhetoric strategies deployed in the speech, see also Ober (1994). On the historical background and origin of the quarrel, see MacDowell (1990, 1–37) and Harris (2008, 75–87).

to those performed by Meidias and reaffirmed his assertion by enumerating his liturgies to the audience.[36]

We do not have direct evidence of Meidias' own perspective. In general, we do not have much evidence of how presumed tax evaders rebuked such accusations or deflected suspicions, or of how they attempted to legitimise their behaviour. One obvious possibility is that they denied these accusations altogether. However, this strategy might not always have proved easy, as liturgists were publicly visible to the magistrates, their fellow liturgists and the Athenian people, depending on the kind of liturgy. To wrongfully claim to have undertaken a certain liturgy was hence difficult. Other possible rhetoric strategies are indirectly revealed by information contained in the speeches of opponents, such as in the case of Demosthenes. In the oration *Against Meidias*, Demosthenes states that he cannot bear the arrogance of Meidias and he mimics Meidias' regular exclamation (uttered "in every assembly meeting") as follows: "We are the rich! We are those who pay the *eisphora* tax in advance!".[37] If we assume that Demosthenes' quotation is based on words uttered by Meidias, such a proud remark before the assembly might at first appear to be a flawed strategy for winning the favour of the audience. But insistently highlighting the contributions one had already paid for the good of the *polis* could also be a way to divert attention from the contributions one had evaded, or an implicit strategy to beg forgiveness with the excuse that one had already given enough.

This relates to a strategy of defence that we can reconstruct from the orators' hints at tax evasion. This strategy consisted of claiming that past fiscal commitment had been so burdensome that it had led to impoverishment. The supposed evader argued that he was unable to accept new duties after he had lost all (or a good part) of his property by bearing the costs of liturgies and taxes. It is from this perspective that we should interpret the words of Aeschylus in the aforementioned passage of Aristophanes' *Frogs* concerning the rich man who "wrapped in rags weeps and claims he is poor". We do not know how frequently the display of poor clothing before the court occurred, but the rhetoric of poverty was indeed often deployed in order to evoke the sympathy and the pity of the audience.[38] We find an echo of this rhetoric also in literary genres other than oratory. The anonymous author of the late fifth-century pamphlet *The Constitution of the Athenians* – a sympathiser of

36 Dem. 21.154–157. On the hostile feelings evoked by liturgy evasion in court speeches, see Sanders 2012, 376–379.

37 Dem. 21.153: εἰ μέν ἐστιν, ὦ ἄνδρες Ἀθηναῖοι, τὸ λητουργεῖν τοῦτο, τὸ ἐν ὑμῖν λέγειν ἐν ἁπάσαις ταῖς ἐκκλησίαις καὶ πανταχοῦ 'ἡμεῖς οἱ λητουργοῦντες, ἡμεῖς οἱ προεισφέροντες ὑμῖν, ἡμεῖς οἱ πλούσιοί ἐσμεν,' εἰ τὸ τὰ τοιαῦτα λέγειν, τοῦτ' ἔστιν λητουργεῖν, ὁμολογῶ Μειδίαν ἁπάντων τῶν ἐν τῇ πόλει λαμπρότατον γεγενῆσθαι: ἀποκναίει γὰρ ἀηδίᾳ δήπου καὶ ἀναισθησίᾳ καθ' ἑκάστην τὴν ἐκκλησίαν ταῦτα λέγων.

38 For a presumed case of display of poor clothing (perhaps rags) before the court, see [Dem]. 44.3-4. In general, on law-court "dramas", Hall (1995); on the rhetoric of seeing in court speeches, O'Connell (2017). On the portrayal of the defenceless in court speeches, Rubinstein (2013); on the rhetoric of poverty in Attic oratory, Cecchet (2015, 141–226).

oligarchy – refers to the impoverishing of rich Athenians as a phenomenon caused by the burdensome liturgies the *polis* imposes on them.[39] The Athenian citizen Charmides, in Xenophon's *Symposion*, refers to himself as having been "a slave" of the *polis* when rich.[40]

But let us return to oratory. In the course of the fourth century, the portrayal of the "poor liturgist" had become a *topos*. The speeches of Demosthenes are particularly rich in self-portrayals of "poor liturgists", including the author himself. In his second speech *Against Aphobus* (364/3 BC), Demosthenes explains: "I mortgaged my house and all my property, and paid the cost of the service in question [...]".[41]

Demosthenes attacks here one of his legal guardians, Aphobus, who had fraudulently deprived him of his property after the death of his father. In this context, he mentions one of the liturgies he had undertaken when younger, which had been a very significant burden. Similarly, in the speech *Against Polycles* (delivered between 360 and 358 BC), the orator and wealthy liturgist, Apollodoros, highlights how he had been obliged to mortgage his property and run up other debts in order to perform the trierarchy:[42]

> 7: Having mortgaged my property and borrowed money, I was the first to man my ship, hiring the best sailors possible by giving to each man large bonuses and advance payments [...] 13: I mortgaged my farm to Thrasylochus and Archeneus, and having borrowed thirty minae from them and distributed the money among the crew, I put to sea...

Selling or mortgaging property in order to bear the costs of liturgies and *eisphorai* is a practice to which orators often refer. In the pseudo-Demosthenic speech *Against Evergus and Mnesilochus* (355 or 354/3 BC), the plaintiff describes how his opponents broke into his house to seize his property but found much less than they had expected:[43]

> They thought to get, not so much merely, but far more, for they expected to find the stock of household furniture, which I formerly had; but

39 [Xen.] *Ath. Pol.* 1.13.

40 Xen. *Symp.* 4.32.

41 Dem. 28.17: ἀπέτεισα τὴν λητουργίαν ὑποθεὶς τὴν οἰκίαν καὶ τἀμαυτοῦ πάντα, βουλόμενος εἰς ὑμᾶς εἰσελθεῖν τὰς πρὸς τουτουσὶ δίκας.

42 [Dem]. 50.7 and 13: [7] ὑποθεὶς δὲ τὴν οὐσίαν τὴν ἐμαυτοῦ καὶ δανεισάμενος ἀργύριον πρῶτος ἐπληρωσάμην τὴν ναῦν, μισθωσάμενος ναύτας ὡς οἷόν τ' ἦν ἀρίστους, δωρεὰς καὶ προδόσεις δοὺς ἑκάστῳ αὐτῶν μεγάλας. [13] ὑποθεὶς δὲ τὸ χωρίον Θρασυλόχῳ καὶ Ἀρχένεῳ, καὶ δανεισάμενος τριάκοντα μνᾶς παρ' αὐτῶν καὶ διαδοὺς τοῖς ναύταις, ᾠχόμην ἀναγόμενος...Cf. Lys. 19.25-26: Demos, son of Pyrilampes, takes a loan of 16 minae in order to pay a trierarchy. For a collection and discussion of cases, see Gabrielsen (1994, 146–172).

43 [Dem]. 47.54: ᾤοντο μὲν γὰρ οὐ τοσαῦτα μόνον λήψεσθαι, ἀλλὰ πολλῷ πλείω: τὴν γὰρ οὖσάν μοι ποτὲ κατασκευὴν τῆς οἰκίας καταλήψεσθαι: ἀλλ' ὑπὸ τῶν λητουργιῶν καὶ τῶν εἰσφορῶν καὶ τῆς πρὸς ὑμᾶς φιλοτιμίας τὰ μὲν ἐνέχυρα κεῖται αὐτῶν, τὰ δὲ πέπραται.

> because of my public services and taxes and my liberality toward you, some of the furniture is lying in pawn, and some has been sold [...].

These stories might either show the dire case of "impoverished" rich Athenians or, more probably, they reflect a strategy of selling property in order to gain liquidity to realise other aims, such as profitable investments, or in order to make wealth "less visible". In the first speech *Against Stephanus* (350/49 BC), Apollodorus accuses his opponent, Stephanus, of avoiding liturgies by hiding cash in the bank of Pasion:[44]

> This course of action, involving so great disgrace, he has adopted, men of Athens, with a view to evading his duties to the state and to conceal his wealth, that he may make secret profits by means of the bank, and never serve as choregus or trierarch, or perform any other of the public duties which befit his station. And he has accomplished this object. Here is a proof. Although he has so large an estate that he gave his daughter a marriage portion of one hundred minae, he has never been seen by you to perform any public service whatever, even the very slightest [...].

In some other cases, orators refer to sales of land as a strategy to avoid liturgies and *eisphorai*.[45] In fact, the strongest proof of individual wealth in classical Athens – and in the majority of the Greek cities – was land ownership, despite the fact that Athenians could acquire wealth from a variety of sources and investments.[46] Lack of landed property could thus be advocated as proof of relative poverty among the rich, regardless of the fact that it might not have reflected economic poverty at all. The orator Aeschines in the speech *Against Timarchus* (346/5 BC) says:[47]

> For the father, afraid of the special services [i.e. liturgies. L.C.] to which he would be liable, sold the property that he owned (with the exception of the items I have mentioned)— a piece of land in Cephisia, another in Amphitrope, and two workshops at the silver mines, one of them in Aulon, the other near the tomb of Thrasyllus.

44 [Dem]. 45.66: ταῦτα μέντοι τὰ τοσαύτην ἔχοντ' αἰσχύνην, ὦ ἄνδρες Ἀθηναῖοι, ἐπὶ τῷ τὴν πόλιν φεύγειν καὶ τὰ ὄντ' ἀποκρύπτεσθαι προῄρηται πράττειν, ἵν' ἐργασίας ἀφανεῖς διὰ τῆς τραπέζης ποιῆται, καὶ μήτε χορηγῇ μήτε τριηραρχῇ μήτ' ἄλλο μηδὲν ὧν προσήκει ποιῇ. καὶ κατείργασται τοῦτο. τεκμήριον δέ: ἔχων γὰρ οὐσίαν τοσαύτην ὥσθ' ἑκατὸν μνᾶς ἐπιδοῦναι τῇ θυγατρί, οὐδ' ἡντινοῦν ἑώραται λῃτουργίαν ὑφ' ὑμῶν λῃτουργῶν, οὐδὲ τὴν ἐλαχίστην.

45 Gabrielsen (1986, 99–114); cf. also Gabrielsen (1994, 53–60); on visible and invisible wealth, see also Ferrucci (2005, 145–169).

46 Harris (2002, 67–99); Taylor (2017).

47 Aesch. 1.101: φοβηθεὶς γὰρ τὰς λῃτουργίας ἀπέδοτο ἃ ἦν αὐτῷ κτήματα ἄνευ τῶν ἀρτίως εἰρημένων, χωρίον Κηφισιᾶσιν, ἕτερον1 Ἀμφιτροπῆσιν, ἐργαστήρια δύο ἐν τοῖς ἀργυρείοις, ἓν μὲν ἐν Αὐλῶνι, ἕτερον δ' ἐπὶ Θρασύλλῳ.

Indeed, we cannot know if Aeschines was right here about the motives for the sale of the property by Timarchus' father as such sales could also have served to obtain cash for profitable investments. Overall, it is difficult to assess how frequently wealthy Athenians sold property to avoid tax liability.[48] It was probably not widespread as land ownership remained a strong sign not only of economic wealth but also of prestige. Given also the paucity of land in Attica and the loss of Athenian land overseas after defeat in the Peloponnesian War, wealthy landowners would not easily sell their ancestorial estates. The wealthy Phaenippus, whom the unnamed speaker of [Demosthenes'] oration 42 accuses of violating the rules in the procedure of *antidosis*, apparently preferred hiding the wood, wine and grain which were stored on his farm by providing false information in the inventory of his property and by making up debts (according to Demosthenes). But he certainly did not sell his large farm in order to conceal his wealth.[49]

What we know for sure is that wealthy Athenians did not suddenly become "poor" in the fourth century. And, despite the fact that some of them lost their overseas assets after 404 BC, fourth-century Athens was characterised by a thriving economy. The wealthy had multiple options for investing their money.[50] It is clear that in some cases orators are playing with the vocabulary and concept of poverty when describing fiscal oppression. In the speech *Against Leptines* (355/4 BC), Demosthenes warns against the arguments which might be used by his rival Leptines who in 356 BC had passed a law that cancelled all exemptions from liturgies:[51]

> Well, perhaps Leptines might possibly try to distract you from this point by making the following argument: liturgies are now falling on poor men, but as a result of this law, the richest men will perform liturgies.

According to Demosthenes, Leptines would probably argue that exemptions from liturgies were contributing to the maintenance of – unjust – financial

48 Epigraphic documents provide evidence mainly of sales of public land (see Lambert 1997) and sales of confiscated property (*Agora XIX*, 58–60 and *Catalogue*), while *horoi*-security inscriptions attest to different kinds of mortgage (*Agora XIX*, 37–52). We know little about land transactions among private citizens in Athens, let alone the case of *hypothekai*. A related question concerns the existence of registers of private land in Athens; for discussion, Faraguna (1997).

49 According to the speaker, Phaenippus never performed a liturgy ([Dem.] 42.3). Violating the procedure of *antidosis*, he carried away stuff from his storehouses, namely, wine and grain (([Dem.] 42.2, 19 and 30), wood (42.9) and possessions from inside the house (42.26). He also made up debts (42.9 and 27-28).

50 See, for example, Aristarchos, in Xen. *Mem.* 2.7.2–12: after losing his land in the civil war of 404/3 BC, he set up a family business of wool working. For discussion, Taylor (2016, 267–269).

51 Dem. 20.18. Trans. Harris (2008): τάχα τοίνυν ἴσως ἐκεῖνο λέγειν ἂν ἐπιχειρήσειε Λεπτίνης, ἀπάγων ὑμᾶς ἀπὸ τούτων, ὡς αἱ λητουργίαι νῦν μὲν εἰς πένητας ἀνθρώπους ἔρχονται, ἐκ δὲ τοῦ νόμου τούτου λητουργήσουσιν οἱ πλουσιώτατοι…For comments on the passage, Kremmydas (2012, 216–217). Cf. Cecchet (2015, 213–214) and Canevaro (2016, 218–219).

pressure on the "the poor" (*penetes*). But the poor in question were still members of the liturgical class, i.e. Athenians with fortunes of no less than three talents! This "flexible" and exaggerated use of the label "poor" is based on the relative nature of the concept of poverty in discursive practice. Thus, a wealthy Athenian might comfortably describe all those who were below his level of wealth as poor (*penetes*). This discursive practice is widely attested also in private court cases (in particular in those concerning inheritance litigation), where it was aimed at evoking the sympathy of the jurors, many of whom had probably never performed a liturgy.[52]

But interesting for us here is the anticipated argument of Leptines, which referred to questions of (un)fair taxation. If exemptions from liturgies were maintained, the "poor" would have to bear their costs. This implies that if the "poor" in question were accused of evading taxes and liturgies, they would probably attempt to defend their position by pointing to exemptions from liturgies as a cause for inequity and excessive burden on their shoulders.

Demosthenes used a similar rhetoric strategy when he presented the liturgists as *penetes* (poor) in *On the Crown* (330 BC). In the following excerpt, Demosthenes reminds the audience of the law with which he had proposed the trierarchy of 340 BC:[53]

> I saw, Athenians, that your fleet was falling apart, that while small payments left the wealthy practically untaxed, citizens of moderate and small means were losing their property, and further, that the situation was causing the city to miss opportunities. I proposed a law through which I compelled some, the rich, to assume their fair burden, stopped the unjust treatment of the poor, and brought about what the city most needed—armed forces ready for action.

The "unjust treatment of the poor" was the problem Demosthenes had identified in the previous trierarchy system. Recalling the situation prior to 340, he claimed that the wealthy had been left "practically untaxed". Instead, those who lost their property were the citizens who were forced to sell or mortgage it. Reading between the lines, we can recognise the complaints of the liturgists who lamented losing "all they had". It is not difficult to envisage

52 On the relative nature of the concept of poverty and the role of the reference group in discursive practice, see Cecchet (2015, 13–48); on the rhetoric of poverty in court speeches, see ibid., 141–224.

53 Dem 18.102. Trans. Yunis 2005: ὁρῶν γάρ, ὦ ἄνδρες Ἀθηναῖοι, τὸ ναυτικὸν ὑμῶν καταλυόμενον καὶ τοὺς μὲν πλουσίους ἀτελεῖς ἀπὸ μικρῶν ἀναλωμάτων γιγνομένους, τοὺς δὲ μέτρι' ἢ μικρὰ κεκτημένους τῶν πολιτῶν τὰ ὄντ' ἀπολλύοντας, ἔτι δ' ὑστερίζουσαν ἐκ τούτων τὴν πόλιν τῶν καιρῶν, ἔθηκα νόμον καθ' ὃν τοὺς μὲν τὰ δίκαια ποιεῖν ἠνάγκασα, τοὺς πλουσίους, τοὺς δὲ πένητας ἔπαυσ' ἀδικουμένους, τῇ πόλει δ' ὅπερ ἦν χρησιμώτατον, ἐν καιρῷ γίγνεσθαι τὰς παρασκευὰς ἐποίησα. For sources attesting the contents of the law, see footnote 28 above.

how they replied to accusations of evading liturgies by pointing out their lack of means and by stressing the unjust character of the current system.

One last – and even more refined – example of this kind of rhetoric is contained in Demosthenes' speech *Against Androtion* (354 BC). Here, a certain Diodoros attacks Androtion, a wealthy Athenian who was in charge of collecting the arrays on an earlier *eisphora*. Diodoros claims that Androtion treated the *eisphora* payers who had defaulted their payments unfairly. He takes up their defence by presenting the audience with a set of rhetoric questions. The first reads as follows:[54]

> And yet, men of Athens, what do you think when a poor man— or even a rich man who has spent a lot and is perhaps likely to be short of money in some way— either goes up over the roof to reach his neighbors or slips under his bed to avoid being physically seized and dragged off to prison? Or when he suffers the kind of indignities appropriate for slaves, not free men?…

Those who had no money, so the argument goes, should not be imprisoned or treated as criminals (as Androtion had done) because they defaulted on taxes (*eisphora*), particularly as these impoverished citizens were not the ones doing the real harm to the *polis*, as Diodorus suggests in his second question, which is fictively addressed to Androtion:[55]

> Take two kinds of people: men who farm and are frugal but fall behind in paying taxes [*eisphorai*, L.C.] because they spend money on raising children or household expenses or other liturgies, and then men who steal money from those who wish to pay the tax and from our allies, then waste it. If someone asked him which group he thinks commits the greater crime against the city, he would certainly not be so bold (despite his utter shamelessness) as to claim that those who do not pay the tax on their own property commit a greater crime than men who steal public funds.

We here find a portrayal of Athenian liturgists and *eisphorai* payers as members of a middle class of small farmers, tilling their own land and, at the

54 Dem. 22.53. Trans. Harris (2008): καίτοι, ὦ ἄνδρες Ἀθηναῖοι, τί οἴεσθ' ὁπότ' ἄνθρωπος πένης ἢ καὶ πλούσιος, πολλὰ δ' ἀνηλωκὼς καί τιν' ἴσως τρόπον εἰκότως οὐκ εὐπορῶν ἀργυρίου, ἢ τέγος ὡς τοὺς γείτονας ὑπερβαίνοι, ἢ ὑποδύοιθ' ὑπὸ κλίνην ὑπὲρ τοῦ μὴ τὸ σῶμ' ἁλοὺς εἰς τὸ δεσμωτήριον ἕλκεσθαι, ἢ ἄλλ' ἀσχημονοίη ἃ δούλων, οὐκ ἐλευθέρων ἐστὶν ἔργα…

55 Dem. 22.65. Trans. Harris (2008): εἰ γάρ τις ἔροιτ' αὐτὸν πότερ' αὐτῷ δοκοῦσ' ἀδικεῖν μᾶλλον τὴν πόλιν οἱ γεωργοῦντες καὶ φειδόμενοι, διὰ παιδοτροφίας δὲ καὶ οἰκεῖ' ἀναλώματα καὶ λητουργίας ἑτέρας ἐλλελοιπότες εἰσφοράν, ἢ οἱ τὰ τῶν ἐθελησάντων εἰσενεγκεῖν χρήματα καὶ τὰ παρὰ τῶν συμμάχων κλέπτοντες καὶ ἀπολλύντες, οὐκ ἂν εἰς τοῦτο τόλμης δήπου, καίπερ ὢν ἀναιδής, ἔλθοι, ὥστε φῆσαι τοὺς τὰ ἑαυτῶν μὴ εἰσφέροντας μᾶλλον ἀδικεῖν ἢ τοὺς τὰ κοίν' ὑφαιρουμένους.

same time, struggling to cope with the high financial pressure of liturgies and *eisphorai*. This picture is, largely, a distortion of reality. Demosthenes plays here with a real fact: as we mentioned in the beginning of this chapter, the *eisphora* was also levied from citizens who were less rich than those qualifying for liturgies. The threshold of 2,500 drachmae probably indicates the upper part of the middle classes. It thus by no means applied to the poor, as the above portrayal claims. Yet again, Demosthenes deploys the well-consolidated *topos* of the poor taxpayer. Rather than mirroring reality, this *topos* reflected the intensive debate about the criteria used for fiscal distribution among the wealthy and the arguments of those who claimed the existing system was unjust. The fact that Demosthenes' trierarchy law of 340 was finally passed confirms that the Athenians felt an urgent need to improve the system and concentrate fiscal pressure on the wealthiest stratum of the "liturgical class".

1.4 Conclusion

This chapter attempted to reconstruct the defence strategies of presumed tax evaders based on information contained in court speeches. One chief strategy involved claiming impoverishment after bearing the costs of financial duties. Other arguments consisted of stressing the burdens individuals had carried in the past and indicating the unjust distribution of fiscal pressure among the different groups of the wealthy. This last argument was at the heart of an intensive debate concerning the criteria adopted in the distribution of financial duties. This debate culminated in several attempted or successful reforms of the *eisphora* and the trierarchy system in the fourth century. The reform measures were aimed at reducing fiscal pressure for the less wealthy and concentrating it on the very rich.

Whatever opinions wealthy Athenians might have had on liturgies and *eisphorai*, they never publicly questioned the very legitimacy of these institutions before the court or the assembly. Rather, the wealthy always had to come to terms with the audience they were addressing in public speeches. This audience consisted, largely, of middle and lower class citizens who had never performed liturgies or paid *eisphorai*, but who were aware of the importance of these contributions for the financial well-being of the city. One of the cornerstones of Athenian democratic ideology was that individual liberty was possible only within the limits of the civic obligations intended to preserve the common good of the city and the civic community. Carrying the burden of liturgies and *eisphorai* was, for the rich, one of these obligations.

References

Akrigg, Ben. 2011. Demography and Classical Athens. In *Demography and the Graeco-Roman World*, eds. Claire Holleran and April Pudsey, 37–59. Cambridge, New York: Cambridge University Press.

Akrigg, Ben. 2019. *Population and Economy in Classical Athens*. Cambridge, New York: Cambridge University Press.

Canevaro, Mirko. 2016. *Demostene, "Contro Leptine", introduzione, traduzione e comment storico*. Berlin: De Gruyter.

Canevaro, Mirko. 2018. What was the Law of Leptines' really about? Reflections on Athenian Public Economy and Legislation in the Fourth Century BCE. *Constitutional Political Economy* 29: 440–464.

Cecchet, Lucia. 2015. *Poverty in Athenian Public Discourse. From the Eve of the Peloponnesian War to the Rise of Macedonia*. Historia Enzelschriften 239. Stuttgart: Steiner.

Christ, Matthew R. 1990. Liturgy Avoidance and *Antidosis* in Classical Athens. *Transactions of the American Philological Association* 120: 147–169.

Christ, Matthew R. 2006. *The Bad Citizen in Classical Athens*. Cambridge: Cambridge University Press.

Christ, Matthew R. 2007. The Evolution of the *Eisphora* in Classical Athens. *Classical Quarterly* 57: 53–69.

Davies, John K. 1971. Athenian Propertied Families 600-300 B.C. Oxford: Clarendon Press.

Davies, John K. 1981. *Wealth and the Power of Wealth in Classical Athens*. New York: Arno Press.

Duplouy, Alain. 2006. *Le prestige des élites. Recherches sur les modes de reconnaissance sociale en Grèce entre les Xe et Ve siècles avant J.-C.* Paris: Les Belles Lettres.

Faraguna, Michele. 1997. Registrazioni catastali nel mondo greco: il caso di Atene. *Athenaeum* 85: 7–33.

Fawcett, Peter. 2016. "When I Squeeze You with Eisphora". Taxes and Tax Policy in Classical Athens. *Hesperia* 85: 153–199.

Ferrucci, Stefano. 2005. La ricchezza nascosta: osservazioni su ἀφανής e φανερα οὐσία. *Mediterraneo Antico* 8.1: 145–169.

Finley, Moses I. 1973a. *Problèmes de la terre en Grèce ancienne: recueil de travaux*. Paris: Mouton.

Finley, Moses I. 1973b. *The Ancient Economy*. Berkeley: University of California Press.

Gabrielsen, Vincent. 1986. Φανερά and ἀφανης οὐσία in Classical Athens. *Classica&Medievalia* 37: 99–114.

Gabrielsen, Vincent. 1987. The *Antidosis* Procedure in Classical Athens. *Classica&Medievalia* 38: 7–38.

Gabrielsen, Vincent. 1994. *Financing the Athenian Fleet: Public Taxation and Social Relations*. Baltimore: Johns Hopkins University Press.

Günther, Sven and Franziska Weiße. 2014. Zwischen aristokratischem Führungsanspruch und demokratischem Gleichheitsideal: Überlegungen zur Gymnasiarchie im 5./4. Jahrhundert v. Chr. In *Sport und Recht in der Antike. Beträge zum 2. Wiener Kolloquium zur Antiken Rechtsgeschichte, 27.-28.10.2011*, eds. Kaja Harter-Uibopuu and Thomas Kruse, 59–87. Wien: Holzhausen.

Hall, Edith 1995. Lawcourt Dramas: the Power of Performance in Greek Forensic Oratory. *BICS* 40: 39–58.

Hansen, Mogen Herman. 1999. *The Athenian Democracy in the Age of Demosthenes. Structures, Principles and Ideology*. London: University of Oklahoma Press.

Harris, Edward M. 1989. Demosthenes' Speech 'Against Meidias'. *Harvard Studies in Classical Philology* 92: 117–136.

Harris, Edward M. 2002. Workshop, Marketplace and Household: the Nature of Technical Specialisation in Classical Athens and Its Influence on Economy and Society. In *Money, Labour and Land. Approaches to the Economies of Ancient Greece*, eds. Paul Cartledge, Edward. E. Cohen, and Lin Foxhall, 67–99. London: Routledge.

Harris, Edward M. 2008. *Demosthenes, Speeches 20–22.* Austin: University of Texas Press.

Kierstead, James and Roman Klapaukh. 2018. The Distribution of Wealthy Athenians in the Attic Demes. In *Ancient Greek History and Contemporary Social Science*, eds. Mirko Canevaro, Andrew Erskine, Benjamin Gray, and Josiah Ober, 376–401. Edinburgh: Edinburgh University Press.

Kremmydas, Chrystos. 2012. *Commentary on Demosthenes' Against Leptines.* Oxford: Oxford University Press.

Lalonde, Gerald V., Merle V. Langdon, and Michael B. Walbank. 1991. *Inscriptions: Horoi, Poletai Records and Leases of Public Lands.* Agora XIX. Princeton: The American School of classical Studies at Athens.

Lambert, Stephen D. 1997. *Rationes Centesimarum: Sales of Public Land in Lykourgan Athens.* Amsterdam: Gieben.

Liddel, Peter P. 2007. *Civic Obligation and Individual Liberty in Ancient Athens.* Oxford: Oxford University Press.

MacDowell, Douglas M. 1986. The Law of Periandros about Symmories. *Classical Quarterly* 36:438–449.

MacDowell, Douglas M. 1990. *Demosthenes: Against Meidias (Oration 21).* Oxford: Clarendon Press.

Ober, Josiah. 1989. *Mass and Elites in Democratic Athens: Rhetoric, Ideology and the Power of the People.* Princeton: Princeton University Press.

Ober, Josiah. 1994. Power and Oratory in Democratic Athens: Demosthenes 21, *Against Meidias.* In *Persuasion: Greek Rhetoric in Action*, ed. Ian Worthington, 85–108. London: Routledge.

Osborne, Robin. 1985. *Demos. The Discovery of Classical Attica.* Cambridge: Cambridge University Press.

Osborne, Robin. 2010. *Athens and Athenian Democracy.* Cambridge: Cambridge University Press.

Pritchard, David M. 2019. The Democratic Control of Public Spending in Classical Athens. In *200 Years after August Boeckh's "The Public Economy of the Athenians". Perspectives of Economic History for the 21st Century. Proceedings of an International Workshop held at the ZiF in Bielefeld 2017. Journal of Ancient Civilization 34*, eds. Sven Günther and Dorothea Rohde, 229–243. Changhun: Changhun University Press.

Rhodes, Peter. J. 1981. *A Commentary on the Aristotelian Athenaion Politeia.* Oxford: Clarendon Press.

Rhodes, Peter J. 1982. *Problems in Athenian* Eisphora *and Liturgies. American Journal of Ancient History* 7: 1–19.

Rohde, Dorothea. 2012. Bürgerpflicht und Gleichheitsideal. "Besteuerung" und ihre diskursiven Grundlagen in Sparta und Athen. In *Ordnungsrahmen antiker Ökonomien. Ordnungskonzepte und Steuerungsmechanismen antiker Wirtschaftssysteme im Vergleich*, ed. Sven Günther, 23–40. Wiesbaden: Harrassowitz.

Rohde, Dorothea. 2019. *Von der Deliberationsdemokratie zur Zustimmungsdemokratie. Die öffentlichen Finanzen Athens und die Ausbildung einer Kompetenzelite im 4. Jahrhundert v. Chr.* Berlin, Heidelberg: Springer.

Rubinstein, Lene. 2013. Evoking Anger through Pity: Portraits of the Vulnerable and Defenceless in Attic Oratory. In *Emotions in Greece and Rome: Texts, Images, Material Culture*, ed. Angelos Chaniotis, 135–165. Stuttgart: Steiner.

Sanders, Ed. 2012. He is a liar, a bounder, and a cad: The Arousal of Hostile Emotions in Attic Forensic Oratory. In *Unveiling Emotions: Sources and Methods for the Study of Emotions in the Greek World*, ed. Angelos Chaniotis, 359–87. Stuttgart: Steiner.

Stanley, Peter V. 1993. Release from Liturgical Service in Athens. *Laverna* 4: 26–44.
Taylor, Claire. 2016. Social Dynamics in Fourth-Century Athens. Poverty and Standards of Living. In *Die Athenische Demokratie im 4. Jahrhundert. Zwischen Modernisierung und Tradition*, ed. Claudia Tiersch, 261–277. Steiner: Stuttgart.
Taylor, Claire. 2017. *Poverty, Wealth and Well-being. Experiencing Penia in Democratic Athens.* Oxford: Oxford University Press.
Thomsen, Rudi. 1964. Eisphora. *A Study of Direct Taxation in Ancient Athens.* Humanitas 3. Copenhagen: Gyldendal.
Van Wees, Hans. 2011. Demetrius and Draco: Athens' Property Classes and Population in and Before 317 BC. *Journal of Hellenic Studies* 131: 95–114.
Wallace, Robert W. 1989. The Athenian *Proeispherontes. Hesperia* 58: 473–490.
Whitehead, David. 1977. *The Ideology of the Athenian Metic.* Cambridge: Cambridge Philological Association.
Yunis, Harvey. 2005. *Demosthenes, Speeches 18 and 19.* Austin: University of Texas Press.

2 The *Alcabala* Sales Tax Administration

Avoidance Strategies in Bourbon Colonial Mexico (1723–1754)[1]

Rodrigo Gordoa de la Huerta

2.1 Introduction

From the late sixteenth century until the first decades of the nineteenth century, the sales tax known as the *alcabala* was one of the most important revenue sources of Spanish America.[2] This fiscal instrument was imposed on all mercantile transactions, mainly on sales and barters of European and Asian goods at a tax rate that shifted from an original 2% – established in 1575 on all transactions – to a 6% fixed rate by the 1630s.[3] Due to the impact of the *alcabala* on most of the commercial activities in all cities, towns and villages of Colonial Mexico, and the absence of a customs system or centralised administration by the Spanish royal treasury, Spanish merchants controlled the sales tax administration by signing tax farming contracts to reduce tax payments. Other strategies of fiscal reduction or evasion existed, as discussed below.[4]

These practices have so far not been comprehensively studied by Mexican or Spanish historiography. Instead, there are a number of specific studies on the sales tax administrations in Mexico City (controlled by a powerful merchant elite represented by a traders' guild) and in Puebla.[5] There are also some monographic studies about tax fraud and its judicial consequences in Mexico City.[6] Overall, we have an incomplete understanding of the structure and function of the sales tax administration before the Bourbon Reforms from the late eighteenth century, as the existing studies have focused on general income trends and on the relation between tax farming and the interests of local merchant and mining elites. Otherwise, research has focused on the

1 This research was supported by public funds from the Mexican state, particularly the Fondo Sectorial de Investigación para la Educación (Proyecto "Gobierno y administración de la Real Hacienda de Nueva España, siglo XVIII" A1-S-18810) of the Consejo Nacional de Ciencia y Tecnología (CONACYT) (Mexico).

2 Garavaglia and Grosso (1987, 6).

3 Sánchez Santiró (2013, 132–135).

4 Valle Pavón (1999).

5 Valle Pavón (1997); Celaya Nández (2010).

6 Schell Hoberman (1991); Bertrand (1999).

DOI: 10.4324/9781003333197-4

origin of New Spain's administrative structure in the late seventeenth up to the eighteenth century.[7]

In contrast and in addition to the existing literature on Colonial Mexico's tax administration and on tax fraud in Mexico City, this chapter aims to offer a comprehensive analysis of the main strategies used by taxpayers to reduce or avoid the *alcabala* during the first half of the eighteenth century. This period was in between the Habsburg reign in Spain and Spanish America during the seventeenth century, and the transition into Bourbon rule.

The chapter begins with a description of the origin, tax base and the application of the *alcabala* system in Colonial Mexico, in order to understand why practices to avoid, evade or reduce its payment had important economic, social and political implications. Second, it reflects on the establishment of the first administrative structures in Colonial Mexico based on a mixed system composed of royal treasuries, accounting offices and courts, and a great diversity of tax collectors: tax farmers, district judges and royal officers.[8] The last section of the chapter is a concise analysis of some tax avoidance strategies, mainly legal and judicial practices based on a casuistic legal system that included tax disputes.

2.2 The *Alcabala* Sales Tax: Origin, Tax Base and Its Application in Colonial Mexico

The *alcabala* sales tax was established in 1323 as a temporary contribution to finance the Castilian Crown's war expenses, and was integrated as a regular part of the royal treasury in the fourteenth century. This sales tax was levied at a 10% rate on the sale, barter and movement of merchandise, with a broad range of exemptions concerning food and other goods (weapons, books, riding horses, etc.).[9] In 1522, during the first stage of Spanish expansion into the continental region of the so-called Indies, Emperor Charles V gave the Spanish settlers a royal exemption from the *alcabala* payment.[10] However, during the rule of King Philipp II, the Spanish Crown suffered a severe financial and political crisis which was accentuated between 1568 and 1571.[11] In November 1571, the king sent a royal decree to his vassals in the Indies and declared that his royal treasury was "[…] exhausted because of the many and continued expenses destined to sustain great armies and armadas for the defence of Christianity and the preservation of his kingdoms and lordships".[12]

7 TePaske and Klein (1987); Garavaglia and Grosso (1987); Sánchez Santiró (2013).

8 Celaya Nández (2010); Gordoa (2019, 65–100).

9 Sánchez Santiró (2013, 131).

10 This sales tax was established in 1323 as a temporary contribution to finance the Castilian Crown's war expenses. It was integrated into the royal patrimony in the fourteenth century. Garavaglia and Grosso (1987).

11 Muro Romero (1982, 47–68); Ramos (1986, 1–61).

12 Royal decree of Philip II, signed 1 November 1575, as cited by: Garavaglia and Grosso (1987, 65–66) (Author's translation).

Three years later, in 1574, the Viceroys of New Spain (*México*) and Peru (*Perú*) were ordered to establish the collection of a 2% sales tax in the Indies, as a response to the financial crisis.[13] The king appealed to the loyalty and love of his vassals and reminded them that their Castilian counterparts were paying as much as 10% in sales taxes on the value of most of the goods traded in the kingdom.[14] This colonial version of the sales tax was imposed on a broad variety of trade goods, most of them of European origin. The collection of this fiscal revenue was regulated by the 1571 decree issued by Philipp II, and by other laws like the Castilian Laws and the *Leyes de Indias*.

The *alcabala* was imposed on "all goods sold and contracted in the Indies [...] and all freights brought to our lands, all the first and successive sales of all the products from plantations, cattle raising and craftsmanship sold, bartered and hired in our domains".[15] Despite the apparent universality of this sales tax, the moral and political order of the Spanish Crown led to many subjects being exempted, such as the clergy, monasteries, religious orders and the "Indian" population. Exemptions were also applied to some basic goods like maize, bread, riding horses, books, weapons and mint silver.[16] The exemption for the Indian population was first declared as provisional, but it remained until 1821. This fiscal benefit was established as a royal privilege to those vassals considered as "miserable people" and because of the heavy tax burden that the natives already suffered due to other taxes such as the *tributo* (a sort of poll tax imposed on all male vassals from 18 to 50 years of age), the *servicio* (compulsory work that was later permuted into a monetary expense), the *medio real* (an increase on the tribute destined to pay judicial representation) and the *diezmo eclesiástico* (tithe).[17] Despite this "gracious act", the fiscal exemption only applied to the first sale of maize, chili, beans, salt, baskets and other local products. If an Indian trader sold Spanish (European) or Asian goods, the *alcabala* was imposed on the transactions.[18] As I explain below, the complex structure of this exemption system was an opportunity for some Spanish traders to use indigenous proxies in small trade deals. Once the particular exemptions had been made, the royal treasury began with the collection of the *alcabala* at a fixed 2% tax rate that lasted from 1574 until the 1620s. Soon, during the seventeenth century, the financial turmoil caused by constant military expenses led to two successive increments in the tax rate.

The Thirty Years' War (1618–1648) had a direct impact on the *alcabala* rate modifications. As part of a financial project destined to involve New Spain and Peru in the Hispanic monarchy's military expenses, the Count-Duke

13 Ramos (1986, 1–61).

14 Artola (1982); Garavaglia and Grosso (1987).

15 Royal decree of Philip II, signed 1 November 1575, as cited by Garavaglia and Grosso (1987, 67) (author's translation).

16 Garavaglia and Grosso (1987, 68).

17 Miranda (1980); Sánchez Santiró (2013, 130–140).

18 Garavaglia and Grosso (1987, 11–18).

of Olivares decided to create a new armada and a land army in the Spanish possessions in America in order to defend the Peruvian and Mexican viceroyalties from Dutch and English attacks. Both defensive projects were financed by the Spanish American vassals.[19] One of the main elements of this fiscal-military project consisted of an initial increment of the sales tax rate from 2 to 4%. This rise in *alcabala* was known as the *Unión de Armas*, which referred to the destination of these funds: the construction of a naval force to defend the Caribbean. The sales tax rate increment met with considerable opposition from Mexico City's council and the traders' guild. After a long dispute, the tax rise was negotiated with both of them. The negotiation involved the signing of a new tax farming lease between the royal authorities and Mexico City's council, as detailed below. The *Unión de Armas* was first collected together with the *alcabala* between 1632 and 1633.

This *alcabala* rise was insufficient to cover military expenditure in the Americas. As a response to the growing military costs, King Philip IV ordered a special tax increment to sustain the Spanish fleet, the *Armada de Barlovento*.[20] Again, the Crown faced an intense period of negotiations with Mexican and Peruvian elite groups and corporations to find a way (*arbitrios*) to finance the new armada. After a series of unsuccessful tax reforms, both the royal authorities and the local corporations determined that the best way to finance the growing military spending in the Indies was to increase the *alcabala* rate from 4 to 6%.[21]

The final 6% tax rate continued without significant changes in the 1630s and was upheld until 1748. The 6% rate was charged in most of New Spain's territory, with some exceptions like the Campeche port in south-eastern New Spain and the Septentrional villages and towns, considered as a "war zone" or borderland with the so-called *indios bárbaros* or semi-nomad Native American cultures. In these territories, the sales tax remained at its original 2% rate as a way to promote Spanish expansion to the north. Such developments demonstrate that the *alcabala* was a tax that was deeply related to military spending in the colonies. By the mid-eighteenth century, the *alcabala* represented the most important source of fiscal income in Colonial Mexico and could only be compared in quantity and importance with the *tributo*.[22]

2.3 The *Alcabala* Collection: Tax Farming and the Royal Administration

The collection of the *alcabala* was managed through an internal customs system known as *suelo alcabalatorio*.[23] This system divided New Spain into several internal fiscal districts known as *alcabalatorios*. These districts were composed

19 Alvarado Morales (1983); Sánchez Santiró (2012).
20 Sánchez Santiró (2013, 136).
21 Ibid., 136–138.
22 Ibid., 130.
23 Ibid.

by a variable number of *suelos* that each had a centralised regional tax office established at an important village or town, the *cabecera*. In addition to this territorial division, the *alcabala* collection was organised in four different ways: (1) direct administration by royal officers, (2) collection by district judges, and two modalities of tax farming, (3) the *arrendamiento* (individual tax farming by a leasing contract) and (4) the *encabezamiento* (corporate tax farming managed by city councils and the trade guild).[24] Both forms of tax farming remained operational from the 1590s until the centralisation and suppression of the *alcabala* tax farming system in 1776.[25] Since the establishment of the *alcabala* in New Spain in 1574, the Crown had designated the royal treasury officers as being at the top of the administrative procedure. The collection of the *alcabala* posed many difficulties due to the vast territory of the viceroyalty and the inexistence of an effective customs system. Despite the original intention to establish a unified system of collection and accounting control under the royal treasury, the royal officers soon faced a complex reality, far from the original project. In view of the limited territorial authority, the high costs of establishing a network of direct delegates or tax collectors, and the weak effective control of these royal officers who were only based in Mexico City and some towns located in its outskirts, the fiscal authorities decided to delegate the sales tax administration to district judges or *alcaldes mayores*.[26]

This indirect system caused a series of abuses and frauds that soon affected the royal treasury in Mexico City. As a response to these problems, the royal authorities decided to create a special court and accounting office, the *contaduría de alcabalas*.[27] This accounting office conducted administrative tasks and possessed jurisdictional authority as a fiscal tribunal. In addition, between 1587 and 1593, the Crown negotiated the first tax farming leasing contracts with the city councils of Mexico and Puebla.[28] The tax farming system given to the councils and the local trade corporations, the *encabezamiento*, had first been successfully used in Spain by King Philip II in 1568 as an alternative to direct administration. Due to the success of the general tax farming system or *encabezamientos generales* in the Castille region, in 1593, the sales tax farming system was also established in Mexico, together with the creation of the traders' guild in Mexico, as colonial traders were the main taxpayers.[29]

Between 1600 and 1615, all the main cities of New Spain were designated by the Crown to collect the *alcabala*. The tax farming system was established in the cities of Puebla (1601), México (1602), Oaxaca (1603) and Zacatecas (1603).[30] Only the royal treasuries installed to collect the sales taxes in the

24 Smith (1948); Valle Pavón (1997); Valle Pavón (2016).
25 Sánchez Santiró (2001a).
26 Celaya Nández (2010).
27 Gordoa (2019).
28 Valle Pavón (1997); Celaya Nández (2010).
29 Valle Pavón (1997).
30 Pastor (1977).

mining centres remained under the control of royal officers because of the strategic impact of the mining activities for the Spanish Empire. In some towns, the sales tax administration was delegated to local traders in a system known as *arrendamiento*, mainly in towns with a small Spanish population.[31]

This multiplicity of tax collectors, and the great distance between some towns and villages in Colonial Mexico and the capital, caused many collection difficulties and a great deal of fraud. During the late seventeenth century and the first decades of the eighteenth century, the *Audiencia de Mexico* (the appeals or high court) and the *contaduría de alcabalas* (the sales tax tribunal) received constant complaints about excessive charges, fraud and bankruptcies.[32] The most notorious case was the bankruptcy of the main sales tax administration: that of Mexico City. The *alcabala* from the Mexican capital were administered by the traders' guild from the late 1660s onwards, after the Mexican city council proved unable to pay the city's debts to the royal treasury and declared bankruptcy. By 1693, the traders' guild had obtained a new tax farm from Mexico City's tax administration to levy the *alcabala*. This corporation controlled the *alcabala* in the viceregal capital until 1754, with the signing of subsequent tax farming contracts.[33] The rest of New Spain's towns, villages and cities remained under different administrations managed by district judges, individual tax farmers and royal officers.

Thus, during the first half of the eighteenth century, the *alcabala* was levied by a great diversity of administrations, controlled by different kinds of tax collectors and with a limited customs system. The only cities that had internal customs offices were Mexico and Puebla.[34] Tax farming by traders' guilds played a major role. In addition to a heterogeneous and decentralised administration, the lack of effective supervision offered a perfect opportunity for tax evaders, whose strategies were constantly reported to the *contaduría de alcabalas* (the specialised accounting office and tribunal) and to the *Audiencia de Mexico* (Appeals Court).

Even though there is enough evidence to portrait some of the main strategies of tax evasion (hiding commodities, trafficking products during the night in Mexico City's outskirts, introducing contraband into coastal towns, etc.), taxpayers had an even wider range of strategies to avoid or reduce their tax burden in some specific situations. These cases will be analysed in the following.

2.4 Alternatives to Fiscal Evasion: Negotiation, Fraud and Judicial Controversy

There is a vast corpus of judicial documents in Spanish and Mexican archives that are vivid testimonies of the constant struggle between taxpayers and tax collectors. Faced with authorities who sought to collect the *alcabala* as part of the royal treasury's revenue (either as officers of the king or as tenants who

31 Garavaglia and Grosso (1987); Gordoa (2019, 65–100).

32 Ibid.

33 Valle Pavón (1997); Sánchez Santiró (2001b).

34 Valle Pavón (1997); Celaya Nández (2010).

had to comply with a contractual agreement with the royal treasury), the contributors (mainly the Spanish merchants in Colonial Mexico) employed a series of strategies to avoid paying a tax which they considered to be pernicious to commercial activities, given its direct impact on the circulation of goods and the final prices.[35] In New Spain, a great diversity of taxpayers were confronted with the *alcabala*, such as merchants, hacienda owners, real estate owners, slave traders and livestock owners.

The following section focuses on the tax evasion strategies used by a particular group of contributors in New Spain: the merchants, who were organised in local corporations or *diputaciones de comercio*. Such a focus provides a first glance into the multiple cases of smuggling, tax evasion and tax resistance which we can find in the Latin-American archives of the Spanish colonial period, and which indicate the complex economic, social and political reality portrayed in the fiscal documents of the Spanish Crown.

In the face of such a burdensome tax (6% of the total value of all the goods traded by a merchant), the New Spain merchants developed a series of strategies that fit the "abide, but do not comply" formula, or that were supported by a legal tradition of the *Ancien Régime* in which privileges, particular rights and a complex casuistry prevailed. In this jurisdictional order, written norms coexisted with traditions or local customs; these were then interpreted by a judge whose ruling prevailed in a particular case.[36]

The first strategy employed by Spanish merchants to reduce or avoid payment of the *alcabala* was to become tax collectors themselves. Through their representation in the traders' guild of Mexico and the *Diputaciones de comercio* (trade deputies), the richest merchants controlled the most important cities and towns of the viceroyalty and managed to gain control of sales taxes through the signing of leased agreements in towns.[37]

This sales tax farming system consisted of a fixed fee to be paid annually by all local merchants who owned a store. The tax collectors were under the control of a specialised court known as the *contaduría general de alcabalas*. For a good part of the eighteenth century, merchants negotiated the conditions under which they would collect and deliver annual fixed fees on all their commercial activities with the representatives of the royal treasury. Under this management modality, merchants and landowners in the viceregal cities established a second fixed fees system with the local tax collector known as *igualas*.[38] This deal involved each trader paying an annual fee based on an average annual income, contained in a document known as *relación jurada*. The *relaciones juradas* had a double function: first, as an accountable source designed to calculate the amount of taxes that a certain merchant had to pay to the local tax farmer or *alcalde mayor*; second, as a judicial document, since each trader declared under oath that the tax information provided was true.

35 Garavaglia and Grosso (1987).

36 Garriga (2004, 13–44).

37 Valle Pavón (1997); Archivo General de Indias (from now on: AGI), México, 711.

38 Sánchez Santiró (2001, a).

In case of inconsistencies, or if a tax farmer sued a taxpayer, these *relaciones* were used as evidence.[39]

The tax farming system was usually managed by local merchant elites. Hence, the members of the *diputación de comercio* had great fiscal advantages over their foreign competitors. The fixed annual fees established for each merchant were significantly lower than the actual tax fee that merchants from other cities had to pay, because this system modified the nature of the tax itself. Instead of the indirect – sales – tax based on trade, so-called *igualas* were imposed as a direct income tax, based on individual commercial capital. To complete the quotas agreed with the royal treasury, the tax farming and tax collecting merchants exerted fiscal pressure on minor merchants by means of the exhaustive collection of *alcabala del viento,* which was the tax charged to merchants without a fixed location. This collection was executed by an armed deputy with coactive functions.[40]

When they were unable to achieve a beneficial outcome through negotiations with the authorities, leasing contracts and the *igualas* system, colonial merchants resorted to several strategies of tax avoidance. One of these strategies concerned the use of indigenous middlemen to sell their products, thereby abusing the royal privilege that the Crown had granted to the native population at the end of the sixteenth century and that had exempted indigenous groups from the duty to pay the *alcabala* while they were charged with other taxes such as the *tributo,* as has been noticed above.[41] This exception had been decreed by King Philip II, who pointed out that "for the time being", the Indians did not have to pay *alcabala* "for what they sell, negotiate or hire, if it is not from Spaniards or from people who owe *alcabala*". But, as the royal decree continued: "… if they sell something that is not from Indians, but from other persons, they will have to pay *alcabala*". If the indigenous vendors tried to circumvent the law and to cover up such deals, they were to be admonished.[42]

The warning implied in this law can be read as indicating a fraudulent practice that had spread throughout the New Spain Viceroyalty. It consisted of monopolising certain merchandise and hiring a series of indigenous minor merchants to pass on the products acquired by the Spaniards as consumer goods from their communities. One example of this widespread practice is provided by a judicial file against a merchandise hoarder in the indigenous town of Ixmiquilpan (Central Mexico).[43]

On 4 March 1748, Miguel de Larrainzar, tenant of the *alcabala* tax farm of the town of Ixmiquilpan, filed a complaint in the *contaduría de alcabala* tribunal against the gunpowder contractor of that region, Sebastián de Pavola. In

39 Ibid.; Gordoa (2019).

40 Sánchez Santiró (2001, 6–41).

41 Sánchez Santiró (2013).

42 *Recopilación de Leyes de los Reinos de las Indias,* Libro VIII, Título XIII, ley XXVI. (Translation by the author).

43 Archivo General de la Nación (hereafter: AGNMX), Alcabalas, vol. 181, exp. 3.

this document, the first accused the second of having, for at least one year, repeatedly evaded the payment of sales taxes on all the products used to make gunpowder, mainly salt and sulphur. In addition, he presented several local residents as witnesses, who denounced Pavola and several neighbours for monopolising some of the most important staple products sold in the town: chili, beans and baked bread.

According to these testimonies, the Spanish merchant Pavola had established absolute control over the sale of various goods in the market through a practice considered as fraudulent. At the time of installing the *tianguis* or market, Pavola bought all the products brought from other locations in New Spain by small retailers. Afterwards, several indigenous people came to him to distribute the merchandise and sell it on the town square. Hence, the indigenous traders were hired as frontmen – or middlemen – so that Pavola (or any other Spanish merchant) could avoid the *alcabala*. Such a circumvention strategy constituted a serious crime against the royal treasury. For his part, Sebastián de Pavola accused Larrainzar of slandering him and of wanting to ruin him through a series of excesses in the payment of sales taxes. The mutual accusations were serious since both had signed lease contracts (for the local sales taxes and for the production of gunpowder, respectively); thus, in legal terms, both were representatives of the Spanish Crown and members of the Mexican political and economic elite. The litigation extended for more than a year. According to the inquiries of the royal judge, the various means of tax evasion identified in Ixmiquilpan had practically ruined Larrainzar, the tenant of the local *alcabala*.

The first tax avoidance strategy had been employed by Sebastián de Pavola directly, who through a legal ruse devised by his lawyers intended to evade payment of the *alcabala* on the sale of salt and other materials used in the manufacture of gunpowder. Pavola did so by appealing to a clause in his lease contract which declared a tax exemption concerning the sale of salt. However, the royal authorities discovered that the said contract had expired since the beginning of 1748, and that Pavola had not been appointed by the main gunpowder manufacturer as his representative. According to the royal officers, Pavola was, therefore, not a legitimate gunpowder monopolist. For this imposture, he should pay a fine of 1,000 silver pesos. The second form of tax avoidance was practiced by Pavola and other local Spanish merchants through the massive purchase of loads of chili and salt paid for by Pavola, and the subsequent sale of these goods in smaller quantities by several indigenous people. The natives posed as poor merchants who apparently sold the products from their parcels and who were awarded a few coins for their part in this game.[44] Given the sheer quantity of individuals involved in this fraud, the judge of *alcabala* decided that it was convenient to grant coercive powers such as the seizure of property and the ability to imprison debtors to Larrainzar, instead of judging the fraudulent merchants separately. This case is just one example of several testimonies

44 AGNMX, Alcabalas, vol. 181, exp. 3.

involving this type of fraudulent practice by Spanish merchants in regions dedicated to commerce and with a majority indigenous population.

In addition to the use of indigenous merchants (*regatones*) as proxies for their commercial operations, local merchants also employed judicial strategies to delay or avoid the collection of *alcabala*. Among them was the tendency to extend the litigation process against the collectors for apparently violating their rights and by invoking the immemorial traditions granted to them, which were themselves a norm as valid as the royal laws.

Such was the case of pig livestock traders in the Toluca Valley region in 1725, who accused the tax farmer, Nicolás de la Barrera, of making an improper collection of the *alcabala*, since it undermined the customs of the town of Tenango del Valle (México), which established that all livestock sold in Tenango was not to be affected by the sales tax until the animal was killed and that only the slaughtering and the meat were to be taxed.[45] After several months of this kind of refusal from the livestock traders, Nicolás de la Barrera filed two lawsuits in the appeal court against the livestock traders and against other members of the local *diputación de comercio*: the shop owners and the bakers. Since the beginning of the tax farm contract in 1724, none of the Tenango merchants had paid their fixed rate on time, while some had paid a fraction of the previously agreed rates. When the tax farmer Barrera made inquiries, some merchants claimed that they had no obligation to pay their tax rate because their goods were exempt as was the case with livestock and bread.[46] After six months of extrajudicial dispute, the tax farmer decided to sue all the tax debtors in the *contaduría de alcabalas*. Once the trial began, the Toluca tax debtors hired a lawyer from Mexico City and countersued Nicolás de la Barrera. These two lawsuits portrayed the different legal strategies applied by taxpayers to avoid the *alcabala* and the legal instruments that the tax farmers used to gain a favourable judgement either from the *alcabala* tribunal or the Mexican appeals court.[47] First, the local merchants, in a desperate attempt not to pay the tax on the sale of pig livestock, appealed to customary law concerning the sale of livestock, as noted above. This implied that the sales taxes should be paid by the butchers of Mexico City.[48] Invoking a particular tradition or custom was a valid legal argument in the Spanish legal system, since justice in the Spanish Empire was based on a multitude of norms, mainly Roman law, canonical law and customs. This system was based on a jurisdictional order in which a judge acted as an impartial public person.[49] The sentences were given once the local or appeal judge had listened to both parties and compared all the laws. This judicial system was casuistic and particularistic, hence the use of custom as law was just as valid an argument as written laws.[50]

45 AGNMX, Archivo Histórico de Hacienda, caja 20, exp.4.
46 AGNMX, Archivo Histórico de Hacienda, caja 20, exp.4.
47 Rosenmüller (2019, 11–52).
48 Quiroz (2005).
49 Rosenmüller (2019, 11–30).
50 Garriga (2004); Rosenmüller (2019).

In this case, the *alcabala* judge acted as a first instance judge and heard both sides. The competing stories give testimony of two different conceptions about the "correct administration" of the sales tax.[51] From the tax farmer's perspective, the tax debtors had committed fraud against him and the royal treasury. He sustained his claims with reference to written laws and his tax farm leasing contract. According to colonial Spanish laws (*Leyes de Indias*), the livestock sale triggered *alcabala*, and its payment was mandatory in the place where the cattle or pigs were sold. In addition, Nicolás de la Barrera's tax farm contract stipulated that, in case of tax avoidance or resistance, he could appeal to the district judge or *alcalde mayo*r to imprison the debtors and confiscate their goods. In his contract, Barrera had for the time of his contract the faculty to compel the taxpayers with the district judge or with an armed deputy.[52] But, instead of fulfilling Barrera's request, the *alcalde mayor* of Tenango refused to arrest the livestock traders because the tax farmer allegedly disrupted the local order and excessively compelled the debtors to declare the value of their livestock.

After the trial against the livestock merchants, Barrera had to face another attempt to sue from a different group of taxpayers: the bakers, who had just bought the flour needed to make the bread for the Spanish population. According to the *alcalde*'s allegation, the sale of flour and bread was exempt from taxes because it was a staple product. Barrera ignored the customary law of this town, and therefore they resisted his claims constantly.

In contrast, Nicolás de la Barrera denounced the local deputy for conspiring with the merchants against him, allegedly obstructing his administration and forcing him to declare bankruptcy. The main problem in this case seems to have been that the tax farmer was alien to the network of interests of local merchants. Maybe he originated from Mexico City or Spain. Not being local turned out to be a serious problem in this case, because the notion of justice held by the merchants from the village of Tenango differed from Barrera's own conceptions. For the local livestock traders, the sale of their animals was exempt from the *alcabala* tax, not because of a specific written law, but because the custom was to delegate tax payment to the buyers in Mexico City. From their point of view, Nicolás de la Barrera was an abusive tax farmer because he did not respect the customs of his tax district. This was a serious accusation against the tax farmer by the locals. According to the lawsuit, Barrera's abuses were so grave that he threatened the entire local economy and most of the villagers' lives by charging abusive taxes on staple goods like bread and on the main economic activity of the region, namely the pig trade. The local merchants complained that if Barrera ignored local customs and decided to apply the written law, the livestock prices would rise and, thus, their main economic support would be compromised.[53]

51 Gordoa (2020).

52 AGNMX, Archivo Histórico de Hacienda, caja 20, exp.4.

53 AGNMX, Archivo Histórico de Hacienda, caja 20, exp.4.

Despite such dramatic claims, the judge of *alcabala* issued a sentence against the allegations of the merchants. From his point of view, the custom was valid only if it was in accordance with the provisions of the laws of Castille and did not contravene other sources of law such as the *Siete Partidas* or the *Leyes de Indias*. By the end of 1727, the judge declared that all livestock merchants had to pay the *alcabala* in the places where the sale of the animals took place. Regarding the complaints of the bakers, he pointed out that the collection of sales taxes on bread was prohibited, but not on flour. If the tax farmer erroneously taxed bread in the future, he would be sanctioned with a pecuniary penalty of 300 pesos.[54]

Despite this seemingly clear ruling, the tax farmer could not get the locals to cover their debts, because they appealed to the *Audiencia of Mexico*. Although this appeal court reached the same conclusion as the *alcabala* judge, the merchants managed to avoid payment of the taxes until 1729. When Barrera, almost bankrupted by this lengthy dispute, ultimately gave up and handed over the tax farm to local merchants in 1730, the pig traders had their way. Despite not being successful in court, livestock traders were able to sell their animals without paying *alcabala* for the duration of the litigation. Once they were sentenced to pay the tax debts, the traders paid their arrears in instalments and in part, which represented a cost reduction in their commercial transactions, and a deferred payment of the tax.

2.5 Conclusion

This chapter has offered an insight into the wide range of tax reduction or avoidance strategies employed by Spanish merchants in New Spain in order to decrease the economic impact of the sales taxes known as *alcabala*. These strategies were elaborated by the local merchants in a social and economic order regulated in a casuistic and particularistic context. The *alcabala* collection was determined by three types of juridical status: by ethnic origin, trade privileges and class or economic capacity.[55] This discussion has focused on strategies that can be considered as an alternative to direct evasion. The economic actors used a series of legal and political strategies to avoid paying the *alcabala*. The first case was the abuse of ethnic privileges through the use of indigenous middlemen by Spanish merchants to sell certain products monopolised by local elites. This constituted a fraud against the royal treasury. Another strategy was through the royal courts. Since the Spanish judicial system was organised according to an *Ancien Régime* jurisdictional order, taxpayers could appeal to local laws and customs to protect their local interests against other economic agents, mainly tax collectors.

54 Gordoa (2019, 65–100).
55 Sánchez Santiró (2015, 165–186).

Either through the royal courts themselves, or through the abuse of certain privileges, the Mexican merchants defended their economic interests against those of the Crown and their representatives. This was possible thanks to a jurisdictional order in which each specific case was attended by all judges and, many times, led to the general dispositions of the Spanish Empire being overcome or modified. This case study highlights some of the particular characteristics of the Spanish Empire fiscal system between the late seventeenth and early eighteenth centuries: a tax collecting structure in which the vast majority of the taxes were under a tax farming system. The local tax collectors faced a complex and multiethnic social order, and a pluralistic judicial that was only severely modified in the late eighteenth century with a series of administrative reforms known as the "Bourbon reforms".

Archives

Archivo General de la Nación (Mexico) (AGNMX).
Archivo General de Indias (Seville) (AGI).

References

Alvarado Morales, Manuel. 1983. *La ciudad de México ante la fundación de la Armada de Barlovento, 1635-1643.* México: El Colegio de México and Universidad de Puerto Rico/Recinto de Río Piedras.

Artola, Miguel. 1982. *La Hacienda del Antiguo Régimen.* Madrid: Alianza Editorial and Banco de España.

Bertrand, Michel. 1999. *Grandeur et misère de l'Office. Les officiers de finances de Nouvelle-Espagne* XVIIe – XVIIIe *siècles.* Paris: Publications de la Sorbonne.

Celaya Nández, Yovana. 2010. *Alcabalas y situados. Puebla en el sistema fiscal imperial, 1638-1742.* México: El Colegio de México.

Celaya Nández, Yovana. 2010. La cesión de un derecho de la Real Hacienda: la administración del impuesto de la alcabala novohispana en el siglo XVII. Tres estudios de caso, América Latina en la historia económica 17: 93–125.

Garavaglia, Juan Carlos and Juan Carlos Grosso. 1987. *Las alcabalas novohispanas (1776-1821).* México: Archivo General de la Nación and Banca Cremi.

Garriga, Carlos. 2004. Orden jurídico y poder político en el Antiguo Régimen, *Istor.* Revista de Historia Internacional 16: 13–44.

Gordoa de la Huerta, Rodrigo. 2019. Los arrendamientos de alcabalas de la Real Hacienda de Nueva España en la primera mitad del siglo xviii: los arrendatarios particulares como 'recaudadores del monarca'". In *Hacienda e instituciones. Los erarios regio, eclesiástico y municipal en Nueva España: coexistencia e interrelaciones,* eds. Yovana Celaya Nández and Ernest Sánchez Santiró (coords.), 65–100. México: Instituto Mora/CONACYT/Universidad Veracruzana.

Miranda, José. 1980. *El tributo indígena en la Nueva España durante el siglo* XVI. México: El Colegio de México.

Muro Romero, Fernando. 1982. La reforma del pacto colonial en Indias. Notas sobre instituciones de gobierno y sociedad en el siglo XVII, Jahrbuch für Geschichte Lateinamerikas 19: 47–68.

Pastor, Rodolfo. 1977. La alcabala como fuente para la historia económica y social de la Nueva España, Historia Mexicana 27:1–16.

Quiroz, Enriqueta. 2005. *Entre el lujo y la subsistencia. Mercado, abastecimiento y precios de la carne en la ciudad de México, 1750-1812*. México: El Colegio de México and Instituto Mora.

Ramos, Demetrio. 1986. La crisis indiana y la Junta Magna de 1568, Jahrbuch für Geschichte Lateinamerikas 23: 1–61.

Recopilación de Leyes de estos reinos de las Indias. 1987. México: Miguel Ángel Porrúa and Escuela Libre de Derecho.

Rosenmüller, Christoph. 2019. *Corruption and Justice in Colonial Mexico, 1650-1755*. Cambridge and New York: Cambridge University Press.

Sánchez Santiró, Ernest. 2001a. Igualas, producción y mercado: las alcabalas novohispanas en la receptoría de Cuautla de Amilpas (1776-1821), Secuencia 49: 6–41.

Sánchez Santiró, Ernest. 2001b. La hacienda reformada: la centralización de la renta de alcabalas en Nueva España (1754-1781). In *Finanzas y política en el mundo iberoamericano. Del Antiguo Régimen a las Naciones independientes, eds.* Ernest Sánchez Santiró, Luis Jáuregui, and Antonio Ibarra, 143–177. México: Universidad Autónoma del Estado de Morelos/Instituto Mora/Universidad Nacional Autónoma de México.

Sánchez Santiró, Ernest. 2012. La Armada de Barlovento y la fiscalidad novohispana (1636-1749). In *Guerra y fiscalidad en la Iberoamérica colonial (siglos XVII- XIX)*, eds. Angelo Alves Carrara and Ernest Sánchez Santiró (coords.), 65–90. México: Universidade Federal de Juiz de Fora and Instituto Mora.

Sánchez Santiró, Ernest. 2013. *Corte de caja. La Real Hacienda de Nueva España y el primer reformismo fiscal de los borbones (1720-1755). Alcances y contradicciones*. México: Instituto Mora.

Sánchez Santiró, Ernest. 2015. La mirada fiscal sobre el comercio interno: las alcabalas novohispanas. In *La fiscalidad novohispana en el imperio español. Conceptualizaciones, proyectos y contradicciones*, eds. María del Pilar Martínez López-Cano, Ernest Sánchez Santiró, and Matilde Souto Mantecón (Coods.), 165–187. México: Instituto Mora/ Universidad Nacional Autónoma de México/Instituto de Investigaciones Históricas.

Schell Hoberman, Louisa. 1991. *Mexico's Merchant Elite, 1590-1660. Silver, State and Society*. Durham and London: Duke University Press.

Smith, Robert Sidney. 1948. Sale taxes in New Spain, 1575-1770, The Hispanic American Historical Review 28: 2–37.

TePaske, John Jay, and Herbert S. Klein. 1987. *Ingresos y egresos de la Real Hacienda de Nueva España*. México: Instituto Nacional de Antropología e Historia.

Valle Pavón, Guillermina del. 1997. *El Consulado de comerciantes de la ciudad de México y las finanzas novohispanas, 1592-1827*. México: Colegio de México.

Valle Pavón, Guillermina del. 1999. La recaudación de las alcabalas de la ciudad de México por parte del Consulado de comerciantes. In *Las ciudades y sus estructuras. Población, espacio y cultura en México, siglos XVIII y XIX, eds.* Sonia Pérez Toledo, René Elizlde Salazar, and Luis Pérez Cruz (coords.), 151–160. México: Universidad Autónoma de Tlaxcala and Universidad Autónoma Metropolitana-Iztapalapa.

Valle Pavón, Guillermina del. 2016. Ocultación del `fondo de sobras´ del ramo de sobras de alcabalas por los priores del Consulado de la Ciudad de México. In *Mérito, venalidad y corrupción en España y América, siglos XVII y XVIII*, eds. Pilar Ponce Leiva and Francisco Andújar Castillo, 323–348. Valencia: Albatros.

3 Imperial Taxation and Local Agency

Tax Avoidance and Tax Resistance in Seventeenth- and Eighteenth-century Germany (Saxony and Thuringia)

Rachel Renault

3.1 Introduction: Extraordinary Taxes, Ordinary Politics

This chapter discusses tax resistance in early modern Germany, starting from the premise that it is an entry point for analysing popular politics, which contribute to the construction of the singular political forms that characterise early modern Germany. The first two sections analyse the forms and actors of taxpaying and tax resistance, and the configuration of popular agency; the third gives an overview of the anti-fiscal claims and the moral economy at stake in these protests.

The chapter focuses on imperial taxes, that is to say, taxes raised in the name of the emperor (*Kaiser*) in order to finance – mostly – imperial wars against the empire's (*Reich*) enemies. For the period from 1648 to 1806, this mainly referred to France or the Ottoman Empire. Such taxes were called "Roman months" (*Römermonate*) and required the consent of the imperial estates (*Reichsstände*) at the Imperial Diet (*Reichstag*) where the amount due to the emperor was negotiated: they fall therefore under what is known as "extraordinary taxes", as opposed to taxes levied on a regular basis, which have the advantage of legitimacy through customary practice. But the imperial tax was not paid by the respective imperial estates (imperial princes, earls or lords, knights and imperial cities) from their own resources, but instead shifted upon their subjects and levied in the three hundred or so territories that composed the empire. As a result, there was a distortion between those who approved and negotiated imperial taxation and its amount, and those who had to effectively bear the tax burden and were bound by a decision they could not influence, although imperial law on this point was extremely ambiguous.[1] Each prince or imperial estate

1 See Moser (1773, 503–505): "[A]t the question 'Who has to pay the imperial taxes? The Lord and the country together, or the country alone?', the Imperial Law is in contradiction to the custom: It is true that 1. The imperial estates in the past not only helped to support the imperial structures, but that they had to pay for them from their own resources; 2. That according to the newer imperial laws, the subjects were usually only drawn into the concurrence; 3. That until

DOI: 10.4324/9781003333197-5

was free to decide the concrete form of this extraordinary taxation (whether poll, consumption or property tax, for instance) for his own territory, and he was free to change it at each new tax levy.[2] Although the tax requirement was punctual and irregular at the imperial scale, depending on the needs of each war, locally it could take years for the tax to be lifted, so that the last imperial tax had rarely been fully paid when the imperial order to pay the next one arrived. Moreover, the local consequences of imperial taxation are medium- and long-term ones: imperial taxes helped shape political and social practices way beyond the tax raising itself, so that the extraordinary character of the tax was locally counterbalanced by its duration. For all these reasons, the imperial tax was also much more contested than the ordinary taxes – that is to say most of the taxes of the territories, levied by the princes on their subjects to finance their administrative or judicial needs.[3]

I will discuss resistance to these extraordinary taxes at a local scale, in small "territories": the small estates were comparatively overburdened in this regard and had, as we will see, a strong political interest in paying their taxes, which powerful estates lacked.[4] They therefore often paid their tax to the emperor very meticulously. As a consequence, imperial taxation levied in the form of "extraordinary taxes" on a regional and local level weighed more heavily on the inhabitants of such smaller states than those of bigger states, was less legitimate and local taxpayers regularly refused to pay. For this reason, the smaller imperial estates provide a much better vantage point for observing tax resistance to imperial taxation. Observing the empire *from below* is a way to analyse its so-called "monstrous" political body[5] by including the views and actions of its subjects. But it implies a shift from the questions usually addressed to consider taxation predominantly as a "modern state-building" factor; a shift which fits the overarching theme of this volume with its focus on different strategies of "not paying taxes".

The prevalence of this state-building paradigm has contributed to the marginalisation of imperial taxation in the literature: imperial taxes were considered – especially after the sixteenth century – to be of no importance for

now, there has been no imperial law, so that all and every empire tax would be burdened solely on the subjects who pay for it. On the other hand, it is also an equally accepted general imperial custom that all the imperial estates properly demand and raise the complete imperial taxes solely from their subjects, [...] and that the highest imperial courts have already declared several times that the subjects alone have to pay the imperial taxes" (Author's translation from German).

2 About the origins of those Roman months and the political negotiations that accompanied their emergence, see Isenmann (2018); Rauscher, Serles, Winkelbauer (2012); Schmid (1989); Schulze (1975a).

3 Ordinary taxes have been studied far more than extraordinary ones, since they were considered to be essential state-building factors. See Schwennicke (1996).

4 In bigger estates, imperial taxes were relatively low, rarely levied, badly paid and merged with territorial taxation. The imperial "matricle" (*Reichsmatrikul*), defining each estate's financial obligation toward imperial taxes, was calculated according to the size and power of each estate by the mid-sixteenth century, and was only rarely updated. See Schulze (1978).

5 In 1664, Samuel Pufendorf described the Empire as an *irregulare corpus aliquod et monstro simile* ("an irregular body, similar to a monster"). Pufendorf (1664).

state-building because they were irregular, and represented relatively low amounts in comparison to overall imperial finances.[6] This idea seemed even more convincing as the Holy Roman Empire is regarded as having failed to become a "modern state". Paradoxically, the recent controversy about the state character (*Staatlichkeit*) of the Old Empire (*Altes Reich*)[7] did not lead to a huge amount of work about imperial taxation – but rather to the exploration of other fields of state sovereignty such as jurisdiction, the postal service, etc.[8] Historians who have analysed imperial taxation have therefore mostly done so for the period prior to the mid-seventeenth century, and mainly for the fifteenth–sixteenth century.[9] Furthermore, they have interpreted imperial taxation primarily from a "central", that is, Viennese point of view which coincided with their main research interest: why did the Empire "fail" to become a modern state ("*der gescheiterte Steuerstaat*")?[10]

This paper takes a different approach and intends to leave the "state-building" question to one side. First, rather than adopting the Viennese point of view, I examine imperial taxation "from below", from the perspective of ordinary taxpayers in three tiny imperial estates located in the Saxon and Thuringian area and ruled by imperial earls or princes (*Reichsgrafen und-fürsten*). The selected imperial estates are those of Schönburg, Schwarzburg and Reuss. Second, I focus on the period after 1648, when the question of whether the Empire or these small territories would become modern states was no longer relevant (since neither of them followed this path of state building). As a corollary of this and third, if we decide to leave aside questions of "modern state building", other questions related to taxation gain importance. I propose therefore to focus on the *political dimension* of the act of paying the taxes or refusing to do so. Although imperial tax revenue was of relatively little importance for the imperial treasury, whose main resources came from credit, the huge number of conflicts surrounding imperial taxes in these small territories in Saxony and Thuringia[11] either indicates that the tax burden was heavily felt by local taxpayers, or that it was easier and perhaps strategically more interesting to challenge imperial taxes rather than other – ordinary regional or local – taxes.

But most of all, although imperial taxation was not always a heavy load in purely financial terms, its political implications were extremely important

6 Edelmayer, Lanzinner, and Rauscher (2003); Moraw (1986); Rauscher, Serles, and Winkelbauer (2012); Rauscher (2004); Rauscher (2010); Schmid (1983).

7 See the controversy between Heinz Schilling and Georg Schmidt about the *Staatlichkeit* of the *Altes Reich* (Schilling 2001; Schmidt 2001).

8 Behringer (2003); concerning imperial justice, the literature on the subject having become plethoric, we cannot refer here to all the research but mention just: Baumann (2001); Diestelkamp (1999); Fimpel (2000); Sailer (1999); Scheurman (1994).

9 See Edelmayer, Lanzinner, and Rauscher (2003); Moraw (1986); Rauscher (2003, 2004, 2010); Schmid (1983, 1989); and the very seminal research of Schulze (1975a, 1978).

10 Rauscher, Serles, and Winkelbauer (2012, 261). See also Schmid (1983).

11 Imperial cities have been far more investigated in this regard than small territories. Weber (1992) for the period after 1648. Most other studies concern the fifteenth and sixteenth centuries. See Isenmann (1980) and Isenmann (2018).

for the imperial earls and princes, as well as for ordinary subjects, because taxpaying was not only about transferring an amount of money from one group – or state level – to another. It was also a gesture loaded with enormous social implications, especially in *Ancien Régime* societies which were rooted in feudal status and privilege. Social and political status defined who had to pay taxes, how much had to be paid, who could ensure exemption and who lacked the power to avoid taxation, and this in turn helped define this status.[12] From the very bottom of the society – the peasant majority – to its very top – the emperor–, social relations within the imperial body politic were permeated and renegotiated by taxation. Following the money through the lens of tax history enables the historian to observe the different social strategies and struggles that defined an individual's (or a group's) social and political position.

The following paragraphs will centre around three sets of questions:

First, how did ordinary taxpayers oppose imperial taxation? Individual and collective resistance did not obey the same logics, and I will focus on the latter, that is to say mainly on petitions, revolts and judicial procedures. How were they related to each other and were they really as different as the literature usually suggests?

Second, how did taxpayers legitimate their refusal? Since ordinary subjects could not simply refuse to pay the taxes they owed the emperor, they had to develop argumentations (especially in front of a court of law) which involved their rights as subjects. Legitimation strategies are therefore a good vantage point for observing popular political culture and its translation into a common legal culture, but also the demands of ordinary subjects for accountability.

Third, how did the different authorities, be they the emperor, the imperial Circles (*Reichskreise*), the princes or the imperial and territorial courts of law, respond to such practices? *Collective* refusal of taxpayment was considered a threat to the legitimacy of imperial earls and princes (more than to the legitimacy of the emperor, which was rarely explicitly questioned), and therefore required a spectacular response, tasked with reactivating the challenged authority.

3.2 Eager to Pay their Taxes: The Strategy of Distinction by Minor Imperial Princes and Earls

At first, it is necessary to differentiate between attitudes towards tax liabilities in different social layers of "taxpayers", as not everyone tried to avoid payment. The minor imperial estates "with little power" (*mindermächtige*), as they described themselves, were eager to pay the taxes they owed to the emperor as

12 About taxation and production of social status, see Renault (2018).

quickly and as fully as possible.[13] They even sometimes paid a larger amount than they owed, and their subjects would ask them to account for these extra payments. This eagerness to pay can easily be explained, as several crucial operations were at stake for the minor princes and earls when paying their imperial taxes. First, their status as immediate members of the empire (*Reichsunmittelbare Stände*), who depended on and answered to no one but the emperor himself, was perpetually endangered, above all by the efforts of the Elector of Saxony (*Kursachsen*) to "mediatise" them, that is to say to incorporate them in his own territory by suppressing their immediate bond to the empire and the emperor.[14] Paying the imperial taxes was a powerful way for the minor imperial estates in Schönburg, Schwarzburg and Reuss to publicly demonstrate their immediate relationship to the emperor and empire.

Second, in return for their "imperial patriotism" and their zealous payment, these imperial estates expected the emperor to reward them with a service in return, be it by protecting them from Saxony's ambitions, or by granting them different kinds of symbolical or political gratification (for instance in the form of a rank elevation). The timely payment of taxes to the emperor's treasury therefore responded to the logics of aristocratic exchanges in general, which were based on reciprocity, surplus and ostentation. This is confirmed by the following example from the Ebersdorf branch of the Reuss family ("house"), from 1738:

> It is our opinion here that we should not wait until the Circle's official order [*monitorium*] concerning these 50 Roman months arrives. Instead we should send the sum of our house to Vienna as soon as possible, so as not to miss the good opportunity *to get from the imperial court a special meritum*: the reputation of our house will be enhanced if a potential monitorium sent by the Circle office can be answered by stressing that the tax portion of House of Reuss for the 50 Roman months has already been paid to Vienna.[15]

The strategy of the administrator of the House Reuss was clearly to be credited and then rewarded for an anticipated payment and, as we can infer from the response of the delegate from Reuss at the Viennese court, it seems to

13 It is well-known from the literature that *mindermächtige Stände* were far better payers than powerful states. See Schulze (1978) and Renault (2017) (Chapters 1 and 2).

14 So called "mediatisation" (*Mediatisierung*) is a form of annexation of an imperial estate that was "directly" dependent on the empire by another estate: the annexed estate then lost its imperial immediacy.

15 "*Man ist hiesigen Orts der Meÿnung, daß das Creÿß-Ausschreib-Amtliche Monitorium dieser 50 Römer-Monath wegen nicht allererst zu erwarten, sondern die Summa unsers Hauses, so bald, als immer möglich, nach Wien einzusenden seÿn mögte, umb die gute Gelegenheit, beÿ dem Kaÿserlichen Hof sich dadurch ein besonderes meritum zumachen, nicht zu versäumen : Wie dann auch zugedachten unsers Hauses Reputation gereichen wird, wenn auf ein allenfalls einlaufendes Creÿß-Ausschreib-Amts-Monitorium man antworten kan, daß die rata des Gräfl. Reuß. Haußes zu denen Reichs wegen verwilligte 50. Römer-Monathen nach Wien bereits bezahlet seÿen. Schloß Ebersdorf am 11. Januar 1738*", Hauptstaatsarchiv Greiz (HStAG), Gemeinschaftliche Regierung Gera, PP – I – 10, Ebersdorf. Votum, 11 Jan. 1738.

have worked. In his letter back to the earls, he was able to convey the good message that the emperor's vice-chancellor had promised to keep in mind this "ready and most subservient devotion".[16] The payment of imperial taxes was thus embedded in socio-political issues and in an aristocratic gift economy, much more than it depended on strictly financial considerations.

For small imperial earls and princes, paying quickly and correctly was a question of both social identity and political status: the confirmation of their contested status as immediate members of the empire (*Reichsstandschaft, Reichsunmittelbarkeit*) was at stake, which distinguished them from the ordinary territorial nobility. The imperial earls and princes would not only do everything in their power to pay imperial taxes promptly and well, but would also ostentatiously publicise their zealous payment as much as possible. Whenever a new imperial tax was demanded, all these small princes and earls carefully observed one another's tax behaviour, so that everyone knew who had paid, when and how much.[17] Towards their subjects, by contrast, tax levying was made extremely opaque and therefore generated perpetual contestation.

3.3 Tax Resistance: Forms, Actors and Repression

Ordinary subjects used different ways to avoid or resist payment. First, some individuals simply resisted or avoided paying tax; this everyday tax avoidance rarely left traces in the archives and there was often no justification given at all. In the three small territories of Schwarzburg, Schönburg and Reuss, like in the rest of early modern Europe, only a third of all required taxes seems to have been effectively paid.[18] As a result of this ineffective tax collection, earls and princes would very often ask for a much larger sum than they actually owed to the emperor, under the pretext of having to fulfil other payments. This renders the analysis of princely accounting extremely difficult; even the local administrators were regularly confused.

A second option for resisting payment consisted of writing individual or collective supplications and petitions to the authorities. Third, resentment against taxpaying could result in collective riots and lawsuits. Lawsuits and riots involved real defiance to local authorities, as they endangered the earls and princes' reputations on the imperial public stage by casting a suspicion of bad government on them, and because such resistance threatened

16 "*Ihro Excellenz der Reichsvizekanzlar haben gütigst versichert, allerhöchst Ihro Kaÿs. Maÿtt. nicht allein nach aller Billigkeit anzurühmen, daß insonderheit daß hochgräfl. Reußi. Hauß hierunter so fertig und eÿfrig gewesen, seine allerunterthänigste Devotion und Treue werckthätig zu bezeigen, sondern Sie wollen auch den dienst, welche Euer hochedelgeb. dabeÿ zugleich vor das allerhöchste Kaÿ. inter[esse] erwiesen, in gutem andenken aufbehalten*", *ibid.*, Heckenberg to the Earls of Reuss, Vienna, 1 Febr. 1738.

17 See Renault (2017), Chapters 1 and 2.

18 See Renault (2017), Chapter 3 for the German example. For early modern France, see for instance Collins (1988, 201): "In other words, more than half of the parishes sometimes paid quite little, and none paid more than a third of its taxes".

their practical ability to pay the imperial taxes (on time or at all). But most importantly, such practices of resistance questioned their – already endangered – right to raise taxes (*jus collectandi*), which was an important part of their "territorial superiority" ("*Landeshoheit*"), their "immediacy" and their status as imperial estates.[19] This highly symbolically and politically charged meaning of taxation is the reason why any collective and public opposition to imperial taxation triggered spectacular forms of repression by the lords. Conversely, the distinctive importance the earls and princes gave to their ability to pay imperial taxation also explains why taxpayers used it as an important lever for obtaining additional rights.

Due to the much more political character of collective forms of resistance, and since tax resistance is here a way to observe the bonds of political and social domination, I now focus on these modes of resistance. This implies that tax resistance here reveals a problem of tax acceptance rather than an inability to pay, all the more so because, as we shall see, tax resistance regularly implies forms of self-taxation.

3.3.1 Supplication

Individual or communal tax resistance often took the path of a supplication or petition (*Supplik*) in which the supplicating party (individuals, groups, a local community) described all the hardships it had to endure and asked for the lordship's grace and favour to omit or reduce taxation, counting on the princely administration's awareness of the difficulties of paying.[20] Here is an example of such a petition, from the representatives of the city of Franckenhausen (Schwarzburg) during the Seven Years' War (24 March 1759), when they had received the order to pay the new Roman months:

> However, we are not wealthy enough; our city has fallen into great decline in just a few years, so that we have enough to do with the ordinary taxes. The hailstorm we suffered three years ago caused our winter fruits, windows and roofs to be mostly knocked to the ground, and the latter severely perforated. This was followed by the high prices of food, and by the French invasion, which cost us three extraordinary taxes.[21]

19 See Moser (1773, 419): "*Das Besteuerungs-Recht ist ein Stück der Landeshoheit, krafft dessen ein teutscher Landesherr berechtiget ist, seinen Unterthanen Steuren, oder Geld-Abgaben, entweder nur anzusinnen, oder auch würcklich aufzulegen*", although paying imperial taxes is not an unequivocal sign of *Reichsstandschaft*.

20 Holenstein (2003); Brakensiek and Wunder (2005).

21 "Hier zu aber seind wier nicht vermögent; unsere Stadt ist in wenig Jähren in große Abnahme verfallen, das Wier mit den ordinairen Außschreiben gnung zu schaffen haben. Das vor dreÿ Jahren erlittene Hagelwetter wodurch Unsere Winterfrüchte, Fenster und Tächer ersteres größten theils zu boden geschlagen, lezte aber starck durch löchert. Hierauf folgete theuerung wie auch der frantzösische durchzug dieser hat uns dreÿ extraordinaire Außschreiben gekostet." HStAR Geheimes Ratskollegium, C XVIII 2a Nr. 25, Supplik der Vierleute Franckenhausen, 24 March 1759.

This is here a very stereotypical discourse, and many texts used the same *topoi* of natural and social hardships and disorders (war, bad harvest, hail...) in order to beg for a discount or for the extension of a timeline. Taxpayers were often supported by local bailiffs, who relayed or supported the petitions to the central authorities. This creates the illusion of a large consensus about the fact that the tax burden was excessive and the peasants or burghers in misery.[22] As we will see, this impression of consensus is somewhat misled.

Nevertheless supplications did not always fit the pattern of poor and humble subjects begging for grace and mercy. Instead, some of them were quite radical, asking for justice and for the enforcement of what they considered to be their rights. When the authorities refused to concede the reductions or postponements demanded, and especially when they sent troops to enforce taxpayment by military violence (*Steuerexekution*), they opened the way to confrontation. This took two main forms which were not mutually exclusive: legal action and "riot" – or any form of contentious collective action.

3.3.2 Lawsuits and Riots: Negotiating Taxes by Force

Although a lawsuit may, from a modern perspective, look very different to a riot, the actual form of protesting against taxes by waging a lawsuit borrowed the same pattern on a local scale:[23] taxpayers consulted advocates, gathered in assemblies by night or day, designated delegates and representatives, wrote supplications, sent messengers all around, and raised money to finance the collective protest in order to avoid taxation, which is not the least of the paradoxes. In the case of lawsuits, they also had to maintain a correspondence with the court and the lawyer, so that a sort of a parallel administration was set up, in all cases involving quite a complex organization which was independent of the classical local institutions.

Riots were highly ritualised and included the use of violence, but cannot be reduced to it. They were also far from an exceptional practice. In the three territories of Schönburg, Schwarzburg and Reuss, I have encountered at least 13 revolts or riots *against imperial taxation* (there were other revolts for other reasons) in the period from 1648 to 1806, some conflicts lasted several years, and some even several decades.[24] Rioting was therefore almost a regu-

22 Blockmans, Holenstein, and Mathieu (2009); Brakensiek and Wunder (2005); Holenstein (2003).

23 See among others Blickle (1988, 1989); Schulze (1975b, 1982, 1983); Trossbach (1983); Renault (2017).

24 Like that by the Schönburgs between 1651 and 1681. Trying to explain the outbreak of revolts has always been a challenge for social sciences. No simple causal factor (such as the price of wheat or the burden of taxes) is ever sufficient to explain why here, why there, why at this very moment. I have tried to show elsewhere how historical explanation could at least try to contextualise such outbreaks in order to understand them better (Renault 2017, Chapter 4). More generally for social science and the explanation of revolts, see Boltanski (2012); Thompson (1971).

lar event, at least not an extraordinary one. One also observes many interactions between the three neighbouring territories. Around 1680, for example, the Earls of Reuss suspected that their subjects of Obergreiz were conspiring with their neighbours from Schönburg and Bohemia.[25] And de facto, the Obergreiz subjects refer to a judgement given by a lawcourt in Leipzig (the *Oberhofgericht*) in the Schönburg case in 1663, which was in favour of the taxpayers, in order to pressure their own Lords of Reuss.[26]

Many riots included the seizure of a court of law. At such moments, the dimension of the protest changed as it was made official: this is a common feature which is at the core of the juridification (*Verrechtlichung*) paradigm.[27] Once it became official, the news of the riot spread, reports were printed and commented on at an imperial scale. This caused the imperial estates to greatly fear the bad publicity that such an escalation might imply, since their good government was publicly questioned.

3.3.3 Agency

The subjects of the three territories systematically brought their actions in front of different courts of law, imperial jurisdictions (usually *Reichskammergericht*), but also the courts of Saxony (*Appellationsgericht Dresden, Oberhofgericht Leipzig, Schöppenstuhl Leipzig*), and local taxpayers were extremely skilful in turning the authorities' competition with each other to their advantage. *Kursachsen* was always very eager to harm the small imperial estates by interfering in their fiscal matters and therefore regularly fostered popular protest against them. The subjects thus used the mediatisation conflicts mentioned above to their advantage, sometimes with great success. But they also obtained some advantages through imperial justice, where the invoked judicial proceedings could last several decades. Finally, subjects who protested against their tax burden in the three small imperial estates under question also turned towards Bohemian jurisdiction, especially the Appeal Court of Prague whose potential authority in such matters was based on the status of some of the fiefs (*Böhmische Reichsafterlehne*). The taxpayers, by collectively refusing to pay, fuelled the intervention of other authorities inside the *arcana* of the government of the imperial princes and earls. Thereby, they helped weaken the already fragile and contested authority of their lords but at the same time, protesting taxpayers risked being exposed to very harsh repression.

25 "*Und mann hierneben einige Nachricht erlanget, daß gemelte UnterGräitzische Pauern, mit denen Schönburgischen, und zugleich beÿde mit denen damahls rebellirenden Böhmischen Bauern heimblich conspirirten*", HStAG Paragiatherrschaft Köstritz, Kap. 6, Nr. 592, [s.d., after 1680, before 1682].

26 HStAG Hausarchiv Ober- und Untergreiz, Schrank II, Fach 20, Nr. 846, fol. 1-4 [petition 5 September, 1680].

27 Schulze (1975b).

3.3.4 Repression. "And Repel Violence by Violence": The "Fiscal Execution"

Anti-tax endeavours were heavily repressed in the small imperial estates, regardless of whether the protests took the forms of riots or attempted to start judicial proceedings. Imperial earls and lords complained to the emperor or to the neighbouring princes about the "renitence" of their subjects, who refused and contested the payment of their tax liabilities. As a consequence, the earls and lords of the small states regularly sent military troops not only to collect the taxes owing, but also to occupy and plunder the obstinate communities and spread terror – the apogee being a case of torture in 1664 committed by Schönburger soldiers.

From a legal perspective, the imperial estates were authorised to send their own troops or troops from a neighbouring territory, sometimes Saxony, if all other efforts to recover the taxes had failed.[28] In fact, military force was regularly used as a means to terrify the population. The soldiers were sent to the houses of the known leaders (*Rädelsführer*) and arch-rebels (*Erzrebellen*), or to the houses of delegates elected or designated to represent communities of taxpayers before a court of justice *(Syndici)* in order to intimidate and imprison them. The advocates were also targeted and arrested. A quite rare document records a discussion held in 1680 between two councillors (*Räte)* from the neighbouring territories of Schönburg and Reuss on how to proceed with the military enforcement of tax collection (*Steuerexekutionen*). The parties involved in the discussion were Councillor Mürhardt, who represented the Lords of Schönburg, and Councillor Paßel for the Earls of Reuss. The document shows that the enforcement procedure envisaged by these two councillors included confiscation, punishment and terror tactics. Their conversation is reported by Paßel to the Earls of Reuss:

> 2. [...] since, if you treat them mildly, the peasants believe that they are right or that you are afraid of them, [...] the imperial tax therefore should be collected by taking away their cattle.
>
> 3. Concerning the village where the execution [military enforcement] was to be carried out, he [Mürhardt] agreed with me [Paßel] that

28 So that the authorities claimed that: "If the recalcitrant stubborn subjects [...] had paid this tax according to their duty, they would not have suffered this execution, which is very much authorised and used in all the world against defaulting and recalcitrant people [...], and they would not have had to pay for it nor suffer any inconvenience. About them is rightful to say: *Damnum quod quis sua culpa sentit, non videtur sentire*." ("*Hätten nun die wiederspenstige harnäckige Amptßunterthanen [...] diese steüer ihrer unterthänigen Schuldigkeit nach abgetragen, so hätten sie solche execution, die wieder säumige und wiederspenstige Leüte ein zurecht zuläßiges und in aller weldt gebräuchliches Mittel ist, [...], nicht erleiden, noch diesertwegen einige Kosten tragen oder auch einige ungelegenheit außstehen dörffen. Solcher gestaldt aber heißet es mit ihnen billig: Damnum quod quis sua culpa sentit, non videtur sentire*") HStaG Hausarchiv Ober- und Untergreiz, Schrank IV, Fach 6d, Nr. 3, fol. 23–30, 27 Febr. 1685.

> it should only be Freÿreuth, [...] because this place has always dragged the others towards sedition [...]. Once the people of Freÿreuth see that this calamity will always befall only them, they will finally get tired of stirring up the others, or of plotting plans against the lord. [...]
>
> 8. Finally, it would be helpful if those believed to be leaders were arrested and held in detention for as long as it takes to find out at least who drafted [the petition] or who their lawyer is; the latter could then complain to his authority [the lawcourt], claiming that he is prevented from defending the peasants.[29]

Considering the risks incurred by those who took part in collective forms of tax refusal, the question arises as to why they still, regularly if not constantly, organised those protests. Since protests lasted for several years, in some cases even several decades, they appear to be a structural means of putting pressure on the authorities, rather than an *ultima ratio* or a rare exception to a government that was otherwise ordinarily consensual and harmonious.[30] In fiscal matters, and even more so for the imperial tax, governments are not inclined towards acceptance,[31] and anti-tax protests were a way to perpetuate tension in everyday social and political relations of domination.

But lawsuits in particular were also a way to perpetuate a certain number of formal rights guaranteed by the empire, such as the right to collect taxes to finance litigation or the right to designate *Syndici*, as two examples.[32] In the cases that I have studied, litigation would turn into riots only when soldiers were sent to the communities, and thus as a consequence of a violent escalation. Sending in military force was perceived by subjects as a rupture with the lords' traditional function of "protection" (*Schutz und Schirm*). Taxes were supposed to finance protection against enemies and the dangers of war. But this feudal "contract" was turned upside down when the lord employed violence against his own subjects: it then appeared a

29 "2° *[...] Nach dem die Bauren so gesinnet, daß wenn man ihnen mit Glimpf begegnet, sie allzeit meinen sie haben recht oder man scheue sich für ihnen, dannenhero [...] die Reichs-Steuer durch Wegnehmung des Rindviehs herauszubringen wäre.*

3° Wegen des Orths, über den die Execution geben solte, war er mit mir eines Sinnes, daß selbiges bloß Freÿreuth seÿn solle, [...] weil dieser Orth die anderen stets zu meher Widersezlichkeit verleutete [...]. Wann dann die freÿreuter sehen würden, daß das Unglück allezeit sie allein betreffen solle, würden sie endlich wohl müde werden, die anderen aufzu wiegeln, oder wieder die Herrschaft was vorzunehmen. [...]

8° Schließlich, so wäre nicht undienlich, wann etliche so man vor die Redelsführer hält, beÿm kopffen nehmen ließe, und so lange in Verwahrung hielte, bis sie wenigst des concipienten oder ihren Advokaten entdeckete; selbiger könte was alß dann wohl beÿ seiner Obrigkeit belangen, daß ihn ferner des bauren zu patrociniren verbothen würde", HStAG, Hausarchiv Ober- und Untergreiz, Schrank II, Fach 20, Nr. 846, fol. 85–86, 25 Sept. 1680.

30 See Thompson (1971) for a similar analysis regarding hunger riots.

31 For a nuanced understanding of government acceptance, see Brakensiek (2005).

32 See Trossbach (1987a).

mere fiction.[33] Refusing to pay taxes therefore became a way to contest the foundations of power legitimacy since, in return, this violence was employed by the subjects as an argument against the legitimacy of taxation. This brings us to the last question: how did taxpayers justify their refusal to pay, in their supplications, before the courts of justice, but also in interrogations and examinations?

3.4 The "Moral Economy" of Taxation: Was Tax Resistance a Political Claim?

Subjects who refused to pay the imperial taxes never pretended that the taxes as such were not legitimate, and the figure of the emperor was almost always spared by their argumentation and accusations, probably because such a protest would have been impossible to defend in the legitimate public sphere, but also because it would have been of no concrete political interest for them. Nevertheless, the claims of the subjects in fiscal matters reveal profoundly political demands, which concern the social and political order of the entire empire. In the following, I classify these demands in three main groups: (1) transparency and publicity; (2) equity and equality; (3) consent and representation. These groups proved quite stable over the period 1648–1806, although the formulation of claims evolved with general political language.

3.4.1 Transparency and Publicity

Taxpayers always suspected the lords of demanding more from them than they actually owed to the emperor. For the reasons mentioned above, this suspicion was not unreasonable, and it actually regularly became reality – all the more so as taxpayers often paid only one third of what had been demanded. Local taxpayers in the small imperial estates under question also suspected that some of the money raised was not sent to the emperor, but was confiscated by the lords. Therefore, they constantly asked to be given access to the registered amounts of collected taxes in order to know "where what is theirs is going".[34] And very often, they stressed the fact that they had already paid their portion – and more – to justify their refusal. Sometimes, the subjects also argued that the tax had changed its name, for example that the war tax (*Kriegssteuer*) they had been asked to pay had become a coronation tax (*Krönungssteuer*), and they would therefore refuse to pay. Or they frequently asked that the imperial tax order should be presented to them including the

33 See Algazi (1996); Renault (2017); Chapter 5. This theory of taxation as a counterpart for protection is in part a fiction intended to legitimise power, but with a very thin empirical foundation. This is, among other things, what the frequency of riots and protests reveals: that the "contract" that should be the basis of power legitimacy is actually rarely fulfilled by the authorities.

34 "Wo das Ihrige bleibt", HStAD Appellationsgericht, 5209, fol. 543, 17 Sept. 1794.

actual tax portion they owed. The following excerpt of a letter from the Lords of Schönburg to the Elector of Saxony in 1663 documents this line of argument:

> Our subjects in the estate of Glauchau, especially in the countryside, were so inclined to cause trouble that they did not by any means want to accept or accommodate any taxes or empire burdens, at least not before the majestic order of the emperor was published and presented to them; they thereby arbitrarily claim such an absurd liberty, which is neither permitted nor granted to any people in the whole Holy Roman Empire nor almost anywhere else under the sun.[35]

More than a century later, during a trial in front of the Dresden Court of Appeal during the 1790s, the advocate for the protesting subjects argued that "publicity" could in no way harm the common good, and that, on the contrary, its absence would enhance mistrust:

> But how could the publicity of the paternal care of a government, which is directed towards the common good, be contrary to the common good, since it rather promotes it, or how could a government [...] find it prejudicial for its dignity?[36]

The demands of the subjects had thus gradually evolved into a demand for accountability of the authorities, which itself implied a new form of political participation.

3.4.2 Consent and Representation

Although imperial taxes had already been approved by the Imperial Diet, the subjects tried to impose their own right of consent to taxation. Even though there were certain estate assemblies (*Landstände*) in some domains of the three territories, they, first, never included representation of the peasants,

35 "*Wie unsere Unterthanen in der Herrschafft Glauchau, sonderlich uffm Lande, sich [...] dermaßen zu turbiren, daß sie sich zu Abtragung einiger Steüern und Reichsbürden keinesweges, od. er zum wenigstens ehe nicht, es werdten ihnen denn der Römischen Keÿßerl. Maÿ. außtrückliche befehlige oder dero Reichspfennigmeister Anordnungen zuvor publiciret und vorgezeigt, accomodiren und bequemen undt solcher gestaldt in eine so ungereümete libertët eigenmächtig sezen wollen, dergleichen keinem Volck im ganzen Heiligen römischen Reich, ja wohl fast unter der Sonne, nicht gestattet noch eingereümet wirdt*", Brief der Herren von Schönburg an den Kurfürsten von Sachsen, July 1663, HSTAD, Reichskammergericht n 41, vol. 2, fol. 345–348b.

36 "*Wie könnte aber die Publizität der väterlichen und zum Zweck des allgemeinen Wohls hinwürckenden Fürsorge einer Regierung dem allgemeinen Zweck entgegen seyn, da sie ihn vielmehr fördert, oder wie könnte eine Regierung [...] etwas ihrer Würde nachtheiliges, wie in dem gegentheiligen ohne Noth geursachten Mistrauen das Vorzügliche eines Landeshoheitlichen Rechtes finden*", HStaD Appellationsgericht, 5209, fol. 118, 22 May 1794.

who were the great majority of local taxpayers, and, second, these territorial assemblies were, except in very special cases, bound by the decisions of the Imperial Diet and could not oppose the levy of imperial taxes.[37] The formal consent to taxes is among the political and fiscal principles of the *Ancien Régime* body politic and guaranteed the legitimacy of taxation. But what was actually and concretely meant by "consent" was a bone of contention. The Lords wanted their subjects to "consent" to taxation, as in "being willing" (*willig sein*) and accepting any tax liability and its payment. The subjects, for their part, claimed they had a right to consent (*bewilligen*), that is to say, to accept and authorise, but also to refuse their lord's tax demands and therefore the payment.

This claim led to a Thuringian variety of the American creed of "No taxation without representation". The practices and claims of the peasants were derived from the governing and legitimising practices of the estates, and they imitated estate assemblies by claiming to represent "the whole country" and to defend "German liberties" against tyranny.[38] In 1778 in Schönburg territory, the subjects protested against "all the unauthorised ordinary and extraordinary taxes" and required to be informed about how the raised tax money was used.[39] Contesting taxation is therefore also a way to *behave and act as if* there were an estate assembly. The lords, though, interpreted this claim as a way to negate their *jus collectandi* and therefore their imperial immediacy, and to unleash never-ending conflicts, which Saxony was very eager to arbitrate.

3.4.3 Equity (Billigkeit) and Equality (Gleichheit)

Finally, the subjects also intended to intervene in the repartition of taxes, which involved disputing the established social order, as the prescription of who owed how much was a way to create and uphold a certain hierarchy. The principle of *Billigkeit* (equity) led to an infinity of conflicts not only between taxpayers and the authorities, but also among taxpayers. The main question was whether the taxes had to be raised according to status (noble or not, land or city etc.) or according to fortune. From the mid-eighteenth century onwards, the subjects increasingly protested against the system of tax exemptions by status, and especially against the exemptions of the lords. An advocate who represented tax protesters in 1793 claimed that the lords wanted to

37 On peasant representation, see Blickle (1973) and the critical review by Press (1975).

38 See Stollberg-Rilinger (1999).

39 "*Wir sind daher gemüssiget [...] wider executivis. Beÿtreibung aller unbewilligter ordinair und extraordinairen Steuern so lange uns nach Vorschrift des Allerhöchst Preÿswürdigsten Kaÿserl. Und Reichs-Cammer-Gerichts Mandtas von 13. Octobr. 1664 nicht gehörig angezeigt worden, wozu die anverlangte ordinair und extraordinairen Steuern eigentlich verwendet werden sollen, und wieviel die von uns zu denen Reichs- und Craÿs-Anlagen zu bezahlen habende Quota betragen möchte [zu appelliren]*", HSTAD, Reichskammergericht 41, vol. 4, fol. 941, 20 March 1778.

"spare" themselves taxation and that they treated demands for equity and the subjects' "fair share" arbitrarily:

> If such excuses [as presented by the lords] could have any substance, and if [the idea of] what is right and fair for raising the sums necessary for public defence and in sub-repartitioning them, could change every now and then, there would soon be an entire regiment of equities. But in actual fact, only ONE EQUITY can exist, when a tax is collected to avert public calamity.[40]

3.5 Conclusion

It is not necessary to go as far as to claim that political equality was invented by rural taxpayers protesting against arbitrariness ("*Willkür*") in the period of the *Ancien Régime*, in order to underline the "political" dimension of such protests.[41] Tax resistance by ordinary Saxon and Thuringian taxpayers shows the high political potential of ordinary people's political action in *Ancien Régime* societies, and the extent of their agency. By contesting imperial taxes, the subjects questioned the power base of their princes and their legitimacy, and revived the conflicts between them and Saxony, in which the emperor himself sometimes intervened. Revolts and trials were fundamentally complementary in the construction of a balance of power with the authorities, and the latter did not replace the former in a great pacification movement. The subjects legitimised their claims by never protesting against the emperor, and instead blamed the government of earls and princes. If tax resistance was made public, it represented a major risk to the reputation of these rulers. In addition, it was of crucial importance that the lords pay their taxes, and pay them zealously, in order to consolidate their threatened political and social status. This is why collective forms of tax resistance were severely repressed: to deter the protesters but, probably even more importantly, to reactivate the power that had been undermined by the challenge. Nevertheless, repression did not discourage contest, which was often successful, whether by winning a court case – which happened regularly in the Saxon courts of law – or by the simple fact that through their self-organisation the subjects asserted forms of political rights (the right of assembly, self-administration and self-taxation, the designation of representatives, etc.). The political claims that legitimised

40 "*Wenn solche Entschuldigungen von einigen Gewicht seyn könnten, und bey Aufbringung der zu Abwendung öffentlicher Drangsale nöthigen Summen und deren Subrepartition bald dies bald jenes billig und recht seyn sollte, so würde es in kurzen ein ganz Regiment von Billigkeiten geben. Bey Einhebung der Contribution zu Abwendung einer öffentlichen Calamitaet kann aber noch wahrhaftig nur eine Billigkeit existiren*", HSTAD, Appellationsgericht, 5209, fol. 443 sqq., 14 September 1794.

41 Unlike French historiography, the political dimension of early Modern protests has long been noticed by German historiography, which nevertheless only rarely focused on the specificities of anti-tax protest in this regard. See Blickle (1988); Trossbach (1985, 1987a, 1987b).

refusals to pay taxes were also an important laboratory for political thought, which was not confined to philosophical treatises: consent, equity and transparency are central and common political concepts, whose concrete content the taxpayers tried to influence in a way that was favourable to their interests. Observing the imperial body from below and delineating the complex network of interests behind the payment of taxes or resistance to their payment shows that, although imperial taxes did not help to build either an imperial or a local state, resistance to such taxes was an important step in the construction of political modernity.

Archives

Hauptstaatsarchiv Greiz (HStAG).
Hauptstaatsarchiv Rudolstadt (HStAR).
Hauptstaatsarchiv Dresden (HStAD).

References

Algazi, Gadi. 1996. *Herrengewalt und Gewalt der Herren im späten Mittelalter : Herrschaft, Gegenseitigkeit und Sprachgebrauch*. Frankfurt am Main, New York: Campus Verlag.

Baumann, Anette. 2001. *Die Gesellschaft der Frühen Neuzeit im Spiegel der Reichskammergerichtsprozesse: eine sozialgeschichtliche Untersuchung zum 17. und 18. Jahrhundert*. Cologne, Vienna: Böhlau.

Blickle, Peter. 1973. *Landschaften im Alten Reich. Die staatliche Funktion des gemeinen Mannes in Oberdeutschland*. Munich: Beck.

Blickle, Peter. 1988. *Unruhen in der ständischen Gesellschaft, 1300-1800*. Munich: Oldenbourg.

Blickle, Peter. 1989. *Studien zur geschichtlichen Bedeutung des deutschen Bauernstandes*. Stuttgart, New York: Fischer.

Blockmans, Wim, André Holenstein, and Mathieu Jon (eds.). 2009. *Empowering Interactions. Political Cultures and the Emergence of the State in Europe 1300-1900*. Farnham, Burlington: Ashgate.

Boltanski, Luc. 2012. Pourquoi ne se révolte-t-on pas? Pourquoi se révolte-t-on? *Contretemps. Revue de Critique Communiste*, 15: 107–121.

Brakensiek, Stefan and Heide Wunder (eds.). 2005. *Ergebene Diener ihrer Herren? Herrschaftsvermittlung im alten Europa*. Cologne, Weimar, Vienna: Böhlau.

Brakensiek, Stefan, 2005. Lokale Amtsträger in deutschen Territorien der Frühen Neuzeit. Institutionelle Grundlagen, akzeptanzorientierte Herrschaftspraxis und obrigkeitliche Identität. In *Staatsbildung als kultureller Prozeß. Strukturwandel und Legitimation von Herrschaft in der Frühen Neuzeit*, eds. Ronald Asch and Dagmar Freist, 49–67. Köln, Weimar, Wien: Böhlau.

Collins, James B. 1988. *Fiscal Limits of Absolutism: Direct Taxation in Early Seventeenth-Century France*. Berkeley: University of California Press.

Diestelkamp, Bernhard. 1999. *Recht und Gericht im Heiligen Römischen Reich*. Frankfurt am Main: Klostermann.

Edelmayer, Friedrich, Maximilian Lanzinner, and Peter Rauscher (ed.). 2003. *Finanzen und Herrschaft: Materielle Grundlagen fürstlicher Politik in den habsburgischen Ländern und im Heiligen Römischen Reich im 16. Jahrhundert*. Vienna, Munich: Oldenbourg.

Fimpel, Martin. 2000. *Reichsjustiz und Territorialstaat. Württemberg als Kommissar von Kaiser und Reich im Schwäbischen Kreis (1648-1806)*. Tübingen: Bibliotheca academica.

Holenstein, André. 2003. *"Gute Policey" und lokale Gesellschaft im Staat des* Ancien Régime. *Das Fallbeispiel der Markgrafschaft Baden(-Durlach)*. Tübingen: Biblioteca academica.

Isenmann, Eberhard. 1980. Reichsfinanzen und Reichssteuern im 15. Jahrhundert. *Zeitschrift für Historische Forschung* (7)2: 129–218.

Isenmann, Eberhard. 2018. Reichsstadt und Steuer. In *Reichsstadt und Geld*, eds. Michael Rothmann and Helge Wittmann, 15–44. Petersberg: Michael Imhof Verlag.

Moraw, Peter. 1986. Der "Gemeine Pfennig". Neue Steuern und die Einheit des Reichs im 15. und 16. Jahrhundert. In *Mit dem Zehnten fing es an. Eine Kulturgeschichte der Steuer*, ed. Uwe Schultz, 130–142. Munich: Beck.

Moser, Johann Jacob. 1773. *Von der Landeshoheit in Steuer-Sachen, wie auch anderen Geld- und Natural-Abgaben, Nach denen Reichs-Gesetzen und dem Reichs-Herkommen, wie auch denen Teutschen Staats-Rechts-Lehrern, und eigener Erfahrung*. Frankfurt, Leipzig.

Press, Volker. 1975. Herrschaft, Landschaft und Gemeiner Mann in Oberdeutschland. *Zeitschrift für die Geschichte des Oberrheins* (123)84: 169–214.

Rauscher, Peter, Andrea Serles, and Thomas Winkelbauer. 2012. *Das 'Blut des Staatskörpers'. Forschungen zur Finanzgeschichte der Frühen Neuzeit*. Munich: Oldenbourg.

Rauscher, Peter. 2003. Die Reichstürkenhilfen von Ferdinand I. bis zum Beginn des 'Langen Türkenkriegs', (1548-1593). In: *Finanzen und Herrschaft: Materielle Grundlagen fürstlicher Politik in den habsburgischen Ländern und im Heiligen Römischen Reich im 16. Jahrhundert*, eds. Friedrich Edelmayer, Maximilian Lanzinner, and Peter Rauscher, 45–83. Vienne, Munich: Oldenbourg.

Rauscher, Peter. 2004. *Zwischen Ständen und Gläubigern. Die kaiserlichen Finanzen unter Ferdinand I. und Maximilian II. (1556–1576)*. Veröffentlichungen des Instituts für Österreichische Geschichtsforschung. Vienne, Munich: Oldenbourg.

Rauscher, Peter (ed). 2010. *Kriegführung und Staatsfinanzen. Die Habsburgermonarchie und das Heilige Römische Reich vom Dreißigjährigen Krieg bis zum Ende des habsburgischen Kaisertums 1740*. Münster: Aschendorff.

Renault, Rachel. 2017. *La permanence de l'extraordinaire: fiscalité, pouvoirs et monde social en Allemagne aux XVIIe-XVIIIe siècles*. Paris: Éditions de la Sorbonne.

Renault, Rachel. 2018. Gleichheit, Gerechtigkeit, Billigkeit. Steuerverteilung, Satus und soziale Ordnung im 18. Jahrhundert. In *Verschränkte Ungleichheit: Praktiken der Intersektionalität in der Frühen Neuzeit*, eds. Matthias Bähr and Florian Kühnel, 303–336. Berlin: Duncker & Humblot.

Sailer, Rita. 1999. *Untertanenprozesse vor dem Reichskammergericht: Rechtsschutz gegen die Obrigkeit in der zweiten Hälfte des 18. Jahrhunderts*. Cologne, Weimar, Vienna: Böhlau.

Scheurman, Ingrid. 1994. *Frieden durch Recht: Das Reichskammergericht von 1495 bis 1806*. Mainz: Verlag Phillip von Zabern.

Schilling, Heinz. 2001. Reichs-Staat und frühneuzeitliche Nation der Deutschen oder teilmodernisiertes Reichssystem. Überlegungen zu Charakter und Aktualität des Alten Reiches. *Historische Zeitschrift* 272: 377–395.

Schmid, Peter.1983. Reichssteuern, Reichsfinanzen und Reichsgewalt in der ersten Hälfte des 16. Jahrhunderts. In *Säkulare Aspekte der Reformationszeit*, ed. Heinz Angermeier, 153–198. Munich, Vienne: Oldenbourg.

Schmid, Peter. 1989. *Der Gemeine Pfennig von 1495. Vorgeschichte und Entstehung, verfassungsgeschichtliche, politische und finanzielle Bedeutung*. Göttingen: Vandenhoeck & Ruprecht.

Schmidt, Georg. 2001. Das frühneuzeitliche Reich - komplementärer Staat und föderative Nation. *Historische Zeitschrift* 273: 371–399.

Schulze, Winfried. 1975a. Reichstage und Reichssteuern im späten 16. Jahrhundert. *Zeitschrift für Historische Forschung* 2: 43–58.

Schulze, Winfried. 1975b. Die veränderte Bedeutung sozialer Konflikte im 16. und 17. Jahrhundert. In *Der deutsche Bauernkrieg*, ed. Hans-Ulrich Wehler, 277–302. Göttingen: Vandenhoeck & Ruprecht.

Schulze, Winfried. 1978. Die Erträge der Reichssteuern zwischen 1576 und 1606. *Jahrbuch für die Geschichte Mittel- und Ostdeutschlands* 27: 169–185.

Schulze, Winfried. 1982. Oberdeutsche Untertanenrevolten zwischen 1580 und 1620. Reichssteuern und bäuerlicher Widerstand. In *Festschrift für Günther Franz zum 80. Geburtstag am 23. Mai 1982, Bauer, Reich und Reformation*, ed. Peter Blickle, 120–147. Stuttgart: Ulmer.

Schulze, Winfried (ed). 1983. *Aufstände, Revolten, Prozesse, Beiträge zu bäuerlichen Widerstandsbewegungen im frühneuzeitlichen Europa*. Stuttgart: Klett-Cota.

Schwennicke, Andreas. 1996. *"Ohne Steuer kein Staat" : zur Entwicklung und politischen Funktion des Steuerrechts in den Territorien des Heiligen Römischen Reichs (1500-1800)*. Frankfurt am Main: V. Klostermann.

Stollberg-Rilinger, Barbara. 1999. *Vormünder des Volkes? Konzepte landständischer Repräsentation in der Spätphase des Alten Reiches*. Berlin: Duncker & Humblot.

Trossbach, Werner. 1983. Bauernbewegungen in deutschen Kleinterritorien zwischen 1648 und 1789. In *Aufstände, Revolten, Prozesse, Beiträge zu bäuerlichen Widerstandsbewegungen im frühneuzeitlichen Europa*, ed. Winfried Schulze, 233–260. Stuttgart: Klett-Cota.

Trossbach, Werner. 1985. *Bauernbewegungen im Wetterau-Vogelsberg Gebiet, 1648-1806. Fallstudien zum bäuerlichen Widerstand im Alten Reich*. Darmstadt: Hessische Historische Kommission.

Trossbach, Werner. 1987a. *Soziale Bewegung und politische Erfahrung. Bäüerlicher Protest in hessischen Territorien, 1648-1806*. Weingarten: Drumlin Verlag.

Trossbach, Werner. 1987b. Bäuerlicher Widerstand in deutschen Kleinterritorien, zwischen Bauernkrieg und Französicher Revolution. Einige Bemerkungen zu Formen und Gegenständen. *Zeitschrift für Agrargeschichte und Agrarsoziologie* 35: 1–16.

Weber, Edwin Ernst. 1992. *Städtische Herrschaft und bäuerliche Untertanen in Alltag und Konflikt: Die Reichsstadt Rottweil und ihre Landschaft vom 30jährigen Krieg bis zur Mediatisierung*. Oberndorf a. N.: Schwarzwälder Druckhaus.

Part II

Resisting and Opposing Taxes

4 Not Paying Taxes in Roman Egypt[1]

Kerstin Droß-Krüpe

4.1 Taxes in the Roman Empire

The importance of taxes for the existence and continuation of the *imperium Romanum*[2] was emphasised already by Cicero in his extant speech *pro lege Manilia* in 66 BC, when he supported the proposal of Gaius Manilius to grant Pompey an extraordinary command during the Third Mithridatic War (89–63 BC).[3] In this speech, Cicero describes taxes as being the nerves of the state. And at the beginning of the third century AD, Cassius Dio in his *History* explains in detail the necessity of tax assessment:[4]

> From what source, then, is the money to be provided for these soldiers and for the other expenses that will of necessity be incurred? […] For

1 I owe thanks to the organisers for providing the stimulus for this chapter. I am most grateful to Prof. Dr Sven Günther (Institute for the History of Ancient Civilizations [IHAC] – Northeast Normal University, Changchun), who read an earlier version of this contribution and kindly helped improve it with his expertise and advice. I am further indebted to Dr Magdalena Öhrman (University of Wales Trinity Saint David [UWTSD], Lampeter) for her useful remarks and her revision of my English. All remaining errors are obviously my own.

2 For a general introduction, see Monson and Scheidel (2015, 229–257).

3 Cic. Manil. 17. *Ancient authors are quoted according* to standard divisions of their works into books and chapters. Their names and *works* are *abbreviated* as in the fourth edition of the *Oxford Classical Dictionary*. 2012, ed. Simon Hornblower, Antony J. S. Spawforth and Esther Eidinow, Oxford: Oxford University Press.

4 Cass. Dio 52.2.1–6: Πόθεν οὖν χρήματα καὶ ἐς τούτους καὶ ἐς τὰ ἄλλα τὰ ἀναγκαίως ἀναλωθησόμενα ἔσται; […] οὐ γὰρ οἷόν τε οὔτ᾽ ἄνευ στρατιωτῶν ἡμᾶς σώζεσθαι οὔτ᾽ ἀμισθί τινας στρατεύεσθαι. Μὴ […] ὅπως ποτ᾽ ἂν πολιτευώμεθα, καὶ ἀργυρίζεσθαί τινα, οὕτω βουλευώμεθα. […] κἀκ τούτου πρὸς πᾶν τὸ λεῖπον φόρον τε ἐπιτάξαι πᾶσιν ἁπλῶς τοῖς ἐπικαρπίαν τινὰ τῷ κεκτημένῳ αὐτὰ παρέχουσι, καὶ τέλη καταστῆσαι παρὰ πᾶσιν ὧν ἄρχομεν. καὶ γὰρ καὶ δίκαιον καὶ προσῆκόν ἐστι μηδένα αὐτῶν ἀτελῆ εἶναι, μὴ ἰδιώτην, μὴ δῆμον, ἅτε καὶ τῆς ὠφελίας τῆς ἀπ᾽ αὐτῶν ὁμοίως τοῖς ἄλλοις ἀπολαύσοντας. (If not stated otherwise, translations of ancient sources are quoted according to the Loeb Classical Library edition.)

This text passage belongs to the last comprehensive assessment of the reign of the first Roman princeps Augustus (27 BC – AD 14), more precisely to the context of the consolidation of power of Augustus, who, after a long period of civil war, advanced the reorganisation of the Roman Empire in political and economic terms. Augustus, whom Cassius Dio considers a paradigm of a good ruler, was in fact responsible for the introduction of various new taxes and a systematisation of taxation. See Günther (2008, 32–34) for an outline of Augustus' fiscal policy.

DOI: 10.4324/9781003333197-7

> we cannot survive without soldiers, and men will not serve as soldiers without pay. Therefore [...] let us assume in our deliberations that, under whatever form of government we shall live, we shall certainly be constrained to secure funds. [...] The next step is to provide for any deficiency by levying an assessment upon absolutely all property which produces any profit for its possessors, and by establishing a system of taxes among all the peoples we rule. For it is but just and proper that no individual or district be exempt from these taxes, inasmuch as they are to enjoy the benefits derived from the taxation as much as the rest.

From at least Augustan times at the turn of the millennium, the then well-established Roman Empire was rich in taxes, which were certainly perceived as being a burden and an imposition. Consequently, examples of resistance to the introduction of new taxes are numerous[5] – for all inhabitants of the Imperium Romanum were liable to tax, although not to the same extent. For Roman citizens (*cives Romani*), tax liability was limited to so-called indirect taxes that were raised on specific occasions (*vectigalia*) – these included the 5% inheritance tax (*vicesima hereditatium*), a 5% tax for the manumission of slaves (*vicesima libertatis vel manumissionum*), the 1% sales tax (*centesima rerum venalium*) and the 4% tax on slave sales (*quinta et vincesima venalium manicipiorum*).[6] Furthermore, they had to pay custom dues (*portoria*), as did every inhabitant of the Roman Empire importing/exporting certain goods, with few exemptions (e.g. private belongings).[7] Due to their exclusive status, other taxes were not levied on Roman citizens. This particularly applies to any form of *tributa* or *stipendia*, i.e. so-called direct taxes raised on the basis of a *census* list.[8] These taxes were of particular relevance for all inhabitants of the Roman provinces aged between 14 and 60.[9] As these people did not hold Roman citizenship, they had to pay the poll tax (*tributum capitis*/λαογραφία).[10] This tax had different rates in the various provinces of the Roman Empire,[11] but is

5 Cf. Corbier (1988, 259–274); Günther (2021).

6 Cf. Günther (2008, *passim*); Günther (2016); Günther (2021, *passim*).

7 Cf. Kritzinger (2015, 11–55).

8 For the discussion of the terms of so-called direct and indirect taxes, see Günther (2016).

9 Cf. P. Lond. 2/259 (AD 94); in some regions up to the age of 65 years. All papyri in the course of this contribution are quoted according to the abbreviations of John F. Oates et al., *Checklist of Editions of Greek, Latin, Demotic and Coptic Papyri, Ostraca and Tablets* (https://library.duke.edu/rubenstein/scriptorium/papyrus/texts/clist.html; last updated 1 June 2011; last accessed 20 October 2020).

10 Cf. Neesen (1980) and Brunt 1990. Even after the granting of Roman citizenship to all provincials by the so-called *constitutio Antoniniana* under Emperor Caracalla in AD 212, things did not change as our sources still demonstrate payment of the poll tax; Buraselis (2007, 94–157).

11 Neesen (1980, 120); Bagnall and Frier (1994, *passim*); Günther (2021, *passim*). The poll tax is mentioned several times in the Gospels of the New Testament, the Gospel of Luke (Lk 2.1–3) being probably the best-known reference. Luke connects the story of Jesus' birth with a first empire-wide *census* under Emperor Augustus. However, Luke misjudges the character of this *census* – it was rather a first provincial *census* (*descriptio prima*), conducted in AD 6 in the course

best documented in Roman Egypt, where certain groups (e.g. the inhabitants of the *metropoleis*) enjoyed the privilege of a reduced tax rate.[12] The poll tax was without doubt one of the most important taxes in the Roman Empire and made up the most significant share of the provincials' tax burden (see below). Regular *census* taking was necessary to evaluate the taxable number of people, as well as their civil rights status, land ownership and other assets that determined the actual level of taxation. Claytor and Bagnall rightly call the *census* in the Roman provinces "one of the most durable and pervasive institutions of the Roman Empire" and "a key component of Rome's control over provincial society".[13]

Since at least in Roman Egypt women children and the elderly were exempted from taxes, but had nevertheless to be registered, tax assessment cannot have been the only purpose of the provincial *census*. Hence, Bagnall and Frier conclude that "[i]t appears, then, that the entire population of Egypt was registered, whatever their status".[14]

The inhabitants of the provinces were required to submit declarations to the local authorities containing their names, ages and other identifying information pertaining to their co-residents every couple of years. Actual responsibility for conducting the *census* lay with the incumbent provincial governors as the Emperor's representatives, who occasionally passed on the task to lower hierarchical levels such as *procuratores*.[15]

4.2 Taxes and Tax Collection in Roman Egypt – Evidence from the Documentary Papyri

As already mentioned above, documents from the Roman province of Egypt inform us particularly about the actual practice of registering taxpayers, as well as about the various types of taxes that affected the local population who did not hold Roman citizenship. The papyri from this region, mostly written in Greek, offer a unique insight into the everyday life of Egypt's population in the period between the conquest of Egypt by Alexander III in 332 BC and the Arab conquest AD 641.[16] In 30 BC, after the defeat of Mark Antony and Cleopatra VII, Egypt became a Roman province. Up to the eighth century

of the incorporation of *Iudaea* into the Roman province of *Syria* after the end of the ethnarchy of Herod Archelaus. Cf. Hirschmüller (1994, 33–68); further Steinmetzler (1954, 971–972); Marquardt (1957, 213). A different, but in light of the lack of reference to an empire-wide *census* in the deeds of Augustus (RG 8) not persuasive position is adopted by Wiesemann (1987, 479–480).

12 Wallace (1969, 116–134); Jördens (2009, 331–354).

13 Claytor and Bagnall (2015, 638).

14 Bagnall and Frier (1994, 12).

15 Braunert (1957, 192–214); Bagnall and Frier (1994, 11–14); Jördens (2009, 62–94).

16 For an outline of the dynamic transformation process after the merging of the Muslim Empire and its conquest of Egypt from AD 642, see Schmidt (2020) (with special regards to the economic impact).

AD, papyrus was the most common writing material in the Mediterranean world – due to the climatic conditions, however, it has survived mainly in the province of Egypt. The region's papyrological record is further supplemented by documents written on potsherds, so-called *ostraca*. So far, about 60,000 Greek papyri and ostraca have been published. In addition to private correspondence, the material includes records of various economic matters and individual trades, legal transactions, administrative acts and literary and religious texts. Through these sources, we gain insights into the economic, social and legal conditions within this province in an almost voyeuristic way. Thanks to these texts we are much better informed about Egypt than about any other region of the Roman Empire or the ancient Mediterranean world in general.

From the papyrological record, we learn that the provincial *census* in Egypt was carried out every 14 years and started with the registration of all individuals – the so-called house-to-house registration (κατ' οἰκίαν ἀπογραφή)[17] that was inaugurated with a promulgation such as the following from AD 104 (Sel.Pap. 2/220 = P.Lond. 3/904, col. 2):[18]

> Gaius Vibius Maximus, prefect of Egypt [declares]: As a house-to-house registration has been authorized, it is necessary to order all persons absent from their homes that they may return to their homes, that they may perform the customary business of registration and may apply themselves to the cultivation of the land, as is their proper duty. I realize, however, that the city [i.e. Alexandria] has need of some of the peasants; and it is my will that all persons who appear to have good reason to remain in the city shall register themselves with Voul[…] Festus, the prefect of the cavalry, whom I have assigned to this duty, from whom those persons who prove that it is necessary for them to remain in the city will receive the necessary authorization […] and all others are to return home within thirty days. Anyone who thereafter is found lacking a permit will be punished without moderation […].

17 Cf. Hombert and Préaux (1952, *passim*); Bagnall and Frier (1994, 1–30); Jördens (2009, 62–94, 64–67).

18 Γ[άιος Οὐί]βιο[ς Μάξιμος ἔπα]ρχ[ος] Αἰγύπτ[ου λέγει·] τῆς κατ' οἰ[κίαν ἀπογραφῆς ἐ]νεστώ[σης] ἀναγκαῖόν [ἐστιν πᾶσιν τοῖ]ς καθ' ἥ[ντινα] δήποτε αἰτ[ίαν ἀποδημοῦσιν ἀπὸ τῶν] νομῶν προσα[γγέλλε]σθαι ἐπα[νελ]θεῖν εἰς τὰ ἑαυ[τῶν ἐ]φέστια ἵν[α] καὶ τὴν συνήθη [οἰ]κονομίαν τῆ[ς ἀπο]γραφῆς πληρώσωσιν καὶ τῇ προσ[ηκού]σῃ αὐτοῖς γεωργίαι προσκαρτερήσω[σιν]. εἰδὼς μέντο[ι ὅ]τι ἐνίων τῶν [ἀπὸ] τῆς χώρας ἡ πόλις ἡμῶν ἔχει χρε[ίαν] βούλομ[αι] πάντα[ς τ]οὺς εὔ[λ]ο̣γ̣ον δο[κοῦν]τα[ς] ἔχειν τοῦ ἐνθάδε ἐπιμένιν [αἰ-]τίαν ἀπογράφεσ[θ]αι παρὰ Βουλ . . .[. . .] Φήστῳ ἐπάρχω[ι] εἴλης, ὃν ἐπὶ το[ύτῳ] ἔταξα, οὗ καὶ τὰς [ὑ]πογραφὰς οἱ ἀποδ[εί]ξαντες ἀναγκ[αίαν α]ὐτῶν τὴν παρου[σίαν] λήμψοντα[ι κατὰ τ]οῦ[τ]ο τὸ παράγγελμ[α] ἐντὸς [τῆς τριακάδος τοῦ ἐν]εσ[τ]ῶτος μηνὸς Ἐ[πεὶφ - ca.13 - ἐ]πανελθεῖν μεθ' ἧ[ς (?)- ca.15 -] ὑπογραφῆ[ς] τοῦ ἐπιλ̣[- ca.16 -] .ρεθηι οὐ μετρίω[ς - ca.11 - εὖ γὰ]ρ οἶδα τὰ ἐντε[- ca.16 -]θαι ὅσο̣ν . . τῇ π[- ca.15 - ἀ]δικοῦντες.

And indeed, another papyrus confirms that at least during the High Empire, severe penalties existed for any failure to register (BGU 5/1210 = Sel.Pap. 206; mid-second century AD):[19]

> Persons who in the household censuses have not registered themselves and those whom they ought are fined a quarter of their property, and if they are reported not to have registered on two occasions, they are sentenced to the same fine doubled. [...] Those who have failed to register slaves suffer confiscation of the slaves only.

As outlined above, the provincial *census* formed inter alia the basis of the taxation of provincial populations. The vast amount of papyri and ostraca from Roman Egypt further reflects the variety of tax burdens for that particular province, as the correct payment of the relevant taxes was always acknowledged to the taxpayers. Thanks to these tax receipts we are comparatively well-informed about the names and actual amounts of the taxes, the period of collection and the administrative apparatus behind it. Nevertheless, compared to later epochs, the source material is still sparse and only offers a glimpse into a section of ancient realities.

However, as the papyrological record demonstrates, the *strategoi* (στρατηγός; governors at nome level) played a crucial role in tax collection in the province of Egypt. While initially the Roman state leased the collection of taxes to private entrepreneurs (*publicani*[20]), who were liable for the farming of taxes, the situation changed in the course of the second century AD, when liability was shifted towards the community. From that time onwards, any tax shortfall was passed on to its capable members in the following year.[21] It seems that this modification in liability addressed and reduced the problem of tax flight, as did the involvement of local elites as tax collectors.

The tax burden of the individual was linked to his or her economic performance but was in principle linear rather than progressive as in modern times. Taxation therefore hit the mass of the rural and artisanal population of the Roman Empire much harder than the comparatively small stratum of the wealthy. This can be illustrated by an example from the province of Egypt, where the unreduced poll tax (λαογραφία) per year varied from 16 to 40 drachmai. Additionally, all male population was obliged to pay the dike tax (χωματικόν) of usually 6 drachmai and 4 obols. For (male and female) craftspeople such as weavers – certainly members of the lower income groups of a rural and artisanal society – an additional trade tax (χειρωνάξιον) was

19 οἱ μὴ ἀ̣π̣ογ̣εγραμμένοι ταῖς [κατ'] οἰκ̣ίαν ἀπογ[ρα]φα[ῖς ἑ]α̣υτούς τε κα[ὶ] οὓς [δ]εῖ τεταρτολογοῦνται, [κα]ὶ̣ ἐὰν δυσὶν ἀπογρ[αφ]α̣[ῖς μ]ὴ ἀπογρα\ψά/μενοι εἰσδοθῶσιν, δ[ὶ]ς τέταρτ[ο]ν ⟦αναλ[α]⟧ [κατακ]ρ̣ίνονται. [...] οἱ μὴ ἀπογραψάμενοι ἀνδράπο[δα μ]όνων τῶν ἀ̣ν̣δ[ρα]πόδω[ν] στέρονται. See also Hombert and Préaux (1952, 97–99).

20 Dig. 39,4,1,1 [Ulpian].

21 Cf. Jördens (2009, 315–317).

imposed. Hence the annual tax burden of a landless male weaver in the province of Egypt – depending on his place of residence within the province – totalled up to 122 drachmai and 4 obols, but was at least 58 drachmai and 4 obols. This sum might have been further increased by other occasional taxes of varying rates such as a property tax (ἀποφορά), the pig tax (ὑϊκή), the guard tax (φυλάκων), income taxes, custom dues and many more.[22] In comparison, the annual living expenses for food, clothing and housing of a single male in Roman Egypt totalled about 158 drachmai during the first century AD, 226 drachmai during the second and 338 drachmai during the third.[23] That the poll tax constituted a particularly heavy burden for the provincial population[24] is further demonstrated by its mention in the Gospels of Mark (Mk 12) and Matthew (Mt 22), when the Pharisees question Jesus about the legitimacy of this tax.[25] Taking all this into account, it is not surprising that different ways and means were sought to evade paying taxes.[26] This can again best be demonstrated by consulting the vast papyrological record from Roman Egypt.

4.3 Tax Fraud in Roman Egypt

The main measure that members of the provincial population of Egypt took to avoid paying taxes was simple flight. The practice of people leaving their own villages is usually referred to as *anachoresis* (ἀναχώρησις, literally "retreat") in the papyrus documents.[27] The fact that there was an actual procedure to announce the removal of an individual from the place where he was officially registered demonstrates how frequently this step must have been taken and how suspicious the authorities must have been that a person might disappear without trace, to evade taxation. Delinquent taxpayers turning fugitive was obviously a thing. This is likewise demonstrated by a list of oracle questions to an unknown deity in another papyrus dating from the

22 For the taxes mentioned, see the relevant sections in Wallace (1969); see also Rathbone (1993, 81–112); for the guard tax, see Homoth-Kuhs (2005, *passim*).

23 Drexhage (1991, 453); on the comparably stable tax burden in the province of Egypt cf. Jördens (2009, 518).

24 Compare Tacitus' account of how delegates from *Syria* and *Iudaea* had campaigned in Rome for a reduction of the tax burden in these regions (Tac. ann. 2.42) or Strabo mentioning a riot in Egypt caused because of the taxes (Strab. 17,1,53). Tax allowance is granted in SB 1/8 (second century AD).

25 Cf. Günther (2021, *passim*). In addition, this touches on one of the crucial theological disputes in *Iudaea* at that time, namely whether it was disobedient to God for the chosen people to pay taxes to the Roman Emperor and thus to acknowledge his rule.

26 In *Iudaea*, the Zealots in particular refused to pay any taxes, refused to be registered in the Roman tax lists and instead retreated into the desert to wage a partisan war against the Roman Empire; Bringmann (1986, 51–53).

27 Cf. Jördens (2009, 304–330); Link (1993, 306–320). A list of the documents pertaining to this practice is appended in Strassi Zaccaria (2008, 76–91).

late third or early fourth century AD (P.Oxy. 12/1477). The questions are numbered consecutively and cover all the principal subjects on which people in Roman Egypt (as elsewhere in the ancient Mediterranean) appealed to the oracle gods for information. Among these standard questions addressed to the deity are: "Shall I take to flight?" as well as "Is my flight to be stopped?". Other questions in the document include social mobility ("Am I to become a senator?" or "Am I to become a beggar?"), indicating that such lists were used by people of very different social strata.

Papyri further demonstrate that if someone left home, the nearest relatives would sometimes report this person to the authorities, stressing that s/he had left no property behind. This was certainly done in the hope of keeping the tax collectors away, however we cannot be sure whether it happened frequently as only about half a dozen cases are documented.[28] P.Oxy. 2/251 dating to AD 44 exemplifies such a report. The papyrus is addressed to two officials in the administration of the *metropolis*[29] and announces the removal of an individual (Thoonis, son of the sender of the report, a certain Thamounion) from the place where he had been formally registered during the *census* (ἀναγραφόμενος) along with the fact that Thoonis no longer possessed any means. His mother Thamounion asks for Thoonis to be enrolled "in the list of persons removed henceforth from this year" – her report is an amendment to the local *census* list (κατ' οἰκίαν ἀπογραφή). Unfortunately, the documents contain no further information that would allow conclusions to be drawn about the social status or profession of the people in question.

Becoming fugitive for reasons of tax evasion was obviously common, since in AD 55 we find 43 men listed as fugitives in the Arsinoite village of Philadelpheia (P.Ryl. 4/595).[30] Thus, approximately every seventh man of Philadelpheia was a fugitive in those days![31]

A more or less contemporary list of a certain Nemesion, son of Zoilos, tax collector in the village of Philadelpheia, records the tax arrears for the poll tax, pig tax and dike tax from the years AD 45/46 to 50/51 (P.Mich. 10/594). The deficit of the poll tax of the year AD 45/46 alone sums up to 28,046 drachmai (line 11). Within a period of five years, however, the sum had been reduced to 3,068 drachmai (line 5).[32] The difficulties to pay the relevant taxes in AD 45/464 may have been caused by tax flight, added to by failed harvests.

28 Lewis (1983, 163–165); on tax flight, see also Lewis (1995, 357–374).

29 Among them the κωμογραμματεύς, i.e. the official, who held the highest rank in a settlement's administration and was responsible for the assessment of land taxes and the *census* declarations. Cf. Derda (2006, 147–168).

30 P.Graux 2 (= SB 4/7462 = Sel. Pap. 2/281; AD 57), a petition to the prefect Tiberius Claudius Balbillus, shows plainly how population shrinkage affected the entire village population. Inhabitants from six villages in the Arsinoite nome tried to obtain a deferral of the tax burden because they had difficulties raising the sums owed; cf. Jördens (2009, 305). Kruse (2002, vol. 2, 645) holds the opinion that the people listed had paid their poll tax but still owed the dike tax.

31 For the size of Philadelpheia's population, see Ruffing (2008, vol. 1, 349) with n. 251.

32 Cf. Oates (1966, 87–95).

Tax policy was thus clearly one of the most prominent factors that led the population to flee their homes. Consequently, the enormous number of tax refugees contributing to tax arrears required action from the Roman authorities. As Andrea Jördens highlighted,[33] a great deal of continuity can be observed in the Egyptian tax administration concerning the key officials – in particular the *strategos* at nome level[34] and the village scribe (κωμογραμματεύς) at village level. This suggests that the Roman administration relied mainly on existing models from Ptolemaic times, not only for the organisation of tax calculation, but also in the recording of the asset bases. During the first decades, individual tax collectors (*publicani*), usually coming from Rome, were entrusted with the farming of taxes following the established example of Rome's proceedings in other provinces. They gained the right to collect taxes for a particular region by auction and paid the approximated tax sums to be expected for their region in advance to the Roman authorities. They had the chance to gain sizeable earnings if they managed to collect more than the amount that they had bid and sometimes earned additional profits by advancing money to the tax-paying cities by means of a loan (e.g. Plut. Lucull. 20 for the province of Asia), receiving interest on this payment at the end of the collection period.[35] This system meant that the *publicani* were personally liable for the tax revenue previously calculated and that any unexpected decimation of taxpayers consequently had a direct impact on their profit. The situation changed – at least in Roman Egypt – in the course of the second century AD, when local tax collectors were established and liability was shifted towards the community. From that time onwards, any tax shortfall was passed on to its capable members in the following year and instead of foreigners, local elite members were entrusted with the task of tax collecting.[36] It seems that these modifications both addressed and reduced the problems of tax flight and tax arrears. However, there is likewise evidence of the need for the Roman authorities to exercise control over the collection of taxes and the people and institutions involved, suggesting that tax collection failed to run smoothly again and again.[37] Yet, every so often, the Roman government was driven to offer tax forgiveness as an inducement for fugitives to return home and to end depopulation of certain areas.[38] An edict by the *praefectus Aegypti* Marcus Sempronius Liberalis dating to the 50s of the second

33 Jördens (2009, 102–103); for later changes: ibid., 264–303.

34 The Egyptian nomes as geographical divisions had already been established in pharaonic times. Even though their numbers and geographical extents were subject to changes, the nomes retained importance as administrative units up to the Byzantine era: cf. Bowman (1986, 59).

35 For a general introduction, see Malmendier (2002).

36 Cf. Jördens (2009, 287–291, 315–317).

37 I.Hibis 4 (AD 68) and BGU 7/1563 (early second century AD); P.Fay. 22 (AD 134); SB 26/16641 (AD 154–159).

38 Lewis (1983, 163).

century AD (BGU 2/372)[39] set out measures which were taken to induce people to return and continue their former lives after they had fled their native settlements to avoid paying taxes. The prefect announced an incentive for refugees to return to their homes and referred to a general amnesty that had been ordered by the Emperor of the time, Antoninus Pius.[40] It has often been suspected that many tax fugitives turned to the city of Alexandria, as Alexandrian territory was not subject to taxation and Alexandrian citizens were exempt from the poll tax – but only if they managed to become officially registered in the city.[41]

The fact that a certain Ptolemaios, son of Diodorus, stressed that he paid his taxes dutifully, even though it was a great sum, may likewise be understood as evidence for a strong tendency of the Egyptian population to evade taxes (P.Mich. 3/174; AD 144–147). However, refusing to pay taxes was not necessarily connected to actually fleeing one's home, as P.Stras. 5/401bis (AD 123) demonstrates. This petition to the *strategos* records that a "discussion" with an unknown weaver concerning the taxes he still owed ended in a brawl with the approaching tax collector.[42]

Apart from the common strategy of flight, however, there are hardly any measures in the papyrus texts referring to what people did to avoid paying taxes. Only a private letter from the third century AD contains a piece of advice from Zenas to his friend Ptolas, not on actual tax evasion but on how to evade supplying the πυρὸς συναγοραστικός (*frumentum emptum*), a tribute in cereals that provincials were obliged to sell to the Roman officials at a fixed (and comparatively low) price (PSI 5/476). Zenas suggests that his friend could avoid this by declaring his land under a different name.[43]

4.4 Dealing with Tax Evasion

At the same time, however, measures were taken to trace tax evaders. This can be seen in a particularly comprehensive documentary papyrus, originating from Panopolis on the eastern bank of the Nile in Upper Egypt and dating back to the late third century AD (P.Beatty Panop. 1). The document provides *in extenso* the outgoing correspondence of the office of the *strategos*

39 Cf. Cowey (1995, 195–199); Jördens (2009, 314–315).

40 For similar attempts to persuade tax evaders to return home, see SB 4/7366 (AD 193–200); P.Oxy. 47/3364 (AD 206); SB 1/4284 (AD 207); P.Mich. 9/529 (AD 235–237). See Jördens (2012, 63).

41 Cf. Jördens (2009, 331–334) as 304 with n. 1 for further literature.

42 PSI 3/222 (late third/early fourth century AD) likewise demonstrates that certain people simply refused to pay taxes and instead used violence against the representative of the Roman authorities.

43 On state acquisitions of cereals in Egypt, see Jördens (2009, 181–211).

of Panopolis, as well as the monthly report on income in money and grain.[44] The text reads (lines 338–341):[45]

> To the nominators of the *metropolis*. So that no hindrance may arise in connection with the persons being sought for by Ammonius also called Ampelius in accordance with the interests of the Treasury, as ordered by Pomponius Domnus, the most eminent *magister rei privatae*, it is necessary that four servants should be provided to the aforesaid to give aid in this duty [...].

It is not certain if these lines refer to taxes to be paid in money or in kind, since taxes were also sometimes collected in kind. What is certain, however, is that defaulting taxpayers were identified by the Roman authorities and were ordered to be tracked down.[46]

Finally, it should be mentioned that the papyrological findings also reveal a tendency to denounce tax fugitives. For example, a decree of the *praefectus Aegypti* Gnaeus Vergilius Capito from AD 48/49 grants a reward from the assets of the accused to those who report a crime.[47] And a petition to the *strategos* from the year AD 207 from a committee of 25 men, acting on behalf of the farmers of the village Soknopaiou Nesos, reads as follows (SB 1/4284):[48]

> We are obligated to work, each of us to the limit of his ability, on the shore land from which the Nile flood has just receded. But a certain Orseus, a violent and headstrong man and his four brothers attacked us

44 Addressee of these reports of the *strategos* was the καθολικός, the highest financial official in the province of Egypt, and not the *praefectus Aegypti* (as e.g. in P.Lips 1/123; AD 136). The office of the καθολικός was created at the end of the third century AD and replaced the διοικητής (see also Dirschel 2004, 226 and 253).

45 συστάταις μητροπόλεως. ὑπ[ὲρ τοῦ] μηδὲν ἐμπόδιον γενέσθαι τῶν ζητουμένων ὑπὸ Ἀμμωνίου τοῦ καὶ Ἀμπελίου κατὰ τὰ δια̣φέροντα τῷ ἱερω[τάτῳ] ταμείῳ ἀκολούθως τοῖς γραφῖσει ὑπὸ Πομπονίου Δόμν\ο/υ τοῦ διασημοτάτου μαγίστρου πριουάτης ἀναγκαῖ[όν ἐστ]ιν τέσσερας ὑπηρέτας τῷ προκειμένῳ δοθῆναι τοὺς ὑπηρετησομένους τῇ χρείᾳ. [...] Transl. Skeat 1964 (= P.Beatty Panop.). Pomponius Domnus, mentioned in the document, was the *Magister rei privatae*, i.e. the supreme administrator of all royal domains throughout Egypt, probably residing in Alexandria. In P.Oxy. 9/1204 (AD 299), we find Pomponius Domnus promoted to the office of καθολικός.

46 Elsewhere in the document, the persons sought by the authorities are referred to as πασσαλιωτικὰ πρόσωπα (lines 155; 199; 202).

47 Hibis 1 = OGIS 665 = SB 5/8248 = Freis Nr. 36.

48 ἐχομένων οὖν ἡμῶν [τῇ] κατεργασίᾳ τῇ ἀποκαλυφθείσῃ αἰγιαλίτι<δι> γῇ ἑκάστων καθὸ δύναμις, Ὀρσεύς τις ἀνὴρ βίαιος καὶ αὐθάδης τυ[γχάν]ων ἐπῆλθεν ἡμῖν σὺν ἀδελφοῖς αὐτοῦ τέτρασι κ[ω]λύων τὴν κατεργασίαν καὶ κατασπορὰν ποιεῖσθαι [...] καὶ ἐκφοβῶν ἡμᾶς, ἵν' [...] [δηλοῦμεν δέ σοι κύριε τὴν τούτων βίαν. οὔτε γὰρ συνείσφοροι γ[ε]ίνονται τῶν [...] γει[νο]μένων [...] καὶ ἐπιβολῶν σι[τ]ικῶν τε καὶ ἀργυρικῶν τελεσμάτων [...] ὅθεν κατὰ τὸ ἀναγκαῖον τὴν [ἐπί] σε καταφυγὴν ποιούμεθα καὶ ἀξιοῦμεν, ἐάν σου τῇ τύχῃ δόξῃ, κελεῦσαι, ἀχθῆναι αὐτο[ὺς] ἐπὶ σ[ο]ῦ καὶ διακοῦσαι ἡμῶν πρὸς αὐτὸν [...] τὸν δὲ Ὀρσέα καὶ τοὺς ἀδελφ[ο]ὺς συνεισφόρας εἶναι τοῖς δημοσίοις τελέσμασι [...]. Transl. Johnson 1936, 119–120.

and prevented us from doing our work and our sowing [...] and so we send you this notice of their lawlessness. They do not pay their share of [...] taxes in money and grain [...]. Wherefore of necessity we fly to you for refuge and ask you, if your Honour please, to order that they be summoned before you and to hear our case against them, so that [...]. Orseus and his brothers may contribute their share to the public revenues [...].

4.5 Conclusion

Taxes were certainly an issue in the Roman Empire. The abundance of Greek papyri from the province of Egypt allows the reconstruction of at least some of both the state's and the individuals' strategies for dealing with the issue of taxes. As there were few legal ways to reduce their tax burden,[49] and as there are no indications that it was possible to negotiate taxes, many Egyptians sought refuge in flight or just refused to pay their taxes. In particular for the rural and artisanal population, the amount of taxes and other charges was sometimes oppressive and threatened people's basic livelihoods, a fact due in no small part to the linear character of Roman taxes. This was, however, a phenomenon likewise common in Ptolemaic times.[50] Additionally, the papyrological record offers insights into countermeasures taken by the Roman state that depended on tax revenues. Tax amnesties are likewise reported and may have served to promote denunciations. However, Rome's imposition of taxation not only secured Rome's welfare, but likewise stimulated regional economies. For, as Keith Hopkins first noted, in order to pay their taxes in money (and not in kind), individuals had to gain money, which was best achieved by selling their produce or manpower.[51] In addition, all inhabitants of the Roman Empire, whether full Roman citizens or holding a "minor" form of Roman citizenship like the provincials, could expect the Roman State to work for their benefit and to reinforce legal certainty, but in turn were expected to be assiduous in paying taxes.[52]

References

Bagnall, Roger Shaler and Bruce W. Frier. 1994. *The Demography of Roman Egypt*. Cambridge Studies in Population, Economy and Society in Past Time 23. Cambridge: Cambridge University Press.

49 Tax exemptions were granted only by the Roman Emperor. However, it was possible to have individual taxes as the trade tax was waived due to disability or age; cf. Jördens (2009, 331).

50 Cf. Clarysse and Thompson (2006, *passim*). The system and overall amount of the levies always took up local traditions from pre-Roman times.

51 Hopkins (1980, 101–125); van Minnen (2000, 205–220). Though some taxes were paid in kind, at least the poll tax and trade taxes were delivered in money.

52 As to be seen in P.Cair. Isid. 1, lines 10–14.

Bowman, Alan K. 1986. *Egypt after the Pharaos. 332 BC–AD 642 from Alexander to the Arab Conquest*. Berkley – Los Angeles: University of California Press.

Braunert, Horst. 1957. Der römische Provinzialzensus und der Schätzungsbericht des Lukas-Evangeliums. *Historia* 6: 192–214.

Bringmann, Klaus. 1986. Steuern und Fremdherrschaft. Judäa zur Zeit Jesu. In *Mit dem Zehnten fing es an. Eine Kulturgeschichte der Steuer*, ed. Uwe Schultz, 51–53. München: Büchergilde Gutenberg.

Buraselis, Kostas. 2007. Θεία δωρεά. *Das göttlich-kaiserliche Geschenk. Studien zur Politik der Severer und zur Constitutio Antoniniana*. Akten der Gesellschaft für griechische und hellenistische Rechtsgeschichte 18. Wien: Verlag der österreichischen Akademie der Wissenschaften.

Clarysse, Willy and Dorothy J. Thompson. 2006. *Counting the People in Hellenistic Egypt*, 2 vols., Cambridge: Cambridge University Press.

Claytor, W. Graham and Roger Shaler Bagnall. 2015. The Beginnings of the Roman Provincial Census: A New Declaration from 3 BCE. *Greek, Roman & Byzantine Studies* 55: 637–653.

Corbier, Mirelle. 1988. L'impôt dans l'Empire romaine, Résistances et refus. In *Forms of Control and Subordination in Antiquity*, eds. Tōru Yuge and Masaoki Doi, 259–274. Leiden: Brill.

Cowey, James M. S. 1995. New Readings in an Edict of M. Sempronius Liberalis (BGU II 372), *Zeitschrift für Papyrologie und Epigraphik* 106: 195–199.

Derda, Tomasz. 2006. *Arsinoites Nomos. Administration of the Fayum under Roman Rule*. Journal of Juristic Papyrology Suppl. 7. Warsaw: Fundacja im. Rafała Taubenschlaga.

Dirschel, Hans Christian. 2004. *Der Gaustratege im römischen Ägypten. Seine Aufgaben am Beispiel des Archiv-, Finanz- und Bodenwesens und der Liturgien*. Pharos 16. St. Katharinen: Scripta Mercaturae.

Drexhage, Hans-Joachim. 1991. *Preise, Mieten, Pachten, Kosten und Löhne im römischen Ägypten bis zum Regierungsantritt Diokletians. Vorarbeiten zu einer Wirtschaftsgeschichte des römischen Ägypten*. St. Katharinen: Scripta Mercaturae

Günther, Sven. 2008. Vectigalia nervos esse rei publicae. *Die indirekten Steuern in der römischen Kaiserzeit von Augustus bis Diokletian*. Philippika 26. Wiesbaden: Harrassowitz.

Günther, Sven. 2016. Taxation in the Greco-Roman World: The Roman Principate. *Oxford Handbooks Online*. DOI:10.1093/oxfordhb/9780199935390.013.38.

Günther, Sven. 2021. Steuern. *Reallexikon für Antike und Christentum* 31: 114–166.

Hirschmüller, Martin. 1994. Der Zensus des Quirinius. *Jahrbuch für die Evangelikale Theologie* 8: 33–68.

Hombert, Marcel and Claire Préaux. 1952. *Recherches sur le recensement dans l'Égypte romaine*. Papyrologica Lugduno-Batava 5. Leiden: Brill.

Homoth-Kuhs, Clemens. 2005. *Phylakes und phylakon-Steuer im griechisch-römischen Ägypten*. Archiv für Papyrusforschung Beih. 17. München/Leipzig: De Gruyter.

Hopkins, Keith. 1980. Taxes and trade in the Roman Empire. *Journal of Roman Studies* 70: 101–125.

Johnson, Allan Chester. 1936. *An Economic Survey of Roman Egypt*. London: Johns Hopkins Press.

Jördens, Andrea. 2009. *Statthalterliche Verwaltung in der römischen Kaiserzeit. Studien zum* praefectus Aegypti. Historia Einzelschriften 175. Stuttgart: Steiner.

Jördens, Andrea. 2012. Government, Taxation, and Law. *Oxford Handbook of Roman Egypt*. ed. Chr. Riggs, 56–67. Oxford: OUP.

Kritzinger, Peter, 2015. Das römische Zollwesen bis in das 3. Jh. n.Chr. In *Studien zum römischen Zollwesen*, ed. P. Kritzinger et al.,11–54. Duisburg: Wellem.

Kruse, Thomas. 2002. *Der königliche Schreiber und die Gauverwaltung*. Archiv für Papyrusforschung Beih. 11. München/Leipzig: Saur.

Link, Stefan. 1993. Anachoresis. Steuerflucht im Ägypten der frühen Kaiserzeit. *Klio* 75: 306–320.

Malmendier, Ulrike. 2002. *Societas publicanorum – staatliche Wirtschaftsaktivitäten in den Händen privater Unternehmer*. Köln et al.: Böhlau.

Marquardt, Joachim. 1957. *Römische Staatsverwaltung*. Darmstadt: Wissenschaftliche Buchgesellschaft.

Monson, Andres and Walter Scheidel. 2015. *Fiscal Regimes and the Political Economy of Premodern States*. Cambridge: Cambridge University Press.

Neesen, Lutz. 1980. *Untersuchungen zu den direkten Staatsabgaben der römischen Kaiserzeit (27 v.Chr.–284 n.Chr.)*. Antiquitas, Reihe I: Abhandlungen zur Alten Geschichte 32. Bonn: Habelt.

Oates, John F. 1966. Fugitives from Philadelphia. In *Essays in Honor of C. Bradford Welles*. ASP 1, ed. American Society of Papyrologists, 87–95. New Haven: American Society of Papyrologists.

Rathbone, Daniel. 1993. Egypt, Augustus and Roman Taxation. *Cahiers du Centre Gustave Glotz* 4: 81–112.

Ruffing, Kai. 2008. *Die berufliche Spezialisierung in Handel und Handwerk: Untersuchungen zu ihrer Entwicklung und zu ihren Bedingungen in der römischen Kaiserzeit im östlichen Mittelmeerraum auf der Grundlage griechischer Inschriften und Papyri*, 2 vols., Rahden/Westf.: Marie Leidorf.

Schmidt, Stefanie. 2020. Between Byzantine and Muslim Egpyt. Mobilizing Economic Resources for an Embryonic Empire. *Journal of Ancient Civilizations* 35(2): 241–266.

Steinmetzler, Franz Xaver. 1954. Census. *Reallexikon für Antike und Christentum* 2, 971–972.

Strassi Zaccaria, Silvia. 2008. *L'archivio di Claudius Tiberianus*. Archiv für Papyrusforschung Beih. 26. München – Leipzig: C.H. Beck.

van Minnen, Peter. 2000. Agriculture and the 'taxes-and-trade' model in Roman Egypt. *Zeitschrift für Papyrologie und Epigraphik* 133: 205–220.

Wallace, Sherman LeRoy. 1969. *Taxation in Egypt from Augustus to Diocletian*. New York: Greenwood.

Wiesemann, Timothy Peter. 1987. 'There went out a Decree from Caesar Augustus…' *New Testament Studies* 33: 479–480.

5 "Taxing" the Tribes in the Ottoman Empire

The Case of the Tribes of Mutki (1839–1908)

Yener Koç

5.1 Taxation and Reforms in the Ottoman Empire

The proclamation of the recte (which literally means reorganisation) edict in 1839 was the harbinger of a comprehensive reform process throughout the Ottoman Empire. During the so-called Tanzimat Period (1839–1876), the Ottoman Empire's state structure underwent significant political change.[1] The reforms were aimed at establishing a centrally coordinated and efficient system of taxation, administration and military conscription, which would enable the central government to penetrate the entire realm and establish direct access to its subjects. In an age of internal challenges, fiscal crises, territorial losses and the spread of nationalism, the reforms aimed to expand central state authority throughout the imperial domains, to increase the capacity of the state treasury through various revenues and to promote the notion of equal citizenship in order to keep the multiethnic and multireligious structure of the empire intact.[2] The reform process continued into the Hamidian era (1876–1909), especially concerning the construction of infrastructure such as railroads, telegraph lines, schools and hospitals.[3]

With regard to fiscality, the Tanzimat reforms envisaged a new tax system which would make each Ottoman subject fiscally responsible only towards the central government. In other words, the reforms were aimed at minimising the tax share and authority of the provincial notables (*ayan*) while increasing the share of the central government.[4] The Tanzimat edict explicitly defined individual property and wealth as tax bases. For this purpose, land, property and income (*temettuat*) surveys were carried out to assess the wealth and incomes of the Ottoman subjects during the early Tanzimat years.[5] Accordingly, a series of land

1 İnalcık (1976). For a brief account of the expansion of modern state power in distant provinces of the Ottoman Empire during the second half of the nineteenth century, see Rogan (1999, 2–17).

2 İnalcık (1976). For studies about the institutional reforms in the Ottoman Empire during the Tanzimat period, see Davison (1963); Shaw and Shaw (2002, 55–172).

3 Zürcher (2003, 77–78).

4 İslamoğlu (2000, 19–20).

5 Güran (2000).

DOI: 10.4324/9781003333197-8

reforms were put into practice. The Land Code of 1858 was intended to secure the property rights of individuals and make them directly responsible to the state with regard to taxes.[6] Following the Tanzimat edict, centrally appointed officials were charged with the tax collection process, while local councils were formed at provincial level to supervise the tax collection.[7] Tax farming, which had been a great source of revenue for local notables, was reorganised several times during the Tanzimat and Hamidian periods in order to increase the revenue share for the central state treasury.[8] A rural police organisation (*asâkir-i zabtiye*) was established in the 1840s and a gendarmerie institution was set up in the late 1870s in order to provide domestic security, as well as to assist in the collection of taxes in the countryside.[9]

The reforms of the second half of the nineteenth century also aimed to gain access to the hitherto untouched resources of the more distant provinces of the empire. The large estates of hereditary dynasties[10] and local notables, tribal spaces, mountainous and frontier zones were envisaged by the central Ottoman government as potential new sources of revenue. In particular, nomadic and settled tribal groups with their large human and economic resources were perceived as new important sources of revenue for the exchequer and manpower for the army. Thus, starting from the early Tanzimat years, the provincial and central bureaucracies engaged in a large-scale sedentarisation campaign tackling the nomadic and semi-nomadic tribes of the Anatolian, Syrian and Iraqi provinces of the Empire, in order to establish more control over them and tax them more efficiently.[11]

While relations between the tribes and Ottoman imperial state were not always antagonistic, taxes and military services became major sources of contention in several regions of Ottoman Kurdistan, Albania, Syria and Iraq.[12] Here direct taxation as well as the new land tenure system, which envisaged the use of title deeds to register land to smallholders, challenged the tribes in several ways. The centralisation not only threatened the economic authority of the tribal chiefs over tribal commoners, but also burdened the commoners with new taxes. Thus, local resistance was inevitable in several tribal spaces. This chapter aims to discuss the contentious taxation of the Kurdish and Zaza tribes of the district of Mutki, which were located in a mountainous and frontier zone in the Ottoman East. It discusses why taxes, particularly the tithe (*aşâr*) and the sheep tax (*ağnam*), remained major sources of contention

6 Terzibaşoğlu (2006, 132).
7 Çadırcı (2007, 259–285).
8 Özbek (2015, 29).
9 Özbek (2008, 1) and Paz (2010, 19).
10 In the Ottoman East, the hereditary dynasties, also known as the emirates, were the Kurdish families who governed large tracts of lands in a hereditary way until the implementation of the Tanzimat reforms.
11 Lewis (1987); Köksal (2006); Haj (1997); Toksöz (2010).
12 Koç (2020, 182–236).

between Ottoman state officials and the tribes of Mutki during the second half of the nineteenth century. It argues that tribes who had lived in a tax-free zone before the Tanzimat era perceived the administrative and fiscal centralisation of the Ottoman Empire as a challenge to their political and economic power.

The chapter provides, first, information about the geography, demography, state perception and the taxes of Mutki. Then, it examines different modes of taxation during the second half of the nineteenth and early twentieth centuries. Section Three explains how officials of the early Tanzimat period relied mostly on military expeditions to maintain taxation and conscription in the region. Section Four focuses on the attempts to increase state infrastructure in the region during the 1870s to ease the taxation and administration of the region. Section Five discusses how state circles increasingly moved to negotiations with tribal circles since the reform expeditions of the Tanzimat period and attempts to increase state infrastructure did not result in any permanent success in tax collection.

5.2 Geography, State and Taxes in Mutki

The district of the Mutki is situated in a highly mountainous and rough zone, which is part of the south-eastern Taurus mountain chain. During the nineteenth century, most of the settlements of the district were located at elevations between 1,500 and 2,500 metres and were dispersed as nucleated villages. As a frontier and mountainous district, Mutki was far away from the surrounding major administrative centres during the early Tanzimat years. On foot, it took nearly 52 hours to travel from Mutki to the city of Erzurum, the closest provincial capital.[13] The administrative status of the region changed several times during the nineteenth century, due to attempts by the central government to exercise more pervasive control over the region. The region was organised either as a sub-district (*nahiye*) or as a district (*kaza*) and was administrated as part of the province (*vilayet*) of Kurdistan first, then of Erzurum and finally of Bitlis.

During the Tanzimat and Hamidian periods, the district was composed of 60 to 70 villages, whose economy was based mostly on self-sufficient agro-pastoralism. Although semi-sedentary and sedentary Kurdish and Zaza tribes dominated the demographic composition, there were also sizable numbers of settled, non-tribal Armenian residents.[14] According to an Ottoman report prepared by the Council of State (*Şura-yı Devlet*) in 1873, there were

13 Okcu and Akdağ (2010, 436); Salnâme-i Vilâyet-i Bitlis, 1308 (1892/1893), 99.

14 The Ottoman and British sources used in this article define the tribal population of the region as Kurdish and they do not differentiate between Kurds and Zazas as two different ethnic identities. Sykes, however, states that the majority of the tribes of Mutki were Zazas, see Sykes (1908, 466).

nearly 6,300 male residents in the 66 villages of the district, of which 5,000 were Muslims and 1,300 Christians.[15] The Muslim population was composed of Kurdish and Zaza tribes, while Christians were exclusively Armenians. However, these numbers are highly speculative since many inhabitants did not appear during the censuses, being frightened of possible taxes and military services.[16] The Kurdish population of the district was mostly organised in several smaller tribes such as Keyburan, Bubanli, Kusan, Rutchaba, Zeydan, Mala Olo and Mermendler.[17] Each of these small tribes was composed of four or five villages and ruled by its chief.

The Ottoman authorities assessed the villages of Mutki as inaccessible and "illegible", and most importantly, as untaxable.[18] Ottoman official correspondence of the second half of the nineteenth century defined the territory as a "mountainous and stony region" (*sengistân ve kuhistân mahal*), "inaccessible terrain" (*suubü'l mürur mahal*) and "land of tribes and clans" (*mahal-i aşâir ve kabâil*).[19] Officials described the inhabitants of the region as "savage" (*vahşi*), "mountainous" (*dağî*), "rebel" (*asi, bagi*) and "ignorant" (*cahil*).[20] From their perspective, the tribes differed in their customs (*adet-i melufe*) from the surrounding towns and villages. It was alleged that these customs made them reject state authority, and that they were prone to commit crimes such as the seizure of properties (*gasb-ı emval*), murder (*katl-i nüfus*) and hijacking (*kutta-i tarik*). The regional tribes' disregard for the state administration and their avoidance of taxation and conscription were conceived, explained and even sometimes justified by their "uncivilised nature", their traditional customs and/or the inaccessible nature of the region.[21] Such official descriptions, however, not only expressed the difficulties in maintaining an efficient system of administration and taxation in the region. They also indicated the alleged cultural and social inferiority of the locals compared with the inhabitants of lowland regions, towns and urban centres. While lowland communities were

15 BOA, Irade Şura-yı Devlet (I. ŞD hereafter) 26/1166, 21 Zilkade 289, (20 January 1873).

16 BOA, Yıldız Sadâret Resmi Maruzat (Y.A RES hereafter) 80/111, 22 Temmuz 1311, (2 August 1895) and Y.A RES 54/26.

17 Sykes (1908, 466), Salnâme-i Vilâyet-i Bitlis, 1308 (1892/1893), 99.

18 For a discussion on the concept of illegibility, see Scott (2009).

19 BOA. I.DH 363/24021, 24.R.1273 (22 December 1856). The division of the land between governmental and tribal spaces was not peculiar to the Ottoman East. For the case of Morocco, Ernest Gellner argues that the country was divided into two different zones: *siba* and *makhzen*. According to him, *siba* (institutionalised dissidence) was used to refer to the High Atlas Mountains of Morocco, a region untouched by central rule until 1933. In *siba,* tribes did not pay taxes to the central government, while the *makhzen* was under the control of the Moroccan government. See; Gellner (1969, 1–2). Yet, scholars also criticise the clear-cut division of land into governmental and tribal spaces and argue that the transition might have been fluent; see Tapper (1990, 70).

20 For a discussion on Ottoman state rhetoric during the Tanzimat era, see Reinkowski (2005, 199–211).

21 For discussions on Ottoman notions of civilization, see Makdisi (2002), Deringil (2003), and Kuehn (2011).

described as obedient people (*ahâli-i mutia*) who paid taxes on time, served in the army and obeyed the laws and regulations of the imperial state, the highland tribal populations were generally described as bandits (*ahâli-i eşkiyâ*) who had rejected any kind of state authority since ancient times.[22]

Sources about the economic organisation of the district of Mutki for the pre-Tanzimat period are scarce if not entirely non-existent. Tribal groups (both chiefs and commoners) did not pay taxes directly to the Kurdish dynasties, governors and other power holders of the neighbouring provinces. Mutki and the mountainous regions of Sason and Huyut were politically and economically more autonomous than the surrounding lowlands, which were ruled by hereditary Kurdish dynasties like family estates (*yurtluk-ocaklık*) before the implementation of Tanzimat reforms. The tribes of Mutki remained largely exempt from paying sheep tax (*ağnam*) and tithes (*aşâr*), the two ancient Ottoman taxes, during the pre-Tanzimat period. The tribal chiefs, however, had the customary right to impose taxes or drudgery (*corvée*) etc. on their ordinary tribal members as well as on the Armenian peasantry.[23] A collective petition, written by a group of Armenian notables in 1856 to the central Ottoman government, reveals the extraordinary taxes paid by Armenian peasants to the Kurdish chiefs of Mutki.[24] The Armenian peasants also paid a protection tax known as *hafir* to the Kurdish tribal chiefs, although information on the amount is lacking. This tax was collected by the Kurdish chiefs even during the early twentieth century.[25]

The early Tanzimat reforms challenged the political and economic power of the chiefs in Mutki in several ways. On the one hand, the new tax system sought to make each subject directly liable to the central state for taxes, not to the tribal chiefs anymore. Moreover, the tribal commoners, who had been largely exempt from tax liability to the central government in the pre-Tanzimat period, perceived the new sheep tax and tithe as a burden, and thus the chiefs could easily mobilise them against the imposition of these taxes. The question of how the central authorities determined the tax base remains, however, unclear. Property and income surveys seem never to have been conducted in the region during the second half of the nineteenth century. Thus, the taxes were based not on a solid survey, but rather on rough estimations by state officials. Tithe imposition amounted to about 40,000 piasters in the 1850s and 50,000 in the 1890s; the sheep tax liability was approximately 57,000 piasters during the late nineteenth century.[26] The total amount of annual taxes to be paid by the tribal inhabitants of Mutki was calculated as 131,867 piasters (around 1,320 pounds sterling) by state officials

22 BOA, I. ŞD 26/1166, 9 Kanun-ı Sani 1288, (21 January 1873).
23 BOA, I. ŞD 26/1166, 9 Kanun-ı Sani 1288, (21 January 1873).
24 BOA, İrade Dahiliye (I. DH hereafter) 364/24114, 73 (1856).
25 Foreign Office 424/220, Inclosure 2 in No 106. Bitlis, (17 August 1909).
26 BOA, DH. TMIK 33/72, 4 Haziran 313 (26 June 1897). The Armenian peasantry also paid an amount of 29,085 piasters poll tax in 1854. See BOA, ML.VRD.CMH: D 1388.

in 1873.[27] During the early Tanzimat years, the taxes of the region were generally entrusted to tax farmers through auctions. But because of the tax collection difficulties, no more tax farmers interested in this region could be found in the following decades. As a consequence, villagers were made directly responsible for tax collection and payment. It was only during the late nineteenth century that some of the tribal chiefs became tax farmers of the villages which they had previously controlled.

By that time, Ottoman officials had long begun to send in military expeditions, increase state infrastructure and engage in negotiations with tribal chiefs to maintain taxation in Mutki. All three methods were in practice during the second half of the nineteenth century, but with different emphases in different decades. Military expeditions were more prevalent during the early Tanzimat period and Hamidian officials paid more attention to negotiations with tribal chiefs to maintain the flow of taxes. The build-up of state infrastructure, which was regarded as an essential part of taxation and administration, started in the 1850s and gained momentum only after the 1870s.

5.3 "Reform Expeditions" of the Tanzimat Period

Although the first attempts of centralisation in the Ottoman East were initiated in the 1830s, the Tanzimat reforms could not be put into practice in Mutki before 1846, during and following the pacification of the Kurdish hereditary dynasties.[28] Once the grand Kurdish dynasties such as the Bohtan and Soran had been defeated, exiled and replaced by centrally appointed officials, the Ottoman authorities could direct their attention to mountainous and tribal zones like Mutki, Hoyut, Sason and Dersim. As mentioned above, the reforms envisioned the collection of taxes by appointed tax officials or through tax farmers, who were to be aided by rural police (*asâkir-i zabtiye*). However, because of the tribal resistance, tax collection and conscription during the early Tanzimat years were mostly carried out through military expeditions with the participation of regular army divisions (*asâkir-i nizamiye*). These expeditions, which were also called reform expeditions (*harekat-ı ıslâhiye*), or discipline and punishment (*tedip ve tenkil*) expeditions, took place at certain intervals and became the common method of pacification, tax collection and conscription among resistant tribal populations of the Ottoman Empire during the Tanzimat period.[29]

27 BOA, I. ŞD 26/1166, 9 Kanun-ı Sani 1288, (21 January 1873). In the 1840s, in the markets of the province of Erzurum a sheep was equal to 45–50 piasters, a cow was equal to 100–150 piasters. See FO 78/703.

28 For information on the pacification of the powerful Kurdish hereditary dynasties, see Bruinessen (1992, 175–180) and Atmaca (2019).

29 Such military expeditions were not peculiar to the Ottoman East. In the 1860s, a Reform Division (*Fırka-yı Islâhiye*) under the command of Cevdet Pasha undertook several military expeditions to pacify, settle, tax and conscript the nomadic Turcoman tribes of Southeast Anatolia. See Özbek (2005) and Toksöz (2010).

One of the earliest reform expeditions to Mutki took place in 1856. In 1853, civil and military officials of the Ottoman Empire had already engaged in a heated debate about how to bring the tribes of Mutki under state control, establish permanent rule in the region, conscript and tax the population. As mentioned before, the annual tithe sum was calculated as 40,000 piasters. However, in 1854, the tithes due amounted to 300,000 piasters because of former tax avoidance of the tribes.[30] According to official correspondence in 1856, the taxes of the region had not been paid properly since 1846, when the region had been finally brought under the Tanzimat programme.[31] After an intense exchange of correspondence between the central Ottoman government and provincial authorities in Erzurum, a large-scale military expedition was organised in 1856 with the participation of regular and irregular soldiers from the provinces of Erzurum and Kurdistan. During the expedition, taxes amounting to 1,200 purses of coin (*akçe*) were collected, while 61 men from Mutki were recruited for the imperial army. Finally, 48 "bandits" of Mutki including their leader were captured and imprisoned. Just after the expedition, a director (*müdir*) was appointed to the district and a district council was established, in accordance with the administrative reforms of the Tanzimat.[32]

Mehmed Emin, the governor (*kaymakam*) of the sub-province of Muş, to which the Mutki district belonged administratively, gave a detailed report on the necessity and consequences of this "reform expedition". He informed the central state that "for over four and five years, they (the tribes) had been in a state of rebellion, rejecting the appointed administrators, not paying their taxes, not allowing conscription".[33] According to Mehmed Emin, the inhabitants of the region had been living in a state of ignorance and lacked any knowledge about religion and the imperial state, which was the reason why they refused any kind of state rule and did not pay their taxes. Bringing the region under permanent control would, thus, require the elimination of ignorance (*izâle-i cehl*). To this end, a mosque and a *medrese* were built in the village of İğin and a school in the village of Kenzü for the education of Muslim and Christian children, respectively. Mehmed Emin stressed the importance of such institutions for making inhabitants of the region understand what "state" and "religion" really meant *(din ve devletimizi bildirmek)*.[34]

However, the military expedition of 1856 and the subsequent administrative reorganisation brought neither permanent rule to the region nor permanent success with regard to tax collection. The need for a new military expedition was widely mentioned among the officials of the provinces of Erzurum and Kurdistan in the following years. Official correspondence

30 BOA, A.MKT.MVL 69/26, 28 S 71 (20 November 1854). In the 1850s, 100 Ottoman piasters were equal to one pound sterling.

31 BOA, A.MKT.UM 241/20, 23 L 72 (28 June 1856).

32 BOA, A.MKT 70/99, 2 RA 73 (31 October 1856).

33 Ibid.

34 Ibid.

from 1860 held that the "savage and mountainous Kurds of Mutki" had been resisting local government, not paying their taxes and engaging in all kinds of brutal acts, including murder and theft in surrounding districts. At first, the expedition was to be postponed since the majority of the Fourth Anatolian Army was stationed in Beirut and Aleppo because of the conflicts there.[35] Provincial authorities warned against sending large numbers of the regular army to the region as they wanted to avoid a military confrontation with tribal groups. Nevertheless, in October 1860, a second reform expedition under the command of Colonel Ismail Bey from the Fourth Anatolian Army entered the region. Under this military pressure, several villages accepted the necessity of paying their taxes and also of performing their military services.[36] According to the administrative council of Erzurum, those who resisted the army in the mountains were arrested after clashes and their small and large livestock were confiscated in return for their due taxes.[37]

Six years later, in March 1866, the governor of Muş demanded an immediate reform expedition be sent, not only to punish the crimes that had been committed by the tribes but also to enforce taxation and conscription in the region. As usual, he appealed to the Fourth Anatolian Army and asked for regular soldiers to discipline the tribes. He argued that the region's tax debt (*vergü*) amounted to 526,270 piasters. The tithe and sheep tax amounts owing were estimated to be even higher.[38] Likewise in May 1867, the administrative council of Bitlis prepared a report in which it demanded a military expedition to collect the due taxes of the district.[39] According to the council, the total tax arrears amounted to 800,000 piasters. Although religious authorities (*ulema*) and tax collectors had visited the region several times to convince the tribes to pay their taxes, they had consistently refused to do so. The council concluded that under such circumstances, taxes could only be collected through the force of the imperial army (*Kuvve-i Cunudiye-yi Hazret-i Şahane*).[40]

5.4 Increasing State Infrastructure

Although attempts to increase state infrastructure in Mutki had started in the 1850s, state influence leading to, for instance, the building of mosques and schools, could only be felt in the area during the reform expeditions. In the 1870s, however, the reform expeditions were abandoned. They were not only costly but also failed to bring permanent success. The central and the provincial administrations concluded that a permanent administration should

35 BOA, A.MKT.UM 435/98, 1277 S 22 (9 September 1860).
36 BOA, MVL 604/29, 1277 R 5 (21 October 1860).
37 BOA, MVL 608/29, 1277 (1860).
38 BOA, A.MKT. MHM. 353/25, 4 Şevval 1282 (20 February 1866).
39 BOA, A.MKT. MHM. 387A/50, 5 Muharrem 1284 (9 May 1867).
40 Ibid.

be established immediately for more effectiveness. Thus, in 1872, the Council of State (*Şura-yı Devlet*) proposed a new reform package for the region, which clearly differed from earlier reform attempts in terms of its scope and practice. Instead of depending solely on military force to subjugate the tribes, the Council of State decided to increase the infrastructural power of the state in the region.[41] To this end, the administrative status of the Mutki region was upgraded from sub-district to district and a district governor, Dede Bey, was appointed with a monthly salary of 2,000 piasters. The council also proposed the construction of a government building, military barracks for the accommodation of two troops and schools for the education of tribal children. It was argued that this was urgently needed:

> Until now, it has been attempted several times to ameliorate their [the tribes, Y. K.] conditions. However, these attempts just relied upon the false assurance of the said leaders who, only after having been threatened, claimed that they would quit opposition and obey the orders of the government and collect the taxes as much as possible with the help of imperial soldiers. Thus, these attempts were not enough for their conditions in the future, or to include them in the circle of the civilization...[42]

It was thought that the existence of such government buildings at the heart of Mutki would not only eliminate the rude nature of the tribal chiefs, but also familiarise them with civilized knowledge *(malûmat-ı medeniye)*. This would bring the tribes under direct state control, and also ease the collection of due taxes which had accumulated to an amount of 1,029,000 piasters.[43]

During the last quarter of the nineteenth century, the "civilising mission" dominated the minds of the state officials appointed to the tribal zones. In the case of the Arab provinces of the empire, Usama Makdisi argues that the contemporary Ottoman reforms "created a notion of the pre-modern in the empire that resembled the way in which European colonial administrators represented their colonial subjects".[44] He argues that the imperial capital treated its Arab provinces as "backward and [...] not yet Ottoman".[45] Accordingly, the extension of Ottoman rule was accompanied not only by a civilising mission but also by the wish to Ottomanise the frontiers of the empire. Likewise, Selim Deringil emphasises how the extension of imperial rule in tribal spaces was accompanied by a discourse of bringing civilisation to these regions.[46] He argues that Ottoman bureaucrats and intellectuals

41 For a discussion on the infrastructural power of the state, see Mann (1993, 59).
42 BOA, I. ŞD 26/1166, 9 Kanun-ı Sani 1288 (21 January 1873).
43 BOA, I. ŞD 26/1166, 9 Kanun-ı Sani 1288 (21 January 1873).
44 Makdisi (2002, 769).
45 Makdisi (2002, 770).
46 Deringil (2003, 317).

adopted a colonialist approach towards the people of the empire's periphery.[47] Yet, such a "colonial" approach, which he defines as "borrowed colonialism", was a survival tactic and cannot be compared to the colonialism of the aggressive industrial empires of the West.[48]

Although tribal spaces like Mutki were not direct colonial spaces of the Ottoman Empire, the civilising mission occupied the minds of the Ottoman officials appointed to such spaces. In 1890, the governor of Bitlis, Mehmed Rauf, informed the imperial capital that the tribes of Mutki had been in a state of rebellion (*hal-i serkeşi*), neither obeying the imperial state nor paying their taxes. The governor added that for effective rule, the tribes needed to be civilised through education, which required the construction of five schools and five mosques in the villages of the district. Soon, his proposal was discussed in the Special Council (*Meclis-i Mahsus*) of the central government. Likewise, the Council emphasised the importance of such institutions to turn the tribes into subjects loyal to the imperial state.[49] Thus in the 1890s, nearly 19 mosques were built, some of which were enabled by the charity of Sultan Abdulhamid II, as the Yearbook of the Bitlis Province (*Salnâme-i Vilâyet-i Bitlis*) reported.[50]

While some of the tribal chiefs expressed their content with the construction of such educational and religious buildings, others perceived the growth of state infrastructure as a threat to their power and authority. A document prepared by the administrative council of Bitlis in 1897 reveals that dissatisfied tribes not only burnt down the public buildings and military barracks of the district, but also killed the appointed district governor.[51] Tribal members also seemed to have continued with their customs in solving intertribal conflicts, rather than abiding by the Ottoman law and authorities. In 1886, the Council of Ministers (*Meclis-i Vükela*) decided to relocate the Court of First Appearance (*Bidayet Mahkemesi*) of Mutki to Hizan, a nearby district in the province of Bitlis, since only a few cases were brought before the court by the inhabitants of Mutki.[52]

5.5 Sheiks and Aghas: Mediation for Tax Collection

The third method of tax collection was through the agency of the tribal chiefs and religious authorities. When the Ottoman imperial capital and the provincial administration realised the difficulties in establishing a permanent administration in Mutki, they sought for other options to extend the

47 Deringil (2003, 313).
48 Deringil (2003, 313).
49 BOA, Irade Meclis-i Mahsus (hereafter I.MMS) 112/4819, 21 Şevval 1307 (10 June 1890).
50 Salnâme-i Vilâyet-i Bitlis, 1308 (1892/1893), 150.
51 BOA, Dahiliye Nezareti Tesri-i Muamelat ve Islahat Komisyonu (hereafter DH. TMIK) M 33/72, 10 Rabiyyü'lahir 1315 (8 September 1897).
52 BOA, MV 44/18, 14 Şevval 1306, (13 June 1886).

rule of the state in the 1860s. In addition to increasing state infrastructure in the region, the central and provincial administrations began to search for tribal leaders and religious authorities who would act as power brokers. In the 1860s, for instance, a certain Emrullah Agha from the locality (*yerlüden*) was appointed to the region as the sub-district administrator, since he was assumed to be familiar with local customs. However, Emrullah Agha had to reside in a Christian village in the district and protected himself with thirty gendarmeries as well as his own retinue. He was able to collect the taxes of some Christian villages and this amount was assumed to be his salary. Yet, his authority was confined to a limited area, as he had no influence over other tribal groups. Thus, the taxes of the other villages remained largely outstanding.[53]

Another important group who acted as power brokers in the region were the religious authorities. The sheiks won tremendous political clout during the second half of the nineteenth century, not only in Mutki, but also in other Kurdish settled areas. Martin Van Bruinessen argues that a power vacuum was created in the Kurdistan by the destruction of the semi-independent Kurdish emirates in the 1840s; this was filled in the following decades by religious leaders mostly from the Naqshbandi order.[54] Especially during the Hamidian era, the central government relied on the authority of the sheikhs to prevent intertribal conflicts, to collect the taxes and to maintain conscription. Sheiks acted as mediators for the central and provincial administration's communication with those tribes which were beyond its reach. Communication with the subjects through religious leaders was not only a breakdown from the centralist policies of the Tanzimat period but was also in line with the Islamic policies of the Sultan Abdulhamid II, as the following example shows.

In March 1897, the deputy district governor of Mutki, İsmail Bey, arrived together with 50 soldiers and 100 gendarmeries at Mutki in order to register and collect the sheep tax.[55] According to the governor of the Bitlis, the taxes of Mutki had been owed for over 12 years and had accumulated to tax liabilities of 1,382,000 piasters. The due amount of sheep taxes alone totalled 650,000 piasters for 12 years, of which only 337,000 piasters had been collected.[56] The newly appointed district governor was determined to collect the remaining taxes. During their mission, the expedition was attacked by 400 Kurds in the village of Kuslan. Tribal members killed the deputy district governor and the sergeant of the gendarmerie and severely injured the lieutenant (*mülâzım*). They also seized the sheep tax registers and official documents besides military equipment.[57] In response, a large squad composed of regular soldiers and

53 BOA, A.MKT.MHM 353/25, 8 Şubat 81, (20 February 1866).

54 Bruinessen (1992, 228–234).

55 BOA, Bab-ı Ali Evrak Odası (hereafter BEO) 946/70925, 29 Mart 313 (10 April 1897).

56 BOA, DH. TMIK 33/72, 4 Haziran 313 (26 June 1897).

57 BOA, BEO 946/70925, 1314.Z.3, (5 April 1897).

gendarmerie forces was mobilised within a short time under the command of the chief of gendarmerie (*alay beyi*), Arif Bey, not only to provide security throughout the region, but also to help the officials to collect the sheep tax. However, after their arrival at Mutki, they were attacked in a similar way by a large group of tribal militias. Arif Bey and several gendarmeries were killed. Finally, the army left the region and returned to the centre of the district.[58] Different segments of the provincial administration accused each other of bearing responsibility for the incidents. The chief commander of the army argued that the events happened because of the maladministration of the tax collectors.[59] A notable from Bitlis argued that the district governor's mistreatment of one of the tribal chiefs was the flashpoint. Finally, the administrative council of Bitlis stated in its report that the tribes of Mutki, who ultimately had accepted government rule after great efforts, had been provoked *(tahrik)* by some people who had lost their influence over the tribes.[60]

The above-mentioned events led to a heated debate among the civil and military officials of the Ottoman Empire. While the administrative council of the province of Bitlis demanded an immediate military expedition to punish the tribes, the army and central government were in favour of more flexible policies. Military intelligence reports from the region underlined the possibility of a unification of the tribes of Mutki with those of Sason and Huyut in the case of any military intervention. The commander-in-chief (*serasker*) of the general Ottoman armies stated that there was no need to use military force to spill blood among Muslims. Besides, the use of military force would only provoke the "wild nature" of the tribal groups and further alienate them from the imperial state. Instead, the commander recommended appointing local sheiks as mediators, who would give proper advice not only about the collection of taxes, but also about capturing the culprits of the rebellion.[61]

Following the events of 1897, the army developed a plan to rely even more on the local elites in the attempt to enforce its rule, and the central government shared this idea. As a result, the governor of Bitlis held meetings with powerful and influential chiefs of the region, like Faris Agha and Reşid Agha, who according to the governor declared their loyalty to the imperial state.[62] These two aghas were also tax farmers, who bought the right to levy taxes in certain villages at low prices at the turn of the century, probably because of their close connections with the provincial administration and because there was no outside offer for tax farming in these villages. And with the encouragement of tribal leaders, 580 people from Mutki agreed to work on the construction of the roads of Bitlis for four days in 1902.[63]

58 BOA, BEO 961/72010, 14 Mayıs 1313 (26 May 1897).

59 Ibid.

60 BOA, DH. TMIK. M 33/72, 1314 Z 24 (26 May 1897).

61 BOA, BEO 1014/76048, 1 Ca1315 (28 September 1897).

62 BOA, Y.MTV 181/70, 23 Ağustos 314 (4 September 1897).

63 BOA, DH. TMIK.34/50, 26 Nisan 317 (9 May 1901).

5.6 Conclusion

This chapter has discussed why taxation remained a source of conflict between the Ottoman central government and various tribes of Mutki during the second half of the nineteenth century, and what kind of methods were implemented by Ottoman officials to maintain the tax flow. The district of Mutki, which was a mountainous and inaccessible region, was largely a non-state zone before the Tanzimat period. The new tax system brought in by the Tanzimat reforms, however, not only threatened the economic power of the tribal chiefs, but also meant double taxation for those who had been paying customary taxes to the tribal chiefs. Since the tithe and sheep taxes under the Tanzimat reforms were mostly new for the inhabitants of the region, tribal chiefs were able to mobilise against the tax officials. At the same time, the tax resistance of the tribes was part of their general opposition against the centralising and modernising attempts of the Ottoman Empire. Although there were no large-scale tax uprisings, the new taxation regime was clearly resisted.

Starting with the early Tanzimat years, the civil and military officials of the Ottoman Empire adopted several "unusual" methods to combat tax evasion among the tribal groups. Due to fierce tribal resistance and a lack of success with flexible policies, early attempts at administration, taxation and conscription were mostly carried out through military expeditions. From the 1850s onwards, state officials also paid attention to increase the infrastructural capacity of the Empire in the region. The construction of government buildings, military barracks, schools and mosques in the region were regarded as important institutions by state officials. Such institutions were perceived as critical in creating loyal Ottoman subjects in order to facilitate administration and taxation throughout the region. Towards the late nineteenth century, during the Hamidian era, the imperial capital adopted more flexible policies to pacify tribal resistance and to collect taxes. Appointing locals as district governors, appealing to the chiefs and sheiks as powerbrokers and rewarding local notables who accepted government authority were the methods used to ensure taxation in the region.

Each tax collection method that was put into practice in this area during the second half of the nineteenth century had its own dilemmas. The reform expeditions of the early Tanzimat period were costly as they required the participation of large numbers of soldiers. Increasing state infrastructure, which was also an expensive undertaking, was influential only if the local population appreciated it. Appealing to the authority of the local sheiks or tribal leaders brought some success towards the end of the century. However, since the region was inhabited by various different tribes, who often had conflicts with one another, this method also ran into difficulties. Nevertheless, taxes and military conscription remained sources of tension between tribal groups and provincial authorities even during the early twentieth century.[64] During the Second Constitutional Period (1908–1918), state officials had to apply a combination of these three methods to ensure the taxation of the region.

By examining the taxation of tribes by the Ottoman Empire, this chapter also contributes to the literature on state-society relations during an age of modernisation and political reform. It exemplifies how plans and projects drawn up by imperial circles had to be changed and redefined at a local level because of tribal responses. The state and tribes are, however, not regarded as always mutually exclusive categories. Although taxes and conscripts largely remained sources of contention between the tribes of Mutki and the imperial state, there were also situations where tribal chiefs were integrated into the Ottoman provincial and fiscal administration. Especially during the late nineteenth century, tribal chiefs began to buy the taxes of the villages that had been formerly under their control, so that imperial tax farming and the tribal tax system overlapped. These were also the moments when the boundary that divided the tribes and the state became blurred.

Archives

Bab-ı Ali Evrak Odası (BEO).
Dahiliye Nezareti Tesri-I Muamelat ve Islahat Komisyonu (DH. TMIK).
İrade Dahiliye (I. DH).
Irade Meclis-i Mahsus (I.MMS).
Irade Şura-yı Devlet (I. ŞD).
Türkiye Cumhuriyeti Cumhurbaşkanlığı Devlet Arşivleri Başkanlığı, Istanbul (BOA)
Yıldız Sadâret Resmi Maruzat (Y.A RES).

References

Atmaca, Metin. 2019. Resistance to centralisation in the Ottoman periphery: the Kurdish Baban and Bohtan emirates. *Middle Eastern Studies*. https://doi.org/10.1080/00263206.2018.1542595

Çadırcı, Musa. 2007. *Tanzimat sürecinde Türkiye: Ülke yönetimi*. Ankara: İmge Kitabevi.

Deringil, Selim. 2003. "They live in a state of nomadism and savagery": The late Ottoman Empire and the post-colonial debate. *Comparative Studies in Society and History* 45(2): 311–342.

Gellner, Ernest. 1969. *Saints of the Atlas*. London: Weidenfield and Nicolson.

Güran, Tevfik. 2000. Yüzyıl temettuat tahrirleri. In *Osmanlı Devleti'nde bilgi ve istatistik*, eds. H. Inalcık and Ş. Pamuk, 73–95. Ankara: T.C. Başbakanlık Devlet İstatistik Enstitüsü.

Haj, Samira. 1997. *The Making of Iraq, 1900-1963: Capital, Power and Ideology*. Albany: State University of New York Press.

İnalcık, Halil. 1976. *Application of the Tanzimat and Its Social Effects*. Lisse: The Peder de Ridder Press.

64 BOA, Y.MTV 273/169, 21 Nisan 321 (4 May 1905).

İslamoğlu, Huri. 2000. Property as a contested domain: A reevaluation of the Ottoman Land Code of 1858. In *New Perspectives on Property and Land in the Middle East*, ed. Roger Owen, 3–62. Cambridge, Massachusetts, London, England: Harvard University Press.

Köksal, Yonca. 2006. Coercion and mediation: Centralization and sedentarization of tribes in the Ottoman Empire. *Middle Eastern Studies* 42(3): 469–491.

Lewis, Norman. 1987. *Nomads and Settlers in Syria and Jordan, 1800-1980*. Cambridge: Cambridge University Press.

Makdisi, Usama. 2002. Ottoman orientalism. *The American Historical Review* 107(3): 768–796.

Mann, Michael. 1993. *The Sources of Social Power, The Rise of Classes and Nation States, 1760-1914*. Cambridge: Cambridge University Press.

Özbek, Nadir. 2008. *Policing the Countryside: Gendarmes of the Late-nineteenth-century Ottoman Empire (1876-1908)*. International Journal of Middle East Studies 40. New York, Cambridge: Cambridge University Press.

Özbek, Nadir. 2015. *İmparatorluğun bedeli: Osmanlı'da vergi, siyaset ve toplumsal adalet (1839-1908)*. İstanbul: Boğaziçi Üniversitesi Yayınevi.

Reinkowski, Maurus. 2005. The state's security and the subjects' prosperity: Notions of order in Ottoman bureaucratic correspondence (19th Century). In *Legitimizing the Order: The Ottoman Rhetoric of State Power*, eds. M. Reinkowski and H. Karateke, 195–212. Leiden: Brill.

Rogan, Eugene. 1999. *Frontiers of the State in the Late Ottoman Empire: Transjordan, 1850-1921*. New York: Cambridge University Press.

Okcu, Naci and Hasan Akdağ (translators). 2010. *Salnâme-i vilâyet-i Erzurum, (1287/1870, 1288/1871, 1289/1872, 1290/1873) Erzurum il yıllığı*, Erzurum: Atatürk Üniversitesi İlahiyat Fakultesi.

Scott, James. C. 2009. *The Art of Not Being Governed, An Anarchist History of Upland Southeast Asia*. New Haven & London: Yale University Press.

Shaw, Stanford J., and Ezel Kural Shaw. 2002. *History of the Ottoman Empire and modern Turkey, Volume II: Reform, revolution, and republic: The rise of modern Turkey 1808-1975*. Cambridge: Cambridge University Press.

Sykes, Mark. 1908. The Kurdish tribes of the Ottoman Empire. *The Journal of Royal Anthropological Institute of Great Britain and Ireland* 38: 451–486.

Tapper, Richard. 1990. Anthropologists, historians and tribespeople on tribe and state formation in the Middle East. In *Tribes and state formation in the Middle East*, eds. Philip S. Khoury and Joseph Kostiner, 48–73. Berkeley, Los Angeles, California: University of California Press.

Terzibaşoğlu, Yücel. 2006. Eleni Hatun'un zeytin bahçeleri: 19. yüzyılda Anadolu'da mülkiyet hakları nasıl inşa edildi? *Tarih ve Toplum Yeni Yaklaşımlar* 4: 121–147.

Toksöz, Meltem. 2010. *Nomads, Migrants and Cotton in the Eastern Mediterranean: The Making of the Adana-Mersin Region 1850-1908*. Leiden, Boston: Brill.

Zürcher, Eric J. 2003. 3rd ed. *Turkey a Modern History*. I.B. Tauris.

6 Tax Evasion as a Means of Resistance in Occupied Greece, 1941–1944

Vasilis G. Manousakis

6.1 Introduction

When Greece was liberated in October 1944, the country was a shambles. A large percentage of its infrastructure was destroyed, about 5–8% of the population was dead and the economy was in ruins with unprecedented inflation and a worthless currency. This economic destruction was a direct consequence of the war and the ruthless exploitation of Greece's resources by the Axis powers. Germany and Italy had forced the country to pay high occupation expenses at a time when state income was in steep decline, while Bulgaria practically annexed part of north-eastern Greece. A neglected aspect of the economic history of occupied Greece is the study of the reasons behind the decrease in state income, and more specifically of tax resistance/evasion. This chapter tries to explain the failure of tax collection during the Occupation by looking at the economic and political reasons behind it. The first section of the chapter presents a brief overview of the political and economic conditions in 1941–1944 followed by estimates of the decline in state revenue during the Occupation. The following section deals with the efforts to reform the tax system and the role of the occupation authorities. The last two sections examine the status of the unpopular Greek Occupation governments and the role played by the resistance.

6.2 The Setting: Greece under German and Italian Occupation

After managing to turn back the Italian invasion of October 1940, the Greek army fought for about half a year inside Italian-occupied Albania before the German invasion into Greek territory began in April 1941. By the end of April fighting on the mainland was over. Crete, the only remaining free Greek territory, was conquered by 1 June. By then the exhausted Greek economy had already started to overheat. However, it was after the start of the joint German-Italian-Bulgarian occupation that inflation

DOI: 10.4324/9781003333197-9

soared.[1] Soon food shortages started to become so acute that people starved by the thousands during the first occupation winter.[2]

Before the war, Greece had imported between a quarter and a third of its necessary food but after the start of the Occupation, imports of food (as well as other critically important goods such as fuel) were greatly reduced. Transport infrastructure was severely damaged, while most of the country's vehicles were either destroyed or taken over by the occupiers. The division into German, Italian and Bulgarian zones proved an additional impediment to the movement of goods. Furthermore, the Greek military mobilisation of 1940 had caused problems in the farming sector due to the lack of manpower and draught animals, leading to decreased food production in 1941, although the extent of that decrease is difficult to calculate with precision. Last, but certainly not least, the occupation forces extracted significant quantities of Greek goods, ranging from luxury goods and fuel to clothes and foodstuff. If such goods were not confiscated outright, they were paid for with occupation currency (Italian Mediterranean Drachmas and German *Reichskreditkassenscheine*), at least for the first four months of the occupation. These notes effectively increased money circulation by more than 40% within a few weeks, contributing directly to the explosion of inflation.[3] After the summer of 1941, payments through the occupation expenses accounts forced inflation even higher. Between the autumn of 1941 and the autumn of 1942, the purchasing power of the average worker's income was reduced to less than a quarter of its pre-occupation value.[4]

Shortages became almost immediately noticeable as many goods practically disappeared from shop windows and could only be found on the black market at very high prices. For the first few weeks of the occupation, the economy froze, and tax income (especially from indirect taxes) was severely reduced.

The "occupation government" of Lieutenant General Tsolakoglou had to deal not only with food shortages and mounting inflation but also with the rapidly rising public deficit. The demands of the German and Italian authorities for occupation payments were the main cause of the high public expenses. Every year between 1941 and 1944, the official cost of the

1 The evolution of the prices of various goods differed significantly, but an examination of the price of gold is indicative of the general trend in prices. One British gold sovereign was worth about 1,100 drachmas before the war; the price climbed to almost 1,500 drachmas just before the German invasion, and it reached 20,000 by the end of 1941. In early November 1942, it skyrocketed to more than 600,000 and exceeded 1 quadrillion during the final days of the occupation.

2 There is a wide variation in the estimates of deaths, ranging from about 100,000 to close to half a million – the latter number being an obvious overestimation (Hionidou 2008, 26). An often-mentioned estimate is 300,000 (see for example Voglis (2006, 23), but this number includes deaths that were indirectly attributed to hunger and malnutrition.

3 Μανουσάκης [Manousakis] (2019, 26–27).

4 Palerait (2000, 40–48).

occupation absorbed between a third and a half of the Greek budget.[5] The real value of all the Greek resources taken by Germany and Italy is difficult to estimate accurately, but it could be as high as half of the country's wartime GDP. It is no surprise, therefore, that the deficit skyrocketed from less than 4% in 1938–1939 to more than 80% in 1942–1943 and to more than 94% in 1943–1944.[6] The occupation government could do little about the excessive demands of the occupation authorities. An effort was made, however, to address the other side of the deficit problem, namely the diminishing revenues from taxes caused by the rising inflation, the general economic downturn and increasing tax evasion.

6.3 Greek Tax Revenue during the War and Occupation

Even before the war, the tax burden (especially the percentage of indirect taxes) was relatively high, probably as a result of the necessity to pay the already accumulated Greek public debt, which accounted to between 83 and 93% of the annual national income.[7] In 1930, the tax burden reached 24.5% of the national income and nine years later, when the country's war preparations were in full swing, it climbed to 26.14%, a percentage that was considerably higher than that of many other European states.[8] In comparison with the other Balkan states, Greece had a reasonably well-developed tax system, which had been modernised in 1919 and partially reformed a few times since. The state treasury, however, still relied to a significant degree on indirect taxes for revenue. The roots of the problem lay in the largely underdeveloped nature of the economy (self-consumption and barter were still relevant in the 1930s), problems with registering transactions and suppressing evasion, and distinct political choices. Thus, even though direct taxes were progressive in nature, a significant percentage of the taxes (primarily the indirect ones) fell to a disproportionate degree on the shoulders of the middle class and the poor.

5 Εθνική Τράπεζα της Ελλάδος [National Bank of Greece] (1948, 98).

6 Μανουσάκης [Manousakis] (2019). See esp. 37–44. There were no official occupation payments in the zone effectively annexed by Bulgaria.

7 According to the official statistics in 1938, public debt amounted to 52,055,654,000 drachmas (Statistique Générale de la Grèce 1940, 315). At the time, the national income was estimated at 62,867,000,000 drachmas (ΕΛΙΑ, Αρχείο Κ. Ζαβιτσιάνου [K. Zavitsianos Archive]), file 3.2, Υπόμνημα επί της Οικονομικής και δημοσιοοικονομικής καταστάσεως της Ελλάδος [Memorandum on the economic and fiscal situation of Greece] (November 1941). A modern estimate raises the amount to almost 55.7 billion (Κωστελλένος et al. [Kostellenos et al.] 2007, 141).

8 For comparison: the percentage for the UK in 1930 was 17.5%, for France 20.4%, for Italy 17.4% and for Yugoslavia 13.2%. Σμπαρούνης [Sbarounis] (1950, 51–52). Sbarounis, who at the time was a high-ranking counsellor at the Ministry of Economics, calculated that the tax burden for 1941 had climbed to almost 40% of the national income (54–55). However, that estimate is inaccurate, as he overestimated the decline of national income (compare Σμπαρούνης [Sbarounis] (1950, 54–55) with the GDP estimates in Μανουσάκης [Manousakis] (2019, 37–44).

When war broke out in Europe, new taxes, like the temporary tax on the profits of shipowners and a 1–2% tax on agricultural production, were imposed in order to finance war preparation.[9] Efforts were also undertaken to increase agricultural production, chiefly aimed at reducing the country's dependence on food imports, but with the added benefit of slightly increasing tax revenue.

Once Greece was conquered, however, these measures proved worthless. The revenue from the taxation of shipping activities, for example, became negligible as most of the Greek ships either joined the government in exile or were sunk. Furthermore, taxes were not adjusted consistently enough to keep up with inflation. Direct taxes were based on the previous year's transactions and thus by the time they were paid, their real value was insufficient to cover the government's needs. An additional problem was that a significant – and growing – percentage of transactions took place in cash on the black market and was never reported to the taxing authorities. The general downturn of the economy and the difficulty of tracking sales meant that revenue from indirect taxes and movement of capital declined after the start of the war and during the early occupation period. However, revenue from direct taxes also decreased, especially after 1942. The state was thus forced to count more and more on indirect taxes, at a time when commerce and production were both shrinking (Table 6.1).

Table 6.1 Greek state revenues: budgeted receipts of each category as % of total revenue

Fiscal year	*Direct taxes*	*Indirect taxes*	*Monopolies*	*State rights, properties, services and stamp duties*	*Special and other revenue*	*Total*	*Movement of capital*	*Total*
1938–1939	19.2	42.8	4.5	12.9	7.6	87.0	13.0	100.0
1939–1940	19.9	41.1	4.9	14.7	8.7	89.3	10.7	100.0
1940–1941	21.6	38.4	4.9	15.6	12.3	92.8	7.2	100.0
1941–1942	24.7	35.8	6.3	14.3	17.2	98.3	1.7	100.0
1942–1943	16.2	41.1	9.7	14.3	9.9	91.2	8.8	100.0

Source: *Statistique Générale de la Grèce* [N.D.], 29. The sinking revenue from the movement of capital after 1938–1939 was caused by the outbreak of the Second World War.

The real revenues from direct taxes were even lower, as a growing proportion of direct taxes were never actually paid. The percentage of direct taxes that were actually collected fell from almost 90% in 1939–1940 to less than 70% in the year 1942–1943, as the comparison between actual and budgeted receipts in Table 6.2 shows. The situation became much worse in 1943–1944, but unfortunately, the precise numbers are missing from the statistical series.

9 Αναγκαστικός Νόμος [AN - Emergency Law] 2288 and 2287 (respectively), both on: ΦΕΚ 118A, 6/4/1940.

Table 6.2 Greek state revenues: actual receipts as % of budgeted amounts

Fiscal year	*DT*	*IT*	*M*	*SD*	*SR*	*SS*	*SP*	*S&O*	*Tot*	*MoC*	*Tot*
1938–1939	88.34	99.01	100.00	99.05	79.96	99.82	90.64	80.06	94.19	32.83	87.17
1939–1940	89.36	99.87	100.00	98.98	81.42	99.94	92.40	72.73	93.45	94.81	93.56
1940–1941	75.59	99.47	100.00	98.71	80.53	98.77	80.31	76.90	88.65	85.31	89.81
1941–1942	74.76	99.70	100.00	99.13	84.85	97.40	92.00	84.82	88.95	54.50	88.85
19421943	69.15	98.82	99.82	99.98	90.10	88.97	94.49	80.30	89.93	99.97	90.74

Source: *Statistique Générale de la Grèce*, [N.D.], p. 29. DT: Direct Taxes, IT: Indirect Taxes, M: Monopolies, SD: Stamp Duties, SR: State Rights, SS: Revenue from State Services, SP: Revenue from State Property, S&O: Special and Other Revenue, MoC: Movement of Capital.

The biggest drop in revenue came from the taxation of land. In the first fiscal year of the occupation, less than 50% of the estimated revenue from taxes related to land were translated into actual state revenue. In the following fiscal year, the percentage dropped to a mere 34% (Table 6.3). The real value of tax receipts was considerably lower as, by the time tax liabilities were actually paid, their monetary value had been significantly reduced by inflation. Even the decision that some taxes had to be paid in several instalments before the end of the year could not prevent the devaluation.

Table 6.3 Percentages of actual receipts from direct taxation in relation to estimated revenue from direct taxation

Fiscal year	*Of net revenue*	*Of land revenue*	*Of turnover*	*Of revenue*	*Of Movement of capital*	*Additional on direct taxes*	*Special taxes*	*Total*
1941–1942 (IV–III)	75	47	96	72	87	79	-	75
1942–1943 (IV–III)	81	34	98	77	97	88	-	69

Source: Table compiled by author. Calculations based on data from Statistique Générale de la Grèce [N.D.], p. 30.

6.4 Plans for Tax Reforms and the Role of the Occupation Authorities

Many of the measures taken early in the war (new taxes for shipowners and for agriculture) and in first months of the Occupation (increases in the taxes on stocks, wages, company turnover, entertainment activities and real estate sales) soon proved to be of limited usefulness. Nonetheless, the first Greek occupation government appeared reluctant to make more drastic changes, for fear that rising taxes would damage the economy, or alienate the Greek public even more. The Tsolakoglou government also rightly argued that the economic problems would never be solved if occupation expenses were not reduced.

The occupation powers wanted to preserve the image of legitimacy of the government they had installed in the country, but at the same time increase its revenue. They thus offered their official assistance in the effort to improve the state of Greek finances. The German and Italian interest in strong Greek tax revenues was no surprise since a complete collapse of Greek public finances would have prevented the country from further financing its occupation. The Axis powers thus promoted tax reforms with the hope of increasing revenue so that they would be able to extract more resources from the country.

The first relatively major reform took place after the visit of a German economic commission in November 1941. The focus of the commission's recommendations was the adaptation of the tax system to inflation and to the demands of wartime. An effort was made to further increase the taxation of company profits, the advanced payment of some taxes was introduced and a new tax auditing authority was proposed. New measures to combat tax evasion were also imposed, including a decree that made the use of checks compulsory for transactions over 30,000 drachmas.[10] The measure was received with a lot of scepticism and had limited results. The major Greek banks did not believe in its success and indeed experienced a drop in new deposits, which they attributed at least partly to the new provision.[11]

Overall, efforts to limit liquidity and thus alleviate the pressures of inflation failed, as did the attempt to root out the black market, despite the German hopes for general economic improvement and an increase in state revenue of about 3.8 billion drachmas to balance the budget. The German authorities blamed the Greek government for not showing support for the reforms or for delaying the adoption of the measures. They also blamed the civil servants for resisting the reforms that were adopted.[12]

The next major tax reform took place around early 1943, after a joint German-Italian intervention in the Greek economy. Most labour-intensive but low-yielding tax cases were to be dropped in order to focus on the few that could yield higher results. In this way state revenue would be increased and the amount of cash in the market reduced. Again, however, the results were limited. This time, the German authorities also blamed the Italians for allegedly acting very slowly and for "trying to limit the effectiveness of the

10 The penalty for breaking the decree was at least two years in prison and a penalty fee equal to the amount of the transaction. Νομοθετικό Διάταγμα [ΝΔ - Legislative Decree] 771/41, ΦΕΚ 416Α, 1/12/1941 and 915/42, ΦΕΚ 2Α, 10/1/1942 (amendment). Also ΝΔ 1941/42, ΦΕΚ 278Α, 30/10/1942 (partial abolition).

11 According to the National Bank of Greece (NBG), there were only 8,693,000 drachmas in new deposits in cash in the period 2–15 December 1941 (the first 15 days of the measure), as opposed to 114,312,000 drachmas in the period 2–15 November. ΙΑΕΤΕ, Α1Σ32Υ1Φ17, the Governor of the NBG to the Minister of National Economy, 29/12/1941.

12 AA-PA, R 27320, "Das Finanzwesen einschließlich der Besatzungskosten in Griechenland während der Deutschen Besatzungszeit", 1941-1944, von Oberregierungsrat Dr. S. Nestler, 139–149.

measures". One of the measures promoted by the Italian side was a tax on capital with the aim of reducing liquidity by an estimated 10%, thus limiting inflation.[13] All Greek banks had to increase their capital by 10% and other limited companies by 20%. The stocks created in this way or the equivalent of their value had to be transferred to the state in the form of taxes.[14] Banks and other limited companies protested heavily against what they considered to be an attempt by the occupiers to take over their companies. The benefits for the state proved limited, as the companies stalled for time and the revenues collected were insufficient.[15]

A further attempt to force the banks to sell the stock portfolios and give the proceeds to the state encountered even more decided resistance because it was perceived as a gift to the occupiers or their collaborators who would buy the stocks, thus a thinly veiled robbery. When rumours circulated about a compulsory "donation" (later a loan) of 40% of the stock portfolios to the state, banks, resistance groups – especially the National Liberation Front (*Εθνικό Απελευθερωτικό Μέτωπο*, EAM) – and even former politicians protested so vehemently that the measure was watered down. In the end about a quarter of the portfolios were sold in order to supply the state with a bank loan.[16] In 1944, after Italy had collapsed, a further series of new, stricter tax laws was introduced, but to little effect since hyperinflation was by then out of control.[17]

In other respects, the occupation authorities actually impeded the collection of taxes by the Greek government. The Italians withheld tax payments from the Ionian and the Cyclades islands, areas which they were planning to annex after the war. The Germans merely took note of this and remained mostly passive towards their ally's behaviour.[18] At the same time, some people who collaborated with the Axis powers showed complete disregard for the Greek state and its tax collectors. As a Greek politician noted in October 1941, certain members of the Vlach minority told the tax collector who came to their village that they considered themselves to be Romanian, not Greek, and therefore they refused to pay. In a nearby milk-producing area, the Roman Legion, a small Vlach armed organisation supported by the Italians, went even further and substituted the Greek authorities by issuing permits for the transport of milk, keeping the taxes from this transaction.[19] The occupation authorities also indirectly contributed to the loss of state revenue by using, as in the rest of occupied Europe, black marketeers to procure goods

13 Ibid.

14 ΝΔ 2021/1942, ΦΕΚ 321Α, 20/12/1942 and ΝΔ 2159/1943, ΦΕΚ 42Α, 24/2/1943 (amendment).

15 See, for example, the memorandum of NGB, in ΕΛΙΑ, αρχείο Κ. Ζαβιτσιάνου; file 3.2, Εκθέσεις υπομνήματα και σημειώσεις I [reports, memos and notes I] (1941–1944).

16 For more information see: Συνοδινός [Synodinos] (2007, 134–160).

17 Kilian (2017, 304–305).

18 AA-PA, R 105897, S. Nestler, Notiz betr: Griechische Steuereinnahmen, 16/10/1941.

19 Αβέρωφ [Averoff] (1948, 93, 123–125).

that had disappeared from the "official" market, and by protecting some of these marketeers when the Greek authorities tried to punish them.[20]

Contractors or suppliers working with the occupation forces also took advantage of their special relationship in order to avoid paying taxes. This practice became so widespread that, after several months of looking the other way, the German authorities issued a statement in the Greek newspapers reminding their Greek allies of their tax obligations.[21] However, tax evasion by Axis collaborators apparently continued. In 1943 it was agreed – despite strong resistance from the Wehrmacht – that the Axis authorities would send all available information about payments to contractors and suppliers to the Greek Ministry of Economics in order to make taxation possible.[22]

6.5 Unpopular Puppets

Despite proclamations of popular sovereignty, it was immediately obvious to everyone that the Greek government did not represent the interests of the Greek population.[23] Even though Tsolakoglou was congratulated by some opponents of the preceding Metaxas dictatorship, who welcomed anybody who would end it, it proved difficult to form a government with some semblance of legitimacy. Diplomat Felix Benzler, who was initially intended to be Reich Plenipotentiary for Greece, noted in a telegram to the German Minister of Foreign Affairs Ribbentrop that "[…] rebuilding the Greek government has been very difficult till now, because it is very difficult to persuade civilians of a certain stature to participate in any way".[24] Tsolakoglou

20 When in 1942 the Greek authorities convicted a black marketer who was supplying a German hospital in Crete with groceries, the German authorities complained and asked the name of the judge, probably in order to punish him (IAK, Αρχείο Γερμανικής Κατοχής [Archive of German Occupation]: File Γ́. Αρχεία Γερμανικής Στρατιωτικής Διοίκησης Κρήτης [Archives of the German military command of Crete] 1941–1942, Δεσμίς [Bundle] 26: letter of the general secretary of the governor of Crete of the district attorney in Chania, no 51, 11/1/1942).

21 *Πρωία*, 4/12/1941.

22 AA-PA, R 27320, Nestler, "Das Finanzwesen einschließlich der Besatzungskosten in Griechenland während der Deutschen Besatzungszeit" p. 147. In 1943, the law for contractor's taxes also changed in an effort to curb tax evasion (*Οικονομολόγος*, 23/1/1943). German and Italian payments to contractors and suppliers in Greece were of course part of the occupation expenses.

23 For Tsoloakoglou: ΦΕΚ 146A, 29/4/1941. For the proclamations of Logothetopoulos (December 1942 to April 1943) and Rallis (April 1943 to October 1944) see: ΦΕΚ 307A, 2/12/1942 and ΦΕΚ 81A 7/4/1943 respectively.

24 AA-PA, R29612, Benzler to Ribbentrop, 29/4/1941. Ribbentrop had telegraphed the same day that Pezopoulos, the prefect of Attica (the capital region), wanted to become prime minister and asked that a suggestion be made by Bezler to Tsolakoglou to include him as a minister (Ribbentrop to Benzler, 29/4/1941). He was not included.

even had to annul the recent (1938) election of the Archbishop of Athens because he had refused to swear in his government.[25]

Ordinary people viewed the New Greek government with contempt. Musician and musicologist Minos Dounias notes in his diary, for example, that it was a "government of puppets" led by the general who "without [...] permission surrendered our heroic Greek army of Albania and Macedonia to captivity".[26] Even the new Archbishop (Damaskinos) was reluctant to support the regime: in July 1941, when Tsolagoglou asked for the Orthodox Church's support against his opponents, he received the following evasive answer: "Without wanting to deny the fact that the population is not very sympathetic towards the government, we think that this discontent has less to do with political views and judgments and more with the serious internal situation that resembles a stalemate, which has arisen from the occupation, and to a large degree, because of it".[27]

That internal situation became much worse in the autumn and especially in the winter of 1941, when thousands of people starved to death. Whatever little credibility the Axis-appointed government might have still possessed practically disappeared as its efforts to reduce the death toll failed. The general impression was that the country's government was controlled by hostile powers and therefore unable or unwilling to help its citizens, and this was strengthened by the fact that other organisations managed to provide some assistance. The International Committee of the Red Cross played an important role by helping with food imports and distribution. Employees of big companies or state organisations formed cooperatives in order to supply their members with necessities. The Greek Orthodox Church created its own organisation, the National Organisation of Christian Solidarity, to help starving Greeks. These organisations operated alongside the government, but separately from it.

More importantly, the starving population was provided with significant support by the resistance movement. EAM, the largest of these organisations, created its own aid structure, the National Solidarity (*Εθνική Αλληλεγγύη*). After 1943, an entire parallel state was formed in the considerable areas controlled by EAM/ΕΛΑΣ, with its own government and taxes.[28]

25 Mazower (1993, 19). In 1938, Metaxas had intervened to overturn the election of Damaskinos, whom he considered an opponent, in favour of Chrysanthos. Tsolakoglou annulled the election of the latter in favour of the former.

26 Δούνιας [Dounias] (1987, 26).

27 Τσολάκογλου [Tsolakoglou] (1959, 226–227).

28 The ΕΛΑΣ (Greek People's Liberation Army, *Εθνικός Λαϊκός Απελευθερωτικός Στρατός*) was the military branch of EAM.

6.6 Tax in Kind and the Battle for the Crops

It quickly became clear that not only would the unpopular government find it difficult to convince its population to comply, but also that many of the economic measures taken would further alienate parts of the population. Given the agricultural nature of the economy, the need for food and the greater presence of resistance in rural Greece, the issue of agricultural taxes became vital. Tsolakoglou had decided to continue the pre-war policy of centralising the collection (*συγκέντρωση*) and sale of certain agricultural and industrial goods.[29] In the interwar period, *συγκέντρωση* had been voluntary. Its aim was to distribute food and other necessities to the urban population at prices below those of the "free" market. In the 1930s, the programme had been a relative success because the state had guaranteed producers fair prices for the goods collected in this way. Before the war, approximately one quarter of annual production had been voluntarily delivered to the state authorities.[30] When war seemed imminent, new measures were introduced, increasing the role of the state, but the prices remained fair and until 1940–1941, only a small proportion of the harvest had been concealed. Thus, the approach continued to function and the loss of state revenue from taxes related to agricultural production was minimal.[31]

After 1941, the Tsolakoglou government hoped that fear of punishment, combined with a sense of civic duty, would make farmers continue to surrender their goods to the state. However, this was not the case. Inflation and lack of food meant that the fixed state prices were now much lower than those on the free (or black) market and most farmers regarded the measure as an unfair loss of income, not unlike a taxation in kind. The pre-war voluntary delivery of part of the agricultural production to state authorities soon began to fail and was made compulsory. New laws and decrees were implemented for the compulsory centralised collection of goods like olive oil, causing considerable loss of income to those who complied.[32]

By the spring of 1942, the forced delivery of production to the state authorities came to be called the "withholding" or "deduction" (*παρακράτημα*), which probably better suited a measure that resulted in losses for the producers. At same time, a tax resembling the Ottoman tithe (*δεκάτη*) was also introduced, which forced the farmers to deliver part of their valuable production

29 The trade with fuel, chemical and some other industrial products had also been centralised, with rations introduced and prices fixed by the state.

30 With the exception of the years 1937 (14.4%) and especially 1936 (a mere 6.3%), the estimates for the 1930s range from 25.9 to 28.7%. Ευελπίδης [Evelpidis] (1944, 151–152), as cited in Μαργαρίτης [Margaritis] (1993, 69–70).

31 AN 2476/40, ΦΕΚ 239A, 3/8/1940.

32 ΝΔ 779/41, ΦΕΚ 424A, 6/12/1941.

as additional tax on top of the *παρακράτημα*.[33] Law-abiding producers could thus essentially lose half their crop or more to the state.[34]

These measures were met with decided aversion. First, major reason was the low prices that were paid for the forced cession of products. These payments were often delayed for weeks or even months, which meant additional, severe losses due to the high inflation.[35] Second, the farmers remained in constant fear that surrendering their production would expose them to hunger. Third, there were plenty of indications that not all the food collected was used for the benefit of the Greek people. In some cases, the products stayed in warehouses for a long time (sometimes rotting) due to the breakdown of the transport network, at the very time when people in the cities were starving. Fourth, rumours abounded that members of the government or the occupation authorities embezzled money, sold food on the black market or were otherwise involved in illegal or at least unethical activities. Finally, the German and Italian authorities purchased foodstuffs at lower, pre-war prices (mostly using Greek money from the occupation expenses accounts) or they outright confiscated it, further fuelling public displeasure.

This popular displeasure helped the resistance, which focused on these measures to attack both the government in Athens and the occupiers. An introductory brochure of EAM accused members of the government of using "the pretence of saving something from the disaster" to secure a good life for themselves and their families while simultaneously helping the occupiers to plunder the country.[36] During the last year of the occupation, EAM put the fight against the *παρακράτημα* and the agricultural tax at the centre of its campaign for the "battle for the crops". Providing armed protection as well as help with the harvest and concealment of the crops, EAM called on the Greek people to help keep the agricultural produce "away from the invaders and the traitors".[37] As a local resistance newspaper put it: "No [village] president or civil servant should become knowingly or unknowingly a collaborator

33 ΝΔ 1207/42, ΦΕΚ 83Α, 14/4/1942. A new law (Νόμος 231, ΦΕΚ 166Α, 5/6/1943) followed the next year. Other agricultural products were taxed based on their bulk prices.

34 When, in November 1942, the prefect of Achaia tried to soothe olive-oil producers, he estimated the combined loss from both tax and *παρακράτημα* to each farmer was "only" 32% of the crop, or close to 50% if one included all the other expenses (*Νεολόγος Πατρών*, 5/11/1942). At the end of the Occupation, a resistance brochure estimated that the loss for grain producers was even higher: 10% tax, 25% *παρακράτημα*, and another 25% for harvesting, thrashing and transport, for a total of nearly 60% (Βιδάλης [Vidalis] 1944, 16).

35 From late 1942, for example, up to 75% of payment for agricultural products collected by the state was often made with special promissory notes payable up to six months later – a significant time period during high inflation (ΝΔ 1984/42, ΦΕΚ 300Α, 26/11/1942).

36 Γλυνός [Glynos] (1944, 28–29). The brochure was first published in 1942 without mentioning the name of the author. At times BBC broadcasts also expressed similar views (Hionidou 2006, 76).

37 Βιδάλης [Vidalis] (1944, 11–22).

of the bandits, an enemy of the people. Not one stremma [of production] should be reported by the farmers".[38]

The state authorities tried to fight back by blaming the "propaganda of agents of the previous regime" of misinforming the population. Producers were said to have succumbed to the "erroneous belief" that the Axis and members of the Greek government were exploiting them. Simultaneously, the occupation government threatened to root out every farmer who incited "rebellion".[39] After 1942, the government's propaganda focused on the "anarcho-communists" as the "enemy agents" that were blamed for various kinds of tax resistance.[40] The occupation authorities, for their part, tried to pressure the Greek state and the civil servants by openly criticising them for their inability – or unwillingness – to effectively deal with the situation.[41]

Despite these efforts, however, civil servants and those who had been temporarily assigned to execute the collection of taxes on agricultural production showed little enthusiasm for their task. Committee members assigned to oversee collection of the tax in kind and the *παρακράτημα* under-recorded as much as 50–60% of the production, retaining part of the unreported foodstuffs to supplement their meagre wages. Liquor was often used to distract the Italian and German soldiers who sometimes oversaw the procedures.[42] Troops would also be bribed as their official pay cheques had been reduced by hyperinflation to the point that it was hardly possible for them to buy anything on the free market.[43]

By 1942–1943, many tax collectors began to adopt the views of the resistance. A member of the committee that oversaw oil presses on the island of Chios remembers that he consistently under-recorded the olive oil produced so that it would not end up in German hands.[44] In another case, a teacher appointed by the government to keep the tax registers of his village described what happened when a few representatives of the resistance movement entered his village in northern Greece in the spring of 1943. The register and all other papers related to taxation were collected at the village square and set on fire,

38 *Σπίθα*, 8/8/1944. Stremma is a unit of land area used in Greece, equivalent to 1,000 square metres. Reporting agricultural production was a key part of the centralised collection (and taxation) of foodstuffs and other agricultural goods.

39 See, for example, *Ελεύθερον Βήμα* and *Πρωία* newspapers, 28/6/1941.

40 Interestingly enough, Jews were not often targeted as resistance fighters by the Greek government, although they participated importantly in the resistance movement.

41 See, for example, the article of a certain Thissenhausen in the *Deutsche Nachrichten für Griechenland* newspaper, translated and published by Πρωία, 10/9/1941.

42 *Σκαλιδάκης* [Skalidakis] (2012, 99) (the thesis was published in book form in 2014, but it does not include this passage). For a different case in another part of Greece, see: Φιλοσόφου [Filosofou] (2010, 150–151).

43 AA-PA, R 27320, Nestler, "Das Finanzwesen einschließlich der Besatzungskosten in Griechenland während der Deutschen Besatzungszeit", 92.

44 Hionidou (2006, 77).

while people started singing and dancing around them.[45] The same ritual was repeated several times, usually with little to no resistance from local officials – indeed often with their participation.[46] Sometimes ΕΛΑΣ [ELAS] units went even further. When after a nearby battle the Italians retreated from the town of Almyros, an ELAS unit captured stores containing produce collected by the authorities. The ELAS did not stop at redistributing the produce to the local population, but also burned the records of the Agricultural Bank in order to erase every trace of the agricultural loans.[47]

Under these conditions, the centralised collection and taxation of agricultural goods fundamentally failed much more spectacularly than taxation in urban areas. The widespread underreporting and hoarding of production during the occupation makes it difficult to calculate the exact percentage of compulsory deliveries from the Greek countryside. In the case of wheat, deliveries were probably close to 10% of total production, a percentage that was considerably lower than what the authorities had intended.

Finally, brief reference needs to be made to the success achieved in overthrowing the Axis' plans for extracting another kind of tax in kind. In early 1943, a German order forced Greeks to work in Axis projects, regardless of the distance from their places of residence. When the plans for this civil mobilisation of the Greek labour force leaked to the public, a series of strikes and demonstrations organised by the resistance paralysed the civil sector. Despite the violent reaction of the police and the occupation forces, the protestors tried to break into the Labour Ministry and succeeded in storming Athens town hall, with the aim of burning the electoral polls so that they could not be used for the civil mobilisation.[48] As a result, the second occupation government collapsed and the plan for a general mobilisation of the Greek labour force had to be abandoned.

The failure of all these taxes did not just cause problems to the Greek state. It also hampered the Greek economic "contribution" to the Axis war effort, while the growth of the resistance led to an increased need for troops to guard the area.

6.7 Conclusion

This chapter has focused on the issue of tax resistance and tax evasion during the Axis Occupation and its causes. It argues that these causes are to be found,

45 Κούφης [Koufis] (1982, 49).

46 Even when there was a small armed presence of the authorities in the village, the result was often the same. E.g. in spring 1943, in central Greece, a small number of resistance fighters convinced or forced a tax collector and the policeman escorting him to hand over the taxes that had been collected and to destroy all the papers related to taxation (Μπέσκος [Beskos] 1987, 25).

47 Αρσενίου [Arseniou] (1999, vol. 1, 269).

48 Mazower (1993, 114–120).

on the one hand, in the economic conditions (inflation, starvation) and, on the other hand, in the lack of government legitimacy. The government's failure to improve economic realities for the average Greek and the growing power of the resistance movement further undermined the ability of the state and the occupation authorities to collect taxes, especially since both monetary taxes and taxes in kind were considered (not entirely unjustifiably) to be providing resources to the Axis.

After the war, members of the Greek occupation government tried to present themselves as guarantors of state continuity and the resistance as a danger whose actions could continue to disrupt normality long after the war was over. Tsolakoglou wondered how "those who for four years have learned to consider the state as their enemy" are going to become tax-paying law-abiding citizens again.[49]

However, when the first post-war government, in which EAM held significant ministerial posts, tried to raise new taxes, the greatest resistance came from those who had gained the most during the Occupation and had avoided joining the resistance. Taxes on war profits were meant to be the primary source of income for the first post-war government, since the near complete economic collapse impeded increasing the collection of revenue from traditional sources. However, only a very small percentage of these taxes was collected. Tax revenue would take years to recover and the economy would continue to struggle well into the next decade.

Archives and Official Statistical Publications

AA-PA (Auswärtiges Amt - Politisches Archiv, Berlin).

ΕΛΙΑ (Ελληνικό Λογοτεχνικό και Ιστορικό Αρχείο - Greek Literary and Historical Archive, Athens).

ΙΑΕΤΕ (Ιστορικό Αρχείο Εθνικής Τράπεζας - Historical Archive of the National Bank of Greece, Athens).

ΙΑΚ (Ιστορικό Αρχείο Κρήτης - Historical Archive of Crete, Chania).

Statistique Générale de la Grèce. [N.D.]. *Bulletin mensuel de statistique publié par la Statistique Générale de la Grèce.* No 1-12 (147), Janvier – Décembre 1943, 1944. Athens: Imprimerie Nationale.

Statistique Générale de la Grèce. 1940. *Annuaire Statistique de la Grèce 1939.* Athens: Imprimerie Nationale.

Newspapers

Ελεύθερον Βήμα [Elefthero Vima]. Athens. 1941.

Νεολόγος Πατρών [Neologos Patron]. Patras. 1942.

Οικονομολόγος [Oikonomologos]. Athens. 1943.

Πρωία [Proia]. Athens. 1941.

49 Τσολάκογλου [Tsolakoglou] (1959, 225).

Σπίθα [Spitha]. Veria. 1944.
ΦΕΚ (*Φύλλο Εφημερίδας της Κυβερνήσεως [Fyllo Efimeridas tis Kyverniseos]* - Official Government Gazette). Athens. 1940–43.

References

Αρσενίου, Λάζαρος Αρσ. [Arseniou, Lazaros Ars.]. 1999. 3rd ed. *Η Θεσσαλία στην αντίσταση*. [Thessaly in Resistance]. Larisa: Έλλα [Ella].

Αβέρωφ, Ευάγγελος [Averoff, Evangelos]. 1948. *Η πολιτική πλευρά του κουτσοβλαχικού ζητήματος* [The political aspect of the koutsovlach issue]. Athens: Εργοστάσιο γραφικών τεχνών Γερ. Σ. Χρήστου [Ger. S. Christou Graphic Arts Factory].

Μπέσκος, Νώντας [Beskos, Nontas]. 1987. Το ΕΑΜ ΕΛΑΣ στον Ερινεό Πατρών [EAM ELAS at Erineo of Patras], *Εθνική Αντίσταση magazine*, συλλογή 55.

Δούνιας, Μίνως [Dounias, Minos]. 1987. *"Έπειτα από 120 χρόνια ελεύθερης ζωής, είμεθα πάλι σκλάβοι'. Το ημερολόγιο κατοχής της Μίνου Δούνια* ['After 120 years of freedom we are again slaves'. The Occupation diary of Minos Dounias]. Φιλολογική επιμέλεια Κυριάκος Ντελόπουλος. Athens: Εστία [Estia].

Ευελπίδης, Χρυσός [Evelpidis, Chrysos]. 1944. *Η γεωργία της Ελλάδος: οικονομική και κοινωνική άποψις* [Greek agriculture: economic and social aspect]. Athens: Λόγος [Logos].

Φιλοσόφου, Μαρία [Filosofou, Maria]. 2010. *Κατοχή και αντίσταση στην Αχαΐα: κοινωνικές και εκπαιδευτικές διαστάσεις* [Occupation and resistance in Achaia: social and educational dimensions]. Unpublished PhD thesis. Department of Educational Sciences and Early Childhood Education, University of Patras.

Γλυνός, Δημήτρης [Glynos, Dimitris]. 1944. *Τι είναι και τι θέλει το Εθνικό Απελευθερωτικό Μέτωπο* [What is the National Liberation Front and what it wants]. Athens: Ο Ρήγας [O Rigas].

Hionidou, Violeta. 2006. *Famine and Death in Occupied Greece, 1941-1944*. Cambridge: Cambridge University Press.

Hionidou, Violeta. 2008. Famine in Occupied Greece: Causes and Consequences. In *Bearing Gifts to Greeks. Humanitarian aid to Greece in the 1940s*, ed. Richard Clogg, 653–654. Basingstoke: Palgrave Mackmillan.

Kilian, Jürgen. 2017. *Krieg auf Kosten anderer. Das Reichsministerium der Finanzen und die Wirtschaftliche Mobilisierung Europas für Hitlers Krieg*. Berlin: De Gruyter Oldenbourg.

Κωστελλένος, Γιώργος [Kostellenos, Giorgos], Κουναρης, Εμμανουήλ [Kounaris, Emmanouil], Πετμεζάς, Σωκράτης Δ. [Petmezas, Sokratis D.], Σφακιανάκης, Μιχάλης [Sfakianakis, Michalis], Βασιλίου, Δημήτριος [Vasiliou, Dimitrios]. 2007. *Ακαθάριστο Εγχώριο Προϊόν 1830-1939* [Gross Domestic Product 1830-1939]. Athens: Κέντρο Προγραμματισμού και Οικονομικών Ερευνών [Centre of Planning and Economic Research].

Κούφης, Παύλος [Koufis, Pavlos]. 1982. Η πρώτη εμφάνιση ανταρτών στα Άλωνα Φλώρινας [The first appearance of antartes in Alona Florinas], Εθνική Αντίσταση magazine, συλλογή 30.

Μανουσάκης, Βασίλης Γ. (ed.). [Manousakis, Vasilis (ed.)]. 2019. *Στο Νότιο Προπύργιο του Ράιχ. Ο απολογιστικός φάκελος του γερμανικού οικονομικού επιτελείου για την Ελλάδα της Κατοχής* [In the Southern Bastion of the Reich. The evaluation file of the German economic staff for occupied Greece]. Iraklio: Πανεπιστημιακές Εκδόσεις Κρήτης [Crete University Press].

Μαργαρίτης, Γιώργος [Margaritis, Giorgos]. 1993. *Από την ήττα στην εξέγερση. Ελλάδα: άνοιξη 1941-φθινόπωρο 1942* [From defeat to rebellion. Greece: spring 1941-autumn 1942]. Athens: Ο Πολίτης [O Politis].

Mazower, Mark. 1993. *Inside Hitler's Greece. The experience of Occupation, 1941-44*. New Haven: Yale University Press.

Palerait, Michael. 2000. *The Four Ends of the Greek Hyperinflation of 1941-1946*. Copenhagen: Museum Tusculanum Press, University of Copenhagen.

Σμπαρούνης, Αθανάσιος [Sbarounis, Athanasios]. 1950. *Μελέται και αναμνήσεις εκ του Β΄ Παγκοσμίου Πολέμου* [Studies and memories from the Second World War], Athens: [N.P.].

Σκαλιδάκης, Γιάννης [Skalidakis, Giannis]. 2012. *Πολιτική Επιτροπή Εθνικής Απελευθέρωσης. Ένας τύπος επαναστατικής εξουσίας. Πολιτικές, οικονομικές και κοινωνικές παράμετροι (1944)* [Political Committee of National Liberation. A type of revolutionary power: political, economic and social parameters]. PhD thesis. School of Political Sciences, Aristotle University of Thessaloniki.

Συνοδινός, Ζήσιμος Χ. [Synodinos, Zisimos Ch.]. 2007. Η Μάχη των Χρεωγράφων (Οκτώβριος 1943). Κορυφαία αντιστασιακή πράξη των εργαζομένων στην Εθνική Τράπεζα [The Battle for the Debt Securities (October 1943). Ultimate resistance action of the workers of National Bank. *Αρχειοτάξιο* [Archiotaxio] *(Journal of Contemporary and Social Archives)* 9: 134–160.

Τράπεζα της Ελλάδος [Trapeza tis Ellados – Bank of Greece]. 1948. Έκθεσις του διοικητού της Τραπέζης [Report of the Bank Governor] Athens: *Τράπεζα της Ελλάδος* [Bank of Greece].

Τσολάκογλου Γιώργος Κ. [Tsolakoglou, Georgios K.]. 1959. *Απομνημονεύματα* [Memoirs]. Athens: Akropolis.

Βιδάλης, Κώστας [Vidalis, Kostas] 1944. *Η Μάχη της Σοδειάς – Μάχη Θρίαμβος* [The Battle for the Crops – Thiumpant Battle]. Athens: Ο Ρήγας [O Rigas].

Voglis, Polimeris. 2006. Surviving Hunger: Life in the Cities and the Countryside during the Occupation. In *Surviving Hitler and Mussolini. Daily Life in Occupied Europe*, eds. Robert Gildea, Olivier Wieviorka, and Anette Warring, 16–41. Oxford: Berg.

7 Women's Protests against Colonial Taxation in the Eastern Provinces of Nigeria

Daniel Olisa Iweze

7.1 Introduction

This chapter explores the gendered dimension of women's protest against colonial taxation in November 1929 in the Eastern Region of colonial Nigeria, discussing existing research literature. The women's protest of 1929 has received some attention from scholars and is documented in the literature as an anti-colonial riot by women and as a political protest against the British administration. This chapter first addresses the British perspective: why did the colonial government start to impose taxes on the people of the Eastern Provinces of Nigeria in 1928? Did the colonial authorities plan or intend to extend taxation to women, who until this time had not been taxed in Nigeria? Second, the chapter explores the women's motives to resist: was their protest directed against the imposition of taxes on the province's female inhabitants, against the warrant chief system or against the colonial administration in general? In the latter case: did the women protest against what they perceived as an exclusion from colonial administration compared to their traditional role in society? Third, the chapter aims to inquire into the riot's consequences: did the protests modify colonial taxation and both the colonial and native administration in the Eastern Provinces and if so, in which respect? And what role did the women's protest play in the decolonisation process during the nationalist movement in Nigeria? Fourth, did this protest have an influence on the political position of women in the Eastern Provinces today, as compared to other parts of Nigeria?

The chapter adopts a qualitative approach as the data was collected through close reading of extensive literature on the British colonial government's taxation policy in Nigeria and Africa. As sources, contemporary publications by the colonial government are also examined. The text is structured as follows. The first section presents a brief history of the British colonial government's introduction of taxes in Nigeria. The second section deals with the imposition of direct taxation in the Eastern Region in 1928, while the third section examines the people's resistance to taxation throughout Nigeria. The fourth section focuses on the establishment of the Commission of Inquiry about the riots in 1930 and is followed by a general conclusion.

DOI: 10.4324/9781003333197-10

7.2 Colonial Rule and the Introduction of Colonial Taxation in Nigeria

British colonial administration was introduced in the territory that later became Nigeria in 1900. The area, which had until then been governed by the British "Royal Niger Company", was now divided into three separate units. The first unit was the *Colony and Protectorate of Lagos* which comprised Lagos and the current states in the Western Region, with Lagos defined as the seat of the colonial government. The second unit was formed by the *Protectorate of Southern Nigeria* which comprised the current states in the Eastern Region and Midwest Region, while the *Protectorate of the Northern Region* was the third unit. In 1906, the *Colony and Protectorate of Lagos* were merged with the *Protectorate of Southern Nigeria* to form one administrative unit known as the *Protectorate of Southern Nigeria*, while the Northern Protectorate was administered as a separate political unit. For administrative convenience, each protectorate was divided into provinces and divisions.[1] Each province was administered by a British resident officer who was assisted by other administrative officers in the districts. On the local level, indirect rule was practised: each district was under the control of traditional rulers and chiefs who were responsible to the district officers, who in turn were responsible to the colonial governor through the resident officers.

7.2.1 How Was Colonial Rule Financed?

In the early years of the British colonial administration in Nigeria, the indigenous population was urged to pay financial contributions and provide forced labour for the construction and maintenance of roads and other public works. Local inhabitants were conscripted for the building of railways, for which they were paid fixed and very low wages. This practice was also common in the Portuguese colonies of Angola and Mozambique in East Africa, where colonial authorities used enforced labour to raise revenue and even coerced indigenous people to migrate for this purpose.[2] However, these forms of taxation were neither sustainable nor sufficient because of the colonial government's growing demand for revenue. Additionally, growing abuses and corrupt practices among members of the administration triggered the people's resistance to forced labour. Pressure due to public opinion in England and the media elsewhere in Europe was one further reason why forced labour was finally condemned by the colonial office or central government in London. But relinquishing tax revenue was not an option for the colonial powers either. The British Empire justified colonial rule with the argument that each of its colonies in Africa would be made self-supporting in providing revenues to cover the costs of administration.[3] Thus, new forms of taxation had to be developed, also in British Nigeria.

1 Utuk (1975, 13–14); Falola and Heaton (2008).
2 Alexopoulou and Juif (2017, 220).
3 Gardner 2012; Bush and Maltby (2004); Frankema (2011, 2019); Frankema and Booth (2020).

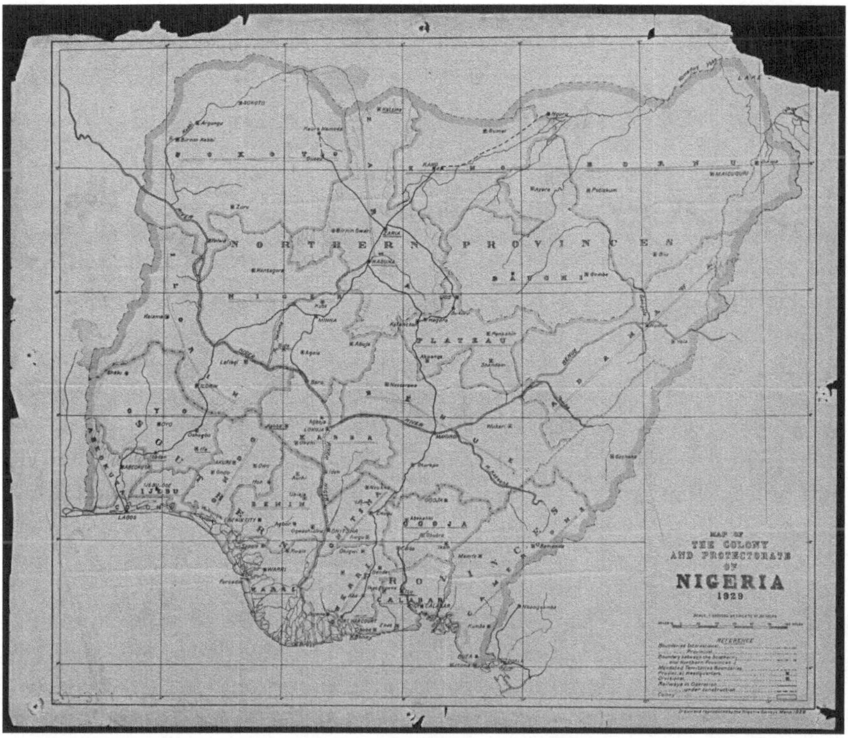

Figure 7.1 Map of the Colony and Protectorate of Nigeria 1929

Source: Drawn and reproduced by the Nigeria Surveys, March 1929, BM Archives Basel Mission/ Mission 2021, Public Domain, https://www.bmarchives.org/items/show/100201454#, accessed Oct. 24, 2022.

Frederick Lugard, the first Governor-General of the British colonial administration and architect of the indirect rule system in Nigeria, paved the way for direct taxation by legitimising it as a boon for the colonised. He praised it as one of the veritable features of extending civilisation to uncivilised regions.[4] In his 1922 book, *The Dual Mandate in British Tropical Africa*, Lugard justified taxation as a right bestowed on a sovereign power in a colonised territory. Emphasising the central role of taxation in stimulating the development of colonies, he legitimised taxation as a means of self-reliance for the colonised subjects: "no tax, no treasury, no self-government".[5] Lugard's approach to taxation was based on the idea that taxation was an innovation that would take the colonies on "the path of progress and civilization".[6] He emphasised the role of taxation in modernisation when he claimed that tax

4 Abdulkadir (2014, 92).
5 Lugard (1922, 70).
6 Ibid., 167

was of "moral benefit to the people by stimulating industry and production".[7] He believed that taxation would develop the economy by encouraging the use of currency and providing revenue which could be used for roads, railways and other public works.

Inhabitants of Nigeria, however, referred to the historic US-American tax rebels and revolutionaries who had argued that colonial taxation was akin to subjugation and enslavement, and that taxation without representation was illegal.[8] Furthermore, local Nigerian inhabitants also argued that taxation was alien to their customs and traditional practices. So conflicts were inescapable when taxation was put into practice.

Governor Lugard enacted the Native Revenue (Amendment) Ordinance in April 1927, which provided the legal framework for the introduction of taxation in the Northern Province of Nigeria and was later extended to the Western Province.[9] The Eastern Province was, at first, exempted because it was considered not yet ripe for taxation. Despite the provisional disclaimer, Lugard only waited for an appropriate moment to introduce direct taxation in the Eastern Provinces as well. To further this aim, he could rely on a census of all the men in the Eastern Provinces that Graeme Thompson, then the Divisional Officer at Bende, had in November 1924 decided to perform in order to gather tax-relevant data. The administration did not balk at lies to ensure a smooth process: during the census of the Oloko clan in 1926, the people were told that the procedure had nothing to do with taxation. Contrary to this promise, direct taxation was introduced among the Oloko in Owerri Province in 1927.

The Native Revenue Ordinance of 1927 dictated the collection of direct taxes in the whole of Nigeria, ultimately also including the Eastern Provinces. A capitation and an income tax were imposed on every male adult from the age of 16 and above. This involved the headcount of adult males per hut and the assessment of their economic wealth in each village and district. A village was marked out as a tax unit and placed under a warrant chief or village head who served as a tax agent. The tax to be paid was between four and seven shillings per person.[10]

7 Ibid., 66.

8 Osgood (1898); Bell (2013).

9 Naanen (2006, 70).

10 Afigbo (1972, 232); Ekundare (1973, 125). It is difficult to compare this amount with the average cost for foodstuff, because the colonial administration was able to gather such statistics: "It is impossible to give any useful figure for the cost of foodstuffs, as food is not sold by weight, but by arbitrary measures or by number. [...] Prices vary somewhat from day to day and from market to market". However, the average living costs in Nigeria in 1935 were estimated by the colonial government to vary between 2 and 4 pennies a day. The yearly taxes of five to seven shillings of 1928/29 (1 shilling = 12 pennies) thus amounted to between 15 and 42 times the average daily living costs. See Annual Report on the Social and Economic Progress of the People of Nigeria, (1935), published by His Majesty's Stationery Office, 1936, 59. However, this report of 1935 does not give any fixed amount of taxes per person but reports that in the Northern Provinces "each man pays according to his income" (91).

A lump sum was demanded from each village sub-unit, according to the nominal roll or the number of taxable adult males in that unit. The sum expected from each village was declared publicly and the sum expected from each household was made known to the village head or warrant chief. Then the chiefs distributed the levy according to the income capacity of each individual. The head of the compound collected the tax from members of his household and handed it over to the warrant chief/village head,[11] who in turn remitted it to the district officer. But it turned out that no one, including the village heads and elders, wanted to pay a progressive rate. Hence the tax burden was distributed equally and thus ultimately became a poll tax.[12]

In the Northern and Western Provinces, the 1927 Ordinance was applied without major incidents or resistance, while it met with stiff resistance in the Calabar and Owerri Divisions of the Eastern Region. The different responses and reactions of the colonised resulted from the pre-existing political institutions in the different parts of the colony. The Northern Provinces had, in pre-colonial times, been ruled by a centralised emirate system with a long tradition of taxation and tribute payment in accordance with Islamic law.[13] Therefore, forced labour had worked well in the northern part of the colony, where the British gave directives to the emirs, who passed them down to the district heads, ward heads and their subjects. The Western Provinces also had applied a centralised political system. Their large political units were ruled by Obas, the paramount rulers, who were assisted by palace chiefs who passed down the colonial administration's instructions to their subjects. In these two territories, the introduction of direct taxation was an easy task, in contrast to the Eastern Provinces of Nigeria with their completely different pre-colonial democratic system with no tax or tribute traditions. Common duties in this traditional system had been financed through the provision of free labour and services for the development of common goods.[14]

7.3 Introduction of Direct Taxation in the Eastern Provinces in 1928

On 1 April 1928, the British Legislative Council extended the Native Revenue Ordinance to the Eastern Provinces of Nigeria and introduced direct taxation there. The lieutenant governor of Nigeria, Fitz Herbert Ruxton, delegated the colonial resident officer, William Edgar Hunt, to explain to the people of Eastern Nigeria the provisions and objectives of the new ordinance in advance, showing that the colonial administration feared that problems might arise.[15] In December 1928, the collection of capitation

11 See Onwumere (2002).
12 Naanen (2006, 75), Afigbo (1972, 231–232)
13 Naanen (2006, 72–73).
14 Afigbo (1972, 228).
15 James (2018, 20).

taxes on male subjects was started in the four provinces of Owerri, Onitsha, Ogoja and Calabar. The British administration was assisted in the collection process by warrant chiefs who had been appointed since 1916 by the colonial government, and who were intended to play a decisive role in consolidating colonial taxation in the region. It is hardly a surprise that in the eyes of the population the warrant chiefs were corrupt and inefficient.[16]

The warrant chief system had been created after the conquest of Igboland in 1916 to serve as an instrument of pacification and to further consolidation of the British colonial administration. Those who were appointed or selected were not the traditional leaders of their people. The warrant chiefs comprised different types. A first group consisted of strong, energetic and promising men who could comply with the directives of the colonial government. A second category of men was arbitrarily appointed by the colonial government without prior consultation with the people who they were supposed to rule. A third group was selected through consultation with the people and the village assemblies, while a fourth category comprised men who were considered by the local communities to be social misfits. They were selected by the communities hoping that this would lead to them either being killed or being sold into slavery by the colonial officers.[17] Apart from serving as agents in the collection of taxes, the warrant chiefs performed other roles by making frequent visits to the district headquarters to obtain directives from the district commissioners and reporting to them.[18] The collection of the first tax in 1928 was executed without serious disturbance, although there were a few areas where the supposed taxpayers resisted. This was the case in the Ihiala court area, in the provinces of Agbaja in the Enugu Division; in Oji River, Abakiliki, Achi and Afikpo in the Abakiliki Division; in Ezza, Izzi, Calabar and Ogoja. The people in these areas at first refused to pay any taxes but were later coerced by the colonial police to do so. The colonial officer negotiated and persuaded the people to pay ten pounds per village, while the tax evaders were arrested, tried and punished.[19] Resistance or refusal to pay tax was considered as a revolt against the colonial authorities.

7.4 Resistance to Colonial Taxation All over the Colony

All over Nigeria, this first round of direct taxation was quite a success in the eyes of the British colonial administration. By the last quarter of the 1928 tax year, the sum of £365,000[20] had been collected in the Eastern Provinces, according to other data £357,267, against the colonial government's expected

16 Afigbo (1972, 59).
17 Ibid., 59–63.
18 Ibid., 70.
19 Ibid., 232–235.
20 Ozigbo (1999, 54).

sum of £288,630.[21] The tax revenue was divided in half between the native courts and the British authorities in London, which held irremediably to the aim of covering all the costs of colonial government from within the colony. But only a small part of the revenue which stayed in the country was used for the maintenance of roads and improvement of navigable waterways.[22]

Although the collection of direct taxes started quite successfully by and large, far from all supposed taxpayers complied with their tax duties. Whereas some people paid taxes without resistance or after initial opposition that could easily be suppressed, others reacted by adopting tax evasion, tax avoidance or tax resistance. One widespread practice of tax avoidance in the whole colony involved the under-declaration of taxpayer's economic wealth and income to the tax collectors and/or warrant chiefs. Another strategy consisted of hiding in the bushes or forests during the day and coming out only at night in order not to be assessed by the tax collectors. Others emigrated from their homeland villages to areas, districts or regions with lower tax rates. This was the case in the Kano emirate in the north where the tax rates were extraordinarily high,[23] aimed at skimming revenue from the traditionally prosperous trade route and fertile crops. Many who were liable to colonial taxation preferred to migrate to neighbouring areas with lower taxes, such as Katsina, Daura or Dutse. Others migrated southwards to Nupe, Bida, Ilorin Bauchi and other parts of the Northern Region and even to the neighbouring communities in French Niger where they established permanent settlements. In Rano, some farmers had to sell their farmlands in order to pay taxes and those who could not pay migrated to Wamba in Nassarawa Province. In Igalaland in the Northern Province, the high tax rate compelled many people to seek a new livelihood in the Western Region where they began to work in the cocoa plantations.[24] The British colonial government did nothing to curb the tax-induced population shift in the Northern Provinces. Instead, the colonial authorities ensured that captured tax evaders and defaulters were punished through forced payment of taxes in arrears, the confiscation of their property and livestock, or brutal flogging.[25]

Such harsh measures by the British colonial government caused reactions which, in some areas, escalated into violence in the following years. In the Southern Province, especially in Lagos where there was a long tradition of

21 Afigbo (1972, 49).

22 Native courts were established to administer "native law and custom" and to act as final arbiters of all kinds of disputes, disagreements or misunderstandings, but in practice, the procedure of the native court was modified by the British mainly to suit the colonial officer's interests, see Afigbo (1966, 541). The people perceived the native court as "native" only in name because its administration was untraditional and contrary to the customary laws of the people.

23 Taxes were so high in Kano because it had the largest population and was the most prosperous emirate in the Northern Provinces of Nigeria. It was also a flourishing emporium of trade and commerce during the trans-Saharan trade. It had fertile soils that yielded abundant food crops such as maize, millet, cotton and groundnut, see Abdullahi (2012).

24 Abah and Adihikon (2015, 176); see also Abah and Adihikon (2020).

25 See Abdulkadir (2014, 163); Abah and Adihikon (2015, 179).

anti-colonial resistance against taxation and tributes, the enforcement of the 1927 Ordinance led to widespread anti-tax protests. As early as 1908, the population of Lagos had protested against the introduction of a new water scheme, which was intended to replace traditional means of water supply and was linked to newly introduced taxes on water.[26] Anti-tax protests in the Western Provinces of Nigeria had also taken place in Oyo in 1916 and in Abeokuta in 1918. The people had protested against the British colonial authorities giving enormous powers to the *Alafin* (ruler) of the town of Oyo and the *Alake* (ruler) of the city of Abeokuta, who were assigned to collect taxes in areas outside their own territories, to enforce tax compliance and to punish defaulters.[27] These rulers had even gone to the extent of publicly stripping both men and women naked to ascertain whether they had reached taxable age.[28] Their violent treatment and humiliation of women had further alienated the people from these traditional rulers in Yorubaland of the Western Region, who had become intermediaries of colonial power. The people's discontent with the traditional rulers led to the destruction of colonial infrastructure such as telegraph and railway lines. Anti-tax revolts would later take place in the Dekina, Ankpa, Ofante and Biraidu parts of Igalaland in 1940.[29] Again tax defaulters were arrested, tortured and imprisoned. Between 1925 and 1935, the number of reported cases of the imprisonment of tax evaders and protesters, both male and female, increased considerably.[30]

When direct taxation was introduced, the situation became more tense in many regions, and the British tried to suppress the waves of dissent by arresting, charging and jailing some of the village heads of the Akpanya in the Igalaland Division of the Northern Province who served as tax collectors and were well known for their unscrupulousness. Those that were jailed were warned not to return to their district after serving jail terms because they had to fear retaliation from their former inferiors. Other tax collectors were dismissed in 1929 for inefficiency in tax collection and were replaced with other village heads.[31]

A gender aspect of the protests can be observed in several Nigerian regions and on different occasions. Resistance against taxation was more persistent in those areas of Nigeria where not only men but also women were liable to taxation. In the Igala Division of the Northern Province, which shared a border with Northern Igboland,[32] the Akpanya women in the Adoru district

26 Oladejo (2019, 80).
27 See Falola and Heaton (2008, 133).
28 Ibid., 133.
29 Abah and Adihikon (2015, 177–178).
30 Ibid., 178; Abdulkadir (2014, 163).
31 Vaaseh and Abah (2016).
32 In Igboland, there was already an Aba women's tax protest in 1929. The protest was quelled by the colonial police and some ringleaders were arrested and detained for two days before they were released. The British colonial administration promised to use the occasion to review the tax duty for women, but the result of this review was that women in the area continued to pay tax equivalent with their income. This resulted in many Igbo women migrating out of the area to avoid taxation, see Abdulkadir (2014).

were not only taxed, but over the course of time, the incidence of the tax for women was even increased, leading to the Akpanya tax revolt in 1940. The anti-tax protest was the Igala women's reaction against increased taxation amid the sharp fall in global prices of palm oil and palm kernels which were the mainstay of their income and economic wealth. During these protests, allegedly over 600 women from the Akpanya and Amaka zones of the Adoru district marched to the office of the divisional officer in Nsukka chanting war songs[33] to declare their discontent with the implemented tax system.[34] This protest of 1940 was described in the literature rather recently but had a famous predecessor: the women's tax riot of 1929.

7.5 The Women's Protest in the Eastern Provinces in 1929

Unlike in the Northern and Western Provinces, where in some areas a poll tax was imposed on both men and women, in the Eastern Provinces of Nigeria, only men were taxed and compelled to pay under the 1927 Ordinance. This was linked to the region's decentralised political system based on village democracy and representative local administration. However, women bore an indirect share of the tax burden on men through supporting their husbands and sons in paying taxes and upkeeping their families. And precisely because women already shared the tax burden on men, "imposing a tax upon women themselves was more than they could bear", as Korieh has observed.[35]

7.5.1 Causes of the Women's Protest

The causes of the women's protest of 1929 have been an issue of vivid debate among scholars. Afigbo (1972) and Mba (1992) believe it was caused by socio-political factors, while Ekundare (1973), Korieh (2001) and others argue that the triggers were mostly economic. Both perspectives are convincing. On the one hand, the newly appointed warrant chiefs were extremely unpopular, especially amongst women. Before the advent of British colonial rule, Igbo women and others in the region played complementary roles to men and were influential in socio-political institutions and self-reliant in the economic sphere. Women's economic and political significance was undermined by the British colonial government because colonialism reinforced the male patriarchy, thereby making women feel inferior and subordinate to men. Nina Mba asserts that "women were invisible within the colonial

33 Nsukka was inhabited by Igala and a significant Igbo population. The British authorities appointed Igala men as warrant chiefs in Nsukka which was administered as part of the Onitsha Province. The proximity of the Adoru district to Nsukka made the Akpanya women march in protest to the colonial officer there.

34 Vaaseh and Abah (2016).

35 Korieh (2001, 150); Afigbo (1972, 239).

administration".[36] This reinforced women's resentment against colonial administration structures. Thus, the colonial warrant chief system introduced by the British became the symbolic object of female resistance.

On the other hand, the harsh British tax policy has to be contextualised within the worldwide agrarian crisis preceding and introducing the Great Depression of the late 1920s and early 1930s. Due to advanced technology, such as the application of fertilisers, agricultural production had grown massively with the consequence that world market prices for agrarian goods like coffee and palm oil, and – to a certain extent – also cotton, dropped heavily in the second half of the 1920s. This caused protests in a number of British colonies, also in India. In Nigeria, especially palm products like oil were affected by the price declines, as were export goods in general – with negative consequences for the farmers who based their economic livelihoods on this crop. The ordinary population's incomes shrank by between 70 and 80%,[37] while the prices of imported goods like salt, kerosene, soap, machinery and textiles increased massively, also due to increasing import duties. This caused a reduction in the consumption of these imported goods. Between 1932 and 1934, the consumption of kerosene dropped by 58%, of salt by 26% and of soap by 57%. The volume of imported textile materials dropped by 39%.[38] Due to their declining agricultural incomes, the inhabitants of the colony could no longer afford to buy these everyday products. Thus, according to Korieh, "the women protested against tax imposition because it was a threat to the agricultural basis of their economy. It was a matter of survival in an increasingly precarious situation".[39] In this severe and tense situation, when the population expected a reduction of tax rates or even a complete lifting of taxes, rumours about the new, additional taxation of women had a telling impact.

7.5.2 The Uprising

In 1929, the aforementioned warrant chiefs undertook a new census to count not only men, but also women and domestic animals. The inhabitants of the Eastern Regions interpreted this – erroneously – as a signal that the taxation of female subjects was planned.[40] It was the warrant chief's misleading transfer of information and their misinterpretation of colonial directives that caused the rumour which mobilised a purely female protest movement in various parts of the Eastern Region in November 1929.[41]

An unlucky personal constellation among the British colonial administration might have contributed to their insensitive behaviour and the

36 Mba (1992, 77), as cited in Korieh (2001, 121).
37 Abdulkadir (2014, 163).
38 Ekundare (1973, 211–213). See Abdulkadir (2014, 143).
39 Korieh (2001, 162).
40 Ibid., 148.
41 For more details, Afigbo, Naaen (2006), James (2018).

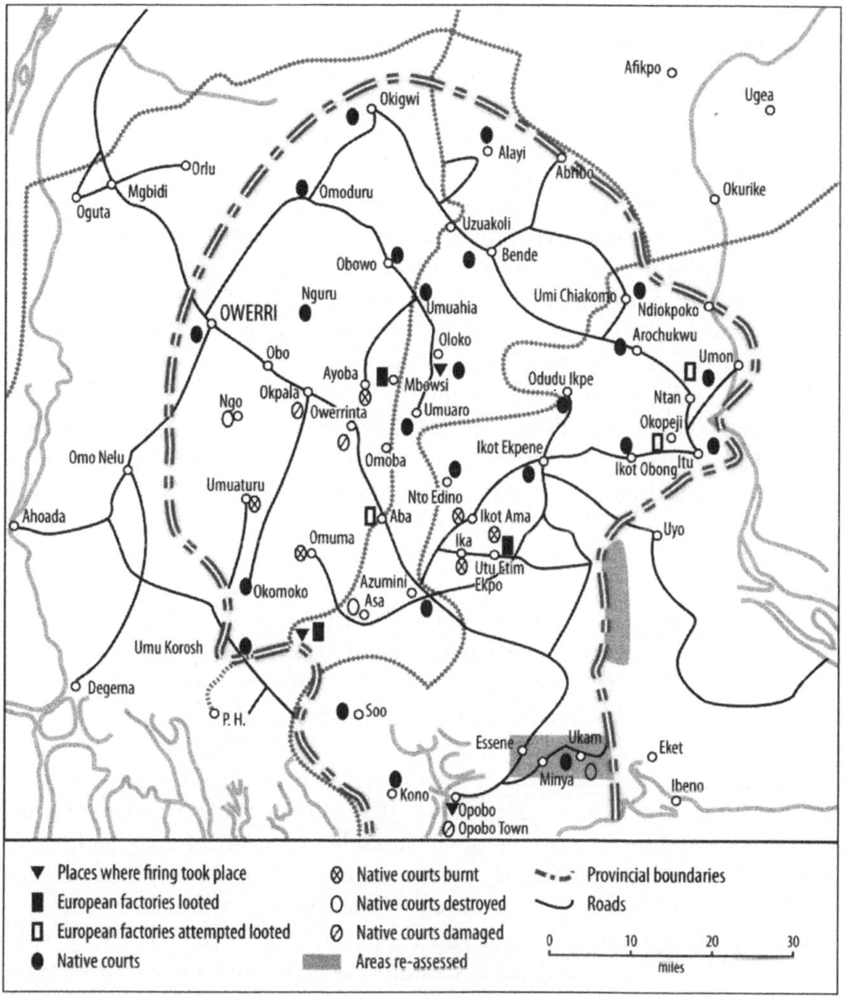

Figure 7.2 Map of Events – Women's War, 1929

Source: Falola and Paddock 2011, p. x. Reprinted with permission of publisher.

subsequently tense situation. The district officer of the Bende Division A. L. Weir was on leave and had been substituted by an assistant officer, John Cook. The inexperienced Cook checked the results of the 1928 tax collection and concluded that the revenue was too low. On 14 October 1929, he thus instructed the warrant chiefs to conduct a new and more comprehensive count of the number of taxpayers, their wives, children and livestock. The announcement of this extended census was disseminated to all the districts by the colonial officers from a car mounted with loudspeakers. Native gongs, the traditional means of communication, were also used to spread the news.

The instructions also reached Chief Ori and Chief Ananamba in Oloko in Bende Division. They therefore announced a meeting with the tribal elders in Oloko. At this meeting, Chief Ananamba gave the people the impression that the census's aim was to tax all registered persons.[42] This interpretation seemed quite convincing given the earlier experiences of the population with the colonial government: in the Oloko case, a census had preceded the introduction of direct taxation even though the government had previously denied such an intention. With these experiences in mind, the warrant chiefs misinterpreted their orders and misinformed the population, explaining that the purpose of counting the women was to tax them.[43] The rumour that the colonial government planned to impose taxes on women spread rapidly, also to other parts of Igboland and Ibiobioland.

The women's protest broke out on 16 November 1929, at Oloko in the Bende Division of Owerri Province. As elsewhere in the region, Chief Okugo, the warrant chief of the Oloko native court, had been instructed by the assistant district officer of Bende to conduct a recount of the adult males in the villages for a fresh tax register. As elsewhere, rumours had already been spread that the purpose of the recount was the taxation of women. Chief Okugo had delegated Mark Emeruwa, a local mission teacher, to execute the census. When Emeruwa, who was also in charge of the tax register, tried to register a woman for the census, this was the spark that finally ignited the riot.[44]

In his research of the riot, Raphael James (2018) collected oral data from the sons, grandchildren and relatives of the women that led the protests at Oloko. He thus gives a very detailed description of the situation. The altercation between the two wives of Mr Ojim and Emeruwa, the tax collector, triggered the protest on 16 November 1929. Emeruwa went to Mr Ojim's house to conduct a headcount of his household members and to collect a supposedly pending tax debt. Mr Ojim's younger wife, Nwanyeruwa, argued that her husband had no money to pay the tax since he was not an employee of the colonial government. Emeruwa approached the elder wife to pay for her husband, but Nwanyeruwa reiterated that women had never been taxed before and should not be taxed now.[45]

The dispute attracted other women in the neighbourhood and Nwanyeruwa informed them that Emeruwa had requested her to pay tax in their husband's place and that if she refused he threatened to beat her up. She further informed the other women that Emeruwa was acting on behalf of Chief Okeugo, and that the warrant chief planned to use the colonial police to seize the property of those who would not pay taxes. The women did not allow Emeruwa to tell his own version of what had transpired and he finally

42 Afigbo (1966, 552); James (2018, 7).
43 Ozigbo (1999, 54).
44 Ibid., 54.
45 James (2018, 4); Afigbo (1966, 553).

escaped to Chief Okeugo's house.[46] The angry village women assembled at Chief Okeugo's house to demand Emeruwa and to "sit on" him – a traditional way for Igbo women to fight injustice, usually in the form of domestic violence.[47] The women thus utilised existing female agency to fight potential male oppression. Okeugo pleaded with the aggrieved women and reassured them that there was no plan to tax women and domestic animals, but they rejected all his entreaties and demanded his cap, the symbol of his authority. It was then that the police officers shot in the air to disperse the crowd and in the process some women were injured. The women dispatched "palm fronts" to other surrounding villages which attracted over 10,000 women to Oloko on 24 November 1929.[48] The riot quickly spread to Aba, Okigwe, Opobo and Abak in Calabar Province and other parts of the Igbo and Ibiobio lands. Women from the ethnic groups of Igbo, Ibibio, Andoni, Ogoni, Bonny and Opobo participated.

On 24 November, women from Bende, Aba, Owerri and Ikot-Ikpene Divisions assembled at Chief Okeugu's residence to "sit on" him. They danced around Chief Okeugo's compound, chanting war songs, insulting his manhood and declaring their grievances against him, and vandalised his hut by plastering it with mud. The "sitting on" Chief Okeugo lasted over a month, during which time they undermined his powers, denounced him to the colonial officers as illegitimate and relinquished him to dishonour and desecration. The Igbo folkloric songs and dances were greatly enriched during the protest. Women composed songs embodying their grievances, and they chanted traditional male war songs like *Nzogbu Nzogbu, Enyimba Enyi* ("We are elephants, marching to the battle, crushing obstacles on our way"), a song that became very popular during the protest.[49]

On 2 December 1929, more women from other villages arrived at Oloko. The protests were now led by Ikonanya Nwanyiukwu Enyia, Nwannedia, Nwugo and Pelinah Nuji, who later were stylised as heroines. The women protesters, though unarmed, destroyed colonial property, stations, native

46 Afigbo, 237; James (2018, 4).

47 Ozigbo (1999, 54). To "sit on a man", the women of a community would come together and dance circles around the man who had disrespected a woman and sing to the spirits, see Matera, Bastian, Kent, Kingsley Kent (2012, 1). This was done to force the man to reflect on what he had done. They never touched him nor spoke to him, but simply sang and chanted their demands for, essentially, an agreement that he would change his ways and do the right thing. They would sing all day to disrupt the man's daily activities and force him to acknowledge their presence. Sometimes the women burnt down the man's hut. This ritual of "sitting on a man" could last for days, depending on the man's willingness to respond to the women's demands, Uzondu (2015, 184f).

48 Mba (1992, 77); Hagen nd, 4. "Palm fronts", women raising the palm of their hand, were sent as messengers to the neighbouring villages to invite other women to come and join the protest against warrant chiefs. Through this passing of the palm, women created a chain of networks that helped to mobilise women in Oloko.

49 Uzondu (2015, 200).

courts and infrastructure. But the riot was brutally quelled by the British colonial troops. The fights left about fifty women dead and an equal number wounded. However, the protests continued to be directed mainly against the hated warrant chief, Okeugo. The assistant officer, John Cook, who had ordered the census, now received complaints from some women demanding that the warrant chief should be dismissed because of his disrespectful behaviour. Okeugo was in fact very quickly put on trial at the Bende court and on 4 December 1929 was dismissed and sentenced to two years in prison. His trial was witnessed by about 4,000 women who requested and were given his cap, the symbol of his office and power.[50]

7.6 The Establishment of Commissions of Inquiry in 1930

With the return of normality to the troubled areas of Oloko, Aba and Umuahia in Owerri Province and Ikot Ekpene in Calabar Province, in January and February 1930, the colonial authorities set up two commissions. The aim was to investigate the causes of the protests, the legitimacy of the warrant chiefs and the workability of the indirect rule system in the Eastern Region, and to make recommendations concerning its reform. The commission investigating the protest in Calabar Province comprised William Gray and Henry Backwall, while a six-man commission led by Chief Justice Donald Kingdom investigated the protest in Aba.[51] After collecting testimonies from the women protesters, in the "Notes of Evidence", the commissions of inquiry requested the district officers to commission an anthropological study on the history and culture of Igbo societies in order to understand the traditional political and judicial institutions and to recommend how the tribes could govern themselves in a traditional manner. The British government anthropologist for Northern Nigeria, Charles Kingsley Meek, was commissioned to carry out the study.[52]

The women felt they were struggling for survival, and they expressed their frustrations to the Aba commission in the following words: "How could women who have no means themselves to buy food or clothing pay tax? How could we pay tax? We depend upon our husbands; we cannot buy food or clothes ourselves: how shall we get money to pay tax?"[53] The Aba commission's report attested these economic reasons for the uprising. Taxation of men continued but was reformed according to people's ability to pay, following the commission's recommendation.

50 Ibid., 199.
51 Ozigbo (1999, 56).
52 Nigeria Commission of Inquiry appointed to inquire into the Disturbances in the Calabar and Owerri Provinces, December, 1929. 1930; Ozigbo (1999, 56).
53 Nigeria (1930, 12) as cited in Korieh (2001, 150–151).

The Aba commission report also condemned the indirect rule system applied by the British colonisers in the Eastern Region and recommended the reinstatement of the traditional system with its handed-down socio-political institutions. It revealed that the women's discontent with the warrant chiefs was one of the causes of the protests. Based on the commission's recommendations,[54] in 1933, the new colonial Governor of Nigeria, Donald Cameron (appointed in 1931), enacted the Native Authority Ordinance and Native Courts Ordinance which reinstalled the traditional structure of the native treasuries and native courts. The region's inhabitants thus were allowed to choose their leaders autonomously and mainly appointed the heads of villages and kindred as chairpersons on the native authority councils and native courts, amongst them also women. The protest therefore paved the way for women's participation in the governance of their communities. The British realised that removing the Igbo and Ibiobio women from their traditional positions of power was inefficient, because they would resist the new male-dominated warrant chief system even more decidedly than their men did, and would never agree to be subjected to those men who drew legitimisation from their cooperation with the colonial power. Thus women were appointed to the native courts for the first time in the history of the British colonial administration in Africa. A prominent woman leader who was appointed to this task was the so-called Miss Chinwe, the only female member of the 13-strong Nguru Mabaise native court. In the Umuakpo native court area, three of 30 members were women, while at the Okuala native court, the nine members now included one woman. The only exception was in Oloko, where the protest had begun. Here the British authorities did not appoint any women to the native court. Uzondu considers that the British deliberately wanted to punish Oloko women for instigating the protest that not only engulfed most of the Eastern Region but also undermined colonial authority.[55]

However, until 1935, different forms of native administration emerged in the south-eastern part of Nigeria, most of them administered by traditional clan or village councils.[56] Further recommendations of the commission of inquiry were implemented through into the 1940s and an enlightened system of local government administration was introduced as the basis for reforming local government in the region. Women claimed their positions in the reformed system. One famous example is Ahebi Ugbabe of Enugu Ezike from the Nsukka area who was appointed a village "headman" and later a warrant chief and then became a member of the native authority court in colonial Nigeria in the 1930s.[57] Ahebi Ugbabe later even became the "King" of Enugu-Ezike and in this function upset gendered politics in the

54 Ozigbo (1999, 56–57).

55 Uzondu (2015, 199).

56 Afigbo (1972, 133); Ekundare (1973, 126).

57 Uzondu (2015, 199).

community. As a female king, Ahebi Ugbabe had the reputation of displaying female-masculine power which surpassed all male political authorities in the community.[58]

This is an indication of how the women's tax resistance produced heroines and influential women leaders in the Western and Eastern Provinces of Nigeria who then played an immense role in the Nigerian independence movement in the 1940s and 1950s. Some of them, including Fummilayo Ransome-Kuti, attended the constitutional conferences in London to agitate for independence with other Nigerian political leaders. The women played pivotal roles that led to the formation of women's wings of major political parties where they articulated their interests between 1950 and 1960. Among the leading women on the National Council of Nigeria Citizens (NCNC) was Margret Ekpo, who was elected to the National Executive Council of NCNC. She served as a special member of the Eastern House of Chiefs in 1959 and as the Vice-President of the NCNC Women's Wing of Eastern Nigeria. Another prominent woman was Janet Mokelu who served as the Secretary of the Eastern Region NCNC Women's Association. She was also appointed as a special member of the House of Chiefs. Both women were elected to the Eastern House of Assembly in 1961.[59] Although these women and others had not participated in the women's protest at Oloko, the 1929 women's tax protest later inspired their and other women's political participation. Additionally, the women's tax resistance largely inspired a generation of lgbo women to engage in various professions as lawyers, medical doctors, educationists, diplomats and so on.

7.7 Conclusion

The British colonial officers had not planned to tax the women in 1929. However, female opposition to taxation was triggered by a downturn in the economy caused by the sharp fall in the prices of palm oil and palm kernel and worsened by the effects of the Great Economic Depression of the 1920s. The women also objected to the governance structure that excluded them and were opposed to the creation of warrant chiefs by the colonial administration. Protests against the supposed taxability of women were used to articulate and popularise older grievances, and the traditional ritual of "sitting on" the chief was used for this purpose. Even if the protest was violently suppressed, the women's tax riot of 1929 proved to be extraordinarily successful in the long run. First, taxation of women was never implemented in the Eastern Provinces of Nigeria. Second, even if the women's anti-tax protests did not result in the cancellation of men's taxation, the principle of capacity to pay was adopted and

58 For full details of the History of Ahebi Ugbabe, see Nwando Achebe (2011); Ogechukwu Ezekwem (2016).

59 Allen 1962. As cited in Uzondu (2015, 201).

became the main element of the Eastern Nigeria tax system due to the Native Authority Ordinance. Furthermore, taxes were henceforth collected by the traditional leaders. Taxation nonetheless remained a focal point of conflict. In 1949, the average daily incarceration rate in the three prisons in Igalaland for those who attempted to revolt against taxes was 119.95 for men and 8.60 for women. In the following year, the number decreased to 109.8 for men, but increased to 19.8 for women. By 1951, it had jumped to 134.31 for men and was 11.76 for women.[60] The reasons adduced for the increase in the number of those imprisoned were, among other things, people's inability to pay taxes due to the high rates coupled with the general lack of economic means to raise the money in European currency for the sole purpose of paying taxes. Third, the warrant chief system was abolished and replaced by a traditional system of rule by the village and community elders. Fourth, the women got a voice by choosing qualified men in their communities to appoint them as members of the native courts in the 1930s.[61] Fifth, some women were even chosen for political functions, so that the protest has to be understood as a significant watershed that enhanced their ascendency into political authority in the reformed native authority system from the 1930s to 1950s. Finally, the 1929 uprising established a tradition of anti-colonial tax resistance that inspired further uprisings in the 1930s, 1940s and 1950s in the region and in the Igala district of the Northern Provinces of Nigeria.

References

Aba Commission Report 337/300. Cited in Korieh, Chima J. 2001. The Invisible Farmer? Women, Gender, and Colonial Agricultural Policy in the Igbo Region of Nigeria, c. 1913-1954. *African Economic History* 21: 117–162.

Abah, Danladi and Adihikon, Tanko A. 2015. A Historical Prognosis of British Colonial Taxation in Twentieth-century Igala Land of Nigeria. *DEGEL: The Journal of the Faculty of Arts and Islamic Studies* 11: 161–181.

Abah, Danladi and Adihikon, Tanko A. 2020. Avoidance, Evasion and Refusal: Women Tax Resistance Movement in Colonial Igalaland of Northern Nigeria, 1900-1960. *Lapai Journal of Humanities* 11(5): 54–80.

Abdulkadir, Mohammed S. 2014. *An Economic History of Igalaland Central Nigeria: 1896-1939.* Zaria: Ahmadu Bello University.

Abdullahi, Fatima. 2012. *Economic History of Rano in the 20th century: A Study of the Administration of Colonial Taxation in Rano District, Kano Emirate 1903-1960.* Saarbrücken: LAP Lambert Academic Publishing.

Achebe, Nwando. 2011. *The Female King of Colonial Nigeria: Ahebi Ugbabe.* Bloomington, IN: Indiana University Press.

Afigbo, Adiele E. 1966. Revolution and Reaction in Eastern Nigeria: 1900-1929: (The Background to the Women's Riot of 1929). *Journal of History Society of Nigeria* 3(3): 539–557.

60 Abah and Adihikon (2015, 178).

61 Uzondu (2015, 199).

Afigbo, Adiele E. 1972. *The Warrant Chiefs: Indirect Rule in Southeastern Nigeria, 1891-1929.* London: Longman Group Ltd.

Alexopoulou, Kleoniki and Juif, Dácil. 2017. *Colonial State Formation Without Integration: Tax Capacity and Labour Regimes in Portuguese Mozambique (1890s–1970s)*, Cambridge: Cambridge University Press.

Annual Report on the Social and Economic Progress of the People of Nigeria. 1935. No. 1763, published by His Majesty's Stationery Office, Nigeria 1936, https://wellcomecollection.org/works/u85cdc3x. Accessed November 22nd, 2021.

Bell, J. L. 2013. No Taxation without Representation Part 1". *Journal of the American Revolution*, https://allthingsliberty.com/2013/05/no-taxation-without-representation-part-1/.

Bush, Barbara and Josephine Maltby. 2004. Taxation in West Africa: transforming the colonial subject into the "governable person." *Critical Perspectives on Accounting* 15: 5–34.

Ekundare, R.Olufemi. 1973. *Economic History of Nigeria: 1860-1960.* London: Methuen and Co.

Ezekwem, Ogechukwu. 2016. Review of The Female King of Colonial Nigeria: Ahebi Ugbabe, (review no. 1393), http://www.history.ac.uk/reviews/review/1393. Accessed September 5, 2020.

Falola, Toyin and Paddock, Adam. 2011. *The Women War of 1929: A History of Anti-Colonial Resistance in Eastern Nigeria.* Durham: Carolina Academic Press.

Falola, Toyin and Heaton, Matthew M. 2008. (eds.) *A History of Nigeria.* New York: Cambridge University Press.

Frankema, Ewout and Booth, Anne (eds.). 2020. "*Fiscal Capacity and the Colonial State in Asia and Africa, C. 1850-1960*". Cambridge Studies in Economic History. New York: Cambridge University Press.

Frankema, Ewout. 2011. Colonial taxation and government spending in British Africa, 1880-1940: Maximizing revenue or minimizing effort? *Exploration in Economic History* 48: 136–149.

Gardner, Leigh A. 2012. *Taxing Africa: The Political Economy of British Imperialism.* Oxford: Oxford University Press.

James, Raphael, 2018. "The Aba Women Riot of the 1929", (Part One) Covering Oloko Women Uprising Like Never Before, https://www.drraphaeljames.com/2018/07/the-aba-women-riot-of-1929-part-one.html?showComment=1532727628270#c5220084056642706214 (Accessed Jan. 15, 2021, blog is not active anymore).

Korieh, Chima J. 2001. "The Invisible Farmer? Women, Gender, and Colonial Agricultural Policy in the Igbo Region of Nigeria, c. 1913-1954" *African Economic History* 21: 117–162.

Lugard, Frederick. 1922. *The Dual Mandate in British Tropical Africa.* London: Frank Cass.

Matera, Marc, Bastian, Misty L., Kent, S. K., and Kent, Susan Kingsley. 2012. *The Women's War of 1929: Gender and Violence in Colonial Nigeria.* New York: Palgrave Macmillan.

Mba, Nina E. 1992. Heroines of the Women's War. In *Nigerian Women in Historical Perspective*, ed. Bolanle Awe, 73–88, Ibadan: Bookcraft.

Naanen, Ben. 2006, You Are Demanding Tax from the Dead: The Introduction of Direct Taxation and Its Aftermath in South-Eastern Nigeria, 1928-39. *University of Wisconsin Press Journal Division* 34: 69–102.

Nigeria. 1930. *Report of the Commission of Inquiry Appointed to Inquire into the Disturbances in the Calabar and Owerri Provinces, December, Lagos 1929*: Lagos: Government Printer. http://www.opensourceguinea.org/2014/10/nigeria-report-of-commission-of-inquiry.html. Accessed Nov. 22nd, 2021.

Nigeria. Commission of Inquiry appointed to Inquire into the Disturbances in the Calabar and Owerri Provinces, December, 1929. 1930. Notes of Evidence Taken by the Commission of Inquiry Appointed to Inquire into the Disturbances in the Calabar and Owerri Provinces. London: Waterlow & Sons.

Oladejo, Mutiat Titilope. 2019. *The Women Went Radical: Petition Writing and the Colonial State in Southwestern Nigeria, 1900-1953*. Ibadan: Bookbuilder. Editions Africa.

Onwumere, Obinna. 2002. Transitions in Political System of Igboland: The Warrant Chief System, 1900-1929. In *Nigeria in The Twentieth Century*, ed. Toyin Falola, 171–182, Durham: Carolina Academic Press.

Osgood, Herbert Levi. 1898. The American Revolution. *Political Science Quarterly* 13: 44–58.

Ozigbo, Ikenga. 1999. *A History of Igboland in the 20th Century*. Enugu: Snaap Press.

Utuk, Efiong Isaac. 1975. *Britain's Colonial Administrations and Developments, 1860-1960: An Analysis of Britain's Colonial Administrations and Development in Nigeria*. Unpublished Master of Science in Teaching in History, Portland State University.

Uzondu, C. 2015, The Eastern Nigeria Women's Resistance of 1929 (Misnamed Aba Women's Riot). In *Igbo Nation: History and Challenges of Rebirth and Development*, eds. T. Uzodinma Nwala, Nath Aniekwu, and Chinyere Ohiri-Aniche, 140–158, Ibadan: Kraft Books Limited.

Vaaseh, Godwin A. and Abah Danladi. 2016. Akpanya Women Revolt of 1940 in Igala Land: A Study in Women Resistance Movement to Colonial Rule in Nigeria. *POLAC Historical Review* 1(1): 84–98.

Part III

Avoiding Tax Avoidance: Counter Strategies by State Authorities

8 Verbally Resisting Taxes in Medieval England

Arguments, Anger and the (In)Ability to Prevent Tax Avoidance in the Reign of Henry III[1]

Christina Bröker

8.1 Introduction

> But in the morning of All Soul's Day, when the magnates of England came together, the king with most pressing manner again asked for pecuniary aid from them; as they had been so often wronged and deceived, they opposed him in his presence.[2]

With these words, the Benedictine monk and chronicler Matthew Paris described in his *Chronica maiora* the reactions to the tax requests of King Henry III (1216–1272) of England in 1244. According to the chronicle, written between 1240 and 1259, these pecuniary aids were the subject of lively debates between the king and the magnates; and they were often resisted. The barons' resistance to Henry's demands was based upon earlier statutes relating to feudal aid. These aids were a significant part of the tax system in England, which referred to certain instances of need when the king could ask for additional money.[3] These instances concerned the knighting of his first-born son, the marriage of his first-born daughter and the ransoming of his person, as fixed in the Magna Carta of 1215.[4] The Carta also stipulated that such monetary demands required the consent of a council of tenants-in-chief, the king's direct vassals.[5] Even though the relevant article 12 was left out of later issues, this remained accepted custom in the reign of Henry III.[6] Magna Carta, thus, offered extensive possibilities of intervention by the council, both in terms of general approval of whether a certain tax could be

1 I would like to thank the editors of this volume for all their helpful and detailed comments on drafts of this essay which contributed a lot to the improvement of it and opened up new perspectives on the topic.

2 CM IV, 395. *In crastino autem Animarum, convenientes magnates Angliae, rex cum instantissime auxilium pecuniare ab eis iterum postularet, totiens laesi et illusi, contradixerunt ei in facie.*

3 Cazel (1988, 613).

4 Magna Carta, Art. 12.

5 Ibid., Art. 14.

6 Carpenter (2020, 30); Maddicott (2010, 120).

DOI: 10.4324/9781003333197-12

allowed at all, and in terms of the exact assessment of it.[7] In addition to these cases, the king could ask for gracious aid for the realm's needs, which was equally dependent on the barons' consent.[8]

The role of the council's consent in Henry's reign concerning pecuniary aids has been discussed extensively in research, especially by Sydney Knox Mitchell. He outlined how consent changed from theoretical to practical and emphasised that the tenants-in-chief in fact could refuse taxes corporately and did so regularly.[9] Apart from focusing on the development of consent, earlier studies investigated the question of why consent was required for specific taxes and the process of how they were levied on the king's subjects.[10] John R. Maddicott stated: "Provided that they acknowledged the necessity, his [the King's] subjects could not deny his claim; but the need for them to make that acknowledgement opened the way for debate and for a sort of consent."[11] However, the course of these debates with their arguments and the king's reactions have not been examined in detail yet, although the significance of such debates should not be neglected as they expose the reasons and perceived reasons for the failure of tax levies. It is, thus, argued that through the debates about taxes, the fundamental lines of conflict were revealed not only to the opposing parties but even to outsiders like Matthew because in these debates dissenting understandings of rulership clashed directly.

Since the *Chronica maiora* offers a detailed insight into the verbal exchange between the king and the barons, and since this exchange is nowhere so strongly thematised as in the discussions about pecuniary aids, it is worth taking a closer look at it. Wrongdoing on the part of the king seems to be one reason for the barons' resistance, at least from the perspective of Matthew Paris as in the above cited passage. Matthew was a monk from the Benedictine abbey of St. Albans and probably lived from 1200 to 1259, when his chronicle ended.[12] As a contemporary of Henry III, he might therefore have gained information about these events as an eyewitness and second-hand through official documents, such as letters.[13] Nonetheless, what he wrote can be seen as anything but a mere factual account. The chronicler is well-known for making up details, and he often dramatised his account in order to enhance readability more than other contemporary English historians.[14] Furthermore, Matthew Paris's attitude towards the persons described is strongly critical. This is true for his portrayal

7 Wareham (2012, 914); Mitchell (1951, 111f).
8 Cazel (1988, 613).
9 Mitchell (1951, 10).
10 Barzel/Kiser (2002, 474).
11 Maddicott (2010, 122); similar Harris (1975, 32/33).
12 Vaughan (1958, 2, 11).
13 Ibid., 12f.
14 Weiler (2009, 254).

of the various popes, and also of King Henry III. Criticism of Henry's alleged proneness to wasting money plays a significant role in the chronicle.[15] Accordingly, it is necessary to critically consider the extent to which Matthew Paris's representation was manipulated, also regarding the king's behaviour in the discussions. M.T. Clanchy has already emphasised the importance of comparing Matthew Paris's chronicle with other sources to better assess the facticity of Henry III's political speeches as depicted in the *Chronica*.[16] An analysis of the tax discussions described by Matthew Paris thus offers a revealing insight into a contemporary judgement of why Henry was not able to prevent tax avoidance and what standards he was supposed to meet.

Pecuniary aids were debated in more than forty councils, later named parliaments,[17] between 1234, when his minority ended, and October 1258.[18] In only four of those council meetings (1235, 1237, 1245, and 1253) did the magnates grant pecuniary aids.[19] 1258 was a turning point as Henry had to swear on the Provisions of Oxford, which included various articles that restricted the king's power. For instance, a more permanent council of 15 barons was created to advise the king. Apart from this major change, it was decided that the king's household should be reformed and important offices such as the justiciar, chancellor and exchequer should be filled with baron-friendly individuals.[20] The Provisions, therefore, provided the council with better control over the king's budget. The frequent resistance against pecuniary aid in the preceding period thus already foreshadowed the conflict that later arose between the king and the magnates and culminated in a war between the two parties (1264–1266).

This chapter therefore focuses on the failed negotiations between 1234 and 1258 and explores the value of Matthew Paris's report in order to understand the reasons for the failure. First, the arguments for the barons' resistance according to the *Chronica* will be investigated and compared to information from other sources such as annals and letters. Next, King Henry III's reaction is analysed and the extent to which financial aspects met a fundamental political conflict is shown. These sections serve primarily to highlight the substance of the arguments and to examine the plausibility of Matthew Paris's account. The last section is concerned with the representation of the debate, particularly of the king's behaviour, because negative behaviour could diminish the king's position too.

15 Weiss (2015, 63).

16 Clanchy (1968, 204).

17 The name "parliament" first appeared in 1237 in the *Chronica maiora*, cf. for its development Carpenter (1996, 382).

18 See the helpful list by Maddicott (2010, 454f).

19 As far as can be identified, cf. ibid.

20 The clauses of the Provisions of Oxford can be found here: Documents 1973, No. 5, 96–113.

8.2 A Question of Policy

In the following, the argumentation strategies of the two opposing parties, the English ruler Henry III on the one side and the barons' council on the other, are examined. The council meetings involved a certain circle of individuals and included the king's direct vassals, both clerical and secular barons.[21] A small circle of council members thus decided on the taxation of all property owners.[22] In most cases, taxes, described as "auxilium pecuniare" in Matthew's chronicle, were levied on movables, but also by *scutage*. The tax on movables was assessed as a percentage on the property owned by property holders with the exemption of the lower clergy. The percentage varied and the type of goods included in the calculation also differed.[23] *Scutage* was shield money demanded by the king to compensate for missing war services. At first, *scutage* had been a lump sum, but by the time of Henry's reign, it was linked to the worth of the knight's fief, on a percentage basis.[24] If these pecuniary aids did not yield successful revenues the king could also use *tallage*, a tax levied on the royal demesne, but *tallage* was not as profitable as levies on movables.[25] The reasons for pecuniary aids varied in Henry's reign. He repeatedly requested them for war in Gascony to suppress the rebellions rising there, and for the so-called Sicilian Business, a project of the papacy to secure the throne of Sicily for Henry's second son, Edmund.[26]

The sources rarely describe tax discussions in as much detail as Matthew Paris, but just inform the recipients of the chronicle that they took place. The monastic annals of Winchester (for the period of 519 to 1277) report that the magnates did not consent (*consensere*).[27] The annals of Waverly (for the period from 1004 to 1262) mention that the king had to make concessions.[28]

One source that is particularly suitable for comparison, as it is the only one that also depicts a discussion, is a protocol of a debate between the king and the council. The debate took place around 1261 during the ongoing resistance of Henry against the Provisions of Oxford.[29] The author of this protocol is unknown. The king laid grievances before the council, and both these and the council's replies are preserved in Old French ("The grievances of which the king complains").[30] A comparison between the *Chronica* and this source should not obscure the fact that the latter was written under different

21 Carpenter (1996, 388/389).
22 Mitchell (1951, 179).
23 Ibid., 113.
24 Ibid., 5.
25 Maddicott (2010, 175).
26 Carpenter (2020, 630, 709); Maddicott (2010, 174).
27 Annales Monasterii de Wintonia, in: Annales Monastici I, 95.
28 Annales Monasteriii de Waverleia, in: Ibid. II, 345.
29 Ridgeway (1988, 228).
30 "Les grevancez dont le roy se pleynt", Documents 1973, No. 31, 219–239. A Latin version contains only the king's complaints and differs slightly: Documents 1973, No. 30, 210–219.

circumstances. Nevertheless, it offers a suitable comparison of how both parties argued in Henry's reign and what the essential positions were.

According to Matthew Paris, the magnates often complained that the king had already demanded too much money and would impoverish the kingdom if he continued to do so.[31] Former bad experiences with the king's handling of money are mentioned frequently. When the king asked for taxes to serve the kingdom, they argued in 1237 that the growing indebtedness was the king's responsibility alone, not theirs, and therefore they did not feel responsible for finding a solution to a problem that they had not caused.[32] At a council in London in 1244, the barons named the many times and situations in which the king had demanded pecuniary aid from them.[33]

A similar argument can be found in the "grievances" as well. Henry complained right at the beginning of the document "that the councillors have done nothing to pay off [his] the king's debt and that the king [he] is now spending more than he used to, though he gives away little".[34] The council answered that everything had been organised in order to reduce the debts of the king, such as the justiciar's selling of wardships and marriages. Apart from this, the councillors blamed Henry for certain problems, "for they have often shown that the king should reduce his household expenses, which seem to them too great, but that he will do nothing about their request".[35] The blame for the lack of money was handed from the barons to the king. In the eyes of the barons, the constant requests for pecuniary aids revealed the king's problems in his management of money.

The conclusion that Henry did not act in the interests of the community logically follows the argument that the king wasted too much money. In 1237 and 1242, the barons accused Henry of treating his subjects like slaves and of impoverishing the kingdom, thus, not acting for the benefit of the whole realm.[36] This argument alluded to the principle of a "gracious aid", namely that the money had to be used for the necessity or benefit of the whole kingdom.[37]

Another important and recurring argument used by the barons held that the king did not ask for their advice before he undertook action. According to Matthew, in 1242, the magnates mentioned that the king had decided on

31 E. g. CM IV, 187.

32 CM III, 381: *nec debuerant esse poenae participes qui fuerant a culpa immunes.*

33 Ibid. 373/374.

34 Documents 1973, No. 31, 220/221.

35 Ibid, 220.

36 CM III, 381: *a naturalibus hominibus suis, quasi a servis ultimae conditionis [...] pecuniam [...] extorqueret* [.]; IV, 182, same phrase.

37 Mitchell (1951, 220); Harris (1975, 38).

a military campaign to Poitou without consulting the council.[38] Concerning taxation for the kingdom of Sicily to support the claim of his son Edmund to the crown of Sicily in 1257, the Annals of Burton copy a text referring to a meeting of the clergy. In this text, the clerical barons also argue that they had complied with the king's wishes enough. They had previously even agreed to pecuniary aids for the king although he had never consulted them concerning the subject in advance.[39] In 1258, shortly before the Provisions of Oxford, the council claimed, according to Matthew Paris, that Henry could not demand money for Sicily because the king had not consulted the barons beforehand to obtain their approval for this undertaking.[40] They argued that they would have discouraged him from this project. In the "grievances", the king complains that concerning the "Sicilian business", his son Edmund lacked the necessary financial support and would therefore lose his claim.[41] The council answered that they had never advised Henry to agree to his aspirations in Sicily;[42] the substance of this argument is similar in different sources.

Magna Carta provided the basis for the barons' arguments in matters of taxation, which is why the barons also decried that Henry did not respect the Carta.[43] Accordingly, whenever Henry promised to preserve the charter, compromises occurred, although this was rare. Such was the case, for instance, in 1237 when a thirteenth on movables was granted.[44] In 1255, the barons demanded to choose their own chancellor, justiciar and treasurer for the acceptance of taxes.[45] These demands, which are reported by Matthew Paris, appear in the Annals of Dunstable and the Annals of Burton as well, and are thus highly plausible.[46]

The nature of the magnates' arguments, as described in the *Chronica*, seems plausible and can be summed up concerning two main points: they did not just state that Henry had already levied many useless taxes, but they named them concretely. Second, they offered to allow the king to raise taxes under certain conditions, naming and listing these conditions explicitly. In other words, they gave constructive suggestions; and even more, they turned the tables by making demands themselves.[47] The fundamental attitude of the barons can be also revealed: they based their commitment

38 CM IV, 181.
39 Annales de Burton, in: Annales Monastici I, 391.
40 CM V, 680.
41 Documents 1973, No. 31, 230–233.
42 Ibid.
43 CM V, 373.
44 CM III, 382; also 1257 V, 8, 623. Holt (2015, 330/331); Maddicott (2010, 152).
45 CM V, 494.
46 Annales de Dunstaplia, in: Annales Monastici III, 189; Annales de Burton, in: Annales Monastici I, 336.
47 Mitchell (1951, 163).

on the frequency of pecuniary aids, essentially on Henry's management of money. Moreover, their attitude rested on the important precondition that they were consulted prior to costly political decisions by the king. Their stance, thus, twisted from concrete grievances to a general criticism of the king's policy during the tax discussions.

8.3 A Question of Interpretation

How did the king react to the barons' resistance? First, it must be mentioned that his reaction was not limited solely to the verbal level but included non-verbal communication and strategies, which Matthew Paris described in detail. The verbal communication and the nature of his arguments will be discussed here first, however, as they can be better verified by other sources, before Henry's behaviour and its background are discussed.

Henry only partially addressed the barons' arguments in concrete terms. From the understanding of a gracious aid, it was important to clearly state the necessity of the funds for the kingdom; a point which the barons always mentioned in their arguments. The recognition of a need would thus lead to recognition of the aid itself.[48] What corresponded to a necessity, however, was not clearly defined and therefore open to interpretation.[49]

The king acknowledged that justifying his fiscal demands as being of necessity for the whole realm was important, as a royal letter shows with which the magnates were summoned to a council in London in 1242.[50] But Henry's understanding of this necessity differed from that of the barons. In the "grievances", "necessity" was also a point of discussion: Henry complained that the profit of the realm had been neglected and therefore he and the realm were "grievously abused and impoverished".[51] The council, on the other hand, wanted the king to declare how the kingdom was suffering and they would then remedy it. It is not possible to read exactly what the different understandings of "necessity" were from the sources because neither the arguments of Henry nor of the barons are presented in detail concerning this subject. When Henry, according to Matthew Paris and the "grievances", referred to necessity for the realm and came closer to the perspective of the barons, no further explanations are provided.

In the same way, the amount of consultation needed was a subject of debate. Henry's position did not seem to be clear. On the one hand, he argued, according to the "grievances" and Matthew Paris, that the council had not advised him well enough or had excluded him from their deliberations. But on the other hand, also according to Matthew, Henry argued in 1244 that

48 Maddicott (2010, 122).

49 Harris (1975, 32/33).

50 CR 1237–1242, 428: *negociis nostris statum nostrum et tocius regni nostri specialiter tangentibus[.]*

51 Documents 1973, No. 30, 236/237.

he had only started the war with Gascony on the advice of the barons.[52] The barons, in return, wanted to be better included in the king's decisions, as explained above.

One main reaction of Henry to the council's resistance was to insist on his position as king. The same problem as with the interpretation of the necessity of monetary payments arises: understandings of the way in which this position was executed varied. While the discussions around necessity are more concretely about taxes, the argument of authority took the discussions to a general political level.

Henry argued that it was the duty of his subjects to make these payments. In 1248 and 1253, according to Matthew Paris, Henry stated in a similar vein that he would no longer be a king but a slave if he made the required concessions.[53] During a quarrel with Cistercians about delivering money for the pope in 1256, Henry argued similarly: "How is it abbot, that you have refused me pecuniary assistance when I am in need of it and humbly ask it of you? Am I not your patron?"[54] In the "grievances", Henry referred to his kingly dignity (*dignite*) as well: "Further, they deprived the king of his power, dignity and regality, so that little or nothing is done at his necessary commands."[55]

However, this argument did not seem to convince his opponents. According to the *Chronica*, the abbot of Buildwas replied to Henry's question: "Would that you were a patron, a father, and a defender, but it is not proper for you to injure us by extorting our money from us, but rather ought you to ask the aid of our prayers [.]"[56] In 1261, the council of the barons answered thoughtfully, as well, to the king's accusation:

> they obey the king as their lord and do not intend that his dignity, regality, or power should be taken from him, and if there is anyone who does not obey his reasonable commands, let the king, if it please [sic] him, say who, or in what matter, and they will put it right as is due to their lord.[57]

The answer is interesting because they agreed with the king but differed in important details. To the council, it was not simply a question of interpreting the king's scope of competence. That Henry should decide in cooperation with the barons did not mean a loss of royal dignity in their eyes but was simply part of the king's duties. Such underlying, competing understandings of rulership can also be found in various mirrors for princes, which on the one hand saw the king's authority as legitimised by God, but on the other

52 CM IV, 362.
53 CM V, 20; 378: *quod non foret rex*.
54 Giles (1854, 169); CM V, 554: *Nonne sum patronus vester?*
55 Documents 1973, No. 31, 225.
56 CM V, 554, transl. Giles, 169/170.
57 Documents 1973, No. 31, 224/225.

hand brought criticism of the ruler to the fore and did not see him as above the law.[58]

It is difficult to conclude what the king's general policy was. M. T. Clanchy and David Carpenter already debated this issue, and their interpretations differ. While Clanchy ascribed an absolutist model of government to Henry, Carpenter saw him as a ruler who was responsive to the barons and cooperated with them.[59] Regarding the tax discussions, both positions can fit, as Henry on the one hand included the barons in the decision, but at the same time did not want to accept their resistance.

As the advisory role of the tenants-in-chief had been under discussion since Magna Carta, the king's position here was based on a tradition that had already been revised. Rather, as Maddicott has put it, the king could no longer invoke his *vis et voluntas* (force and will) alone but was dependent on the advice of the barons.[60] Or in Mitchell's words: "Henry believed that he should call the barons into council but that the final decision rested with him alone [.]"[61]

At first, it seems that Henry's opponents were not concerned with the position of the king in general, but with concrete objections. Later in the "grievances", the barons even pointed out several times that they would like to investigate the accusations or that he should give specific reasons why, for example, his honour had been violated.[62] Unfortunately, we do not know whether the king responded to any of these demands. In general, the barons gave constructive advice for the future and named concrete grievances.

While the description of Matthew Paris portrays them as highly talkative during these parliaments, in contrast the king is depicted as rather silent. Even when he spoke, he rarely reacted with specific arguments to the verbal resistance of the magnates. He simply mentioned, for example, that they were not allowed to resist him, but did not explain why exactly.[63] Nevertheless, it is significant that the barons were appeased when in 1252 Henry argued that it was not because he was their lord that they should grant the demanded tax, but for the church.[64] This argument worked, according to the chronicler's narrative.

It can be said that the conflict over taxes was ultimately orientated around the question of the degree of baronial involvement and revealed questions of principle. Tax debates, thus, offered room for fundamental criticism of the ruler's way of governing, and led to criticism because the king's handling of money was under direct observation. The negotiations turned from questioning the proper exercise of the king's duties to questioning the king's general scope of competence and a wish to limit it.

58 E.g. John of Salisbury (1993, 234).
59 Clanchy (1968, 215); Carpenter (1985, 40).
60 Maddicott (2010, 169).
61 Mitchell (1951, 221).
62 Ibid., 234/235.
63 CM V, 20/21.
64 CM V, 326.

8.4 A Question of Evaluation

Previous research has strongly devalued the king's reactions in comparison to the barons' position in the debate of 1261 as childish, petulant and unscrupulous.[65] Maddicott described the king's argumentative strategy in general as hectoring and pleading.[66] Such judgements might also result from Matthew Paris's narrative. He adds a non-verbal level to the king's verbal communication: strategies and emotions.

Because Henry could not convince the barons as a group, he tried to convince them individually in several parliaments, according to the chronicler, such as 1242, 1252 and 1257.[67] To implement this tactic, Henry even delayed the negotiations to increase his opportunities.[68] He often did not speak directly to the council, but rather through others, such as William Raleigh.[69] In 1244, he tried to extort money by force from the Londoners and made up, according to Matthew, an argument that the Londoners owed him money for a past incident.[70] Matthew Paris changed such critical passages to a more neutral form in a revised version of the chronicle.[71] During the Parliament of 1253, Henry reminded the attendants how much he had supported some of them and that they were now in his debt.[72] It was more an attempt to influence and appeal to guilt than to convince argumentatively. In 1255, Matthew Paris informed the reader that the king "although the abbot had answered him wisely, laid plans in secret against all the Cistercians abbots".[73] It seems that the king, as he was not able to convince the barons verbally, tried to complot against a part of the clergy. Asking the magnates individually can be considered as comprehensible, however, (despite Paris's portrayal), because originally consent had been given on an individual basis anyway before this changed to corporate consent.[74]

Matthew Paris's description also adds emotional outbursts to Henry's reactions, especially when the barons reminded him of having omitted consulting them.[75] According to Paris, he erupted in anger after giving his short speech in 1248 that he risked no longer being a king should the magnates

65 Treharne (1971, 253).
66 Maddicott (2010, 175).
67 CM IV, 182: *Et sic, quos non potuit universos, singulos singillatim enervatos [...] conabatur [.]*; V, 330, 554.
68 CM V, 521.
69 CM III, 381; CM IV, 365.
70 CM IV, 395.
71 Ibid. 396.
72 CM V, 374.
73 transl. Giles, 170; CM V, 554: *Rex autem, licet satis eleganter respondisset abbas, tamen abbatibus Cisterciensibus tacitus insidiabatur universis.*
74 Mitchell 1951, 2.
75 CM IV, 184: *His rex auditis in iram excanduit vehementem [.]*

resist his demand.[76] In the Parliament of 1252, he "ran furiously away from all who were in his chamber".[77] Although he could be temporarily appeased, according to the chronicle, he soon became angry again.[78] His anger is mostly reported during a parliament where the king tried to convince someone individually, in the case of 1252, the bishop of Ely. When the bishop did not want to give in, another outburst of the king's rage was the consequence, Matthew Paris states.[79] Although rarely, annals also report the emotional character of the debates in the taxation parliaments, and thus make Matthews's description appear (more) plausible. The annals of Osney, for instance, state for the Parliament of 1255 that the king left the venue enraged (*iratus*) because the magnates' answers did not meet his expectations.[80]

If it were a matter of evaluating the king's argumentation technique from a modern point of view, we would indeed call the king's arguments sham arguments, fallacies,[81] and see his evasion into non-verbal communication and strategies as a sign of weakness, similar to Maddicott and Treharne. The interesting question, also from a history of mentalities perspective, is whether contemporaries also perceived the king's behaviour as objectionable and worth of criticism. This brings us to the next point of analysis. How does Matthew Paris's critical view of Henry affect the evaluation of both positions in the discussion?

The chronicler's stories are verifiable and plausible up to a certain point. His narrative is further substantiated by references to letters and information obtained through royal contacts, such as the king's brother Richard of Cornwall.[82] At the same time, Matthew Paris's portrayal must be treated with caution, at least concerning his characterisation of the king. But what exactly were the king's failures, in general, according to the chronicler?

Miriam Weiss has analysed the specific points of criticism. These include favouring foreigners, appointing the wrong people to spiritual offices, not taking advice and the financial plundering of his subjects.[83] The last two points are strongly expressed in the debates about taxes, as has been shown. Weiss adds that the king was criticised personally, his anger, his extravagance and his ability to be influenced.[84] These aspects again were shown in the tax discussions examined. No final judgement can yet be made as to whether this fundamental attitude of Matthew Paris was strengthened because of these

76 CM V, 21: *in iram conversus vehementem [.]*

77 CM V, 326.

78 CM V, 328: *ira incanduit vehementiori.*

79 CM V, 332: *Cum autem haec audisset rex, quasi alto vulnere saucius, nec adhuc rationi adquiescens, exclamavit inordinate nimis* [.]

80 Annales Monasterii de Osneia, in: Annales Monastici 4, 109.

81 "deficient moves in argumentative discourse". Cf. Eemeren (2001, 295).

82 Vaughan (1958, 12f).

83 Weiss (2015, 63); Vaughan (1958, 139).

84 Weiss (2015, 63).

debates or whether, the other way round, his attitude actually shaped the narrative of the discussions.

Matthew Paris often reveals his general criticism when describing the conflicts, for example in the Parliament of 1242, when he mentions that the king had often shamelessly demanded money, or in 1253, when he suggests that demons (*sathanae*) spoke to the king.[85] The chronicler, indeed, does not hold the king's arguments in high esteem, as shown by the fact that Henry's exact arguments are rarely reported and the *Chronica* just states that they were false. Furthermore, they are characterised as "pretended speeches" (*simulati sermocinationes*) and "usual twisted trickeries" (*consuetae conversus cavillationes*).[86] Matthew Paris, in this case, refers to a person's bad character to discredit him: the *ad hominem* fallacy.[87] The use of alliterations reinforces the bad image of Henry as an incapable orator (and lord) on a rhetorical, textual level.

English mirrors for princes can serve as evidence that fluency in conversation was important to a ruler in the period. Matthew Paris at least knew Gerald of Wales's work *De Principis Instructione* written between 1191 and 1216.[88] Whether the magnates knew this and John of Salisbury's work *Policraticus* from ca. 1159 cannot be proven, but these mirrors for princes reflect contemporary ideas. John of Salisbury claimed that it was important for a ruler to react moderately to criticism, thus showing foresight, an important quality in a ruler.[89] He should also be affable (*affabilis*) in words.[90] Gerald of Wales outlines that "in no human activity is there greater need of care than in speech". He cites Solomon: "[…] he that moderates his lips is most wise. He who guards his mouth, guards his soul; but he who is careless in speech shall meet with evils [.]".[91] Thus, Gerald considered a certain sharp-wittedness as an advantage and some rhetorical abilities as a helpful capability for a king. These are all qualities that are not attributed to Henry in the *Chronica maiora*. The emotionality of the king's reactions was also crucial for the perception of the king's position in the conflict. Although the barons are described as angry or desperate because of the difficult negotiations, Matthew Paris did not ascribe to them as excessive outbursts of emotion.[92]

However, the pure use of the term *ira* (anger) need not necessarily indicate an emotional outburst by the king. It could as well only point to a political action rather than an emotion: in royal letters, "anger" (*ira*) simply signified that someone had fallen into disgrace.[93] As far as the understanding

85 CM IV, 182; V, 378.
86 CM IV, e. g. 366, V, 521.
87 Walton (2001, 1).
88 Marshall (1939, 471).
89 John of Salisbury (1993, 228).
90 Ibid., 259.
91 Gerald of Wales (2018, 44/45).
92 E.g. CM III, 381.
93 Barton 2005, 388.

of a ruler's anger is concerned, there were different perspectives on this emotion, depending on whether Seneca's or Aristotle's theory of anger was employed.[94] Anger could be noble anger, and concerning its expression, a moderate (Aristotelian) public display of emotions is often recommended in mirrors for princes.[95] Gerald of Wales sums up the image of an ideal ruler's behaviour as reserved: "So the ruler [...] is bound to rule and govern his mouth, his eyes, every limb, and every gesture of his body in such a way that he will not offend the eyes of anyone among so many thousands".[96] And also John of Salisbury remarks that even in punishing a ruler should always control his emotions completely.[97] Important characteristics of an ideal ruler are, thus, prudence, moderation[98] and temperance.

Karl Schnith interpreted Henry's gestures at the 1252 parliament as an indication that the king was not able to observe the ceremonial niceties and was personally inadequate.[99] A comparison with mirrors for princes supports that such behaviour was not beneficial in tax debates and could not further the king's ambitions to avoid tax resistance. Expressive anger instead weakened Henry's position. Above all, the depiction of a ruler who can hardly control himself can be regarded as encouraging the bad image of Henry III. In the given context, this bad image can be specified further: the outbursts portray the king in a state of uncontrollability and incompetence and thus support the barons' accusations regarding the management of money in the narrative.

Even if the king's words were worthless for Matthew Paris in many places (and therefore not mentioned or detailed), they were not necessarily so in practice. They provoked reactions and could well have exercised an appeasing effect, even according to the chronicler. The few parliaments in which the king could convince the barons are, characteristically, the ones in which he responded to their demands, resulting in functional communication. In 1237, he swore an oath to observe the Carta and promised concessions, without resorting to an emotional outburst.[100] In 1253, Henry admitted that he had made a mistake and had not complied with the customs; again, no emotions are mentioned in the *Chronica*.[101] On both occasions, the taxes were approved by the barons. Moreover, the opposing party was appeased in the

94 Ibid., 373/374, Gerald of Wales (2018, 77).

95 Gerald of Wales, 152/153: *Modestia vero, que et temperancie pars est, sed sicut illa ad frenandos ire impetus* [.]

96 Gerald of Wales, 44/45: *Princeps igitur [...] sic os, sic oculus, sic membra singula gestusque corporis omnes, ut nec unum in tot milibus oculum offendat, regere tenetur et moderari.* Also 56/57 with reference to behaviour.

97 John of Salisbury (1993, 262).

98 Gerald of Wales (2018, 152/153); John of Salisbury (1993, 258f).

99 Schnith (1974, 203).

100 CM III, 382.

101 CM V, 374.

few moments when the king provided the appropriate arguments. Such was the case in 1252, when Henry argued that the barons should allow the tax for the honour of the church and not because he was their master.[102]

Thus, Matthew Paris's portrayal of the events and the verifiable parts of his narration show how contemporaries perceived the tax debate between the king and his vassals under post-Magna Carta conditions, demonstrating that they criticised a certain form of kingly behaviour as undeserving and not legitimate. Competent fiscal management was obviously highly important to the chronicler, which might derive from the fact that the tax burden rested on all individuals with property, not only the upper classes. Even if it did not affect the lower clergy,[103] including monks like Matthew Paris, the tax could still fall on St Albans Abbey in general. This would explain why the chronicler's depiction of contemporary tax debates was of interest for the small circle of the abbey, probably the *Chronica's* first and foremost readership.[104] Accordingly, Matthew Paris criticised the Pope's mandate for Henry's project to install his son Edmund as king of Sicily as hateful (*exosus*) and detestable (*detestabilis*), because it resulted in 1252 in a crusading tenth and revenues from "the whole English church".[105] The king and the council decided on pecuniary aids for individuals that could not participate in the discussion and, thus, provoked indirect reactions.

However, Henry's emotional and angry behaviour during some of the council's debates on taxation in the *Chronica* should not be judged as decisive for the outcome of the discussions. The chronicler's lens merely signifies which moves complicated the levying of taxes. The analysis shows that a king could not simply bypass the arguments by bursting out in rage. Such behaviour caused disapproval and did not foster consent, but just renewed and strengthened resistance. To turn it around: if the king had communicated competence through his words and gestures, and even more importantly through his acts, the discussion could have been successful on his part.

8.5 Conclusion

Several levels can be observed in the discussions on pecuniary aids, which repeatedly led to failed negotiations. The barons' criticism largely referred to the king's fiscal management. Questioning the administration of money in particular casts doubt on the king's political competences per se. Whereas the king, from his point of view, acted for the necessity of the realm, the barons saw the frequent demands for taxes as an indication of a lack of ability and, based on Magna Carta, wanted to become more involved in political

102 CM V, 326.
103 Mitchell (1951, 179).
104 Weiss (2018, 186/187).
105 CM V, 324/325.

decisions. This in turn led to the revelation of a deeper problem: both parties understood the king's scope of action and thus his position differently. Understandings of rulership collided here. Henry was reluctant to allow further interference by the council in political and personnel decisions, as this would also lead to a de facto loss of power. However, it was the only way to reach consent and became a method of controlling the king.[106]

In the eyes of contemporaries, this line of argumentation casts further doubts about Henry's competences on an additional level. While the barons argued precisely and with examples and had pivotal points to which they always recurred, the king did not give examples or communicate a plan about how he would manage and avoid pecuniary aids in the future. However, mirrors for princes show that good articulation was important for a ruler and indicated competencies such as foresight.

This factor goes hand in hand with the last level at which communication failed: non-verbal communication. According to those mirrors for princes, such a failure could also show incompetence. An evaluation is difficult in this case since the information is only derived from Matthew Paris's subjective description. Nevertheless, these very descriptions, whether they are true or not, show that the behaviour accompanying the discussion was important. Emotional outbursts could testify to a ruler's lack of sovereignty.

Nonetheless, the conflict around taxes cannot be reduced to what happened in the debates. Individual conflicts of interest also played an underlying role.[107] Both Matthew Paris and the magnates went into these conflicts with a certain attitude and posture towards the king. Furthermore, the king certainly had other ways to obtain his money. One could argue in the sense of Carpenter that asking for aid was a concession on the part of the king.[108] That the king was helpless is what the *Chronica maiora* means to convey to its recipients. Ultimately, it proved more important that Henry followed up his words with actions and kept his promises. For we must not forget that the tax discussions only show a part of the relationship between the king and the magnates.

But failed negotiations could not have been in Henry's interest at all. Even if the debates were not necessarily decisive, they revealed the two opposing positions that eventually led, among other things, to the Provisions of Oxford and later the "Barons' War" (1264–1267). The fact that Henry III demonstrated little control over the funds and the situation, as well as little flexibility, intensified rather than diminished the criticism against the king and only deepened the divisions by reinforcing the barons' position.

The tax discussions thus provided a stage to sound out the balance of power and evaluate the ruler's authority on a verbal level that should not be

106 Mitchell (1951, 163).

107 Carpenter (1985, 53).

108 Ibid., 40.

underestimated. In the eyes of critical observers, the king demonstrated his lack of ability to respond to tax refusals, and therefore his lack of ability in governance. Seeking other means to accredit funds solved the immediate problem, but not the conflict between the parties, which was based on dissenting understandings of a ruler's tasks.

Published Sources

Annales Monastici. 1864-1869, ed. Henry R. Luard, 5 vols. Rolls Series 36. London: Eyre and Spottiswoode.

Close Rolls of the Reign of Henry III preserved in the Public Record Office: Henry III, 1226-1272. 1902-1938, 6 vols. London: Eyre and Spottiswoode (CR).

Documents of Baronial Movement of Reform and Rebellion. 1258-1267. 1973, ed. R. E. Treharne/I. J. Sanders. Oxford Medieval Texts. Oxford: Oxford University Press.

Gerald of Wales. 2018. De Principis Instructione/Instruction for a Ruler, ed. Robert Bartlett. Oxford Medieval Texts. Oxford: Oxford University Press.

John of Salisbury, Ioannis Saresberiensis Policraticus I-IV. 1993, ed. K. S. B. Corpus Christianorum Continuatio Mediaeualis 118. Keats-Rohan, Turnhout: Brepols.

Magna Carta. 2015, ed. David Carpenter. Penguin Classics. London: Penguin.

Matthaei Pariensis Monachi sancti albani, chronica majora. 1872-1883, ed. Henry R. Luards, 8 vols. Rolls Series 57. London: Longman&co etc. (CM).

Matthew Paris's English History. From the Year 1235 to 1273, 1854, ed./transl. J. A. Giles, vol. III, London: George Bell&Sons.

References

Barton, Richard E. 2005. Ira, Furor, and Discourses of Power and Masculinity in the Eleventh and Twelfth Centuries. In *In the Garden of Evil. The Vices and Culture in the Middle Ages*, ed. Richard Newhauser, 371–392. Papers in mediaeval studies 18. Ontario: Pontifical Institute of Mediaeval Studies.

Barzel, Yoram and Edgar Kiser. 2002. Taxation and Voting Rights in Medieval England and France. *Rationality and Society* 14 (4): 473–507.

Carpenter, David. 1985. King, Magnates, and Society: The Personal Rule of King Henry III, 1234-1258. *Speculum* 60 (1): 39–70.

Carpenter, David. 1996. The Beginnings of Parliaments. In Ibid., *The Reign of Henry III*, repr. 2006, 381–408. London/Rio Grande: Hambledon Press.

Carpenter, David. 2020. *Henry III. The Rise to Power and Personal Rule 1207-1258*. New Haven/London: Yale University Press.

Cazel, Fred A. Jr. 1988. Taxation, English. In *Dictionary of the Middle Ages*, ed. Joseph R. Strayer, 611–618. New York: Charles Scribener's Sons.

Clanchy, M. T. 1968. Did Henry Have a Policy? *History* 53 (178): 203–216.

Eemeren, Frans H. van. 2001. Fallacies. In *Encyclopedia of Rhetoric*, ed. Thomas O. Sloane, 295–301. Oxford: Oxford University Press.

Harris, G. L. 1975. *King, Parliament, and Public Finance in Medieval England to 1369*. Oxford: Clarendon Press.

Holt, J. C. 2015. 1st ed. 1965. *Magna Carta*. Cambridge: Cambridge University Press.

Maddicott, John R. 2010. *The Origins of the English Parliament, 924-1327*. Oxford: Oxford University Press.

Marshall, Miriam Helene. 1939. Thirteenth-Century Culture as Illustrated by Matthew Paris. *Speculum* 14 (4): 465–477.

Mitchell, Sydney Knox. 1951. *Taxation in Medieval England*, ed. Sidney Painter. Yale Historical Publications Studies 15. New Haven: Yale University Press.

Ridgeway, Huw. 1988. King Henry III's Grievances against the Council in 1261: A New Version and a Letter Describing Political Events. *Historical Research* 61 (145): 227–242.

Schnith, Karl. 1974. *England in einer sich wandelnden Welt (1189-1259). Studien zu Roger Wendover und Matthäus Paris.* Monographien zur Geschichte des Mittelalters 7. Stuttgart: Anton Hiersemann.

Treharne, R. F. 1971. *The Baronial Plan of Reform, 1258-1263.* The Ward Bequest 6/ Publications of the University of Manchester 121/Historical Series 62. New York: Manchester University Press.

Vaughan, Richard. 1958. *Matthew Paris. Cambridge Studies in Medieval Life & Thought New Series 6.* Cambridge: Cambridge University Press.

Walton, Douglas. 2001. Ad Hominem Argument. In *Encyclopedia of Rhetoric*, ed. Thomas O. Sloane, 1–4. Oxford: Oxford University Press.

Wareham, Andrew. 2012. Fiscal Policies and the Institution of a Tax State in Anglo-Saxon England within a Comparative Context. *The Economic History Review* 65 (3): 910–931.

Weiler, Björn. 2009. Matthew Paris on the Writing of History. *Journal of Medieval History* 35: 254–278.

Weiss, Miriam. 2015. *rex [...] magis ac magis [...] deliveravit.* Königskritik in den Chronica maiora des Matthew Paris. In *Idoneität - Genealogie - Legitimation: Begründung und Akzeptanz von dynastischer Herrschaft im Mittelalter*, eds. Cristina Andenna and Gert Melville, 59–76. Cologne: de Gruyter.

Weiss, Miriam. 2018. *Die Chronica maiora des Matthaeus Pariensis.* Trierer historische Forschungen 73. Trier: Kliomedia.

9 How to Create a Taxpaying Spirit

A Transnational Examination of an US American and a Western German Tax Education Film in and after World War II

Korinna Schönhärl

9.1 Promoting Compliance by Tax Education: The Transnational Approach in Historiography

Interdisciplinary tax morale research points out that voluntary compliance is a very meaningful factor in making people pay their taxes, and much more effective than governmental controls or pressure.[1] Fostering voluntary compliance is therefore a major aim of the public relations of financial administrations worldwide. In many countries, this was and is pursued by tax education campaigns that use various media, amongst them films for cinema or TV.[2] The analysis of this kind of tax education material is one important pillar of the research project "International Cultural History of Tax Morale", which examines the differences between norms of taxpayment and their development in Western Germany, Spain and the USA between 1945 and 1990.[3] The project's central idea is that the norms of paying taxes are broached, negotiated and disputed in debates about taxpayment behaviour and within the area of the application and everyday limits of tax law. These norms then depict the nucleus of the relationship between citizens and state. Thus, the project applies a historiographical toolbox to examine, both diachronically and synchronically, the norms of paying taxes in the second half of the twentieth century in these three countries with very different concepts of society and tax systems.

Inspired by the Sociology of Morality,[4] tax morale is defined as a certain group's set of norms concerning the payment of taxes that aims to regulate the selfish behaviour of its members. I do not aim to measure tax evasion in the

1 For an overview of social scientific tax morale research, see Torgler (2007). See also Van Brederode (2020).

2 For historical examinations of tax education campaigns, see e.g. Likhovski (2007); Jones (2018).

3 International Cultural History of Tax Morale at Paderborn University, see https://kw.uni-paderborn.de/en/historisches-institut/neueste-geschichte/forschung/international-cultural-history-of-tax-morale, accessed 15.09.2022.

4 Abend (2010).

DOI: 10.4324/9781003333197-13

past, as economists have tried to do since the end of the nineteenth century.[5] Nor do I endeavour to measure individuals' attitudes towards their tax duty, as empirical social scientists have done since the 1950s[6] and continue to do today, e.g. in the World Values Survey.[7] Rather, my aim is to examine the discourse on honest taxpayment behaviour within different historical, social, political and economic settings. To analyse and compare the norms and their development, I focus on documents of "public moral normativity",[8] e.g. the press, TV, radio, parliamentary debates, tax guidebooks, lobby groups' statements or tax education material. What characterises discussion of tax avoidance or evasion versus tax honesty and compliance, how is non-compliance legitimised or delegitimised? To what extent and why did norms of taxpayment behaviour vary and develop differently in the three countries in the decades under consideration? These questions can be used as a probe into the very heart of societal structures: which ideals of citizens and societies appear in the background of the debates about tax morale? The transnational comparison of tax education material is a suitable instrument to make differences visible, and also to show how different traditions of tax education are historically connected. Thus, as a case study, this chapter examines two tax education films that were produced 11 years apart in the USA and Western Germany during and after World War II: "The New Spirit" (USA 1942) and "Putzke wants to know" (FRG 1953).

9.2 The Films in their Historical Context

9.2.1 "The New Spirit" (USA, 1942)[9]

"There's a Yankee Doodle spirit in the heart of everyone. It's the Yankee Doodle spirit now that's shouldering a gun for freedom and liberty. Your freedom! Your liberty! This is our fighting song!"[10] We see Donald Duck dancing to this song, intoned by Cliff Edward, reflected by several mirrors in the starting scene of the animated short film "The New Spirit" (1942). The film is a piece of World War II propaganda, produced as the first of several Walt Disney productions released through the War Activities Committee of the Motion Picture Industry. It was continued by "The Spirit of '43",[11] and is part of a

5 Meisel (1883).
6 Schmölders (1960).
7 "Can it be justified to cheat on taxes if you have a chance?", in: World Values Survey Database 2019 (http://www.worldvaluessurvey.org/wvs.jsp, last accessed 17.09.2020).
8 Abend (2014, 23).
9 The New Spirit, 7:20 min, produced by Walt Disney, directed by Wilfred Jackson and Ben Sharpsteen, written by Joe Grant and Dick Huemer, music by Oliver Wallace, distributor: War Activities Committee of the Motion Pictures Industry, premiere: January 23, 1942. The film is available at various platforms online.
10 A variation of the popular patriotist US Yankee Doodle songs, see Library of Congress: Song Collection Yankee Doodle, https://www.loc.gov/item/ihas.200000025/, last accessed 17.09.2020.
11 Shull and Wilt (2004, 156).

body of numerous Walt Disney World War II propaganda films like "Food Will Win the War" (1941), "Donald Gets Drafted" (1942) or "Commando Duck" (1944). The Disney Company became part of the American propaganda machine during the war period, producing movies on behalf of various US ministries,[12] even if the artist Walt Disney was worried that the quality of such films suffered under the great time pressure in which they were produced and that this could affect his reputation.[13] Other movie companies in Hollywood such as Warner Bros., Paramount and Columbia, all of whom produced animated short films, contributed to war propaganda too.[14] Secretary of the Treasury Henry Morgenthau Jr. commissioned Disney to produce "The New Spirit" in order to make the payment of income taxes more acceptable to the public.[15] This was absolutely essential because many Americans had to pay income taxes for the very first time in their lives in 1941. A highly progressive income tax had been introduced in the USA in 1916, and had become even more progressive during the New Deal years from 1935 onwards.[16] In 1941, the basis of income tax was significantly broadened to finance the war effort: the number of individual taxpayers soared from 3.9 (1939) to 42.6 (1945) million, and federal income-tax collections leaped from $2.2 to $30.1 billion within this period.[17] In this situation, the Treasury Department took various measures to convince Americans to pay their taxes voluntarily and honestly. Tax education was practised via newspaper coverage, radio addresses, the purchase of saving stamps and the education of schoolteachers,[18] but also by works of art and culture. For instance, the famous composer Irving Berlin was ordered by Morgenthau to write a song with the title "I paid my income tax today", which was then played constantly in radios across the nation as the deadline for income tax declaration on March 15, 1942 approached.[19] "The New Spirit" is another example of this tax education campaign with emotional and patriotic content.[20] The Treasury financed this production with $43,000, a sum that left the Disney Studies with a loss of $4,000 for the film, which was produced in an extraordinarily short time.[21]

12 N. N. (1943).
13 Gabler (2006, 389).
14 Shull and Wilt (2004, 38); Concerning feature films, see Koppes and Black (1987).
15 Gabler (2006, 384–387).
16 Brownlee (1996, 109ff).
17 Brownlee and Boyer (2004).
18 Jones (1996, 111, 117).
19 Ibid., 122.
20 Ibid., 125f; Jones (2018, 207f).
21 Including distribution costs, the Treasury Department spent $80,000 on the film, but Congress did not grant this sum because taxpayers could regard the production of movies in the face of war as a waste of money. Disney was even accused of being a war profiteer, see Schickel (1997, 271). The figures differ in Gabler (2006, 385f). More details on the parliamentary debate in Shale (1976, 29f).

In the movie, Donald suddenly interrupts his dance to listen to the radio announcer, who proclaims a new patriotic spirit. An all-too-enthusiastic Donald is told to support the cause not by joining the army, but by filling in his tax return for 1941, a patriotic act described both as a sacrifice and a privilege. Once Donald has overcome his astonishment, the announcer explains how easy it is to fill in the form, assisted by the personalised figures of dip pen, inkwell and blotter. Donald states his job as "actor", thus abandoning his usual role (with various, fluctuating jobs) to approach a kind of meta-level. His enthusiasm is so great that he does not send the filled-in form via mail to the local tax office but races across the nation from Hollywood to Washington, D.C. to deliver it in person. The second part of the film concentrates on the legitimisation of the governmental tax demands. It shows what the tax revenues are spent on under the motto "Taxes to beat the Axis": weapons and munition for the sea, land and air war against Nazi Germany. Shaped by the strokes of fate from Beethoven's fifth symphony, we are shown how American weapons destroy the Nazi military, marked by swastikas. While the American flag is formed by clouds around a setting sun and "God bless America" is intoned, a summary is given by the speaker, explaining that taxes are necessary to save the American freedoms of speech and worship from want and from fear: "Taxes will keep democracy on the march!" Thus the grounding idea of "The New Spirit" is that of a fiscal contract: what the taxpayers get for their money is the defence of their home country and the American way of life against their enemies. Carolyn C. Jones convincingly interprets the film's message: "Rational Americans, as economic actors, could make a wise consumer decision by buying victory with their tax dollars. The legitimacy of taxpaying obligations was approached as 'a question of domestic morale' in time of war."[22] Because the American way of life was not neutral but a term loaded with morality and emotion, taxes could be advertised as a sacrifice on the one hand but, on the other hand, also as a privilege of citizens living in a free world and able to thus maintain their freedom. This ideal lifestyle requires the ideal citizen, and it is at first sight puzzling that this citizen is embodied by Donald Duck, Disney's most popular animated figure, known for his bad luck and awkwardness but not for his intellectual capacities.[23] Treasury Secretary Henry Morgenthau was initially sceptical whether Donald Duck was the right figure to convince the Americans to pay taxes. He tried to pressurise Disney to introduce a new figure, a "Mr Average Taxpayer" for "The New Spirit", but Disney managed to push the production firm's top star, demonstrating how easy filling in the tax form is (even Donald managed without difficulties!) and at the same time

22 Jones (1996, 115); Shale (1976).

23 It is not accidental that Donald has to pay 13 dollars and has the house number 1313, traditionally associated with bad luck.

brightening the dry matter of tax declaration.[24] But furthermore, Donald in "The New Spirit" incorporated the typical American "common man" as imagined by the American constitution. On the one hand, he is rational and in favour of pursuing his own advantage. On the other hand, and due to his limited intellectual abilities, he cleaves more strongly to his values and norms and therefore embodies the basis of the US democracy.[25] Rife with patriotism, he cares passionately about his democratic rights and is willing to fight for them. The success of the film proved Disney's concept was convincing: "The New Spirit" was (with 24 others) nominated for the best documentary feature at the 15th Academy Awards. The film, which was supplied free, was booked in 11,700 theatres in the six weeks prior to Tax Day on 15 March 1942[26] and thus was seen by 32 million Americans. In a Gallup poll, 37% admitted that the movie had fostered their willingness to pay taxes when they had to fill in their income tax return for the first time in their lives.[27]

9.2.2 "Putzke Wants to Know" (FRG, 1953)[28]

In contrast to America's most popular cartoon character 11 years earlier, Erwin Putzke is in a terrible mood at the beginning of the short film "Putzke wants to know" (1953). The family father and electrician with a workshop of his own is annoyed and upset by the duty of filling in his tax return, grumbling at his wife and daughter and even at their budgie. Whereas the task of filling in his tax return is completely new for Donald Duck, but welcomed with patriotic enthusiasm, Erwin Putzke is familiar with taxpaying duties, but completely demotivated.

The film's tax morale message is conveyed to its audience against the backdrop of a sober post-war reality characterised by allied occupation and the Allies' say in West German tax policies during a period of laborious economic build-up after a lost war.[29] The tax system was partially taken over from the Weimar Republic and the Third Reich, with minor changes by the foreign occupying forces, which removed anti-Semitic excesses from the German tax code. Tax rates were high, with a top income tax rate of up to

24 Schickel (1997, 270).
25 Lammersdorf (2005, 92f). Lammersdorf examines Friedrich (1942, 29–37). See also Lane (1967).
26 Shull and Wilt (2004, 125).
27 Gabler (2006, 385).
28 "Putzke will es wissen". Director: Peter Pewas. Book: Peter Pewas, based on an idea of R. A. Stemmle and H. Wobser. Camera: Klaus Schumann, Heinz Pehlke. Cut: Ulrich Wiedmann. Music: Martin Böttcher. Actors: Max Walter Sieg, Wolfgang Schwarz. Production: Neue Deutsche Wochenschau, Hamburg, by order of the German Civil Liberties Union. Format: 35 mm, black-white. Length: 456m = 17 min. Premiere: January 1953. The short film is available at Filmarchiv im Bundesarchiv Berlin and online at https://videos.uni-paderborn.de/video/Putzke-will-es-wissen-FRG-1952/ac91650c0016c4f244b1566f84dfccae, last accessed Oct. 24, 2022. (Rightsholder: FRG).
29 Muscheid (1986).

95%. In addition to making the Germans pay for occupation costs, the Allies had a strong interest in keeping taxes higher in Germany than in their homelands, which in contrast to Germany had won the war.[30] So they refused all German attempts to reduce taxes, first by the provisional government and after 1949 by the government of the newly founded Federal Republic of Germany (FRG). Both German politicians and the press agreed that under these conditions tax morale was extraordinarily bad in the western part of Germany, although statistics were not available and the figures were only occasionally cited in the debates.[31] One exception was Württemberg-Baden's chief finance president Ludwig Ellinger, who estimated that the taxes evaded in West Germany in 1950 amounted to 4.5 billion German Marks, which was about a quarter of the total governmental budget of 16 billion.[32] How could voluntary compliance be enforced? The Social Democrats called for more controls and penalties. In contrast, the Conservatives argued that it was the high tax burden that was responsible for the dishonest taxpayment behaviour of the Germans. After 1949, the de facto tax burden was slowly reduced, but public opinion about taxpaying did not seem to improve significantly in the wake of this measure – a development that confronted the coalition of conservative and liberal parties with severe problems of argumentation. The Office of the High Commissioner US, Germany (HICOG) also put pressure on the government to take measures to restore the formerly (allegedly) so good German tax morale.[33] The conservative government under Chancellor Konrad Adenauer and Minister of Finance Fritz Schäffer therefore developed the idea that tax morale did not result from bureaucratic failures or was a consequence of flawed policies. Instead the tax morale question was relegated to citizens' individual responsibility and conscience. Citizens therefore had to be educated to understand the obligation to pay taxes. The finance ministry used various media to address the taxpayers and convince them to pay taxes honestly. Citizens were sent requests to return annual tax declarations accompanied by letters in which the purposes of spending were explained in detail.[34] And in 1953, they were shown "Putzke want to know" at movie theatres. This movie was thus part of a larger tax education programme, as "The New Spirit" had been 11 years earlier, even if the dimensions of the German programme were much smaller.

The Western German concept of tax education built on American roots in two respects. First, the film can be understood as part of the re-education campaign for Germany after World War II. The Allies, and especially

30 Ullmann (2005, 179).

31 Schönhärl (2019b, 175).

32 As cited in Willi Lausen (SPD) in the Bundestag, 145. Session, 31 May 1951, p. 5741, available at http://pdok.bundestag.de/, last accessed Oct. 24, 2022.

33 German Bundestag: Allied High Commission for Germany, The Council, Printed Paper No. 845, 21.04.1950, https://dserver.bundestag.de/btd/01/008/0100854.pdf, last accessed Oct. 24, 2022.

34 Schönhärl (2019b, 175).

the USA, tried to democratise and re-educate the defeated Germans and to convert them from their submissive stance to authority into free and responsible citizens, in order to avoid the danger of Germany again succumbing to extremism in the future.[35] Re-education in Germany was practised not only by the staff of the US High Commission, but also by various private associations like the American Civil Liberties Union (ACLU).[36] The aim of this association was to encourage the Germans to protect their civil rights (understood in the sense of the "bill of rights"), even against unjust government demands or decisions. The ACLU wanted to make the Germans understand that these civil rights were closely connected with civil duties like paying taxes. And it was the ACLU that initiated the Foundation of the German Civil Liberties Union (*Bund für Bürgerrechte*) in 1949, which was funded mainly by contributions from the US High Commission, and initiated the production of "Putzke wants to know".[37] Thus, second, the initiators of the German film were in close contact with the US American mother association and so must have been familiar with the US tradition of tax education as described above.

The idea to use the film as a medium for re-education was far from inventive: not only had films been extensively used for propaganda purposes under Nazi dictatorship but they were also shown in the occupation period between 1945 and 1949 to re-educate the Germans.[38] After 1949, some of the newly founded German ministries, amongst them the Marshall Plan Ministry, continued this approach to democratise citizens and to build up public relations. The Ministry of Internal Affairs did so with the film "Country of Light" (about the German Olympic Youth Excursion to Helsinki in 1952), and the Ministry for All-German Questions with "Way of the Cross of Freedom" (1950/51) and "Poste restante Turtle Dove" (1952).[39] At the same time, the Federal Agency for Homeland Service (*Bundeszentrale für Heimatdienst*) produced a series of documentary films such as "The Parliament", "The Daily Routine of an MP" or "How a Law Comes into Existence".[40] And also the HICOG produced several films for re-education, e.g. "The Case Strobel" (1950).[41] "Putzke wants to know" can therefore be understood as part of a whole series of movies to educate Germans to become better (and democratically minded) citizens, and the German Finance Ministry subsidised the production with 60,000 Marks. Peter Pewas (1904–1984) became the film's

35 Fisher (2007).
36 Rupieper (2005).
37 Lammersdorf (2005); Rupieper (1993, 315).
38 Hahn (1997; 2005); Fay (2008); Görl (2009).
39 "Kreuzweg der Freiheit", "Postlagernd Turteltaube".
40 N. N. 25.03.1953, 31f.
41 "Der Fall Strobel". Other productions were planned, but it is unclear if they were indeed produced, see Rupieper (1993, 325).

director.[42] As a commercial artist who had sympathised with the extreme left during the Weimar Republic, Pewas had been accused of high treason and imprisoned twice during the Nazi period, but had nonetheless been able to study at the Film Academy at Babelsberg.[43] After 1945, he co-founded the DEFA film production company at Babelsberg and produced "Street acquaintanceships", one of the popular rubble movies (*Trümmerfilme*).[44] In Pewas' opinion, the German film industry had the duty to foster democracy, to extinguish German arrogance, subservience and militarism, and to provide impulses for building up a new home country.[45] In 1949, he founded his own production company in Munich, which produced about 100 spots for TV advertisements, but he did not manage a real breakthrough as an artist. In the Putzke case, however, it was compliance toward tax duties that Pewas tried to advertise.

What is the movie's narrative and message? Putzke, upset about having to fill in his tax return, thinks about how much taxes reduce his quality of life and living standard because they are levied on everything: alcoholic drinks, cigarettes, cinema, income.[46] But despite these direct and indirect taxes, there is no money available to mend the street in front of his house (which was in very bad condition like much of the infrastructure in the post-war decade). "The high-ups" seem to just throw the money he pays down the drain. Putzke, full of anger, decides to find out why he has to pay and what his money is spent on. He starts with the local tax office, where he is warmly welcomed ("a taxpayer!") and informed that most of his taxes are not spent on the local level but on the federal level, in the German capital Bonn. He goes there and visits the Finance Minister Fritz Schäffer, who performed in person in the film. "Nice that you ask this question, Mr Putzke. To do so is your good right, and I wish that taxpayers in general cared more about it," Schäffer thus compliments Putzke's interest in the topic, handling him the 1,700 pages of the federal government budget for the year 1951. Up to this point, Putzke resembles Donald Duck in "The New Spirit" as an incarnation of the "common man" who cleaves to his values and norms and is willing to fight for his rights.

But this interpretation quickly loses ground as Putzke is not confronted with the simple task of filling in an easy tax return form. Rather, he is hopelessly overwhelmed by Schäfer´s voluminous federal government budget. Despite all his best and sudorific efforts, the solid yet simple craftsman cannot

42 This choice was not self-evident, because Pewas' films were known for heavily questioning bourgeoise virtues like respectable conditions, fixed residence, fixed employment, altruism and public spirit, see Kurowski (1981, 12).

43 Deutsches Filminstitut s.t.

44 "Straßenbekanntschaften", see Straßenbekanntschaften s.t.

45 Pewas (1981, 63).

46 So the German movie also takes indirect taxes into consideration, even though only in passing. These are not mentioned at all in "The New Spirit", which focuses exclusively on income tax.

make sense of the mound of information. The notes that he takes are meaningless little snippets of isolated numbers, which do not capture the overall sense of the publication.

Putzke is relieved from his struggles by a well-groomed young man who turns out to be a representative of the Civil Liberties Union (the initiator of the film). The (unnamed) civil-rights activist is in many ways a contrast to Putzke: too young to be associated with life under the Nazi dictatorship; very well informed about all issues of democratic processes, laws and rules; well educated, eloquent and equipped with elaborate documentation. Even if his profession is not mentioned, it seems likely that he is a professional politician or lobbyist in service of the Civil Liberties Union. This man helps Putzke with the complicated materials. First, he explains the procedures by which the federal budget comes into existence. Putzke understands that spending is controlled and balanced by various democratic, reliable mechanisms. Second, the electrician comes to understand that he himself uses his democratic right to vote to appoint the politicians who are responsible for spending his taxes by good governance. Third, the civil-rights activist explains that only 3% of the budget is spent on administration, whereas the rest is spent on important social and common-good measures. Putzke, more and more persuaded, has to agree that all these procedures make sense and are necessary. In answer to his quite defiant question about why, however, no money is available for the reconstruction of the street in front of his house, the civil-rights activist wafts away in the paternoster, recommending Putzke contact local politicians about this question. In the last clip, we see Putzke again, having finally completed his tax return. At this moment, he and his wife realise that work on their street has just started: "A wonder – due to my taxes!"

Like in "The New Spirit", the idea of a fiscal contract is central to the argumentation of the film: the taxpayer gets many extraordinarily important services from the state in return for the money he or she has to pay. These services had to be explained in more detail, because they are not as easy to grasp as US military spending during World War II, where evil aggressors had to be fought. So the quid pro quo is listed in detail: the defence contribution, as a kind of insurance in the Cold War; common duties which are directed towards the future like building streets and dykes, funding science and the meteorological service, and organising border protection; social purposes, especially assistance for groups like war widows and orphans. Expenses caused by the recent war, like care for war victims as a duty of the community, are given central importance in "Putzke wants to know", explicitly invoking all the traumatic experiences that the spectators themselves had probably gone through. The necessity and reasonability of all these purposes are explained in accentuated transparency, in obvious distinction to the way the public budget was hidden and disguised in the Nazi era. In contrast, narratives legitimising tax evasion or tax avoidance are refuted: tax revenue is *not* thrown down the drain by the government but instead used very carefully and economically. And members of the middle classes like the Putzke family are *not* exploited by exorbitant taxes. Compared with the pitiable war orphans, they are quite well-off – even if only one visit to the cinema per week is possible now instead of two as in earlier times (maybe: under Nazi dictatorship?), as Putzke complains.

But what is Putzke, our ideal citizen, like? Like Donald Duck, he is competent at his job (not as a dubious actor, but as a master craftsman, so much more solidly respectable), concerned about his good life and personal standard of living. And like Donald, he becomes aware of his responsibility for the common good, once he is reminded of this and it is explained to him. But whereas his limited intellectual capacities do not hinder Donald from grasping and immediately doing what is right in the sense of common norms, Putzke is not able to understand by himself. His ineffective, naive attempts to decode the complex financial system even make him deplorable and risible. What he urgently needs to help him understand is the leadership and explanation of a professional politician, here the activist of the Civil Liberties Union. Only with the young man's help is Putzke able to grasp the nucleus of his civil duties and thus act accordingly as a reliable member of the community. This sublimation is immediately honoured by a direct reward, an external motivation for his new behaviour, the street in front of his house is repaired. So Putzke differs considerably from Donald: he is not the "common man", the pillar of US American democracy. Rather he is a "little man", as the founding fathers (and few mothers) of the Second German Republic imagined him or her. After the experiences of the Nazi period, German citizens were suspected of being easily seduced by political extremism because they allegedly lacked the intellectual abilities necessary to be reliable democrats.[47] Thus leadership and advice from professionals (portrayed in the film by the young representative of the Civil Liberties Union) is indispensable for the German "little man", because he lacks knowledge, intellectual capacity and reflection. Society and state in Western Germany were not easy tasks, but complicated and difficult. Putzke is therefore not a pro-active hero of democracy like Donald, but he has to learn to accept it. Following this German conception, after having voted these politicians into office, citizens could quietly lean back and leave business to the politicians' professional, reliable and careful care – an image that fits very well with the authoritarian style of rule of Konrad Adenauer's "chancellor democracy".[48] Thus, the American understanding of civil rights and the duty of citizens to protect them did not fit into post-war Germany, and associations with the purpose of promoting this understanding were short-lived. When the High Commission's funding for the Civil Liberties Union was reduced and finally stopped altogether after the foundation of the FRG in 1949, the umbrella organisation had to halt

47 Lammersdorf (2005, 93f). The term "little man" picks up on the title of the famous book by Fallada (1932).

48 Niclauß (2004, 17–66); Recker (2016, 47–66).

its activities in 1954 (although some local committees continued to exist); despite intensive attempts no other funding could be organised.[49] This may be a sign that the civil-rights approach did not comply with the FRG's democratic understanding that viewed the Federal High Court of Justice, which had in the meanwhile started work, as sufficient to defend civil rights.

"Putzke wants to know" was appended to the box-office hit "Captain Bay-Bay" and shown in German cinemas at the beginning of 1953. But the film was not a success. Neither journalists nor the cinema public reacted enthusiastically. Either the German citizens did not feel they were depicted correctly or they felt this image to be uncomplimentary, uncomfortable and far from enjoyable: they did not like the film. Cinema operators commented very critically too: they described the film as state propaganda, which they wished to avoid after catastrophic experiences of involvement during the Third Reich. In any case, they preferred to play commercial advertisements, for which they could charge money, before and after the main film. There were only a few screenings of the Putzke film.[50] This might have been one reason why "Putzke wants to know" remained the only attempt by the Finance Ministry to employ the medium of film for tax education in Germany.

9.3 Conclusion

The two films "The New Spirit" and "Putzke wants to know" differ greatly in their historical settings and styles. However, both films prominently employ the idea of the fiscal contract, emphasising that taxpayers receive indispensable services in return for their money, be it for purposes of state protection or state building. At the moment when the taxpayers understand what they should do, both main characters behave accordingly – a very Socratic idea: you have only to inform people thoroughly and they will act appropriately. Nevertheless, the role of the taxpayer in the two national democratic systems differed greatly, depending on the main idea of the role of citizens towards the state.

However, this strongly pro-active and optimistic form of tax education in movies seems to be bound mainly to situations where the capacity of taxpayers to satisfy governmental demands is extraordinarily challenged (be it due to an ongoing war or due to the consequences of a lost war in combination with foreign occupation) and important and controversial tax reforms have just taken place or are planned (in the US in 1941, in West Germany in 1953/1954). Governments only seemed willing to bear the high production costs of movies at such challenging points in tax history. This thesis is further supported by the far-reaching tax campaigns that the Spanish government started between 1977 and 1985 after the country's transition to democracy,

49 Rupieper (1993, 315).
50 N. N. 25.03.1953.

using children's books and comic strips as well as TV spots on fiscal purposes. When, in contrast, the public budgeting situation becomes more relaxed and political controversy about the tax system recedes again, than tax education seems to lose its priority. In Western Germany tax education was stopped when the economic miracle gained speed after 1953 and the governmental tax coffers filled without any further effort to educate the taxpayers in compliance.[51] The US-American Internal Revenue Service, however, continued tax education even when after World War II the US Congress decided (in bipartisan consensus) to keep the new tax system beyond the end of the war to finance the American welfare state. Anyway, tax education films prove to be extraordinarily useful source material for examining and comparing understandings of democratic societies, "stripped of all phrases", as Joseph Schumpeter put it.[52]

References

Abend, Gabriel. 2010. What's New and What's Old about the New Sociology of Morality. In *Handbook of the Sociology of Morality*, eds. Steven Hitlin and Stephen Vaisey, 561–584. New York, NY: Springer.

Abend, Gabriel. 2014. *The Moral Background: An Inquiry into the History of Business Ethics.* Princeton: Princeton University Press.

Brownlee, W. E. 1996. *Federal Taxation in America: A Short History.* Washington, DC: Woodrow Wilson Center Press.

Brownlee, Wilson E. and Paul S. Boyer. 2004. Taxation. In *The Oxford Companion to United States History* (Online Edition), ed. Paul S. Boyer. Oxford: Oxford University Press.

Deutsches Filminstitut. s.t. Peter Pewas, http://www.difarchiv.deutsches-filminstitut.de/dt2tp0136.htm, last accessed Oct. 24, 2022.

Fallada, Hans. 1932. *Kleiner Mann - was nun?* Berlin: Rowohlt.

Fay, Jennifer. 2008. *Theaters of Occupation: Hollywood and the Reeducation of Postwar Germany.* Minneapolis: University of Minnesota Press.

Fisher, Jaimey. 2007. *Disciplining Germany: Youth, Re-education, and Reconstruction After the Second World War.* Detroit, Michigan: Wayne State University Press.

Friedrich, Carl J.d. 1942. *The New Belief in the Common Man.* Boston: Little, Brown.

Gabler, Neal. 2007. *Walt Disney: The Triumph of the American Imagination.* New York, Toronto: Vintage Books.

Görl, Simone. 2009. Die Werbefilme des Kölner Interessenverbandes Die Waage, *Geschichte in Köln* 56: 333–353.

Hahn, Brigitte J. 1997. *Umerziehung durch Dokumentarfilm? Ein Instrument amerikanischer Kulturpolitik im Nachkriegsdeutschland (1945 - 1953).* Münster: Lit.

Hahn, Brigitte J. 2005. Dokumentarfilm im Dienste der Umerziehung. Amerikanische Filmproduktion 1945-1953. In *Lernen Sie diskutieren!: Re-education durch Film. Strategien der westlichen Alliierten nach 1945*, ed. Heiner Roß, 19–32. Berlin: CineGraph Babelsberg.

51 Schönhärl (2019a).

52 Schumpeter (1918); See also Martin, Mehrotra and Prasad (2009).

Jones, Carolyn C. 1996. Mass-Based Income Taxation: Creating a Taxpaying Culture, 1940–1952. In *Funding the Modern American State, 1941 - 1995: The Rise and Fall of the Era of easy Finance*, ed. W. E. Brownlee, 107–47. Cambridge: Woodrow Wilson Center Press.

Jones, Carolyn C. 2018. Seeing Taxation in the Mid-Twentieth Century: US Tax Compliance. In *The Leap of Faith. The Fiscal Foundations of Successful Government in Europe and America*, ed. Sven Steinmo, 198–222. Oxford: Oxford University Press.

Koppes, Clayton R. and Gregory D. Black. 1987. *Hollywood Goes to War: How Politics, Profits, and Propaganda Shaped World War II Movies*. New York: Free Press.

Kurowski, Ulrich. 1981. Der Filmregisseur Peter Pewas. In *Der Filmregisseur Peter Pewas: Materialien und Dokumente*, eds. Ulrich Kurowski and Andreas Meyer, 7–12. Berlin: Spiess.

Lammersdorf, Raimund. 2005. "Das Volk ist streng demokratisch". Amerikanische Sorgen über das autoritäre Bewusstsein der Deutschen in der Besatzungszeit und frühen Bundesrepublik. In *Demokratiewunder: Transatlantische Mittler und die kulturelle Öffnung Westdeutschlands 1945 – 1970*, eds. Arnd Bauerkämper, Konrad Jarausch, and Marcus M. Payk, 85–103. Göttingen: Vandenhoeck & Ruprecht.

Lane, Robert E. 1967. *Political Ideology: Why the American Common Man Believes What He Does*. New York: Free Press.

Likhovski, Assaf. 2007. "Training in Citizenship": Tax Compliance and Modernity. *Law & Social Inquiry* 32(3): 665–700.

Martin, Isaac W., Ajay K. Mehrotra, and Monica Prasad. 2009. The Thunder of History: The Origins and Development of the New Fiscal Sociology. In *The New Fiscal Sociology: Taxation in Comparative and Historical Perspective*, eds. Isaac W. Martin, Ajay K. Mehrotra, and Monica Prasad, 1–27. Cambridge, New York: Cambridge University Press.

Meisel, Franz. 1883. *Die Ergebnisse der Finanzstrafjustiz in Österreich seit der Einführung des Gefällsstrafgesetzbuches vom 11. Juli 1835 (1836 - 1879)*. Wien: Hölder.

Muscheid, Jutta. 1986. *Die Steuerpolitik der Bundesrepublik Deutschland 1949 - 1982*. Berlin: Duncker & Humblot.

N. N. 1943 (Jan.). Disney Studio at War. *Theater Arts 27*: 31–39.

N. N. 1953. Putzke will es wissen. *Der Spiegel*, March 25th.

Niclauß, Karlheinz. 2004. 2nd ed. *Kanzlerdemokratie. Regierungsführung von Konrad Adenauer bis Gerhard Schröder*. Paderborn [u.a.]: Schöningh.

Pewas, Peter. 1981. Über das Gesicht des kommenden Films. Vortrag in der Volkshochschule Wilmersdorf 1945. In *Der Filmregisseur Peter Pewas. Materialien und Dokumente*, eds. Ulrich Kurowski and Andreas Meyer, 62–64. Berlin: Spiess.

Recker, Marie-Luise. 2016. *Konrad Adenauer: Leben und Politik*. München: Beck.

Rupieper, Hermann-Josef. 1993. *Die Wurzeln der Westdeutschen Nachkriegsdemokratie: Der Amerikanische Beitrag 1945 - 1952*. Opladen: Westdt. Verl.

Rupieper, Hermann-Josef. 2005. Peacemaking with Germany. Grundlinien amerikanischer Demokratisierungspolitik 1945-1954. *In Demokratiewunder: Transatlantische Mittler und die kulturelle Öffnung Westdeutschlands 1945 – 1970*, eds. Arnd Bauerkämper, Konrad Jarausch, and Marcus M. Payk, 41–56. Göttingen: Vandenhoeck & Ruprecht.

Schickel, Richard. 1997. 3rd ed. *The Disney Version. The Life, Times, Art and Commerce of Walt Disney*. Chicago: Elephant Backpapers.

Schmölders, Günter. 1960. *Das Irrationale in der Öffentlichen Finanzwirtschaft: Probleme der Finanzpsychologie*. Hamburg: Rowohlt.

Schönhärl, Korinna. 2019a. Die Steuermoral weltweit. Eine Artikelserie in der Frankfurter Allgemeinen Zeitung in den Jahren 1963/64. In *Moderner Kapitalismus. Wirtschafts- und unternehmenshistorische Beiträge*, eds. Jan-Otmar Hesse et al., 475–92. Tübingen: Mohr Siebeck.

Schönhärl, Korinna. 2019b. Steuermoral in Westdeutschland nach dem Zweiten Weltkrieg. Eine Diskursanalytische Rekonstruktion. *Leviathan* 47: 169–191.

Schumpeter, Joseph. 1918. *Die Krise des Steuerstaats. Zeitfragen aus dem Gebiete der Soziologie*. Graz, Leipzig: Leuschner Lubensky.

Shale, Richard. 1976. 2nd ed. *Donald Duck Joins Up: The Walt Disney Studio During World War II. 1982*. Ann Arbor: UMI Research Press.

Shull, Michael S. and David E. Wilt. 2004. 2nd ed. *Doing Their Bit: Wartime American Animated Short Films, 1939-1945*. Jefferson: McFarland & Company Inc. Publishers.

Straßenbekanntschaften. s.t. DEFA-Filmdatenbank, https://www.defa-stiftung.de/filme/filmsuche/strassenbekanntschaft/, last accessed Oct. 24, 2022.

Torgler, Benno. 2007. *Tax Compliance and Tax Morale: A Theoretical and Empirical Analysis*. Cheltenham, UK, Northampton, MA: Edward Elgar.

Ullmann, Hans-Peter. 2005. *Der deutsche Steuerstaat: Geschichte der öffentlichen Finanzen vom 18. Jahrhundert bis heute*. München: Beck.

Van Brederode, Robert (Ed.). 2020. *Ethics and Taxation*. Singapore: Springer.

10 "Exceptional" Tax Amnesties

A Common Swiss Way of Fighting Tax Evasion in the Twentieth Century

Aniko Fehr and Sylvain Praz

10.1 Introduction

This volume shows that throughout the world and in different periods of history, states developed strategies to limit the extent of tax avoidance. These measures can be divided into two major categories. On the one hand, state authorities increased their means of control and sanctions and, on the other hand, they introduced measures to strengthen the degree of consent of taxpayers to the tax system. Tax authorities generally portray these two types of measures in a dialectical relationship. For example, enhanced means of investigation are often presented as guaranteeing a more uniform application of the legislation and, consequently, a more equitable distribution of the tax burden. In return, implementing fairer and more equal taxation is supposed to enhance tax consent and disincentivise tax evasion.

This contribution focuses on a particular measure against tax evasion, one which lies at the crossroads between the repression of tax avoidance and the promotion of tax consent, namely tax amnesties. Tax amnesties are not rare or even exceptional. In Germany, especially in the first half of the twentieth century, amnesties were often used as a fiscal policy tool and as an attempt to limit capital flight.[1] In the United States, there has not yet been a tax amnesty at the federal level, but numerous states have decreed such measures since the beginning of the 1980s. Many other countries resorted to such policies in the 1990s and 2000s as well.[2] Tax amnesties are generally considered a convenient way to achieve short-term goals, such as raising additional public revenue. They are often enacted hand in hand with a fiscal reform or a reinforcement of measures intended to fight tax evasion.

Yet, the effects of tax amnesties vary along clear class-based divisions. The ability to avoid taxation is closely linked to types of wealth and revenue, and (low) wage earners in particular are unable to hide a significant proportion

1 The first amnesty for the entire German Reich was in 1913. Subsequent major ones were then held in 1918–1920, 1930–1933, 1949, 1954 and 1988/1990, Barbara Petrick-Rump (1996, 18–37).

2 For a partial overview and an attempt to assess the effects of such policies, see Baer and Le Borgne (2008).

DOI: 10.4324/9781003333197-14

of their salaries from the tax authorities.[3] Accordingly, upper-class taxpayers can benefit more from amnesties than lower-class taxpayers. Additionally, in a progressive tax system, if tax rates are lowered as a consequence of an amnesty – or if the amnesty helps to prevent an increase – taxpayers in the upper brackets gain relatively more (and by the same logic, they also profit more from avoiding taxation in the first place).

In the case of Switzerland, many tax amnesties were granted in the twentieth century at both the federal and the cantonal level. According to the Swiss tax system, a "general" tax amnesty allows for a complete cancellation of the penalties and fines ordinarily applied by the legislation in cases of tax evasion, including any additional tax assessment.[4] Most of the time, these tax amnesties were presented as extraordinary and one-time measures. Yet, a conservative count shows that there were around 40 amnesties between 1917 and 1968 at the cantonal level.[5] On top of this, three general tax amnesties were conducted at the federal level (1940, 1944 and 1968), and from 1934 to 1939, fiscal legislation partially protected taxpayers who voluntarily self-disclosed tax evasions from the past.[6]

On the federal level, the first two amnesties were part of larger tax reforms and acted as a counterpart to the planned strengthening of measures to reduce tax evasion. Furthermore, they were designed to help new legislation pass political veto points, such as the popular vote that was often required to enact the reforms. Amnesties were also considered a way to guarantee sufficient revenue for the state under the upcoming tax regime.

In this chapter, we present two cases of tax amnesty in Switzerland. First, the one granted in the canton of Zurich in 1936 and, second, the national tax amnesty adopted in 1968. These amnesties stand out because both were first included in a larger programme aimed at fighting tax evasion. But in the end, these tax amnesties were the only so-called anti-evasion policy enacted. Who fostered this development, why and using which arguments? The distinct setting common to both amnesties makes them especially suitable case studies to analyse the attitude of tax authorities and the major socio-political actors towards tax evasion in twentieth-century Switzerland.

10.2 The 1936 Tax Amnesty in Zurich

The process leading to the adoption of an overall tax amnesty by popular vote in April 1936 in the canton of Zurich can be divided into three periods. First, in 1933, the cantonal Finance Direction evoked the possibility of

3 On this issue in connection with tax amnesties, Biedermann (1948, 112–119). On the issue of class in connection with tax evasion in the Swiss context, Tanner (1994, 129); Guex (1998, 65–75, 105–128, 257ff); Tanner (2012, 33–36); Guex (2012, 1097, 1105, 1109).

4 Fehr (2017).

5 Gubler (1947, 5); Brupbacher (1968, 155).

6 Gubler (1947, 3–4).

an amnesty several times, as a means of increasing tax revenue, but argued against this policy. In a second period in the years 1934–1935, a tax amnesty was explicitly requested by a member of parliament, but his motion was met with general rebuttal. In the third and final period from the end of 1935 to 1936, tax amnesty reappeared as part of a large financial programme, comprising six different laws.

The following section will try to shed some light on the reasons why a policy that was first largely rejected was in the end adopted with a comfortable majority by parliament and subsequently accepted in a popular vote, whereas other measures to fight against tax avoidance, a major political topic at the time, were all eliminated from the final bill.

10.2.1 The First Attempts and Failures to Promote an Amnesty

In the process leading to the adoption of a tax amnesty in 1936 in Zurich, the earliest consideration that we have identified dated back to July 1933. At the time and as a consequence of the Great Depression, the cantonal authorities were beginning to struggle with growing deficits.[7] The Zurich finance minister, Adolf Streuli, a member of the business-friendly and liberal Radical Party,[8] mentioned the possibility of reducing these deficits by introducing an amnesty. The idea was to enable taxpayers to lay bare their hitherto undeclared wealth or income with no penalties, so as to broaden the taxable base and boost fiscal revenue. However, A. Streuli dismissed this solution as “unfair”, “amoral” and encouraging tax evasion in the long run.[9] The reason why A. Streuli evoked an amnesty if he was against it remains unclear. One hypothesis would be that this option was being considered by other political actors, perhaps influenced by the German amnesties of the time. Perhaps it was also viewed as a means to render a softening of sanctions against evasion – a policy that was promoted by the tax administration[10] – more acceptable as a compromise. In December of that year, the Zurich government also rejected an amnesty in its public annual budget report, but instead considered amending the existing legislation by lowering sanctions in a bid to foster tax recovery by facilitating taxpayers’ voluntary self-disclosure.[11]

The first explicit call for an amnesty came in February 1934 with a parliamentary motion from Friedrich Werder, a member of the Democratic Party – a rather diverse party that represented the interests of white-collar employees and certain small business fractions, and which had historically presented a

7 StAZH, M 14 h.10, Nr. 3, Staatsrechnungsprüfungskommission, 14.07.1933.

8 “Freisinnige Partei” (Free Democratic Party).

9 StAZH, M 14 h.10, Nr. 3, Staatsrechnungsprüfungskommission, 26.09.1933, 2.

10 StAZH, M 14 h.10, Nr. 3, Kommission der Staatsrechnungsprüfungskommission, 26.09.1933.

11 Bericht des Regierungsrates an den Kantonsrat zum Voranschlag 1934, 14.12.1933. In *Amtsblatt 1933*, 1028-1030. Some business circles welcomed the proposition, see [s.n.] 1934, Voranschlag und Steuerfuss im Kanton Zürich, *Neue Zürcher Zeitung*, February 2.

progressive agenda. The motion's main goal was, again, to raise tax revenues. Werder argued that a significant share of the taxpayers avoided taxation on income and wealth, and that an opportunity should be given to them to regularise their situation. He added that after this amnesty, anyone who still continued to evade taxation should "be subject to the full force of the law".[12]

This motion met with wide opposition in parliament. Robert Schmid, speaking for the Radical Party, reckoned that an amnesty would be an admission of failure for the tax law in force at the time, which had been largely designed by his party. The main point of that law, adopted in 1917, had been precisely to reduce tax evasion and had already included an amnesty. Accepting that tax evasion was a major issue would also have strengthened the claims of the Socialist Party, who had just criticised the tax administration in an important case of tax evasion in 1931.[13] Furthermore, the Radical Party was not willing to risk larger debates about a tax reform and wanted to prioritise expenditure cuts over raising new revenue. However, in these debates, Schmid only laconically added: "The state must ensure that citizens give it what belongs to it".[14]

Finance Minister A. Streuli, speaking for the government, also rejected the proposal. He argued that the financial benefits of an amnesty might not be very substantial, considering the losses it would involve due to missing fines and fees. He also stressed, as in 1933, that an amnesty was unfair, not only to the honest taxpayers but also with regard to those tax dodgers who had already faced penalties. A. Streuli expressed fear that an amnesty would in fact not help reduce tax evasion at all, but would be regarded as a kind of collusion between the state and the tax evaders. It would create the expectation of recurring amnesties and "the granting of the amnesty under the current law would be a direct incentive for increased tax evasion".[15] In the parliamentary debates, no party explicitly supported an amnesty. The Socialists and Communists in particular insisted on the need to tighten taxation procedures, but without making concessions to the tax evaders.

During all these debates, since July 1933, many voices, including that of Finance Minister A. Streuli, wanted to amend the law and lower or even abolish fines in cases of voluntary self-disclosure instead of granting an amnesty.[16] Between October 1934 and October 1935, the government

12 PKR, 26.02.1934, 964.

13 SoZA, Tätigkeitsbericht der Sozialdemokratischen Fraktion des Kantonsrates pro 1931/1932, 31.12.1932.

14 PKR, 26.02.1934, 964.

15 PKR, 26.02.1934, 967.

16 This was mainly inspired by a provision that could be called a "permanent tax amnesty" in the tax law of the canton St. Gallen. There, any taxpayer could, at any time, avoid all fines and fees if s/he self-disclosed past evasion. Germany was also influential. See for example: E. L. 1936. Steuerbelastung und Steueramnestie. *Neue Zürcher Zeitung*, January 25. The term "permanent tax amnesty" has also been coined by Petrick-Rump (1996, 219).

attempted to amend the tax law to that effect, but the parliament refused to pass such a reform.[17] Up to this point, the idea of a tax amnesty or any concession toward tax evaders seemed to face widespread rejection across the political spectrum.[18]

10.2.2 The Return of the Amnesty as a "Sweetener"[19]

But things changed in November 1935, when the government presented a vast finance programme addressing the continuously growing budget deficits. From then on, the fiscal reform was included in a larger legislative package that contained important expenditure cuts on the one hand and measures to increase revenues on the other. Examples of revenue-raising measures included an increase in inheritance taxes, a new cantonal crisis tax (a short-term progressive tax on high incomes), and a few other smaller taxes and excises. In this context, the government also wanted to reinforce the fight against tax evasion, mainly with the introduction of compulsory wage statements, the publishing of the names of refractory taxpayers and tax evaders, and a tax amnesty.[20] This time, the cantonal government contended that this amnesty would be justified since the package simultaneously strengthened the means to fight tax evasion. The amnesty was also considered a way of incentivising citizens to adopt the whole financial programme, which had to be accepted in a popular vote.

One reason for the government's volte-face in the question of an amnesty probably was that the fiscal administration witnessed an increase in tax evasion and tax resistance at the time.[21] In the city of Zurich, death inventories revealed that around 20% of income and 8% of wealth went undeclared in 1933.[22] Given that these inventories were far from waterproof against dissimulation, the real scale of tax avoidance was probably significantly higher.[23]

17 Gesetz über die Ergänzung des Gesetzes betreffend die direkten Steuern vom 25. November 1917 mit den Abänderungen vom 19. Februar 1922 und vom 2. Dezember 1928. Vorlage des Regierungsrates, 27.10.1934. In *Amtsblatt ZH 1934*, p. 930–938; Gesetz über die Ergänzung des Gesetzes betreffend die direkten Steuern vom 25. November 1917 mit den Abänderungen vom 19. Februar 1922 und vom 2. Dezember 1928. Antrag der Kommission, 08.02.1935. In *Amtsblatt ZH 1935*, 300–301; PKR, 26.08.1935, 212–213; PKR, 14.10.1935, 385–386.

18 See also Klaus (1935).

19 "Zückerchen", in the words of the socialist MP August Ziegler, PKR, 17.02.1936, 765.

20 Bericht des Regierungsrates an den Kantonsrat zum Voranschlag 1936, 22.11.1935. In *Amtsblatt ZH 1935*, 1117ff., especially 1149–1152 and 1198–1202.

21 Geschäftsbericht (1935, 260–262); StAZH, M 14 h.11, Nr. 1, Kommission für Prüfung des Geschäftsberichtes, 05.09.1935, 8–9; see also Henggeler (1936, 3).

22 Honegger (1942, 10).

23 Within the administration, criticism of the laxness of these death inventories had been raised since their introduction with the tax law of 1917, StAZH, Z 353.14, Aufgaben des Steuerkommissärs gegenüber dem Inventar, 16.09.1921, 2–3, 25–26.

The tax administration's strategy against this problem was mostly not confrontation by law enforcement, but an attempt to negotiate. Symptomatic of this tendency was the 1935 attempt to make a deal with Maggi, a large food industry corporation domiciled in the canton of Zurich, in the hope of obtaining wage lists of Maggi's employees.[24] In exchange for these lists, the tax authorities promised that no penalty would be inflicted on tax evaders among the employees. This example shows how the tax administration took the opportunity to grant an informal amnesty, but one that only applied to a small portion of taxpayers and lacked any legal basis. However, this led to some confusion inside the administration as some employees were fined after all, and the new finance minister – Hans Streuli, also member of the Radical Party – had to declare the promises void.[25] Nevertheless, this case illustrates that Zurich's tax administration supported a strategy consisting of offering a "golden bridge"[26] to taxpayers, allowing them to regularise their situation.[27] Combined with the fact that parliament had only just refused to soften the sanctions, this strategy could explain why the Finance Direction came out in favour of a more generalised tax amnesty.

An even more important explanation for the proposal of this tax amnesty was probably the fact that new taxes were being introduced on the federal level.[28] This would to some extent strengthen the control of the tax administration. Specifically, this federal reform would usher in compulsory wage statements for employees with high salaries. In conjunction with the new cantonal crisis tax and the increase of municipal levels of taxation, it led to a significantly enlarged tax burden for taxpayers with high incomes. At the same time, the tax evasion issue was increasingly utilised by the Socialist Party as an argument against austerity measures.[29] Socialists argued that business income and capital could be much better taxed if more tax officers were employed. This would then render large parts of the finance programme, which were detrimental to wage earners, unnecessary. In this context, the Zurich Chamber of Commerce, among others, demanded that these new federal provisions would not authorise sanctions at the cantonal level and hinted that an amnesty could be called for in this regard.[30] These

24 StAZH, M 14 h.11, Nr. 1, Kommission für Prüfung des Geschäftsberichtes, 15.06.1936, 11.

25 StAZH, M 14 h.11, Nr. 1, Kommission für Prüfung des Geschäftsberichtes, 27.08.1936, 6–9.

26 The term "Golden Bridge" is often used for amnesties, for example: Walter Wettstein (1919, 44); Munz (1944, 29).

27 Exemplary of this tendency from a senior civil servant: Klaus (1935); See also the Chamber of Commerce indicating that in practice most of the time a taxpayer wanting to regularise his situation did *not* face penalties, Zürcher Handelskammer (1935, 21).

28 Volksabstimmung vom 26. April 1936, 27.02.1936. In *Amtsblatt ZH 1936*, 198–199; see also Geschäftsbericht 1936, 95–97.

29 [s.n.] 1935. Für eine gerechte Steuerreform, *Volksrecht*. Dezember 30 and 31; see also SozA, Ar.27.20.2, Report of the Socialist Party for the year 1936, 5.

30 AfZ, IB-ZHK A.3.2.1.8, Vorstand Handelskammer, 29.11.1935, 5.

factors also explain why many other cantons offered amnesties between 1935 and 1938.[31]

10.2.3 The Adoption of the Amnesty and the Path of Least Resistance

In the subsequent legislative period during the winter and spring of 1936, two trends regarding the Zurich public finance programme emerged.[32] First, the Socialist Party tried to slow down the legislative process in a bid to block or delay austerity measures. This tactic, combined with the fact that the cantonal government and the majority of parliament wanted to pass the bills needed to reduce the state deficit as quickly as possible, allowed the Socialist Party to obtain some concessions. In the end, the finance programme reduced expenditure less than initially intended.[33] The second process of interest to us was that, despite the adoption of an amnesty, measures to combat tax evasion had been completely eliminated from the bill.[34]

Quickly, the proposal to publish the names of refractory taxpayers and tax evaders was abandoned, as it was deemed useless and in fact no political party supported it. The core of the matter was rather the compulsory wage statement for all employees. This measure was important for two main reasons. First, the compulsory wage statement had been a point of contention between the tax administration and employers in the year following the enactment of the 1917 tax law. Despite lacking a legal basis, the tax administration had tried to force employers to communicate the salaries of their employees, but was met with fierce opposition by employers.[35] Second, the employee representatives, mainly the Socialist Party and members of the Democratic Party, tried to link the communication of wage lists with corresponding provisions against owners of capital. In particular, employee representatives reacted to attempts to enforce the compulsory wage statement by calling for the lifting of banking secrecy in tax matters.[36]

Finally, this attempt to reform the tax bill opened the door to many other claims regarding the tax law, most notably measures to strengthen the fight against tax evasion and tax breaks for small taxpayers.[37] In short, a more encompassing reform of the tax legislation risked offering the Socialist Party a platform to debate social and fiscal inequalities and thus generating long

31 Meisterhans (1939); Honegger (1942, 54).

32 StAZH, M 14 h.11 a, Staatsrechnungsprüfungskommission, 20.12.1935-21.02.1936; PKR, 17.02.1936, 764–780; PKR 24.02.1936, 784–798.

33 SozA, Ar.27.20.2, Report of the Socialist Party for the year 1936, p. 4–6 and 31; SozA, Ar. 27.15.1, Report from the parliamentary fraction of the Socialist Party for 1935–1938, 3.

34 Keller (1946, 62–64).

35 Praz (2021, 245–248).

36 PKR, 17.02.1936, 764–767, 770–771; Henggeler (1936, 3–4).

37 StAZH, M 14 h.11 a, Staatsrechnungsprüfungskommission, 16.02.1936 and 21.02.1936.

debates and procedures at a time where the majority of parliament and the government wanted to act quickly.

In the end, a circumstantial coalition of parliamentarians who represented employees (Socialists and Democrats) on the one side and business interests (mostly Radicals) on the other side removed all measures for fighting tax evasion from the bill but adopted the amnesty.[38] A significant proportion of those representing the employees declared they would reject the compulsory wage statement if no corresponding measures for the self-employed and owners of capital were introduced, while organised business wanted to avoid any other amendment, especially one targeting capital owners. In order to avoid a long and complicated process and to quickly pass the finance programme, as the president of the Chamber of Commerce commented, "only what did not meet with any opposition, namely the mere tax amnesty, was left standing".[39] In February 1936, the amnesty was adopted in parliament with 81 "yes" against 36 "no" votes and accepted in the popular vote by 63% of the citizens in April.[40]

After stating repeatedly that an amnesty without measures to fight tax evasion would be unacceptable, the government and business circles argued that the new federal tax law did in fact justify the granting of the amnesty.[41] This argument was not very convincing for two reasons. First, only a limited proportion of employees would be affected by the new federal tax law since the exemptions in the bill were set at a relatively high rate of income. Second, the tax administration had in fact by this time already managed to get salary lists from most employers.[42]

Accordingly, the Socialist Party did not oppose the amnesty and left its members free to vote, despite a few remarks commenting that it was unfair to honest taxpayers, among which were most of the workers whose salaries were easy to assess.[43] Essentially, the Socialists accepted the deal, comprising on the one hand reduced expenditure cuts and on the other hand some new taxes to finance social policies designed to meet the economic crisis.[44] For the Democratic Party, although the amnesty itself was viewed as an injustice for honest taxpayers, it was a piece of realpolitik and a way to ensure acceptance of the whole financial programme.[45] Only

38 PKR, 17.02.1936, 764–775; PKR 24.02.1936, 790–794, 797–798.

39 AfZ, IB-ZHK A.3.2.1.8, Vorstand Handelskammer, 26.03.1936, 9.

40 PKR, 24.02.1936, 798; Beschluss des Kantonsrates über die Ergebnisse der Volksabstimmung vom 26. April 1936, in *Amtsblatt* 1936, 367.

41 See for example E. L. 1936. Steuerbelastung und Steueramnestie. *Neue Zürcher Zeitung*, January 25.; AfZ, IB-ZHK A.3.2.1.8, Vorstand Handelskammer, 26.03.1936, 9.

42 PKR, 24.02.1936, 792–793.

43 ibid., 798.

44 SozA, Ar.27.20.2, Report of the Socialist Party for the year 1936, 4–8 and 31; SozA, Ar.27.15.1, Report from the parliamentary fraction of the Socialist Party for 1935–1938, 3.

45 StAZH, W II 41.39, Nr. 3, press releases: "Herzhaftes Ja!", 16.04.1936, and, insisting this was a one-off occasion, "Um die Steuerehrlichkeit. Von oben gesehen", 24.02.1937.

the Communist Party explicitly opposed the amnesty. They considered, as their representative Ernst Walter expressed before the parliamentary vote, that "the only purpose of the amnesty is to let the big tax cheats go and hang the small ones".[46]

In later years, this amnesty was presented by the cantonal government and its tax administration as contributing to the low levels of tax avoidance in Zurich and the canton's good "tax morale" when compared with other cantons.[47] This framing of Zurich's low tax avoidance as the result of – among other factors – tax amnesties is somewhat ironic given that subsequent amnesties continued to yield significant new revenues over the years.[48] Indeed, despite the fact that the rhetoric employed to defend the amnesty stressed that it was an extraordinary one-time opportunity, the 1936 tax amnesty was just one of many that were offered to taxpayers in Zurich. After the amnesties in 1917 and 1936, taxpayers benefitted from three additional ones in 1940, 1944 and 1968. In the end, over fifty years, no less than five amnesties were granted.

10.3 Failure and Success of a General Tax Amnesty (1964–1968)

In the 1960s, Swiss voters were twice called upon to decide whether they wanted to grant a general tax amnesty at the federal level. The first time, in February 1964, 58% of the voters and the majority of the cantons rejected the proposal. Four years later, in February 1968, 62% of those who voted agreed that the federal state should grant a general tax amnesty in Switzerland.[49] As we said earlier, the general tax amnesty is one of the most generous a state could grant, and the one adopted in 1968 was the last of this kind in Switzerland.

The main question this case study intends to answer is why the tax amnesty project that was rejected in 1964 was accepted barely four years later. How can we explain these two opposing votes in a relatively short period of time? To answer this question, we need to better grasp the differences between the two tax amnesty projects of the 1960s, in order to assess whether these differences can explain, at least in part, the two contrasting results.

46 PKR, 24.02.1936, 793.

47 StAZH, RRB 1937/2134, 05.08.1938; Klaus (1939, 331); Report on the accounts. In *Staatsrechnung 1941*, 374–375; Report on the accounts. In *Staatsrechnung 1945*, 334–335; Zürcher Gemeindesteuerverhältnisse (1946, 6); Biedermann (1948, 119); Illi (2008, 227).

48 Statistisches Bureau des Kantons Zürich (1951, 12); Recently, see Krummenmacher, Jörg. 2019. Die reuigen Steuersünder füllen die Staatskassen. *Neue Zürcher Zeitung*, Mai 10; Vonplon, David. 2019. Selbstanzeigen von Steuersündern bringen dem Fiskus Milliarden ein. *Neue Zürcher Zeitung*, Mai 10.

49 For more on these fiscal projects, see Fehr (2015, 2017); Hürlimann (2012, 2020); Vittoz (2014).

10.3.1 The 1964 Tax Amnesty Project

Before the 1960s, at least two other general tax amnesties had been granted by the Swiss Confederation, in 1940 and 1944.[50] These amnesties were introduced by the federal government during the Second World War, in the context of important tax reforms and financial deficits and in a position where the Federal Council had what is called "executive special power".[51]

The tax amnesty project of 1964 came about in a completely different context. First, the federal accounts were in surplus at the time. The finance minister of the time, Roger Bonvin, even referred to "especially abundant financial income" during a meeting of the Financial Commission of the National Council.[52] Second, the tax amnesty project was not the direct product of government action or the activities of right-wing parties. It was the result of a socialist enterprise that began in the early 1960s, and could be seen as part of a left-wing programme to improve the fight against tax evasion in Switzerland.[53] This socialist move led to the publication by the Federal Council of a report on the extent of tax evasion in Switzerland in May 1962, a report we will call here the *Defraudationsbericht* (report on tax evasion).[54] According to this publication, the amount of assets withheld from the Swiss tax authorities amounted to almost 40% of the country's GDP.[55]

The *Defraudationsbericht* was actually elaborated by the finance minister of the time, the Conservative Jean Bourgknecht, and his team at the Federal Finance Department. When it was published, this report was given a highly controversial reception, particularly from the business community in Switzerland. Actually, it was quickly buried by the right-wing majority in parliament, and public discussion about the extent of tax evasion in Switzerland was kind of nipped in the bud.[56] However, one concrete measure emerged as a result of the parliamentary treatment of this publication: a parliamentary proposal, coming again from the Socialists, that the federal government should grant a general tax amnesty, associated with the ability to strengthen the repression of tax evasion in Switzerland.

50 During the First World War, taxpayers were also offered some kind of amnesty, in the sense that the declarations for the newly introduced federal direct taxes could not be used by the cantons, be it retroactively or even for future (!) taxations (Guex 1993, 354).

51 "Vollmachtenregime" in German or "pleins pouvoirs" in French. This implies that citizens did not vote on these amnesties but that they were decided on by the federal government, Tanner (1986, 186-212).

52 SFA, CH-BAR#E6100B-01#1980/49#75*, Minutes of the Financial Commission of the National Council, 17.05.1963.

53 Fehr (2017, 364–367).

54 Rapport du Conseil fédéral sur la motion Eggenberger concernant une lutte plus efficace sur la fraude fiscale (du 25 mai 1962). In FF1962, vol. 1, 1097–1159.

55 Longchamp (2014, 117).

56 Fehr (2017, 367–373).

Why the Socialists demanded a tax amnesty remains somewhat unclear. To better understand this, we have first to specify that their move – the tax amnesty proposal – was heavily influenced by growing pressure since the end of the 1950s, both from the bourgeois parties and from the cantonal finance ministers, for the introduction of a general tax amnesty by the Confederation.[57] It was perhaps to counter this pressure and to take control of the legislative process that the Socialists developed the project of a tax amnesty accompanied by anti-evasion measures. Our hypothesis is therefore that for the Socialists, a general tax amnesty was supposed to be the *sweetener* designed to gain wider support (especially from fractions of the bourgeois parties) for the anti-evasion programme they wanted to introduce from the beginning.[58]

Even if it failed to gain unanimous approval in parliament, a majority accepted this proposal for a tax amnesty in September 1963.[59] There were dissonant voices about the project, among the Liberals in particular.[60] Indeed, we come now to the very heart of the political controversy about the 1964 tax amnesty project. For the majority of those who opposed it, the main issue was not so much to defend a notion of "tax justice" that would be flouted by a general tax amnesty. The main problem was much more the anti-evasion measures that would be developed by the federal administration to accompany this tax amnesty if the latter were to be adopted.

The referendum of February 1964 was about a constitutional project that did not specify the terms and conditions of the general tax amnesty or the exact measures that the law would introduce to prevent tax evasion in the future. The plan was to develop the law once the constitutional basis had been adopted by popular vote. However, before the referendum vote, the Federal Tax Administration published a draft of this planned bill in the summer of 1963, which presented, among other things, new measures aimed at fighting tax evasion in the future.[61]

The divisions between those opposing and supporting a tax amnesty were reinforced by this publication. The Swiss Banking Association, on the one hand, lobbied heavily to minimise federal competences to prevent tax evasion, especially regarding provisions that the banking industry considered to breach Swiss banking secrecy. On the other hand, the political left tried – in vain – to ensure that even tougher measures against tax evaders were introduced.[62]

57 Fehr (2015, 26–33).

58 Ibid., 41–43

59 Arrêté fédéral concernant l'octroi d'une amnistie fiscale au 1er janvier 1965 (du 27 septembre 1963). In FF 1963, vol. 2, 807.

60 We refer here to the representatives of the Liberal Democratic Union (Swiss Liberal Party from 1977), a national political party at that time, whose members were on the right of the political spectrum.

61 SFA, CH-BAR#E6300B#2000/144#2*, Avant-projet de l'Administration fédérale des contributions concernant la loi d'application de l'amnistie fiscale générale, 31.07.1963.

62 Fehr (2017, 373–375).

Prior to the popular vote in 1964, neither side seemed satisfied with the revised version of the bill: it was either too intrusive (for the business community and right-wing parties) or too watered down (for the left and trade unions).

It is thus not surprising that during the voting campaign, which officially began in December 1963, the right-wing parties and the business community worked actively against the tax amnesty project. More surprising though, the Socialists, who were originally behind the proposal, did not adopt an official position for the project and left their members (cantonal parties and supporters) free to vote.[63] In the end, the 1964 tax amnesty and its potential anti-evasion component had very few official supporters and was thus unsurprisingly rejected at the polls.

10.3.2 The 1968 Tax Amnesty Project

This failure in 1964 paved the way for the success of a second general tax amnesty project in 1968. This time, the project did not come from the Socialist Party, but from right-wing representatives.

Indeed, barely a month after the amnesty's failure in 1964, an intervention filed by the Conservative MP Rudolf Mäder regarding the association of the Confederation with tax amnesties at the cantonal level[64] finally led to a new proposal for a general tax amnesty in 1967.[65] This proposal differed from the previous one on two essential points.

First, it did not provide for measures to fight tax evasion; a tax amnesty was to be granted by the federal state but it was not associated with a strengthening of anti-evasion measures in Switzerland, which was largely due to pressure from the representatives of the banking industry.[66]

Second, the legislation governing its implementation, usually decided in parliament *after* the adoption of a constitutional provision in a mandatory referendum vote was, in this case, voted on by parliament *before* the popular vote, which was scheduled for February 1968.[67] This represented a rather exceptional derogation in the functioning of Swiss democracy.[68]

63 *Ibid.*, 376–377.

64 A specific measure called *Anschlussamnestie* in Switzerland, cf. Fehr (2015, 26–31).

65 Motion Mäder, 05.03.1964; Message du Conseil fédéral à l'Assemblée fédérale sur la motion Mäder relative à l'adhésion de la Confédération aux amnisties fiscales cantonales en ce qui concerne l'impôt pour la défense nationale (du 6 juin 1966). In FF 1966, vol. 1, 955–970 ; Arrêté fédéral concernant l'octroi d'une amnistie fiscale générale (du 5 octobre 1967). In FF 1967, vol. 2, 507.

66 SBAA, Minutes of the Board of Directors, 22.09.1967, 8 and 13.12.1967, 14f.

67 Loi fédérale concernant l'exécution de l'amnistie fiscale générale au 1er janvier 1969 (du 15 mars 1968). In RO 1968, 1049–1051.

68 To legitimise this decision, the federal authorities claimed that the 1964 tax amnesty was rejected because the electorate did not know in advance what anti-evasion measures were to be introduced with the tax amnesty.

A tax amnesty project which was exempt from any anti-evasion measures was this time much more appealing to right-wing representatives. This is mainly why, in the campaign preceding the popular vote during the winter of 1967, the business community and all the right-wing parties actively supported the project.[69] On the other hand, the position of the left-wing representatives to this tax amnesty project remained ambiguous, since only the communist Labour Party opposed it. Despite the total absence of anti-evasion measures, the Socialist Party once again failed to take a clear position on the referendum and, as in 1964, the party's supporters and the cantonal parties were allowed a free vote.[70]

In February 1968, 62% of the electorate as well as mot of the cantons voted in favour of the tax amnesty project. This result can be explained by the unity of the front of supporters for a general tax amnesty this time around. In addition, this successful outcome can be better understood when the changed financial context is taken into consideration. Indeed, in 1967–1968, the federal financial situation had deteriorated, and a fiscal project to create more financial resources had been developed by the finance minister at that time.[71] During the campaign, it was thus possible to argue that a general tax amnesty was better than a tax increase, which allegedly was the alternative.[72]

Ultimately, more than the principle of fiscal justice, it appears that the reasons for the failure of the general tax amnesty of 1964 were related to the influence and striking power of the business community and especially the banking industry, the widespread practice of tax evasion in Switzerland, the ambiguous attitude of the Socialists, the financial situation of the Confederation and, above all, its anti-evasion component. It is likely that these same factors – this time coupled with the lack of an anti-evasion policy – were also responsible for the success of the project in 1968.

10.4 Conclusion

What were the results of the two tax amnesties under consideration? In the case of Zurich in 1936, the tax amnesty was generally considered a success.[73] Taxable wealth increased by nearly 450 million CHF, which represented an increase of 7%, and taxable income grew by nearly 31 million

69 Fehr (2017, 377).

70 Linder, Bolliger and Rielle (2010, 297).

71 Message du Conseil fédéral à l'Assemblée fédérale sur l'adaptation du régime des finances fédérales à l'accroissement des besoins (Programme immédiat pour procurer des recettes supplémentaires) (du 7 novembre 1966). In FF 1966, vol.2, 657–676.

72 [s.n] 1968. "Amnistie fiscale: le point de vue de l'Association Suisse des banquiers. De deux maux choisissons le moindre", *Journal de Genève*, February 7; Hürlimann (2012, 60).

73 Geschäftsbericht (1937, 85); see also Meisterhans (1939, 394).

CHF or 3%.[74] The amnesty brought more than 2.3 million CHF of new tax revenue (+6.9%) for the canton, and more than 6 million CHF if we include the municipalities.

Regarding the general tax amnesty of 1968, estimations were published by the federal government in 1972, but these estimates were plagued by methodological problems.[75] According to the Federal Council, difficulties arose especially in the area of income so the Federal Finance Administration refrained from attempting to estimate it. Thus, the Federal Council published only the amount of the wealth newly declared, but no information on the amount of income. The Federal Tax Administration estimated this newly declared wealth to total approximately 11.5 billion CHF at the time, which represented 9.1% of the GDP of 1972 and almost 10% of the total net assets declared in Switzerland in 1968.

This result of the general tax amnesty of 1968 was not diametrically different from the estimations made in the *Defraudationsbericht* published in 1962 regarding the amount of undeclared wealth and assets in Switzerland (between 17 and 23 billion Swiss francs). Indeed, despite fierce right-wing criticism of the allegedly exaggerated results set out in this report, the results of the tax amnesty published in 1972 demonstrated the existence of significant tax evasion in Switzerland.

Both case studies clearly show the class-based aspect of tax amnesties. In the case of the amnesty in Zurich in 1936, only a small proportion of taxpayers, 19,343 from 365,104, used the opportunity offered by the tax amnesty at all. And from this minority, the payments made by the 238 highest income earners (more than 50,100 CHF a year) accounted for almost a third of the new tax revenues.[76] In 1968, from 23,022 taxpayers who used the amnesty in the canton of Zurich, the 58 wealthiest (possessing more than 10 million CHF) accounted for 18% of the newly declared wealth.[77] Furthermore, from the nearly 2 billion CHF in wealth that was newly declared in the canton, less than one third was in the hand of wage earners.

This chapter shed some light on the attitude of Swiss tax authorities and the major socio-political actors towards tax evasion in Switzerland. In the two case studies, we presented here, tax amnesty was first considered within a programme to strengthen the fight against tax evasion, the extent of which was well-known and attested by well-grounded studies – as in the

74 If we compare with the death inventories from 1933 mentioned earlier, we can probably infer that much of the undeclared income remained hidden from the tax authorities despite the amnesty. This supposition is supported by the fact that undeclared income remained higher than 15% in the inventories from the years 1938–1940. In fact, undeclared wealth also remained at above 8% in 1938, before dropping to 4.6% resp. 6.1% in 1939 and 1940. Honegger 1940, 10.

75 SFA, CH-BAR#E6802#1985/126#99*, Rapport aux membres des Chambres fédérales sur le résultat de l'amnistie fiscale de 1969, 1.06.1972.

76 Geschäftsbericht (1937, 85).

77 StAZH, Z 395.152, Auswirkung der Steueramnestie 1969, 25.02.1972.

Defraudationsbericht from 1962 or via the death inventories in Zurich – and, subsequently, by the results of the tax amnesties themselves. But in the end, these tax amnesties turned out to be the only promulgated measures, while the new means of investigation or new sanctions initially envisaged to mitigate tax evasion were abandoned. Indeed, in both contexts, we can observe a coalition against the so-called "inquisition"[78] by the tax authorities, in a rhetoric that placed the state and its administration on one side, and all taxpayers, without distinctions, on the other side. Eventually, the tax amnesty seemed to be the path of least resistance – or the lesser evil – for most of the political representatives in a system with many veto players.

The analysis of these two case studies thus provides a striking insight into the divergence between official discourse on the need to fight tax avoidance and its trivialisation in practice by tax authorities and a major proportion of political actors.

Archives

AfZ: Archiv für Zeitgeschichte, Zurich.
SBAA: Swiss Banking Association Archives, Basel.
SFA: Swiss Federal Archive, Bern.
SozA: Sozialarchiv, Zurich.
StAZH: Staatsarchiv des Kantons Zürich, Zurich.

Published Sources

Amtsblatt: Amtsblatt des Kantons Zürich (Official publications of the canton of Zurich).
FF: Feuille fédérale (Official publications of the Swiss Confederation).
Geschäftsbericht: Geschäftsbericht des Regierungsrates an den Zürcherischen Kantonsrat (Annual report from the government to the parliament of the canton of Zurich).
PKR: Protokoll des Kantonsrates des Kantons Zürich (Minutes of the parliament of the canton of Zurich).
RO: Recueil officiel (Official collection of Swiss federal legislation).
RRB: Regierungsratsbeschlüsse des Kantons Zürich (Resolutions of the government of Zurich).
Staatsrechnung: Staatsrechnung des Kantons Zürich (Annual accounting of the canton of Zurich).

References

Baer, Katherine and Eric Le Borgne. 2008. *Tax Amnesties. Theory, Trends, and Some Alternatives*. Washington DC: International Monetary Fund.
Biedermann, Edwin. 1948. *Die Steuerbelastung im Kanton Zürich*. Zurich: Juris-Verlag.

78 Among many examples, [s.n].1964. Les libéraux s'opposent à l'amnistie fiscale. *Journal de Genève*, January 10.

Brupbacher, Felix. 1968. *Die rechtsstaatliche Problematik der Steueramnestie.* Zurich: Schulthess.

Fehr, Aniko. 2015. *La lutte contre la fraude fiscale ou les origines de l'Arrêté fédéral concernant l'octroi d'une amnistie fiscale générale au 1er janvier 1965 (1958-1964).* Master Thesis. University of Lausanne (dir. Sébastien Guex).

Fehr, Aniko. 2017. Origines, échec et adoption d'un projet d'amnistie fiscale générale en Suisse (1958-1968). *Revue suisse d'histoire* 3: 361–380.

Gubler, Jakob. 1947. *Die Steueramnestie in Bund und Kantonen unter besonderer Berücksichtigung des Bundesratsbeschlusses über die Steueramnestie bei Einführung der Verrechnungssteuer vom 31. Oktober 1944.* Doctorate thesis. University of Fribourg.

Guex, Sébastien. 1998. *L'argent de l'Etat: parcours des finances publiques au XXe siècle.* Lausanne: Réalités sociales.

Guex, Sébastien. 2012. Öffentliche Finanzen und Finanzpolitik. In *Wirtschaftsgeschichte der Schweiz im 20. Jahrhundert*, eds. Patrick Halbeisen, Margrit Müller, and Béatrice Veyrassat, 1077–1129. Basel: Schwabe.

Henggeler, Joseph. 1936. *Das Zürcherische Steueramnestiegesetz vom 26. April 1936.* Zurich: Orell Füssli.

Honegger, Fritz. 1942. *Vergleichende Betrachtungen über das Erhebungsverfahren bei den direkten Bundessteuern. Ein Beitrag zur schweizerischen Steuerpolitik.* Zurich: AG. Fachschriften-Verlag und Buchdruckerei.

Hürlimann, Gisela. 2012. Einträglich und gerecht? Steuern und Umverteilung in Nachkriegsboom, 1970er Krise und darüber hinaus. In *Steuern und umverteilen. Effizienz versus Gerechtigkeit*, eds. Gisela Hürlimann and Jakob Tanner, 55–81. Zurich: vdf Hochschulverlag ETH.

Hürlimann, Gisela. 2020. *Schweizerische Steuerwelten 1955 bis 1979. Gerechtigkeit, Wettbewerb und Harmonisierung im transnationalen Kontext*, Habilitationsschrift bei der Philosophischen Fakultät der Universität Freiburg (Schweiz).

Illi, Martin. 2008. *Von der Kameralistik zum New Public Management. Geschichte der Zürcher Kantonsverwaltung von 1803 bis 1998.* Zurich: Chronos.

Keller, Peter. 1946. *Die veranlagten Staatssteuern des Kantons Zürich seit 1890.* Zurich: tapuscript.

Klaus, Emil. 1935. "Der Weg Zurück" Keine Steueramnestie und keine Milderung der Strafsteuer im Kanton Zürich. *Zentralblatt für Staats- und Gemeindeverwaltung* 11: 249–252.

Klaus, Emil. 1939. Die Bewegung der Steuerkapitalien im Kanton Zürich 1918-1937. *Zentralblatt für Staats- und Gemeindeverwaltung* 13/14: 328–331.

Linder, Wolf, Christian Bolliger, and Yvan Rielle. 2010. *Handbuch der eidgenössischen Volksabstimmung 1848 bis 2007.* Bern: Haupt.

Meisterhans, Emil. 1939. Steuermoral, Steueramnestie. In *Handbuch der schweizerischen Volkswirtschaft II*, 392–394. Bern: Verlag Beteli.

Munz, Hans. 1944. *Steuerhinterziehung – ein Massenphänomen in der Schweiz.* Zurich: Schriftenreihe Landesring der Unabhängigen.

Petrick-Rump, Barbara. 1996. *Ökonomische Wirkungen von Steueramnestien. Untersuchung konkreter Erfahrungen ausgewählter Länder mit dem Einsatz von Steueramnestien anhand eines effizienten Steueramnestieprogramms.* Frankfurt am Main: Peter Lang.

Praz, Sylvain. 2021. "Es wäre nur recht und billig, dass auch der ärmere Bürger [...] etwas steuern müsste, damit er wenigstens auch eher das Recht 'zu schimpfen' hätte". Sujétion fiscale et pratique d'imposition à l'égard des petits contribuables (1870-1952). In *Steuern und Ungleichheit/Fiscalité et inégalités*, eds. Sébastien Guex, Gisela Hürlimann, and Matthieu Leimgruber, 235–249. Zürich: Chronos.

Statistisches Bureau des Kantons Zürich. 1951. *Zürcher Staatsfinanzen 1910-1949*. Zurich: Statistische Mitteilungen des Kantons Zürich.

Tanner, Jakob. 1986. *Bundeshaushalt, Währung und Kriegswirtschaft: eine finanzsoziologische Analyse der Schweiz zwischen 1938 und 1953*. Zurich: Limmat Verlag.

Tanner, Jakob. 1994. Steuerwesen und Sozialkonflikte. Entwicklungen und Diskontinuitäten. In *Financement de l'Etat et conflits sociaux (14e-20e siècles)*, eds. Sébastien Guex, Martin Körner, and Jakob Tanner, 123–135. Zurich: Chronos.

Tanner, Jakob. 2012. Der totaldemokratische Minimalstaat. Zur Geschichte des Steuerstaates in der Schweiz. In *Steuern und umverteilen. Effizienz versus Gerechtigkeit*, eds. Gisela Hürlimann and Jakob Tanner, 27–54. Zurich: vdf Hochschulverlag ETH.

Vittoz, Pierre-Etienne. 2014. *Les amnisties fiscales fédérales des années 1960 au regard de la presse suisse-romande*. Master Thesis. University of Lausanne (dir. Sébastien Guex).

Zürcher Gemeindesteuerverhältnisse: Steuererträge der Zürcher Gemeinden 1879-1944. 1946. Zurich: Statistisches Amt des Kantons Zürich.

Zürcher Handelskammer. 1935. *Bericht über das Jahr 1934*. Zurich: Verlag der Zürcher Handelskammer.

Wettstein, Walter. 1919. *Das neue Zürcherische Gesetz betreffend die direkten Steuern. Gesetz, Vollziehungsverordnung, Sachregister sowie Einleitung*. Zurich: Polygraphisches Institut.

Part IV

Sparing the Rich and Companies from Taxation?

11 "There Is No Wrongdoing in Avoiding Taxes"

The Land Union's Tax Resistance in Great Britain (1900–1930s)[1]

Anna Grotegut

11.1 Introduction

Real estate is generally regarded as a rewarding object for taxation. Land does not change its location and its owner is usually easy to identify. In political debates, present and past, the taxation of land has been and is considered as beneficial. Milton Friedman even described land value taxation – just like the influential land reformer Henry George imagined it – as the least bad tax.[2] However, this assumption is not always justified by reality. In practice, the levying of taxes often causes major problems or provokes resistance. This was also the case with the introduction of the land duties in Great Britain in 1909/1910. In the following, the tax resistance of the Land Union, which was founded for this purpose, will be discussed.

Numerous studies have dealt with these land duties. Often they are examined from a political perspective, such as liberal politics or related to land reform and land policy. The organisation of the Land Union is often mentioned, but usually only in passing.[3] In their political science contribution on veto player work, Ian McLean and Jennifer Nou argue that the failure of land value taxation was caused by an increased number of veto players in British politics. They mention the influence of the landed interests, but do not consider the agitation of the Land Union.[4] This chapter thus contributes to research on organised tax resistance. The first part of the article deals with the distribution of land ownership and the socio-economic conditions which

1 Abbreviated quote, original quote: "There is no wrongdoing either legal or moral, in avoiding taxes which are not clearly and explicitly imposed." The Land Union 1910a, 5. I would like to thank the organisers and the participants of the workshop for their feedback and comments. This article has been written within the framework of the Collaborative Research Centre SFB 1288 "Practices of Comparing. Changing and Ordering the World", Bielefeld University, Germany, funded by the German Research Foundation (DFG), subproject B07, "Comparing in Markets: Practices of Real Estate Valuation in Great Britain and the German Territories, 1750–1950."

2 Friedman (1978, 3).

3 Douglas (1976); Murray (1980); Offer (1981); Packer (2001); Readman (2008); Short (1997); Tichelar (2019); Ward (1976).

4 McLean and Nou (2006).

DOI: 10.4324/9781003333197-16

led to the introduction of new real estate taxes by the Liberal government in 1909. This so-called "People's Budget", which contained the new taxes, faced opposition, particularly in the House of Lords. The second part deals with the foundation and aims of the Land Union and its measures against taxation of land. The third part is about the achievements of the Land Union, especially in the courts. The next part is about the eventual abolition of the land duties and offers a brief look at the history of land value duties up to 1934. The last part provides some concluding remarks.

11.2 Land Distribution, the Liberal Party and the "People's Budget"

In England, private ownership of land was more widespread than in other parts of Europe, including Scotland and Ireland, where feudal ownership was still dominating. After the process of enclosure was concluded in the eighteenth century, there was no longer a right for the common use of land. Instead, a tripartite system of mostly aristocratic landlords, tenant farmers and agricultural labourers had developed.[5] Land ownership was concentrated in the hand of relatively few owners. The contemporaries referred to John Bateman's report from 1873 in which he described that in England and Wales half a percent of the landowners owned about 60% of the land. According to Avner Offer, urban home ownership was underrepresented in these calculations. He estimates that 30% of property values belonged to the big landowners. Even if there were about one million small property owners, a large part of the land belonged to a few 1,000 people. The others were tenants.[6] In the late nineteenth century, there was growing awareness and dissatisfaction with this situation of unequal land distribution. This was due to the fact that the local agriculture suffered from the inflow of cheap American corn which swept the British market as a consequence of free trade policy. The tenant farmers experienced a decrease in incomes, but had to pay the same amount of rent, which brought many into great economic distress. The situation was aggravated by a series of bad harvests due to weather conditions at the end of the nineteenth century. The agricultural crisis forced many people to migrate to the cities, where new problems such as unemployment, poor housing and infrastructural difficulties arose or worsened in the course of industrialisation. The rural population increasingly blamed their landlords for their problems, and land reform ideas gained support and were increasingly appreciated.[7]

When the Liberals came to power in 1905, they faced this and other considerable social challenges. Liberals and Unionists agreed on the necessity to

5 Tichelar (2019, 24–25).
6 Offer (1981, 105–106).
7 Readman (2008, 104).

invest in social expenditures and defence.[8] However, they were completely at odds about how to finance these expenditures. The Unionists were in favour of a broader tax base through new tariff duties, while the Liberals, who were in favour of free trade, wanted to extend direct taxation.[9] For the latter, the taxation of land seemed an obvious solution: landowners were a traditional enemy of the Liberals – especially the radical wing of the Liberals – and in their opinion should now be taxed. The contemporary theoretical background was the assumption that the income of the landowners was not earned by proper work or investment and therefore "unearned". Furthermore, landlords did not make any improvements, and the land was farmed by others who owed them rent. This theoretical background of unearned increment was significantly influenced by Henry George's theory.

In 1879, the US-American land reformer and economist Henry George published his book *Progress and Poverty*, in which he tried to explain the discrepancy between technical progress and simultaneously growing poverty and developed a theory on how poverty could be eliminated. George stated that profit from mere land ownership was the cause of poverty and proposed to confiscate non-productive income through a high land tax. This tax would, according to George, make all other taxes obsolete. In his study, which became an international bestseller, George did not specify how this tax, later known as the "Single Tax", could be implemented in concrete terms, but his theory nevertheless found numerous supporters and influenced land reform movements in many countries. Especially in Great Britain, where he travelled several times and gave lectures, he and his ideas achieved some popularity.[10]

The idea of taxing land according to its value became more acclaimed: In 1906, 518 municipal authorities supported a petition that local rates should be based on site value and not on the annual present-use value of site and building together. These local land taxes, which were an important source of revenue for the municipal authorities, were mostly paid by the occupiers and not by the owners and were particularly onerous for the low-income households. The idea to base the rates on site value was supposed to relieve the pressure on the poorer.[11] The issue of land value taxation also became increasingly important in parliament. In 1906, 280 Liberal and Labour MPs belonged to the Land Values Group, which lobbied for land value legislation in parliament.[12]

8 The Liberal Unionists, which had split from the Liberals in 1886, and the Conservatives worked closely together, officially merging in 1912 and calling themselves Unionists for some time. Douglas (2011, 10).

9 Murray (1980, 21).

10 Douglas (1976, 43–45).

11 Murray (1980, 46).

12 Murray (1976, 40–41).

The Liberal government aimed to introduce a national land value tax. But there was a problem: in order to levy a land value tax, the land would have to be valued first. Usually, a valuation bill would be passed first, and then, when the land valuations were available, taxation of these values could be imposed. But the House of Lords, where landowners were over-represented, would almost certainly veto a valuation bill as they had in the last three years partially blocked Liberal politics by rejecting the Education Bill, the Scottish Smallholdings Bill and the Licensing Bill.[13] To avoid failure, Liberals planned to interlink the valuation of the land directly with a new land value tax and place it in the budget, since the unwritten law did not allow the Lords to refuse financial bills.[14] The Liberal Chancellor of the Exchequer Lloyd George wanted to tax the unearned increment in the value of land that was not owed to the landlord but to public investments, for example through infrastructure improvements such as new railway stations, better transportation, etc. This so-called Increment Value Tax was influenced by the ideas of Henry George, and especially by the concept of the increment value tax (*Wertzuwachssteuer*) that Lloyd George imported from Germany. He was aware of the *Wertzuwachssteuer* that had been levied in Frankfurt since 1904 and had requested a report about the increment value tax in the German Reich, focusing on Frankfurt. The report was submitted to the cabinet in 1908. It stated that the levying of this tax was not causing any major problems and could be carried out simply and without great expense. However, the reporter Bernhard Mallet also pointed out that the conditions in Frankfurt were not the same as in Great Britain. First, the Frankfurt tax was based on purchase prices. These could not be used for Great Britain, as with typical leases there were other ownership structures and land and buildings had to be valued separately. Second, unlike in the German Reich, there were no British land registers (*Grundbücher*) in which sales were recorded.[15]

However, in 1909, the Liberal government needed new sources of revenue to finance both social and military expenses, particularly old age pensions and dreadnoughts. On 29 April 1909, Lloyd George presented his budget to the House of Commons. This so-called "People's Budget" contained seven completely new taxes. Existing taxes for very high incomes were to be increased and the tax burden of middle and working classes reduced. The "unearned incomes" – such as those of landlords – were finally to be taxed as planned. The "People's Budget" clearly was not only intended to be a means of raising revenue, but also to achieve a distinct redistribution of income and wealth in favour of the middle and working classes whose voters the Liberals wanted to address.[16] With this budget, the Liberals criticised the distribution

13 Douglas (2011).

14 Douglas (1976, 143).

15 Bernhard Mallet, Report by Mr. Bernhard Mallet, TNA: IR73/2, 8.

16 Short (1997, 19).

of land in the country up to that date. Lloyd George argued that the landlords had a monopoly on land, would selfishly exploit it and made access to land unnecessarily difficult for entrepreneurs and tradesmen, thus weakening the entire economy.[17] Next to this "unearned incomes" of the "selfish" land-owning class, very high incomes – over £5,000 – were to be taxed with the so-called super-tax. Four of the seven new taxes were taxes on land: the previously mentioned Increment Value Duty and the Undeveloped Land Duty, a Reversion Duty and the Mineral Rights Duty. These taxes were expected to raise only about £600,000 in the first year.[18] This was less than 5% of the total increase in taxation.[19]

The land taxes were considered an affront by the landlords who, accordingly, provoked resistance in parliament. The Unionists rejected the budget because of the land duties. About one-third of the Unionist Party members were landed gentry.[20] Unionist MP Ernest George (E.G.) Pretyman led parliamentary resistance from the very beginning.[21] After long debates – the entire Finance Bill was debated for 640 hours in parliament – the bill was finally accepted in the House of Commons on 4 November 1909. After six days of discussion, on 30 November, the House of Lords rejected the budget by 350 to 75 votes. About two-thirds of the Lords who voted against the budget owned at least 5,000 acres of land.[22] With their budget opposition, the peers caused a constitutional crisis since the authorisation of finance bills had been the preserve of the House of Commons since the fifteenth century.[23] The House of Lords declared that it would pass the bill if elections were held and the newly elected House of Commons supported the bill. General elections followed in January 1910, which gave the Liberals a wafer-thin lead over the Unionists.[24] The House of Lords passed the bill and it was signed by the King on 29 April 1910, exactly one year after its first presentation. The rejection of the budget had an aftermath for the House of Lords as Prime Minister Asquith, among others, saw it as a breach of the constitution.[25] In the following year, the Parliament Act severely restricted the power of the upper chamber: it stated, inter alia that the House of Lords had no right to interfere in financial legislation.[26]

17 Readman (2008, 104).
18 Short (1997, 19).
19 Readman (2008, 22).
20 Short (1997, 23–25)
21 Offer (1981, 367).
22 Short (1997, 24–25).
23 Wende (2001, 57).
24 Douglas (2011, 8).
25 The question of whether Lloyd George wanted to use the budget to provoke the House of Lords into a rejection has been discussed extensively in the research literature. Since the 1950s, however, the prevailing view has been that Lloyd George had no intention of confronting the House of Lords. Murray (1980, 112).
26 Short (1997), 26, HC Deb 2nd December 1909, col. 546.

By 1910, the new land duties were finally enacted. The four new taxes on land had different objectives and were imposed at different stages. First, the Increment Value Duty was set at 20% of the amount by which site value of a plot of land had increased compared to 1909. The tax became due when there was a change of ownership, such as in the case of sale or inheritance. For example, the seller had to pay 20% tax on the "unearned increment" that occurred between 30 April 1909 and the date of sale. Second, the Undeveloped Land Duty had a rate of about 0.21% on the site value of undeveloped land which had to be paid annually. This tax was intended to prevent landowners from resisting the sale of those plots of land that were ready for construction, especially in urban areas where housing was urgently needed, in order to achieve an even higher price at a later date. Third, the Reversion Duty was a 10% tax on the benefit accruing to a lessor on the determination of a lease of land. The fourth tax, the Mineral Rights Duty, which had to be paid annually on the capital value of minerals, had a similar rate of taxation. All four taxes required a valuation of landed properties. However, only the land was supposed to be taxed, not the buildings that existed on it, and permanent charges (e.g. tithes) were to be deducted. To generate this Assessable Site Value, three other values that were criticised for being too theoretical had to be measured. To this end, for all landed properties, the 30 April 1909 was declared the due day for value assessment. This was called the "original valuation".[27]

11.3 The Land Union – Its Goals and Actions

In April 1910, a few days after the law was passed, Unionist MP E.G. Pretyman founded the Land Union and became its president.[28] Through his work in the House of Commons, Pretyman had an excellent knowledge of land duties, knew their weaknesses and was thus able to take action against them. The aim of the Land Union was to repeal the new taxes on land. The self-declared claim of the newly founded organisation was to defend those who saw their interests threatened with regard to land valuation and to offer help and advice.[29] The Land Union described itself as a non-party political organisation which was open to all who were involved in the land business or construction industry through ownership, profession or business. This included house- and landowners, building contractors and their employees, members of building and benefit societies, mortgagees and holders of

27 The Gross Value was the value of the land, free from burdens and restrictions. The Full Site Value was the Gross Value minus the difference between the Gross Value and the value of the cleared site. The Total Value was the Gross Value less the depreciation caused by burdens or restrictions. Short (1997, 68, 82, 89); George (1910, 147).

28 Its predecessor was the Land Defence League, founded by Charles Newton-Robinson in the summer of 1909, which became the Land Union in 1910. Offer (1981, 366–367).

29 The Land Union (1910b, binder).

insurance policies.[30] The membership fee per year was at least 5 shilling. This subscription was chosen "in order that the owner of small property may join the Union."[31] There is no precise information about the exact number of members. According to the Land Nationalisation Society, one of the Land Union's opponents who advocated the nationalisation of land, the organisation grew rapidly. After two months, it is said to have had 1,100 members. Other sources report that by October 1910, after half a year, the Land Union had 50,000 members, among them "the largest landowners in the country."[32]

The Land Union claimed to represent by no means only the interests of the larger landlords: the organisation emphasised that the figures from 1873 on the number of landowners were no longer accurate and that real estate now belonged to many more people including small salesmen and artisans.[33] Nevertheless, its president Pretyman was one of the big landowners. Of the 293 hereditaments[34] in the parish of Keelby in Lincolnshire, Pretyman and a certain Lord Yarborough owned 113 hereditaments – including most of the larger plots. Pretyman owned for example the Manor Farm with 499 acres. The remaining landowners of Keelby usually possessed only one or two hereditaments.[35]

The Land Union pursued its goal of abolishing the land duties in four ways. First, through their work in the House of Commons, where Pretyman and other members of parliament asked critical questions, requested amendments and constantly demanded information about the course of the valuation process. The second strategy was to support the members of the Land Union. In an article in *The Land Union Journal*, Pretyman stated that over 10,000 letters from people seeking advice had been answered.[36] The Land Union strongly recommended its members, for example, not to declare a self-estimated value in Form IV, which homeowners were supposed to fill out, as this could be interpreted to their disadvantage. Instead, they were advised to wait for the Provisional Valuation and then file an objection if necessary.[37] The third main area of activity were court cases. The Land Union supported several cases of general interest, cases that could have resulted in far-reaching judgements and had the potential to become a precedential case. In these cases, the Inland Revenue, which was responsible for the assessment and collection of taxes, suffered some bitter defeats, some of which had far-reaching consequences. Last, the Land Union undertook nationwide information and propaganda

30 The Land Union (1910b, binder; 1910c).
31 The Land Union (1911, 187).
32 The Land Union itself stated that 1,194 new members had joined in 1911. The Times (1912); Ward (1976, 511); Land Values (1910, 95).
33 The Land Union (1910d).
34 Property that can be inherited.
35 Short (1997, 212–213).
36 The Land Union Journal (1911, 9).
37 The Land Union (1910a, 11–12).

campaigns, including the publication of leaflets, brochures, guidebooks and, since 1911, the organisation's own newspaper, *The Land Union Journal*.[38]

The Land Union put forward numerous arguments for the abolition of land duties. In the booklet *The Land Union's Reasons for Repeal of the New Land Taxes and Land Valuation*, for example, the authors based their arguments on classical tax fairness principles such as the ability to pay. The booklet quoted the famous liberal philosopher and economist John Stuart Mill with his claim for an equal distribution of the tax burden. According to the Land Union, the land duties violated this principle by not taxing all capital, but only capital in the form of landed property. Opposing to any kind of taxation land in general, the Land Union criticised the new liberal law on land duties in detail and specifically by invoking Adam Smith's four principles of good taxation from his 1776 publication on *The Wealth of Nations*, to which according to Smith, the state was supposed to comply.[39]

First, there was the demand for equality: the tax burden was to be based on the respective ability of each individual to pay. Over the course of time, however, this maxim was increasingly equated with equity.[40] The Land Union argued that the land duties contradicted this interpretation of equity and criticised that the new law only taxed assets in the form of land, whereas assets invested elsewhere, for example in the rubber plantations in Ceylon, then a British colony, remained tax-free. The second demand, following Smith, was for certainty and the avoidance of arbitrariness; tax laws were to be comprehensible and transparent. Here, the Land Union argued that the new land duties were highly arbitrary and uncertain, in no way predictable and thus contradicted the maxim. The amount of tax was not predictable for the seller, as the valuation was carried out by an expert. Even people working in the real estate sector were stunned by the complexity of the tax assessment. The third demand referred to Smith's maxim of convenience by which a tax was to be as convenient to pay as possible, both in terms of the payment method and the date. The Land Union argued that the new taxes were not only contradicting this maxim, but that in many cases it was even impossible to pay them without borrowing money first. For example, in the case of an inheritance, the Increment Value Duty was to be paid in addition to death duties. In consequence, heirs would likely be forced to take out loans. Finally, in 1776, Smith had demanded that tax paying should not cost citizens much more than it brought in revenue for the state. Among other things, this meant that administrative costs for tax collection were to be kept as low as possible. According to the Land Union, which made this point particularly

38 The Land Union Journal (1911, 9).
39 The Land Union (1910b, 15–16).
40 Sahm (2019, 89).

strong in its argumentation, no other tax system was "more diametrically opposed"[41] to this maxim. The Land Union complained that the valuation of land required a lot of personnel, and that accommodation for the personnel had to be provided throughout the country, which on the whole was very expensive. In addition, numerous court cases were to be expected, with which highly paid judges would have to deal, possibly including the High Court. In addition to these costs for the state, there would also be costs for the landowners, who would have to pay for the valuation of their land themselves.[42] These costs were eventually covered by the state, but in this way, costs were only shifted and would ultimately have to be borne by the tax payers again.

In addition to this theoretical analysis, the Land Union also put forward political, economic and moral objections against the land duties. For instance, it expressed the concern that the taxes were only a foretaste of a possible nationalisation of land and the prelude to the abolishment of individual property. The organisation was of the opinion that the Finance Act could pave the way for universal state ownership and state control, thus threatening the fundamental right of individual property.[43] In addition, the Land Union criticised that the tax revenues would not be available to the local authorities but would disappear "into the bottomless pit of the National Exchequer."[44] The Land Union also found economic reasons for opposing the land duties, asserting that there would be an immediate threat of a decline in the land value and, thus, a decrease in the entire wealth of the country. Furthermore, the Land Union warned against a serious threat of unemployment because the construction sector would stagnate, as would all related industries.[45]

Beyond detailing its complaint against the new land taxes, the Land Union did not shy away from using scandalising language calling the Liberals "Robber Socialists" or "Communists" in its publications.[46] Overall, the Land Union predicted that the new taxes would have disastrous effects: the middle class and the working men would be "robbed", the trade of land would come to a standstill and nobody would be willing to build anymore, which would lead to a housing crisis. The Land Union defended itself against the accusation of "incitement [...] to resist the law"[47] by arguing that "there is no wrongdoing either legal or moral, in avoiding taxes which are not clearly and

41 The Land Union (1910b, 26).
42 Ibid., 24, 26.
43 Ibid., 10.
44 The Land Union (1910c).
45 Ibid.
46 The Land Union (1910b, 14).
47 The Land Union (1910a, 5).

explicitly imposed, since it is the duty of the state to use language of precision when it is imposing liabilities upon its citizens."[48]

11.4 The Land Union's Achievements

The Land Union's efforts did not remain without effect. In a report on alleged undervaluation of landed properties in Birmingham, published in 1913, Chief Valuer of Inland Revenue Edgar J. Harper, stated that the accusations were unfounded and complained that the meetings of the Land Union were one of the reasons for the increase in accusations.[49] As already described, a central field of activity of the Land Union was the work in the courtroom. In total, the Land Union provided assistance in 26 court cases between 1910 and about 1915.[50] The Inland Revenue suffered a number of setbacks in these trials and was put under a severe stress test even if it won in court. The Lumsden Case, for example, received considerable contemporary attention. Indeed, the building contractor R.J. Lumsden had to pay the Increment Value Duty and the Land Union lost the case in his defence. But the Land Union could show that the law was open to interpretation in a way that rendered Lloyd George's promise that building companies would not be affected by the Increment Value Duty meaningless. With builder's profits now being taxed, the Land Union blamed the government, and Lloyd George in particular, for the crisis in the construction sector, the associated unemployment and the impending housing crisis. The Lumsden Case became Land Union's prime example for tax injustices. They confronted the House of Commons about Lloyd George's broken promise and issued a small booklet outlining the Lumsden Case and describing the taxation of building profits as a "gross injustice".[51] Contrary to the Land Union's claim, however, the crisis of the construction sector was not – or at least not exclusively – caused by land duties. Overall, the economic growth slowed in the Edwardian era, wages stagnated and unemployment increased. Economic stagnation, rising interest rates and increasing building costs also led to a housing crisis, with cheap housing becoming a scarce commodity.[52]

Another success of the Land Union was that, in 1914, all previous valuations of agricultural land were declared invalid by the court in the sentence concerning the Commissioners of Inland Revenue v. Smyth case. Lady Emily Smyth, landowner of a farm in Norton Malreward, Somerset, wanted to obtain a lower valuation. The dispute was whether or not the grass on the grazing land should be included in the valuation. In the

48 Ibid. The Land Union here quotes barrister W.h. Aggs. The same quote can be found again in The Land Union (1910b, 8).

49 Harper (1913, TNA: T 171/39).

50 Yardley (1930, 652–655).

51 Short (1997, 31–32); The Land Union (N.d.)

52 Offer (1981, 254, 282).

Court of King's Bench, Justice Thomas E. Scrutton declared the previous basis of the valuation invalid. He ordered new methods, which, however, could not be implemented in practice. As a result, the Undeveloped Land Duty was practically invalidated or its collection had to be reorganised.[53] Nevertheless, 20 million acres of agricultural land were valued after the ruling according to the Finance Act, even though these valuations were not finalised due to the unclear legal situation.[54] In the case of Burghes v. Attorney General, one of the forms for the valuation was declared invalid.[55] In addition, Pretyman, who supported the case on behalf of the Land Union, obtained an extension of the objection deadlines for the valuation because the majority of landowners who could have objected to valuation were serving at war. Thus, the values could not be fixed and therefore no taxes collected.[56]

11.5 The Abolition of the Land Duties

The Great War with all its consequences further delayed land valuation and tax levying. During the war, numerous taxes were raised considerably in order to finance military costs. The land duties were, as described, partially suspended, or brought almost no income. However, the ongoing valuation continued to cost money. Not only the eternal opponents of the new land taxes were slowly running out of patience, but also former supporters grew impatient and demanded a rise or change of the duties. Lloyd George had become Prime Minister in the meantime, but the Conservatives held the majority of seats in parliament since 1918. A Select Committee was founded in 1919 to provide a recommendation as to whether the land duties should be retained, changed or abolished. Pretyman became a member of the committee and temporarily also its chair. Apparently, there was some disagreement within the committee and no recommendation was made, but the statements on the subject requested by various persons and organisations were delivered. The committee received proofs of evidence from several employees of Inland Revenue, from the Surveyor's Institute, the Law Society, the Land Union, the Land Agent's Society and the United Committee for the Taxation of Land Values. The Land Union's report by its secretary R. B. Yardley, barrister-at-law, and the assistant secretaries C. Crofton Black and E. Watson was mainly aimed at describing the negative consequences of the Finance Act and the shortcomings of the valuation. A fundamental point was that the Land Union was against the special taxation of *land*. For them, land was a piece of property like furniture or machinery.

53 Offer (1981, 368–369).
54 Short (1997, 33).
55 The Land Union (1911, 158).
56 Short (1997, 33).

Moreover, land duties raised very little revenue, but valuation was very expensive and overly complex. The complicated rules for the valuation were ambiguous and led to many lawsuits. Overall, the valuations were problematic, new laws could invalidate the values established for 1909, as could fluctuations in the value of money. The tax also had a negative impact on housing supply, the building trade and the construction industry.[57] Other organisations expressed similar opinions. The Surveyor's Institution Council stated that the land duties could not be usefully amended and should therefore be abolished.[58] The Land Agents' Society criticised the calculation of the different values and in the view of the Law Society the taxes were unworkable.[59] In the Select Committees report, the connections between the different organisations become apparent. The assistant secretary of the Land Union E. Watson was also a fellow of the Surveyors' Institution and the witness Edwin Savill a member of the council of the Surveyors' Institution and also a member of the council of the Land Union. Advocating for retention with amendments was James Dundas White, a former Liberal member in the House of Commons.[60] The criticism that these taxes did not generate high revenues was justified. The Undeveloped Land Duty, Reversion Duty and Increment Value Duty together generated only about £1 million of receipts. The Mineral Rights Duty still generated £3 million. But the cost of valuation was £2–3 million until 1915.[61]

Although there was no recommendation from the committee, the land clauses of the Finance Act were abolished in July 1920 at the suggestion of the Conservative Chancellor of the Exchequer Austen Chamberlain. Only the more lucrative Mineral Rights Duty remained. No further taxes were levied and taxpayers were able to reclaim previously paid taxes with an application. Lloyd George, who had introduced the land duties eleven years earlier, now, as Prime Minister, had to abolish them again. During the debate, Josiah Wedgwood, a former Liberal and now a Labour MP, but always a supporter of land value taxation, said that voters were aware that these taxes had been abolished by the landlords – including the landlords in the House of Commons who, Wedgewood hoped, would not outnumber the Commons chamber for much longer. His hopes for renewed or changed land duties were very low at this time, because he felt that the current government "must do what the Land Union tell [sic] them". The Liberal MP C. White added, that the Land Union was "the masters of the Government".[62]

57 Report from the Select Committee (1920, 75, 79–81).
58 Ibid., 64.
59 Ibid., 69, 94.
60 Ibid., 94–96.
61 Ibid., 41–42.
62 HC Deb 14th July (1920, 131), col. 2511–2513, 2517.

The Land Union self-confidently claimed the abolition of the land duties as its own victory. In several newspapers, the Land Union published appreciations for the numerous congratulations "on the successful result of its work".[63] Towards one of its major opponents, the United Committee for the Taxation of Land Values (UCTLV), the Land Union boasted that it was generally accepted that the abolition of the land duties was "largely due to the activities of the Land Union."[64] However, landowners were still not safe from future "attacks", and the Land Union expressed the need to continue its work, otherwise they feared that supporters of the land value taxation would again be able to enforce their plans. The Land Union's attention shifted to local site value taxation.[65] By doing so, the organisation strengthened its raison d'être after the abolition of the land taxes. The Land Union was represented by Pretyman in the House of Commons until 1923 and the organisation continued to publish papers on land valuation.[66] The organisation's members did not stop stirring up fears that if Labour or the Liberals came back to power, land value taxation might be reintroduced.[67] Land Union secretary Yardley expressed this concern in a critical history of the land value taxation movement published in 1930, and thus under a Labour government. Yardley's book was intended to counteract Labour's potential plans by calling land value taxation "a disastrous experiment" or a "fiasco".[68] Land Union's forecast turned out to be true. The Labour government's Chancellor of the Exchequer, Philip Snowden, included land value taxes in his 1931 budget. However, little information is available about this perhaps because only three months later, these taxes were suspended by the National Government and finally abolished in 1934.[69] But according to the Land Union's opponents, they and other lobby groups of landowners were involved – not to mention the MPs, who had always refused land value taxation.[70] Looking at the further work of the Land Union would certainly be interesting, but it is not included in the framework of this chapter. I assume that with the abolition of land duties the Land Union gradually lost importance, as land reform also lost relevance: The Great War forced many aristocrats to sell land, so the number of landowners increased. The Liberals' enemy image of the large landowner began to

63 Land and Liberty (1920a, 391).
64 Land and Liberty (1920b, 482).
65 Land and Liberty (1920a, 391); see page 3.
66 The Land Union Journal was published until 1950, from 1950 it was merged with the Real Estate Journal.
67 Yardley (1930, XIII).
68 Yardley (1930, X).
69 Short (1997, 36).
70 Land and Liberty (1933, 215–216).

disappear, also because the aristocratic landowners lost political influence overall as a result of the extension of the franchise in 1918.[71]

11.6 Conclusion

The Land Union worked in many ways to abolish the land duties. Through its expertise, it was able to identify the shortcomings of the laws and use them for their resistance against the taxation of land. But the main reason for its success resided in the fact that the organisation was supported by the also politically influential group of the land-owning class. The members of the Land Union saw themselves as largely responsible for the abolition of the land duties and the valuation. This point of view was shared by their opponents, such as the liberal MP Wedgwood and the UCTLV. Admittedly, the land duties offered numerous points of attack. Even Harper, the Chief Valuer, later admitted that the valuation was far too complicated.[72] The Land Union was certainly not alone in paving the way for the abolition of land duties. The growing weakness of the Liberal Party, the general crisis in times of the Great War and the overall difficult political situation must also be taken into account. However, the Land Union, through its actions such as the court cases, gave the public the impression that this type of land value taxation was not an appropriate means of tax collection. This impression persisted: except for Snowden's attempt in the 1930s, there was no national land value tax in Britain. The request for it came up occasionally, but the opponents maintained the upper hand, and the reference to the "People's Budget" 1909/1910 was helpful for this purpose.[73] It is therefore rewarding, in researching land duties, to also look at organised tax resistance in the form of the Land Union, which has made a decisive contribution to the perception of the "People's Budget".

The National Archives (TNA)

Edgar J. Harper, Allegation of Under-Valuation in Birmingham, 27 June 1913, TNA: T 171/39.

Bernhard Mallet, Report by Mr. Bernhard Mallet, One of the Commissioners of Inland Revenue, upon Taxation of Site Values in Frankfort, Hamburg, Cologne, and Dresden, Together with a Translation of the Bye-Law Relating to the Tax on Changes of Ownership of Real Property in Frankfort, 1908, TNA: IR73/2.

The Land Union. N.d. *The People's Budget in Operation: Taxation of Business Profits*. London: The Land Union.

71 Tichelar (2019, 204).

72 Harper (1929, 84).

73 Connellan (2004, 50–62); Tichelar (2019, 201).

Printed Sources and Sources Available Online

HC Deb (House of Commons Hansard Sessional Papers) 14th July 1920, 131, col. 2511–2513, 2517. Accessed October 14th 2020: https://parlipapers.proquest.com/parlipapers/docview/t71.d76.cds5cv0131p0-0013?accountid=14488.

HC Deb (House of Commons Hansard Sessional Papers) 2nd December 1909, col. 546. Accessed March 5th 2021: https://parlipapers.proquest.com/parlipapers/docview/t71.d76.cds5cv0013p0-0005?accountid=14488.

Land and Liberty. 1920a. "A Challenge." May, 391. Accessed October 31st 2020: https://www.henrygeorgefoundation.org/publications/land-liberty-archive/1920s/land-and-liberty-vol-21-1920.html.

Land and Liberty. 1920b "Our Friend, the Enemy." September, 482. Accessed October 31st 2020: https://www.henrygeorgefoundation.org/publications/land-liberty-archive/1920s/land-and-liberty-vol-21-1920.html.

Land and Liberty. 1933. "The Lesson." May/June, 215–216. Accessed October 31st 2020: https://www.henrygeorgefoundation.org/publications/land-liberty-archive/1930s/land-and-liberty-1932-33-39th-40th-year.html.

Land Values. 1910. "Here and There." October, 95–96. Accessed October 31st 2020: https://www.henrygeorgefoundation.org/publications/land-liberty-archive/1910s/land-values-vol-13-1910-1911-1911-1912.html.

Lloyd, George. 1910. "The Land and the People. Limehouse, July 30, 1909." In *Better Times. Speeches by the Right Hon. D. Lloyd George, M.P.* London: Hodder & Stoughton.

Report from the Select Committee on Land Values together with the proceedings of the committee, minutes of evidence and appendices, BPP. 1920. (Cmd 556), https://parlipapers.proquest.com/parlipapers/docview/t70.d75.1920-023454?accountid=14488. Accessed October 27th 2020.

The Land Union. 1910a. 5th and rev. and extended ed. *A Guide to Property Owners Calles Upon to Fill in the Government Valuation Forms.* London: n.p.

The Land Union. 1910b. *The Land Union's Reasons for Repeal of the New Land Taxes and Land Valuation.* London: The Land Union.

The Land Union. 1910c. Leaflet No. 1. In *Land Union. A Series of Leaflets.* London: Land Union. British Library, General Reference Collection 8139.ee.46

The Land Union. 1910d. Leaflet No. 13. In *Land Union. A Series of Leaflets.* London: Land Union. British Library, General Reference Collection 8139.ee.46.

The Land Union Journal. 1911. "The Land Union. Second Annual General Meeting." May, 8-10.

The Land Union. n.d. [1911]. *The New Land Taxes and Mineral Rights Duty: The Land Union's Handbook on Provisional Valuations.* London: Vacher & Sons.

The Times. 1912. "The Land Union." April 17th, 7.

References

Connellan, Owen. 2004. *Land Value Taxation in Britain: Experience and Opportunities.* Cambridge, Massachusetts: Lincoln Institute of Land Policy.

Douglas, Roy. 1976. *Land, People & Politics: A History of the Land Question in the United Kingdom, 1878-1952.* London: Allison and Busby.

Douglas, Roy. 2011. "The Lloyd George Land Taxes." *Journal of Liberal History* 73: 4–13.

Harper, Edgar J. 1929. "The Lloyd George Finance (1909-10) Act, 1910: Its Errors, and How to Correct Them." In *Conference Papers Presented at the Fourth International Conference Edinburgh*, ed. International Union for Land Value Taxation and Free Trade, 84–89. London: International Union for Land Value Taxation and Free Trade.

McLean, Ian and Jennifer Nou. 2006. "Why Should We Be Beggars with the Ballot in Our Hand? Veto Players and the Failure of Land Value Taxation in the United Kingdom, 1909-14," *British Journal of Political Science 36*(4): 575–591.

Milton Friedman Gives the Answers, 1978, Collected Works of Milton Friedman Project Records, Hoover Institution Archives. Online accessed on 31st October 2020: http://miltonfriedman.hoover.org/objects/56718.

Murray, Bruce K. 1976. "Lloyd George and the Land: The Issue of Site-Value Rating." In *Studies in Local History: Essays in Honour of Professor Winifred Maxwell*, eds. J. A. Benyon, C. W. Cook, T. R. H. Davenport, and K. S Hunt, 37–47. Cape Town, London, New York: Oxford University Press.

Murray, Bruce K. 1980. *The People's Budget 1909/10: Lloyd George and Liberal Politics.* Oxford: Clarendon Press.

Offer, Avner. 1981. *Property and Politics, 1870-1914.* Cambridge, New York: Cambridge University Press.

Packer, Ian. 2001. Lloyd George, *Liberalism and the Land: The Land Issue and Party Politics in England, 1906–1914.* Woodbridge, Suffolk; Rochester, NY: The Boydell Press.

Readman, Paul. 2008. *Land and Nation in England: Patriotism, National Identity, and the Politics of Land, 1880-1914.* Royal Historical Society Studies in History: New Series. Woodbridge: Boydell Press.

Sahm, Reiner. 2019. *Theorie und Ideengeschichte der Steuergerechtigkeit: Eine steuertheoretische, steuerrechtliche und politische Betrachtung.* Wiesbaden: Springer Gabler. https://doi.org/10.1007/978-3-658-25903-7.

Short, Brian. 1997. *Land and Society in Edwardian Britain.* Cambridge Studies in Historical Geography 25. Cambridge: Cambridge University Press.

Tichelar, Michael. 2019. *The Failure of Land Reform in Twentieth-Century England.* Abingdon, Oxon, New York, NY: Routledge.

Ward, Sadie. 1976. *Land Reform in England 1880–1914.* University of Reading, unpublished Ph. D. thesis.

Wende, Peter. 2001. *Großbritannien 1500-2000.* München: R. Oldenbourg Verlag.

Yardley, Robert B. 1930. *Land Value Taxation and Rating: A Critical Survey of the Aims and Proposals with a History of the Movement.* London: W. H. & L. Collingridge.

12 Populist Ambivalence to Tax Evasion

The 1962 Campaign against Dividend and Interest Withholding in the US

Steven A. Bank

12.1 Introduction

In 1962, President John F. Kennedy called for Congress "to apply to dividends and to interest the same withholding requirements we have long applied to wages".[1] Kennedy was concerned about the tax evasion that had been allowed to run rampant during the 1950s, which included a $3.3 billion shortfall between dividends and interest paid and reported on income tax returns.[2] By requiring withholding, Kennedy hoped to close what was considered one of the "major tax-escape routes for the upper-income brackets".[3]

Kennedy's withholding proposal was not expected to sail through Congress easily, but it at least was expected to be relatively uncontroversial among average taxpayers.[4] Wage earners had become accustomed to withholding since Congress had started requiring it during World War II.[5] Moreover, unlike withholding on wages and salaries, withholding on capital income such as dividends and interest was likely to hit wealthy taxpayers much harder than the average person.[6]

Despite this history, Kennedy's proposal to withhold taxes on dividend and interest payments encountered more public opposition than any measure in recent memory.[7] It was so wildly unpopular that it threatened to kill the 1962 tax bill altogether.[8] Congressional offices were "bombarded" by "an unprecedented avalanche" of letters from constituents opposed to the proposal,[9]

1 Kennedy (1962a).
2 The Tax Bill Battle: Withhold—Or Not? (1962).
3 Zelizer (1998).
4 Withholding for dividends and interest had been rejected in World War II and the early 1950s, but the opposition had primarily come from businesses. Pechman (1959).
5 Current Tax Payment Act of 1943; Zelenak (2018, 52–60); Twight (1995, 369–381); Jones (1988, 697); Doernberg (1982, 602).
6 Stern (1964, 171).
7 Anti-Dividend Tax Letters Flood Senate (1962); The Tax Bill Battle: Withhold—Or Not? (1962, 78).
8 The Tax Bill Battle: Withhold—Or Not? (1962, 80).
9 Id.

DOI: 10.4324/9781003333197-17

with some senators receiving thousands of letters a day in what they called the most mail they had ever received on a single issue.[10] Congress relented and stripped the dividend and interest withholding provision from the bill in favour of new reporting requirements.

Why did dividend and interest withholding generate such a reaction? This chapter explains that the resistance, although initially organised by business interests,[11] reflected populist concern about what some characterised as the "gentle robbery" of dividend and interest withholding.[12] More broadly, the reaction to the withholding proposal illustrated a general tension in anti-tax avoidance efforts. Lower bracket taxpayers resented that the rich could avoid taxes in many ways, but they did not want *their* one way – non-reporting of dividends and interest – foreclosed. Part 2 discusses Kennedy's proposal for withholding on dividends and interest. In Part 3, the chapter examines the letter-writing campaign orchestrated by banks, financial institutions and other businesses to rally popular support against withholding. This might suggest that the populism was orchestrated rather than genuine, but as Part 4 demonstrates, the public's responsiveness to these orchestrated campaigns reflected something deeper than a typical "astroturf", or fake grassroots, movement.[13] Part 5 explores the reasons for this resistance to withholding, situating it in the context of the popular ambivalence about tax avoidance generally.

12.2 Kennedy's Dividend and Interest Withholding Proposal

In 1959, House Ways and Means Democrat Committee Chair Wilbur Mills announced that Congress needed to consider closing avenues for tax avoidance, including the non-payment of taxes on dividends and interest.[14] A Treasury Department study of income tax returns had revealed that almost $1.5 billion worth of dividends and interest had gone unreported in 1956, resulting in a loss of approximately $500 million in tax revenue.[15] The tax gap on dividends was estimated to be 14%, while the gap for interest was almost 50%.[16]

Treasury had launched a dual education and enforcement campaign to try to spur increased reporting.[17] The Internal Revenue Service (IRS), the bureau of Treasury charged with collecting the taxes levied by the Internal Revenue Code, printed 42 million notices explaining the taxability of dividends and interest, which it then asked corporations and banks to distribute

10 Cornell (1962, 6).
11 Martin (1991, 63).
12 Editorial (1961b, 16).
13 See Kollman (1998, 13) (on "astroturf" movements).
14 Otten (1959, 1).
15 Mooney (1959a, 7).
16 Id.
17 IRS Moves to Cut Dividend Tax Loss (1959, C7).

to their stockholders and depositors.[18] The Individual Income Tax Return Form 1040 was changed to specifically include the words "dividends" and "interest" in bold type,[19] while the IRS declared that "underreported and unreported dividend and interest payments" would be "a major target of income tax audit checks" during 1960.[20] It also began working on an early computer system, called an "electronic data processing system", designed to make it easier to match interest and dividends with their recipients for purposes of catching non-reporters.[21]

Treasury claimed that its approach was starting to work,[22] but the election of Democratic President John F. Kennedy in November 1960 ushered in renewed support for dividend and interest withholding.[23] A bill to require withholding for dividends and interest as a tool against tax avoidance had passed the House a decade earlier under Democratic President Harry Truman,[24] but it had been defeated by business lobbying in the Senate.[25] Truman's Republican successor, Dwight D. Eisenhower, was not interested in revisiting the issue in his two terms in office. Concern about tax avoidance, though, had grown in the intervening years, with one *Los Angeles Times* writer indignantly proclaiming that "the government loses a billion dollars a year in taxes not collected on interest payments and dividends alone!"[26] With the change to the Kennedy administration, Treasury also changed its tune regarding its educational programme.[27] Douglas Dillon, the new Treasury Secretary under Kennedy, concluded in his 1961 Annual Report that:

> [T]his gap in tax payments cannot be closed by taxpayer educational programs nor by attempts to apply other collection techniques to the millions of separate dividend and interest transactions. An automatic system similar to tax withholding for employee compensation is essential.[28]

18 Morris (1960, 19); IRS Moves to Cut Dividend Tax Loss (1959); Mooney (1959b, 48); Map Tax Drive on Dividends and Interest (1959, C10).

19 Id.

20 Metz (1960, 35); Income Tax Drive Aims at Dividends Loophole (1960, 27).

21 Income Tax Drive Aims at Dividends Loophole (1960, 27). For background on the use of the electronic data processing system by the IRS, see Smith (1961, 205).

22 Treasury Encouraged by Rise in Taxpayers Voluntarily Reporting Dividends, Interest (1960, 16).

23 Metz (1961a, 85).

24 H.R. Rep. No. 586, 82nd Cong., 1951. Congress Group Urged to Support Withholding Tax on Interest and Dividends to Raise $250 Million (1951, 3).

25 Conferees Drop Withholding Levy on Interest, Dividends, Royalties (1951, 4).

26 Keezer (1960, G19); Metz (1961c, F1).

27 Grimes (1961, 4) ("[IRS Commissioner Mortimer] Caplin politely scoffed at Eisenhower Administration claims, made in Congress last December, of 'significant increases' in interest and dividend reporting on 1959 tax returns as a result of the voluntary-reporting campaign").

28 Annual Report of the Secretary of the Treasury on the State of the Finances for the Fiscal Year Ended June 30 (1961, 25).

Thus, it was not surprising that Kennedy planned to submit a bill that contained a provision for dividend and interest withholding.[29] As the president told Congress in a special message on taxation,

> [T]he application of the withholding principle has remained incomplete. Withholding does not apply to dividends and interest, with the result that substantial amounts of such income, particularly interest, improperly escape taxation. [...] This is patently unfair to those who must as a result bear a larger share of the tax burden. Recipients of dividends and interest should pay their tax no less than those who receive wage and salary income, and the tax should be paid just as promptly. Large continued avoidance of tax on the part of some has a steadily demoralizing effect on the compliance of others.[30]

Under his proposal, which he expected would raise $600 million, dividends and interest would be subject to withholding at a 20% rate.[31] Compliance burdens would be lessened on payers by removing the necessity of issuing withholding statements and arrangements would be made to ease the hardships on recipients not otherwise subject to tax.[32]

12.3 Business Leaders' Resistance

Business leaders vigorously opposed dividend and interest withholding, considering it an assault on savings.[33] Norman Strunk, executive vice president of the United States Savings and Loan League, called it a "tax on thrift", while Gaylord Freeman, president of the First National Bank of Chicago, complained that it would be "discriminatory" against investments that generated interest and dividends.[34] The Vice President of New York's First National City Bank argued that "taking off 20% of a man's interest, without any identification, no W-2 withholding form, no detail at all, no statement to the customer – that's just outright confiscation".[35]

29 Mooney (1961a, 1).
30 Kennedy (1961).
31 Id.
32 Id.
33 Kennedy's Tax Plan on Dividends Assailed (1961, 50); Wall Street Rips Kennedy Taxing Plan (1961, C9); Business Criticism of Plans to Withhold Dividends Expected at Hearings this Week (1961, 3).
34 Dombrowski (1961, C5).
35 Editorial (1961a, 18) (quoting "Vice President Painter"). A W-2 withholding form is the form that employers are required to provide to employees to notify them of the amount that has been withheld from their wages or salary and remitted to the federal government as a credit towards the employee's tax liability.

They were also concerned about the administrative burden. Although the proposal did not require banks to issue receipts,[36] they would still need to collect and remit the taxes from depositors' interest payments. One representative of the American Bankers Association called the plan "unduly burdensome and costly" to banks and savings institutions, while being "inequitable and confusing for taxpayers".[37] Another explained that "no practical, workable withholding system has yet been proposed which would not contribute to confusion and irritation on the part of ordinary taxpayers and would not impose unreasonable hardships or inequities" on individuals and financial institutions.[38] Essentially, a bank did not want to be "pressed into service as a tax collector [...] at its own expense".[39]

Representatives of banks and savings and loans offered dire predictions about the consequences of withholding. There were anecdotal reports that depositors, fearing or even "resenting" the withholding proposal, withdrew their funds to purchase savings bonds.[40] While bond interest would be subject to withholding, bondholders could defer that indefinitely by renewing their bonds rather than cashing them in.[41] This would reduce the funds available for banks to lend out, which they claimed would raise "the cost of home mortgage loans and other types of credit".[42] One bank executive warned that "for every dollar withheld from interest and dividends paid by savings banks and savings and loan associations, the supply of money invested in home mortgages by these institutions would be reduced by 75 cents or more".[43] Another estimated that savings and loans in New York State would have to remit $160 million to the government because of withholding – "enough to finance the purchase of 10,000 homes".[44]

After stalling in late 1961,[45] President Kennedy reissued his call for dividend and interest withholding in his 1962 State of the Union Address.[46] With Kennedy's push, the withholding proposal moved swiftly through the House. Ways and Means adopted the withholding proposal with a 20% rate that exempted savers under age 18 or over age 65.[47] The House passed

36 Metz (1961b, 27).
37 A.B.A. Oppose Tax Withholding (1961, C5).
38 Banks' Views Mixed on Withholding Taxes on Interest, Dividends (1961, 2).
39 Id. (quoting Robert J. Landoll, the Controller's Institute of America); "Tax Plan's Effect (1961, N_B6); Questions Withholding Tax on Dividend Plan (1961, S_B6).
40 Metz (1961d, 18).
41 Id. at 18.
42 Questions Withholding Tax on Dividend Plan (1961, S_B6).
43 Sidelights: Job Peril Seen in Withholding (1962, 48) (quoting Gerald J. Peffert, vice president and controller of Dime Savings Bank of Brooklyn).
44 The Tax Bill Battle: Withhold—Or Not? (1962, 79).
45 Dividend Tax Plan Defeated in Part by House Panel (1961, 3).
46 State of the Union (1962, 16).
47 Burke (1962, A2).

the bill with the dividend and interest withholding provision intact, despite Republican attempts to remove it.[48]

12.4 Taxpayers' "Astroturf" Resistance

As in 1961, the proposal met fierce opposition, but this time, it came directly from taxpayers rather than businesses. Politicians faced a literal "deluge" of letters from individuals opposed to withholding.[49] Described as "a grass-roots revolt of surprising intensity cutting across party lines",[50] some senators reported that they received "3,000 letters of protest a day" with several saying that "it is the biggest volume of mail they ever have gotten on one subject".[51] Paul Douglas, a liberal Democrat, stated that he had "received over 40,000 letters from constituents in Illinois protesting against the withholding tax"[52] with 10,000 letters reportedly coming in the first week of the Senate Finance Committee hearings.[53] Senator Clifford Case, a Republican from New Jersey who had received 5,000 letters in a single day, reportedly had to hire part-time help to answer the letters, while Senate Finance Committee chair Harry Byrd, a Democrat from Virginia, reported that "he had received 100,000 letters opposing the proposal".[54] The Senate Postmaster reported that total mail delivery volume doubled during the Finance Committee hearings.[55]

Few thought that the letter writers were acting on their own initiative. Democrats "said they believed the mail flood resulted from an organized campaign".[56] Senators reported receiving notes from depositors "scribbled on the back of the letter making the request from the financial institution" or "on the back of forms supplied by savings and loan and banking institutions".[57] The *Washington Post* canvassed senators of both parties and concluded that "there is abundant evidence that many of their constituents wrote in only after reading statements on the subject from their savings institution".[58] Given that more than 50% of the population reportedly had money deposited in interest-bearing accounts or invested in bonds or stocks as of 1961,[59] it was not surprising that businesses turned to the average saver and investor in their fight against withholding.

48 Morris (1962, 1).
49 Anti-Dividend Tax Letters Flood Senate (1962, B3).
50 Novak (1962a, 1).
51 Cornell (1962, 6).
52 Hearings before Senate (1962, 4357).
53 Anti-Dividend Tax Letters Flood Senate (1962, B3).
54 Dividend Withholding Defeat Seen in Senate (1962, D2).
55 Albright (1962, A15).
56 Anti-Dividend Tax Letters Flood Senate (1962, B3) (citing Senators Paul Douglas, D-Ill., and Harrison A. Williams, Jr., D-N.J.).
57 Id.; Albright (1962, A15).
58 Id.
59 Mooney (1961b, 18).

The campaign could be traced to a precise date – 26 March 1962 – when a subcommittee of the United States Savings and Loan League decided to seek the aid of their customers in lobbying against withholding.[60] It paired a letter-writing campaign with a campaign against one of the bill's other proposals that would raise taxes on savings and loans.[61] On 30 March, the League's executive vice president, Norman Strunk, sent letters to its 4,800 members announcing the campaign and providing them with sample letters that they were encouraged to use to write letters to all of their 30 million depositors.[62] "Member institutions from coast to coast took up the battle" after receiving the League's request.[63] They sent "Dear-Saver" letters to their depositors, arguing that going after tax evasion by imposing withholding was like "trying to weed the garden with a bulldozer".[64]

The stock exchanges also initiated a public campaign against dividend withholding. After a survey revealed that most shareholders opposed withholding,[65] New York Stock Exchange president Keith Funston asked listed corporations "to urge their shareowners to get in touch with their respective congressmen" and reported that the Pacific Stock Exchange was doing the same thing on the west coast.[66] The Association of Stock Exchange Firms conducted "a full-fledged drive across the country on a regional level".[67]

Mutual funds also tried to "arouse shareholders against" dividend withholding.[68] They included inserts in their quarterly statements "advising shareholders to write their senators".[69] One contained the following:

> You may want to write your Senator in Congress right now about something of vital importance to you which is being decided now. At issue is a bill to withhold 20 per cent of your dividend and interest income. [...] Withholding applied to dividends and interest would, we feel, be unjust, ineffective and enormously complicated and confusing. While the bill would have the benefit of reducing tax evasion, we feel that there are many other alternatives to dividend-interest withholding which would not carry the same hardships to individual taxpayers.[70]

60 Cong. Rec. (1962. Vol. 108, 22971) (reprinting McCartney, "Big Lobby Push").
61 Id.
62 Id.
63 Id.
64 Stern (1964, 171).
65 "Funston Says" (1961, 6).
66 Walsh (1961, B7).
67 Id.
68 Smith (1962, 50).
69 Id.
70 Id. (quoting from a letter sent by David L. Babson Management Corporation, sponsor of the Aberdeen Fund).

The letter went on to warn that because the withholding proposal would be done at a flat rate, "millions would overpay their taxes – would have their money taken away from them and then have to arrange for its return".[71] Mutual funds asked their salesmen to convince clients to lobby against withholding. One securities dealer service publication "recommended that all salesmen warn their clients about the dangers and get them to write their senators protesting such proposed legislation".[72]

The letter writing appeared to make an impression on liberal senators. According to one report, "Democratic members of Congress, [...] surprised at the widespread opposition to the Administration's plan for withholding taxes on dividend and interest income", were taking notice.[73] Senator Paul Douglas later recalled, "we were not prepared for the storm that followed. Suddenly, from all over the country [...] thousands of protests poured into my office".[74] *The Wall Street Journal* observed:

> the real cause of the withholding plan's present problems is an uprising against it by liberals and moderates. This rebellion reflects an influx of anti-withholding letters matched in recent years only by protests against President Truman's dismissal of Gen. MacArthur and the Senate's censure of Sen. McCarthy.[75]

Democrats' wavering reflected the letter-writing campaign's potential to be "a campaign issue of some potency".[76] One senator described as a "liberal-leaning Southern[er]" explained:

> In all honesty, the Treasury has some pretty good arguments for withholding. But this is something the people just plain don't want, and I'm not going to vote for it, particularly in a year when I'm running for re-election. That's what I tell the Treasury.[77]

Another said "it could be the kind of issue that hurts you, especially with people who aren't vitally concerned with other issues".[78] This led some senators to publicly announce their opposition, including Senator Edward Long, a stalwart Democrat from Missouri facing an election challenge, and Administration supporter Stephen Young of Ohio, while Senator Warren Magnuson of Washington reportedly "dispatched 10,000 letters branding

71 Id.
72 Smith (1962, 44).
73 Editorial (1962, 12).
74 Douglas (1967-68, 25).
75 Novak (1962b, 13).
76 Novak (1962a, 18).
77 Novak (1962b, 13) (quoting from the Senator).
78 Novak (1962a, 18).

the withholding plan as unconstitutional".[79] Other senators privately advised Kennedy to drop, or at least shelve, the proposal.[80] Democrats in the Senate had become "so concerned about the flood of mail [...] that [about 25 senators] called a secret meeting" in which they decided to ask Senate leaders to go to Kennedy and privately urge that he intervene.[81]

While Kennedy lashed out at political defectors,[82] the *Washington Post Times Herald* reported that "the surge of opposition mail continue[d] in a concentrated flood".[83] Letter writers may have been inspired by Senator Byrd's decision to break ranks with the president on withholding.[84] By the summer of 1962, the anti-withholding forces gained the upper hand. In August, the Senate "overwhelmingly rejected" withholding on dividends and interest.[85] House conferees made a "perfunctory demand" to reinstate some form of dividend and interest withholding but dropped it in favour of information reporting on interest and dividends in excess of $10.[86]

Kennedy lamented the absence of withholding in the Revenue Act of 1962, which established a new investment tax credit and erected limits on deductions for entertainment expenses.[87] He suggested that he would reintroduce his proposal in a new Congress,[88] but this was quickly dropped to give more time for a trial of the stricter information reporting requirements.[89] Treasury was directed to provide annual reports to Congress "on how successful the system is in combating tax avoidance".[90]

12.5 Understanding the Popular Opposition

Although the industry letter-writing campaign focused taxpayer attention on the issue, it should not have been sufficient on its own to sustain the opposition. In part because of the obvious self-interest of their promoters, top-down attempts to generate grassroots opposition are rarely successful.[91] There is little doubt that the financial institutions opposing withholding

79 Novak (1962b, 13).
80 Senators Urge Kennedy to Scrap New Tax Plan (1962, 22).
81 Albright (1962, A15); Senators Urge Kennedy to Scrap New Tax Plan (1962, 22).
82 Cornell (1962, 6); Kennedy, in Bid to Stem Grass Roots Revolt (1962, 3).
83 Mail Opposition to Dividend Tax Plan Increases (1962, A7).
84 Withheld Interest Tax is Opposed by Byrd (1962, A2); Mail Opposition to Dividend Tax Plan Increases (1962, A7).
85 Senate Crushes Plan to Withhold Tax on Dividends (1962, 1); Hall (1962, 16).
86 Novak (1962c, 3).
87 Kennedy (1962b).
88 Id.
89 Treasury May Not Request Dividend Withholding Tax (1962, 1).
90 Novak (1962c, 3).
91 Kollman (1998, 33).

were self-interested, as they wanted to avoid administrative costs,[92] be able to use the funds prior to payment,[93] and did not want to lose customers to other investments.[94]

Moreover, defeating withholding provided few benefits to the average letter writer.[95] Only 10% of 1959 tax returns included dividends, but 80% of those dividends went to individuals with incomes of $100,000 per year or more.[96] Indeed, taxpayers making $100,000 or more received 30% or more of their adjusted gross income as dividends, while those in the $1 million bracket received over 48% of their adjusted gross income from dividends.[97] Interest income was a bit more evenly distributed, but only 1% of the total tax returns filed – those with incomes of over $20,000 per year – accounted for 55% of all interest.[98]

Despite the obvious self-interest of its sponsors and the disproportionate benefit for upper income individuals, the campaign struck a nerve with the average taxpayer.[99] A variety of factors contributed to making it a populist issue.

First, millions of individuals were potentially affected by the withholding proposal. According to one estimate "more than half the population [had] savings accounts, savings bonds, corporate bonds or stocks".[100] That includes non-filers, but "more than 75 million special notices were mailed to recipients of dividends and interest" as part of the education and information program that Treasury utilised before Kennedy introduced his withholding proposal, suggesting the number of affected taxpayers was still high.[101] As the *Wall Street Journal* noted, the fact that "many millions of ordinary Americans now own stocks and many millions more of moderate means have either savings accounts or stocks or both" meant that Congress should not have been surprised at the "widespread opposition" to the Administration's plan.[102]

Second, lower bracket taxpayers felt targeted by the withholding proposal. In some respects, that is because they *were* being targeted. Kennedy's proposal was designed so that it effectively hit low bracket taxpayers more than other taxpayers. Under the income tax, the lowest bracket was 20% on income up

92 See "Hearings on the President's 1961 Tax Recommendations," 2325–2331 (testimony of Robert K. Wilmouth, member of the Savings Operations Committee of the Savings Division of the American Bankers Association). But see, Nossiter (1962, B9).

93 Douglas (1967/68, 27).

94 Trude (1961, 20).

95 Novak (1962b, 13).

96 Cong. Rec. (1962. Vol. 108, 17776–17777).

97 Id.

98 Id. at 17777.

99 Novak (1962a, 1); Stratemeyer (1962, 20).

100 Mooney (1962, 17).

101 Latham (1960, 16).

102 Editorial (1962, 12).

to $2,000, rising to 91% on income over $200,000.[103] This meant that the 20% withholding rate on interest and dividends captured all of the tax due from low bracket taxpayers, but potentially only a fraction of what was due from high bracket taxpayers.[104] Stanley Surrey, the Assistant Secretary of the Treasury in charge of Tax Policy and a former Harvard Law School professor, suggested in a 1961 interview about the withholding proposal that this was intentional: "We feel that if we have this automatic machinery for getting at those in the lower brackets, we can concentrate on other methods of enforcement to ensure compliance from those in the upper brackets".[105]

Third, low bracket taxpayers viewed withholding as a form of self-help to counter the fact that the "chosen few" could avoid taxes by investing in domestic tax shelters and foreign tax havens.[106] As George Sokolsky of the *Washington Post* noted, one of the reasons the withholding proposal was "something to be angry about" is "because it strikes directly at those who do not have much money. [...] If they want to soak the rich, why don't they go after the numbered accounts in Swiss banks?"[107] "The loss in tax collection," Sokolosky noted, "from American money on deposit in Switzerland, West Germany, Liechtenstein, Monaco, Panama, Hong Kong and other places [...] must be much larger than one billion dollars", which was what some estimated was the amount lost from non-reporting of dividends and interest.[108]

By contrast, dividends and interest were among the few areas where middle and lower-bracket taxpayers were able to avoid taxes. As one contemporary commentator observed:

> The Little Guy, whose wage or salary is his only source of income, really is in a tough spot. He'll have a hard time dreaming up any kind of tax-saving device. If only he owned a few stocks and bonds – that's the one field where he can practice a bit of "withholding" of one's own.[109]

There is some evidence that they took advantage of this. Economist Daniel Holland examined the gap in dividend reporting over time and observed that "the zeal with which people reported their dividend income declined markedly between 1939 and 1952",[110] which he attributed to the change in tax rates over this period.[111] Holland surmised that "more taxpayers were pushed below the margin of honesty as it became more profitable not to

103 Tax Foundation, Federal Income Tax Rates History.
104 Metz (1961e, 6).
105 Interview, "Stanley S. Surrey" (1961, 21).
106 Humphrey (1952, 10).
107 Sokolsky (1962a, A13.)
108 Sokolsky (1962b, 4).
109 Millikin (1963, 153).
110 Holland (1958, 246).
111 Id. at 247.

report dividend receipts".[112] Most significantly, there was "a general tendency for the importance of underreporting to vary inversely with income class", with underreporting higher among the lower-income classes.[113] Although some underreporting in the lower-income groups could "be laid to carelessness and poor record-keeping", Holland concluded that since "overreporting errors averaged only half as much or less than underreporting errors", taxpayers in the lower brackets may have deliberately underreported their dividends to avoid taxes.[114]

Those taxpayers who did omit dividends and interest deliberately often justified it as a form of self-help. Consider the remarks of a 1950s-era insurance consultant:

> The income-tax law is stacked against the professional and the little man in favor of businessmen and owners of stocks, bonds, and other property [...]. While overstating deductions and omitting dividends or interest income will not set things right, no one [...] can properly criticize the disfavored taxpayers from using these devices to offset in a small measure the injustices of the tax laws.[115]

IRS Commissioner Mortimer Caplin concluded that "[i]ndividuals frequently hear of expense accounts, fringe benefits, and persons earning huge sums but paying little taxes. The remark made the other day by a salaried employee is typical: 'Why does everyone have a loophole but me? Why shouldn't I have a window to crawl out of?'"[116]

Fourth, taxpayers resented that withholding seemed to be more about revenue-raising than tax avoidance. Many felt it was designed to obscure an effort to increase taxes on the already "overburdened" average citizen.[117] One columnist reported the "growing feeling" that withholding mechanisms were "mischievous and trouble-making devices which only help hide from the average individual the extent to which he is being taxed".[118] Another complained that "the proposal to put a withholding tax on interest and dividends may look like a scheme to soak the rich to get after the tax-dodger. In fact, it will be a hardship on the widow and orphans, on those who have inherited small amounts and have to live on interest and dividends".[119]

112 Id. at 250.
113 Id. at 253–254.
114 Id. at 256.
115 Hellerstein (1963, 241–242).
116 Caplin (1958, 840).
117 Schilling (1962, A5); Cole (1962, A20).
118 Henry (1962, A1).
119 Sokolsky (1962a, A13).

Furthermore, it appeared that the revenue from withholding was intended to pay for tax breaks for the wealthy.[120] In 1962, Kennedy told Ways and Means Committee Chair Wilbur Mills that "the single-most important provision in the bill would provide a tax credit for new investment in machinery and equipment",[121] which most viewed as primarily a benefit for the high-bracket taxpayers.[122] Withholding, by contrast, was described as a way of funding the new investment tax credit,[123] fulfilling Kennedy's pledge to submit a balanced budget for 1963.[124] One letter writer, identified appropriately as "Anxious Widow", complained to the *Chicago Daily Tribune* that "it would mean real hardship to give up $50 a month just so that Mr. Kennedy can have more to slather around like you know what kind of sailor".[125]

This suspicion about the true motives behind withholding reflected a broader anti-government sentiment. As one individual wrote to the *Los Angeles Times*, "there is a growing resentment as to the way in which our finances are being managed, or rather mismanaged by the administration, and its encroachments on all phases of business and incomes in the form of taxation".[126] Another compared it to military draft in a letter written to the *Wall Street Journal*, asking whether the government has the right to "conscript the services of private citizens at the expense of private enterprises".[127]

Even if withholding helped to curb tax evaders, not everyone viewed them as enemies. As one observer noted, "taxes are so heavy and so complicated that the average citizen has more sympathy than he should have, perhaps, for the tax dodger".[128] Another commented that "[e]verybody wants a smaller tax bill, and the collective response of taxpayers generally to this aspiration is sympathetic".[129] It was true, of course, that some law-abiding citizens resented this attitude. As one individual remarked in a letter to the *Wall Street Journal*, "I find it infuriating to hear people say that they 'never bother to report dividend or interest income.' I suspect that these are the same people who are opposing" the withholding proposal.[130] This apparent erosion of confidence was part of Kennedy's concern when he focused his 1963 tax message on removing some of the "complexities and inequities which undermine the morale of the taxpayer".[131] Nevertheless, withholding for dividends and interest was unlikely to do much to boost taxpayer morale. It only served to

120 Walsh (1961, B7).
121 Kennedy's Letter to Mills on the Tax Bill (1962, 15) (quoting from Kennedy's letter to Mills).
122 Hambrick (1963, 67); Rosacker & Metcalf (1992, 65); McIntyre (1992).
123 Id. Program for Economy: Tax on Dividends (1962, E2); Pollack (1996, 73–74).
124 Mooney (1961c, E6).
125 Anxious Widow (1961, 16).
126 E.D. (1962, A5).
127 Mitchell (1962, 14).
128 Tidal Wave of Protests Rolls in on Dividend Holding Plan (1962, 39).
129 Metz (1961e, 8).
130 Seligman (1961, 6).
131 Kennedy (1963), 6).

align high and low bracket taxpayers in their opposition to serious efforts to curtail tax avoidance.

12.6 Conclusion

The anti-withholding campaign struck a chord with middle class taxpayers who felt that they had been left behind in the hollowing out of the tax base. Not only did millions of people own dividend or interest-bearing investments, but the proposed withholding system's low flat rate effectively targeted the middle and lower-bracket taxpayers. By linking it with an investment tax credit, Kennedy and his fellow Democrats deprived withholding of much of its moral force and encouraged the self-help rationale that contributed to middle-class tax avoidance. Consequently, the rejection of dividend and interest withholding was as much about populist ambivalence toward tax avoidance efforts as it was about the letter-writing campaign that sparked the movement.

This populist ambivalence continued when renewed concerns about the tax gap led to a revival of the dividend and interest withholding proposal in the 1970s and 1980s, first by Democratic President Jimmy Carter and then again by Republican President Ronald Reagan.[132] Congress even went so far as to adopt a withholding requirement in 1982.[133] In 1983, however, in the face of a letter-writing campaign against withholding that resembled the one that took place two decades earlier, Congress ultimately "acquiesced to the opposition" and passed a measure to repeal the withholding requirement over President Reagan's threat of a veto.[134] To this day, withholding generally applies only to wages, and not to dividends and interest.[135]

References

A.B.A. Oppose Tax Withholding. 1961. *Chicago Daily Tribune*, May 27.

Albright, Robert C. 1962. Confusion on Tax Bill Keeps Senators Busy. *Washington Post*, May 4.

Annual Report of the Secretary of the Treasury on the State of the Finances for the Fiscal Year Ended June 30, 1961.

Anti-Dividend Tax Letters Flood Senate. 1962. *Chicago Daily Tribune*, April 22.

Anxious Widow. 1961. Letter to the Editor, Dividend Withholding and One Person. *Chicago Daily Tribune*, April 6.

Banks' Views Mixed on Withholding Taxes on Interest, Dividends. 1961. *Wall Street Journal*, May 29.

Burke, Vincent J. Interest, Dividend Tax Withholding Backed. 1962. *Washington Post Times Herald*, Feb. 24.

132 Twight (1995, 385–390).

133 Rankin (1982).

134 Congress Passes Repeal of Interest Withholding (1983, D7).

135 Kahng (2010).

Business Criticism of Plans to Withhold Dividends Expected at Hearings this Week. 1961. *Wall Street Journal*, May 22.

Caplin, Mortimer M. 1958. Threats to the Integrity of Our Tax System. *Virginia Law Review* 44: 839–855.

Cole, Abigail. 1962. Letter to the Editor, Bread and Water. *Washington Post Times Herald*, May 11.

Conferees Drop Withholding Levy on Interest, Dividends, Royalties. 1951. *Wall Street Journal*, Oct. 11.

Congress Group Urged to Support Withholding Tax on Interest and Dividends to Raise $250 Million. 1951. *Wall Street Journal*, Feb. 7.

Congress Passes Repeal of Interest Withholding. 1983. New York Times, July 29.

Congressional Record of U.S. Congress. 1962. Vol. 108.

Cornell, Douglas B. Tax Foes Lying, Says President, 1962. *Atlanta Constitution*, May 10.

Current Tax Payment Act of 1943, Pub. L. No. 78-120, §2, 57 Stat. 126, 128 (1943)

Dividend Tax Plan Defeated in Part by House Panel. 1961. *Wall Street Journal*, July 14.

Dividend Withholding Defeat Seen in Senate. 1962. *Los Angeles Times*, July 29.

Doernberg, Richard L. 1982. The Case against Withholding. *Texas Law Review* 61: 595–654.

Dombrowski, Louis. 1961. Withholding of Dividend Tax Ripped, *Chicago Daily Tribune*, March 31.

Douglas, Paul. 1967-68. The Problem of Tax Loopholes (Or: My Eighteen Years in a Quandary). *American Scholar* 37: 21–43.

E.D. 1962. Letter to the Editor. Withholding. *Los Angeles Times*, July 20.

Editorial. Political Withholding. 1962. *Wall Street Journal*, May 4.

Editorial. Saving Under Suspicion. 1961a. *Wall Street Journal*, May 25.

Editorial. The Art of Gentle Robbery. 1961b. *Chicago Daily Tribune*, April 24.

Funston Says Survey Backs Big Board Stand on Dividend Tax Rise. 1961. *Wall Street Journal*, April 17.

Grimes, John A. 1961. Tax Agency Calls Drive to Spur Voluntary Reporting of Dividends, Interest a Failure, *Wall Street Journal*, March 29.

H. R. Rep. (Report of House Committee on the Judiciary), No. 586, 82nd Cong., (1951).

Hall, Joe. 1962. Dividend Withholding Taken Out of Tax Bill. *Atlanta Constitution*, Aug. 30.

Hambrick, J. Reid. 1963. The Illusion of Tax Reform. *Duke Law Journal* 1963: 56–97.

Hellerstein, Jerome R. 1963. *Taxes, Loopholes, and Morals*. New York: McGraw-Hill.

Henry, Bill. 1962. The Opposition is Bi-Partisan. *Los Angeles Times*, May 22.

Holland, Daniel M. 1958. Dividend Underreporting on Tax Returns. *Journal of Finance* 13: 238.

Humphrey, Hubert H. 1952. *Tax Loop Holes*. Washington: Public Affairs Institute.

Income Tax Drive Aims at Dividends Loophole. 1960. *Los Angeles Times*, Feb. 17.

Interview, Stanley S. Surrey. The Role of the Tax System. 1961. *Challenge* 9: 20–24.

IRS Moves to Cut Dividend Tax Loss. 1959. *Washington Post Times Herald*, Dec. 11.

Jones, Carolyn C. 1988. Class Tax to Mass Tax: The Role of Propaganda in the Expansion of the Income Tax During World War II. *Buffalo Law Review* 37: 685–737.

Kahng, Lily. 2010. Investment Income Withholding in the United States and Germany. *Florida Tax Review* 10: 315–341.

Keezer, Dexter M. 1960. Our Scandalous Income-Tax Snarl, *Los Angeles Times*, April 10.

Kennedy, in Bid to Stem Grass Roots Revolt, Defends Withholding of Taxes on Dividends. 1962. *Wall Street Journal*, May 10.

Kennedy's Letter to Mills on the Tax Bill. 1962. *New York Times*, March 23.

Kennedy's Tax Plan on Dividends Assailed, 1961. *Atlanta Constitution*, April 21.

Kennedy, John F. 1961. Special Message to the Congress on Taxation, April 20. http://www.taxhistory.org/thp/readings.nsf/ArtWeb/2B727964C0A28BE5852571690051FD23?OpenDocument.

Kennedy, John F. 1962a. Annual Message to Congress on the State of the Union, Jan. 11. https://www.presidency.ucsb.edu/documents/annual-message-the-congress-the-state-the-union-4.

Kennedy, John F. 1962b. Statement by the President Upon Signing the Revenue Act, October 16. https://www.presidency.ucsb.edu/documents/statement-the-president-upon-signing-the-revenue-act.

Kennedy, John F. 1963. Text of President Kennedy's Message to Congress on Tax Reduction and Revision. *New York Times*, Jan. 25.

Kollman, Ken. 1998. *Outside Lobbying: Public Opinion and Interest Group Strategies.* Princeton: Princeton University Press.

Latham, Dana. 1960. Internal Revenue Administration – 1960, *Bulletin of the American Bar Association, Section of Taxation* 14: 7–24.

Mail Opposition to Dividend Tax Plan Increases. 1962. *Washington Post Times Herald*, May 23.

Map Tax Drive on Dividends and Interest. 1959. *Chicago Tribune*, Nov. 23.

Martin, Cathie, J. 1991. *Shifting the Burden: The Struggle over Growth and Corporate Taxation.* Chicago: The University of Chicago Press.

McIntyre, Robert S. 1992. No: Tax Breaks Only Distort Investment and Undermine the Market's Efficiency. *Washington Post*, March 8.

Metz, Robert. 1960. Interest Income to be Target of U.S. Tax Return Scrutiny, *New York Times*, February 15.

Metz, Robert. 1961a. Study May Lead to Tax Changes, *New York Times*, January 9.

Metz, Robert. 1961b. Dissent on Tax Plans. *New York Times*, July 24.

Metz, Robert. 1961c. Tax Agency Spurs Collection Work, *New York Times*, October 22.

Metz, Robert. 1961d. Tax Escape Seen in Savings Bonds, *New York Times*, October 29.

Metz, Robert. 1961e. The Politics of Tax Reform, Challenge 9: 6.

Millikin, H.F. 1963. *The Prudent Man: Tax Dodging as an Art.* London: Abelard-Schuman.

Mitchell, Margaret M. 1962. Is it Ethical? *Wall Street Journal*, May 22.

Mooney, Richard E. 1959a. Loophole Noted in Dividend Tax. *New York Times*, September 19.

Mooney, Richard E. 1959b. U.S. Seeking Unreported Taxes, *New York Times*, November 23.

Mooney, Richard E. 1961a. Kennedy to Urge Business Tax Aid to Spur Investing. *New York Times*, April 9.

Mooney, Richard E. 1961b. Congress is Given Tax Plan Seeking Aid for Business. *New York Times*, April 12.

Mooney, Richard E. 1961c. Budget Debate Grows Sharper, *New York Times*, November 5.

Mooney, Richard E. 1962. Tax Bill is Ready for House Floor. *New York Times*, February 28.

Morris, John D. 1960. Tax on Dividends May Be Withheld. *New York Times*, February 29.

Morris, John D. 1962. House Approves Kennedy's Plan of Tax Revision, *New York Times*, March 30.

Nossiter, Bernard D. 1962. Maverick Bank Likes Withholding, *Washington Post Times Herald*, April 20.

Novak, Robert D. 1962a. Grassroots Report: Voter Revolt is Raging Over Plan to Withhold Interest, Dividend Tax. *Wall Street Journal*, May 2.

Novak, Robert D. 1962b. Tax Bill's Troubles. *Wall Street Journal*, May 22.

Novak, Robert D. 1962c. Conferees Vote Tax Bill Diluting Outlay Credit Plan, Eliminating Proposal for Withholding on Dividends. *Wall Street Journal*, September 26.

Otten, Alan L. 1959. Specialists Mull Ways to Close 'Loopholes' in Present Taxes. *Wall Street Journal*, January 7.

Pechman, Joseph A. 1959. Withholding for Interest and Dividends, in *Tax Revision Compendium, Compendium of Papers on Broadening the Tax Base*. Report prepared for the Committee on Ways and Means, U.S. House of Representatives.

Pollack, Sheldon D. 1996. *The Failure of U.S. Tax Policy*. University Park, Pennsylvania: Pennsylvania State University Press.

President's 1961 Tax Recommendations. Hearings before the Committee on Ways and Means, House of Representatives, 87th Cong., 1st Sess. 2499.

Program for Economy: Tax on Dividends. 1962. *New York Times*, February 25.

Questions Withholding Tax on Dividend Plan. 1961. *Chicago Daily Tribune*, June 25.

Rankin, Deborah. A Closer Look at the New Tax Law. 1982. *New York Times*, October 10.

Revenue Act of 1962. Hearings before the Committee on Finance, United States Senate, 87th Cong., 2d Sess., on H.R. 10650.

Rosacker, Robert E. and Richard W. Metcalf. 1992. United States Federal Tax Policy Surrounding the Investment Tax Credit: A Review of Legislative Intent and Empirical Research Findings over Thirty Years (1962-1991). *Akron Tax Journal*. 9: 59–77.

Schilling, H.F. 1962. Letter to the Editor, Withholding Tax on Dividends: Its Benefits are Pure Guesswork. *Los Angeles Times*, May 21.

Seligman, Edward J. 1961. Letter to the Editor, Dividend Tax, *Wall Street Journal*, July 21.

Senate Crushes Plan to Withhold Tax on Dividends. 1962. *Wall Street Journal*, August 30.

Senators Urge Kennedy to Scrap New Tax Plan. 1962. *Los Angeles Times*, May 7.

Sidelights: Job Peril Seen in Withholding. 1962. *New York Times*, February 13.

Smith, Gene. 1962. Mutual Funds: Drive Against Tax Bill of U.S. *New York Times*, May 7.

Smith, William H. 1961. Electronic Data Processing and Federal Tax Administration. *Proceedings Annual Conference on Taxation, National Tax Association* 54: 205–212.

Sokolsky, George E. 1962a. These Days … How to Protect Yourself. *Washington Post Times Herald*, April 7.

Sokolsky, George E. 1962b. These Days. *El Paso Times*, June 2.

Stern, Philip. 1964. *The Great Treasury Raid*. New York: Random House.

Stratemeyer, George E. 1962. Letter to the Editor, Voice of the People, Kennedy's Mistake? *Chicago Daily Tribune*, May 25.

Tax Foundation, Federal Individual Income Tax Rates History, https://files.taxfoundation.org/legacy/docs/fed_individual_rate_history_nominal.pdf, last accessed Oct. 24, 2022.

Tax Plan's Effect. 1961. *Chicago Daily Tribune*, June 25.

The Tax Bill Battle: Withhold—Or Not? 1962. *Newsweek*, June 4.

Tidal Wave of Protests Rolls in on Dividend Holding Plan. 1962. *Chicago Daily Tribune*, May 27.

Treasury Encouraged by Rise in Taxpayers Voluntarily Reporting Dividends, Interest. 1960. *Wall Street Journal*, December 23.

Treasury May Not Request Dividend Withholding Tax. 1962. *Wall Street Journal*, Nov. 12.

Trude, William E. 1961. Letter to the Editor: Withholding Taxes, *Chicago Daily Tribune*, April 18.

Twight, Charlotte. 1995. "Evolution of Federal Income Tax Withholding: The Machinery of Institutional Change." 14 *Cato Journal* 14: 359–395.

U.S. Congress. Congressional Record 87th Congress, 2d Session. 1962. Vol. 108

Wall Street Rips Kennedy Taxing Plan, 1961. *Chicago Daily Tribune*, April 21.

Walsh, Harold. 1961. Ranks Form to Stop Higher Dividend Tax. *Los Angeles Times*, April 21.

Withheld Interest Tax is Opposed by Byrd. 1962. *Washington Post Times Herald*, May 20.

Zelenak, Lawrence. 2018. *Figuring Out the Tax: Congress, Treasury, and the Design of the Early Modern Income Tax*. Cambridge: Cambridge University Press.

Zelizer, Julian E. 1998. *Taxing America: Wilbur D. Mills, Congress, and the State, 1945-1975*. Cambridge: Cambridge University Press.

13 "I Am a Professional Tax Evader"[1]

Multinationals, Business Groups and Tax Havens, 1950s to 1980s

Boris Gehlen and Christian Marx

13.1 Introduction

Multinational enterprises (MNE) and (family) business groups are often used as negative examples in public and populist discourses about tax morality. The rather casual claim made by Hans Heinrich Thyssen-Bornemisza (1921–2001), the very rich owner of the multinational Thyssen-Bornemisza-Group (TBG), that he considered himself "a professional tax evader" and actually belonged in prison, seems at first glance to confirm such a view. It was not without pride that he told his biographer, the journalist David Litchfield, in a wine-soaked atmosphere sometime in the 1990s, what great efforts he had made to minimise both his personal tax payments and those of his companies.[2]

This episode reveals a lot about Hans Heinrich Thyssen-Bornemisza's personality, but at the same time, succinctly sums up the "tax logic" of multinational companies. First, it shows the extent to which tax planning had become a matter-of-course practice for multinational entities in the second half of the twentieth century. Second, the anecdote sheds light on what a complex and therefore cost-intensive (but obviously worthwhile) undertaking tax avoidance is. And third, the reference to prison, while not an admission of guilt in a legal sense, perhaps testifies to a subliminal awareness of the (moral) questions raised by practices of tax optimisation, which, in the case of Hans Heinrich Thyssen-Bornemisza, could quickly be put aside with the next bottle of red wine.[3]

1 Hans Heinrich Thyssen-Bornemisza, quoted from Litchfield (2006, 406).

2 Hans Heinrich never authorised Litchfield's biography, who instead wrote a book on the Thyssen family after Hans Heinrich had died. It is very well-researched but dispenses with an annotation apparatus in the academic sense, so that it is not clear exactly when Hans Heinrich's statement was made. However, the context reveals that it was made retrospectively. Litchfield (2006, 405–406).

3 Litchfield repeatedly describes such acts of demonstrative nonchalance on the part of Hans Heinrich Thyssen-Bornemisza, who had no problem in switching from thorny topics to the pleasantries of life. This seems to be part of Thyssen-Bornemisza's self-stylisation; see Litchfield (2006).

DOI: 10.4324/9781003333197-18

Actually, Hans Heinrich Thyssen-Bornemisza and his group were not tax evaders, but rather tax avoiders par excellence. They thus fit into a long series of MNEs in the twentieth century that used their multinationality to engage in tax arbitrage and to "optimise", i.e. minimise, their accumulated tax liabilities. In the context of increasing globalisation and the spread of MNEs from the 1960s, international financial relations and possibilities for tax avoidance intensified.[4] Although recent literature can help explain and confirm (global) wealth inequality, it only provides a condensed picture of business action, as the authors often infer the motivation from the result. But with their tax-avoidance measures, did MNEs really *deliberately* reduce state revenues, evade social responsibility or weaken democratic institutions?[5] The simple observation that multinational companies and wealthy families take advantage of a variety of opportunities to reduce their taxes does not explain why and how they do so or how these financial relations emerged from a specific historical context.[6]

The question of the motivation and the scope to evade or to avoid taxes is certainly a normative or moral one. However, from a (simplistic) business view, taxes are nothing but costs and companies always try to reduce costs, especially if there is no corresponding benefit or if they can achieve similar benefits more cheaply elsewhere. As the French economist Céline Azémar puts it: "It is now widely accepted that tax differentials among countries and the interaction of the home and the host countries' tax systems influence not only the location and the amount of capital invested abroad, but also the financing of investment, the repatriation of dividends, and the transactions between related parties, located in different jurisdictions."[7] In short, there have always been several and – what is even more important for historians – time-specific incentives for companies and/or company owners to reduce their taxes in order to generate competitive advantages or to remain competitive – but nation states also act similarly.[8]

In the past, offers of low tax rates encouraged companies to transfer their tax residence to a more convenient country, as indeed they still do today. This is greatly facilitated, for example, by low or non-existent restrictions on capital movements and political and institutional stability (legal certainty). Thus, the tax-relevant political frameworks of nation states – and beyond nation states – matter. The economic literature suggests a link between international tax competition and increased opportunities for multinationals to take advantage of this competition through increasingly sophisticated

4 For empirical evidence, see especially Zucman (2015).

5 Piketty (2015); Sklair (2001).

6 Saez and Zucman (2019).

7 Azémar (2010, 233).

8 E.g. Becker and Fuest (2011). For an historical overview, Huerlimann, Brownlee and Ide (2018). For a more general discussion of the ambivalent relations between nation states and multinationals, see Gehlen, Marx and Reckendrees (2020); Reckendrees, Gehlen and Marx (2022).

intra-company measures to reduce their taxes, especially through intermediary conduit entities (financial subsidiaries, endowments, letterbox companies, etc.).[9] In other words, with the growth of globalisation and economic competition between nation states, opportunities for MNEs to reduce their tax liabilities have grown as well.[10]

Business historians stayed out of these debates for a long time, but have recently become increasingly concerned with the international taxation of multinational companies, especially for British free-standing companies in the time period until the 1960s.[11] By referring to this and other literature, our chapter adopts a business historian "bottom-up" perspective to the following decades and uses archival sources to inquire into the motivations of MNEs for reducing their taxes beyond the obvious desire to reduce costs. This main question is closely connected with an additional one about justification strategies of the (legal) measures that were employed. Furthermore, against the background of a globalising economy, the chapter examines the causes of tax avoidance inherent in the international structures and the organisation of the companies which ultimately led to tax avoidance in a particular state.

Our case study examines "typical" production-based multinationals from the chemical industry (Bayer/BASF), which have been active on the world market since the nineteenth century, and a business group (TBG) which developed from a coal, steel, logistics and utility company into a global investment group during the twentieth century. All were of German origin and emerged from traditional industrial companies. However, this clear assignment to a home country faded during the twentieth century. While by the mid-1920s the TBG could already no longer be clearly classified as a German company, the German domestic market lost much of its importance for "German" chemical companies from the 1970s onwards. The massive expansion of foreign production and the increase in foreign direct investments raised the question of how foreign subsidiaries should be treated in terms of (tax) law – and thus created scope for action. Since we are looking at production-based and finance based multinationals, we can identify similar as well as divergent practices of tax avoidance and in this way improve our historical knowledge of the development of tax practices.[12]

In the following section, we first give an overview of international policy structures for tax optimisation and highlight four interlinked developments. Using the example of Bayer, BASF and the TBG, we then discuss their motives for saving taxes, and consider which international corporate

9 Wamser (2011, 1522).

10 Jones (2008).

11 Mollan and Tennent (2015).

12 This chapter is based on the findings of two major research projects that have been completed. Christian Marx's habilitation thesis dealt with the internationalisation of the chemical industry since the 1960s and Boris Gehlen wrote a monograph – generously funded by the Fritz Thyssen Stiftung – on the (early) Thyssen-Bornemisza-Group. See Marx (2019); Gehlen (2021).

organisations were established for this purpose after the 1950s, before we summarise our results in the conclusion.

13.2 Changes in International Policy Structures Fostering Corporate Tax Planning – with a Special Focus on Caribbean Tax Havens

Motifs and instruments of tax avoidance have changed over time. Until World War I, tariffs were more or less the only tax-related element with a significant impact on multinationals. But the belligerent nations were forced to change their tax policies during the war due to the related costs. Consequently, overall taxation increased nearly everywhere – with the exception of contemporary "tax havens" like the Netherlands and Switzerland – and international double taxation became a serious problem. Many companies transformed their foreign affiliates into subsidiaries to cope with the war and with nationalism in the interwar period. Foreign subsidiaries adapted more closely to the conventions of the host country in order to avoid repression and negative sanctions; in some cases, business relations were temporarily or permanently interrupted by enemy legislation. Although many international business relationships were restored after the war, governments maintained increased taxation in order to pay off war debts. Tax management or tax planning therefore became an essential element of the financial departments of large (especially multinational) companies.[13]

Hence, in the aftermath of World War I, the avoidance of double taxation and the cloaking of assets via foreign holding companies were primarily used to protect property rights.[14] Double taxation became a particular problem of international politics and was discussed at several conferences of the League of Nations as well as by the International Chamber of Commerce. As was the case with many other world economic problems, these debates in the 1920s and 1930s did not go beyond a description of the problem and possible solutions. International cooperation efforts often failed due to nationalistic considerations, for example, at the World Economic Conferences.[15]

As a result of World War II and the subsequent reconstruction phase, which was characterised by a strong nation-state bias in economic terms, international tax avoidance temporarily lost importance for MNEs – especially due to restrictions on capital movements and, as was the case in West Germany, tax relief for companies. Ironically, the upturn in tax havens and offshore locations coincides precisely with this period, as some governments

13 Farquet (2012); Farquet (2019); Forbes, Kurosawa and Wubs (2019); Izawa (2015); Picciotto (1992); Picciotto (1999).

14 Mollan and Tennent (2015, 1061–1062, 1069); Kobrak and Wüstenhagen (2006, 420).

15 For example, a German-Dutch double taxation agreement was not concluded because the Dutch side feared that in this case, German capital would be withdrawn from the Netherlands. Essers (2015, 1).

allowed loopholes to be created in order to increase the future competitiveness of "their" companies. Vanessa Ogle concisely summarised this context as follows: "The motives that inspired governments to selectively encourage offshore leakages were often extremely limited and short-sighted, while the consequences were extensive and long-ranging."[16] Decolonisation created a kind of money panic among white settlers, businessmen and colonial officials who shied away from transferring their assets to their home countries with high tax rates. It thus provided an important share of early post-war tax haven business and offshore finance during the 1950s and 1960s.[17] However, the extent of MNEs in this business remained moderate at the time.

From the 1970s globalisation accelerated and MNEs like our case studies made more and more use of opportunities that could favourably reduce costs. In this context, the tax avoidance of MNEs and business groups turned from what had been a defensive measure into an offensive instrument used to reduce costs and increase competitiveness.[18] To explain this development, we briefly point out four interlinked developments that could be described as changes 1) in the institutional integration, 2) in financial markets, 3) in world market competition and 4) by international tax treaties and tax havens.

First, goods and financial markets were integrated by politically removing barriers to trade and capital movements. In the aftermath of World War II, the Bretton Woods Institutions (IMF, GATT and the World Bank), the European integration process (European Economic Community, set up in 1958) and the establishment of the OECD as a place to develop international economic standards and guidelines (for example, double taxation agreements), to name only the most important institutions, provided incentives for cross-border economic exchange in various ways. The case studies considered here also took advantage of these opportunities, even though their internationalisation initially remained limited as a result of the loss of foreign assets after World War I.

In our second point, we emphasise the development of financial markets. Since the 1960s, credit and capital markets were gradually integrated and globalised, particularly through the unregulated euro-dollar markets that emerged from the 1950s in response to foreseeable difficulties in the Bretton Woods monetary system. The growing US trade deficit led to a steady increase in US dollar assets outside the USA. This market of US dollars defied control by the USA and in particular the Federal Reserve.[19] In view of the weakness of the US dollar, more and more central banks had to raise interest rates in order to stabilise the exchange rate. This made the

16 Ogle (2017, 1433).
17 Ogle (2020).
18 Sævold (2017); Zucman (2015). In reaction to this corporate practice, the OECD Working Party No. 6 on the Taxation of Multinational Enterprises was founded in 1973.
19 N.N. (1969).

cost of capital domestically more expensive, which is why banks and companies always switched to the euro-dollar markets where they could obtain financing more cheaply. These developments also favoured the emergence of offshore centres such as Luxembourg, which attracted capital and financial institutions with low transaction costs (including low tax rates) and institutional stability, guaranteed, for instance, by the Roman treaties. From the 1960s, low transaction costs combined with institutional stability became one driving force of "financialisation", finally symbolised by the "big bang" in the City of London in 1987.[20]

Third, following the collapse of the Bretton Woods monetary system (in 1971/1973) and the gradual transition to flexible exchange rates, competitive pressure on companies and economies increased because the internal and external value of currencies were more closely linked than at times of fixed exchange rates. In the 1950s and long into the 1960s, for example, the (artificial) undervaluation of the DM acted as an export premium for German firms. These opportunities to use monetary policy to subsidise export-oriented industries gradually disappeared with flexible exchange rates. Increasing global competition, fuelled by the investment-seeking capital of oil-producing countries ("Petro-Dollars") and the rise of the so-called Asian tiger economies accelerated structural change in developed economies considerably and brought into political focus, among other things, the cost burden of taxes and social security contributions for companies. In a nutshell, the global competitiveness of developed economies now increasingly depended on the global competitiveness of domestic companies. Thus, politicians had to take into account that if corporate taxes were "too high" this could have negative effects for the national economy and the state budget in the long run. In the face of rising unemployment, MNEs used their growing power to negotiate tax advantages in their home country. In short, the Western tax states had to perform a balancing act in the taxation of multinational companies, attempting to protect their global competitiveness, prevent a transfer of their tax domicile and still generate tax revenue which was perceived as at least adequate. Hence, taxation motivated by redistribution policies, which skimmed off company profits to finance social measures, came increasingly under pressure.[21]

Our fourth point on tax treaties and tax havens also deals with international developments, but it is even more significant in explaining international tax strategies through our case studies. These treaties and agreements are effective if threats of sanctions are credible or if there are other incentives to abandon certain tax avoidance practices. The USA was an especially crucial actor in this political "game". US domestic tax policy initially favoured

20 For an overview about the development of global capital markets: Krippner (2005); Michie (2007); Ogle (2017, 1437–1439).

21 See e.g. for Germany: Ullmann (2005, 195–213).

the emergence of tax havens and the financing strategy of MNEs, but when the negative effects on the domestic economy became apparent the USA pushed for a change in the bilateral agreements with tax havens.

These effects of US tax policy can, for example, be described by the development of Curaçao as a tax haven. This story started in 1951 at the latest, when the Netherlands Antilles introduced legislation designed to attract offshore companies, but the process was accelerated in 1955 when the Dutch-American tax treaty was extended to the Netherland Antilles. Among other things, this treaty exempted dividends, interest and royalty payments (license fees) from the USA to companies based in Curaçao from US withholding tax in whole or in part. Generally, dividends from US corporations paid to a resident of the Antilles were taxed in the USA at a 15% rate, whereas the tax rate decreased to only 5% if 95% or more of the US Corporation was owned by an Antillean parent company. These tax incentives laid the basis for the establishment of offshore holding, investment and financing companies in Willemstad. The Antilles shared common features with most tax havens such as a low tax rate, minimal currency exchange regulation, commercial and banking confidentiality laws and a record of political stability. For many companies operating across borders, this setting offered advantageous financial conditions compared to the genuine host country with comparable benefits.[22]

US American and Western European corporations used their Caribbean subsidiaries both to avoid taxes and to raise capital. In this context, the small group of former Dutch island colonies in the Caribbean took advantage of the opportunities arising from the emerging euro-dollar market. According to Craig Boise and Andrew Morriss, virtually every major US corporation made interest payments to a Netherlands Antilles finance subsidiary in the 1960s and 1970s: "The 'Antilles sandwich' strategy exploited the difference between high U.S. withholding tax rates that applied to interest payments made to most foreign lenders, and the zero rate of tax that applied to U.S. interest payments made to residents of the Antilles under its tax treaty with the United States."[23] More than 200 US corporations established "paper corporations" in the Antilles – borrowing money from foreign investors and lending the borrowed funds to US corporations – to escape the withholding tax on portfolio indebtedness interest. From 1978 to 1982, the amount of borrowing by US corporations from Antillean subsidiaries rose from $1 to $16 billion. In particular, these finance subsidiaries took advantage of the euro-bond market since the Antilles Treaty provided US corporations with the opportunity to raise capital on the euro-bond market through the issuing of debt by an Antillean subsidiary which was then lent to a US company.[24] The expanding euro-dollar and euro-bond markets boosted not only

22 Hampton (1996, 100); Beurden (2018, 81–192); Lang (2001); Schoeller (1988, 496–497).
23 Boise and Morriss (2009, 377).
24 Schoeller (1988, 497–498).

Curaçao, but also other offshore financial centres like the Cayman Islands, Guernsey and Jersey.[25]

In the early 1980s, the US government was increasingly dissatisfied with the existing tax regulations and announced that it would terminate the tax treaty with Curaçao. In 1984, the US administration repealed its 30% withholding tax on interest income paid to foreign persons or corporations, because the tax had raised little revenue but had created implicit costs for US corporate borrowers since domestically issued bonds were subject either to withholding tax or strict information requirements.[26] The tax exemption was intended to allow companies, as well as the US government, to raise capital in foreign capital markets without having to bear the cost of a domestic withholding tax. In particular, it was intended to facilitate access to the euro-bond market for US companies (including foreign subsidiaries of European MNEs in the United States), since until then, raising capital in this important capital market without withholding tax had only been possible through financing companies in the Netherlands Antilles.[27] As one of the consequences, the internal US measures led to the Caribbean subsidiaries of German MNEs losing their role of financing their US subsidiaries. From then on, financing companies in the USA as well as in the European financial metropolises (London and Amsterdam) took over their tasks. Finally, in 1987, the United States unilaterally terminated the tax treaty with the Netherlands Antilles. The Curaçao model and the adaption to new financial conditions demonstrate the global interrelationships of multinational corporate financing and the flexibility with which company management was able to react to new tax regulations.

The shift in US tax policy was part of a larger development. The United States had "stimulated" the emergence of tax havens since the 1950s, as did Great Britain and the Netherlands as well. In a more open world economy since the late 1980s (and with lower tax rates in some developed countries), the perception of tax havens (and corruption) shifted towards a "compliance revolution" putting financial transparency on the political agenda.[28] The USA, other nation states and international organisations like the OECD became increasingly aware of the problem of tax evasion or avoidance and gradually implemented and improved transparency standards. In return, they explicitly accepted the existing leeway granted to tax havens, so that the business volume of tax havens grew significantly despite transparency standards and increasing public criticism.[29] As one effect, profits made in tax havens by multinationals and individuals exponentially increased in the 1990s and 2000s.[30]

25 Beurden (2018, 355).
26 Papke (2000); Schoeller (1988, 499–500).
27 Gerten, Haag and Kornack (2013, 821).
28 Berghoff (2016). For US criticism about tax exemption for MNEs: Fitzgerald (2015, 435).
29 For a contemporary overview, see e.g. Hay (2001).
30 Zucman (2015).

Nevertheless, tax optimisation sounds easier than it actually was, because very specialised and very expensive expertise was required in the global context with its different and dynamic national tax systems, international negotiations and complex global business strategies, which included other objectives in addition to low taxation. Optimising tax payments or avoiding taxes therefore came at a cost. Not by chance, a parallel upswing of globalisation and (global) business consultants can be observed from the 1960s.[31] In sum, from an MNE-perspective, tax avoidance was the result of a complex process of balancing overall corporate strategy with the institutional framework, the relevant market, the global competitive environment, possibly geopolitical considerations not further mentioned yet and the company's own financial and administrative capabilities. This is shown by the German case studies, first of all the MNEs from the chemical industry.

13.3 German Chemical Multinationals and Tax Avoidance

Recent literature increasingly emphasises the genuine economic function of tax havens – not in any way overlooking their detrimental effects such as reducing state capacity and the infamous "race to the bottom".[32] However, as discussed above, tax havens became relevant not only for tax avoidance but also for international corporate financing.[33] These two aspects cannot always be clearly distinguished from one another. German companies undoubtedly intended to save taxes, but in view of the loss of foreign assets that resulted from World War II and a lack of investment capital, they had a particularly strong interest in foreign financing opportunities that allowed them to return to the world market. This was particularly true for the chemical industry, which had already been highly internationalised in the nineteenth century.

In the case of BASF, the Caribbean subsidiary BASF Overzee had held shares in Putnam Chemical Corporation since the late 1950s. Putnam Chemical Corporation was BASF's US subsidiary, had been founded in 1957 and produced dyes and binders using the process knowledge of the parent company. In 1966, this Caribbean finance subsidiary founded the wholly owned Basfin Corp. in New York to expand its access to the US capital market. And only three years later, in 1969, Bayer, BASF and Siemens placed bearer bonds (*Inhaber-Teilschuldverschreibungen*) to the amount of $115 million through their respective foreign subsidiaries in Curaçao: Bayer International Finance N.V. (BIF), BASF Overzee N.V. and Siemens Western Finance N.V.[34]

31 McKenna (2006, 145–164).

32 For an interdisciplinary overview about the tax-haven literature, see Ogle (2017).

33 Ogle (2017, 1447), e.g., points this out by saying "that the well-known story of the 'rise' of U.S. multinational corporations after World War II, first in Europe, then gradually across the globe, would have been impossible without the Euro-market and the offshore economy".

34 Lutter (1972).

One year later, the German chemical group Hoechst, wishing to expand on the US market, also founded a foreign subsidiary called Hoechst Investment and Finance N.V. on the Caribbean island.[35] Hence, by 1970, all three large German chemical MNEs operated in the Netherlands Antilles. The managers wanted to finance their foreign businesses abroad in order to avoid financial risks in the form of revaluations and devaluations, to keep the parent company's indebtedness as low as possible, and to be able to use the domestic capital market (West Germany) primarily for domestic investments. With additional bases in Luxembourg, Switzerland and Canada, they established an international network of finance companies to expand worldwide.

The German Bayer Group and BASF can serve as showcases for such procedures and entanglements. Until the early 1980s, Bayer Foreign Investments Ltd. (Bayforin) in Toronto/Canada mainly held Bayer shareholdings in Western Europe and Latin America, while the US subsidiaries (with exception of the Agfa-Gevaert Group) were held by BIF in Curaçao, which also served as the financing base for capital expenditures in the United States. In addition, Bayer Finance S.A. in Luxembourg and Bayer Capital Corporation (BCC) in Amsterdam/Netherlands provided various loan-financing arrangements.[36] In the 1980s, however, the Caribbean finance subsidiaries lost importance and financing was reorganised in favour of BCC as a result of the termination of the tax agreement between the United States and Curaçao. The BIF's debt of $500 million at the end of 1982 was therefore successively reduced, and BIF was finally liquidated in 1988.[37]

BASF had a similar structure. At the end of the 1960s, the chemical giant had four foreign financing and holding companies, one of them based in Willemstad/Curaçao (BASF Overzee N.V.), two in Zurich (BASF Chemiewerte AG, BASF Holding AG) and one in Panama (BASF Transatlantica S.A.). BASF Overzee was responsible for the subsidiaries in North America, BASF Transatlantica for those in Latin America, and BASF Chemiewerte for those in Asia and Australia.[38] These companies had also been founded to take advantage of tax benefits, to facilitate access to international capital markets and to minimise debt on the parent company's balance sheet. When the situation on the US capital market worsened and the US government announced that it would make massive use of the US capital market at the beginning of the 1980s, the BASF management was able to call on its Caribbean subsidiary. Thus, with its international financing companies, the German multinational had a flexible instrument for raising capital

35 Geschäftsbericht Hoechst (1970, 16).

36 Bayer AG: Corporate History and Archives, Leverkusen (BAL) 384/1–40 Bayer Aufsichtsratssitzung (01.12.1983); BAL 384/1–41 Bayer Aufsichtsratssitzung (12.12.1984); BAL 384/1–43 Bayer Aufsichtsratssitzung (12.12.1985); BAL 384/1–46 Bayer Aufsichtsratssitzung (10.12.1986); Geschäftsbericht Bayer (1983, 71); Bayer Geschäftsbericht (1986, 96).

37 BAL 384/1–48 Bayer Aufsichtsratssitzung (10.12.1987).

38 Abelshauser (2007, 585); Geschäftsbericht BASF (1971, 55); N.N. (1963).

and overcoming temporary weaknesses in national capital markets. In this way, it contributed to the establishment of international financial flows that extended from the Middle East via the European euro-dollar market and Caribbean intermediary companies to the United States (and back again).[39] However, at the end of 1982, BASF's finance department came to the conclusion that the two financing companies BASF Overzee N.V. and BASF Transatlantica S.A. were no longer required to raise funds on the capital market or to make use of tax advantages. The Dutch company BASF Finance Europe N.V., which had now been established, offered better conditions for these purposes. Against this background, the management decided to liquidate both older financing companies in 1986/1987.[40]

Thus, for German chemical companies, the chapter of Caribbean finance companies came to an end in the 1980s. This was due not least to the fact that increasing economic internationalisation was accompanied by a reduction of capital restrictions by Western European governments.[41] The closure of the financing companies on Curaçao by BASF, Bayer and Hoechst between 1985 and 1988 was by no means an expression of de-globalisation. Rather, the economic policies pursued by Western governments after about 1980 contributed to the liberalisation of their (financial) markets and, in combination with new tax regulations, enabled the rise of London and Amsterdam to become international financial centres through which the chemical companies could henceforth finance themselves. Nevertheless, the principle of tax avoidance was not brought to an end by the shift in international financial architecture – it only received a new structure.[42]

13.4 The Thyssen-Bornemisza-Group and Tax Avoidance

From an individual perspective, tax avoidance and the relationship between tax-payers and nation states can be illustrated by Hans Heinrich Thyssen-Bornemisza's (1921–2002) biography. The TBG was established in 1926 when Heinrich Thyssen-Bornemisza (1875–1947), a Hungarian citizen of German origin, inherited those parts of his father's companies which were not involved in coal, iron and steel production. During the 1920s and 1930s, Heinrich managed to create an organic business group almost completely owned by himself.[43] His youngest son, Hans Heinrich, who was born and raised in the Netherlands, inherited most of the shares of the Dutch trading

39 BASF Unternehmensarchiv, Ludwigshafen (UA), PB / B.1.5.2. / 103, Vorstandsprotokolle, Vorstandssitzung (02.02.1982).

40 BASF UA, PB / B.1.5.2. /108, Vorstandsprotokolle, Straffung der gesellschaftsrechtlichen Beteiligungsstruktur (10.12.1982, Anlage 9 zu 26/82).

41 Wirsching (2012, 22, 226–228).

42 Brinkmann (2016).

43 See for business groups: Colpan and Hikino (2018).

and merchant companies (esp. N.V. Transport en Handels Maatschappij "Vulcaan" and Bank voor Handel en Scheepvaart including subsidiaries) as well as those of the German shipbuilding companies (esp. Bremer Vulkan), gas and waterworks (Thyssengas) and tube producers (Press- und Walzwerke Reisholz). From the 1960s, the new head of the TBG restructured the group into a portfolio business group. Instead of inflexible long-term investments in industrial production (mostly in Germany), the group henceforth preferred flexible investments in trade, commerce and securities throughout the western hemisphere.[44] In 1971, Hans Heinrich Thyssen-Bornemisza made the new strategy visible and reorganised his group. He sold the banking activities of the Bank voor Handel en Scheepvaart and renamed the former bank Thyssen-Bornemisza Group N.V., still incorporated in the Netherlands (Amstelveen), which then acted as a holding and investment company.[45] Previously, Hans Heinrich Thyssen-Bornemisza had not appeared as a "professional tax evader", as he much later described himself to his biographer.[46]

But a short glimpse at his biography may foster comprehension – not necessarily sympathy – of how Hans Heinrich got there (and his apparent pride in the fact). In his early days at TBG, beginning in 1940, the nation state (and thus the tax state) appeared to Hans Heinrich as a permanent threat to property rights: the German Reich forced the group to reorganise in 1941, the USA, Great Britain, the Netherlands and other states seized his father's property as enemy assets during World War II, and the Soviet occupation forces expropriated group units in 1945. In 1950, Hans Heinrich, a Dutch native with Hungarian and German ancestors, became a Swiss citizen. With his new Swiss nationality, Hans Heinrich and the family endowment Kaszony, which had been founded in 1926 and was the formal owner of the group's most important holding company, the Holland-American Investment Corporation (HAIC) N.V., were in a position to take advantage of low-income taxes in the Alpine country. But Hans Heinrich, who was married five times to women from five countries, would refer to himself not as living in Switzerland but as living in Lugano, nor did he mention residing in England but rather in London. This worldly attitude towards nation states as well as the negative experience of his early career influenced his perspective on taxpaying (or the avoidance thereof).

However, with regard to corporate taxation, Thyssen-Bornemisza was, at first, not particularly noticeable. This changed during the 1970s. As part of its global investment strategy, in 1974, the TBG acquired 90% of the shares of the Indian Head Inc., a diversified US company, producing textiles and

44 Die Geschichte der Familie Thyssen und ihrer Aktivitäten. Rede von Hans Heinrich Thyssen-Bornemisza, 6.6.1979, 32, Stiftung zur Industriegeschichte Thyssen, Duisburg (SIT) TB/1.

45 For details, see Gehlen (2020).

46 See Litchfield (2006, 405–406).

glass, among other things,[47] and consequently possessed almost equal assets in the USA and in Europe. The group therefore reorganised its structure and established one single top holding above the European (HAIC) and the US-American holding (Thyssen-Bornemisza Inc., Maryland). This new holding was first founded in Luxembourg as the Holland American Investment Corporation, S.A. It not only had the same name as its Dutch equivalent but was also run by the same managers. This Luxembourg company founded – under the law of the Netherland Antilles – the Thyssen-Bornemisza N.V. (without "group" in its name) in Willemstad/Curaçao, which took over all the assets of the Dutch HAIC as well as all the shares of Thyssen-Bornemisza Inc., the US holding, thus becoming the group's new top asset holding. However, the assets were still administered by managers in the Netherlands. This manoeuvre had taxation implications. Usually, the corporate tax rate in Curaçao was 30% but investment companies such as Thyssen-Bornemisza N.V. were only taxed with 3%.[48] However, there was also a considerable push factor: in May 1973, Joop den Uyl had become prime minister of the Netherlands – a left-wing social democrat who proposed a capital-gains tax. Not surprisingly, neither Dutch business in general nor Thyssen-Bornemisza in particular were amused.[49]

In 1978, the TBG was again restructured. This reorganisation had two objectives. First, the property rights of the "beneficial owner"[50] Hans Heinrich Thyssen-Bornemisza had previously not been regulated clearly enough due to the large number of interlinked companies. It was questionable whether Thyssen-Bornemisza could always dispose of his property in the way he saw fit. Second, the TBG wanted to establish "a more favourable holding from a tax point of view".[51] Again, tax avoidance was only one of several objectives.

At the time, the shares of Hans Heinrich Thyssen-Bornemisza were ultimately owned and managed by HAIC S.A. in Luxembourg, the parent company of Thyssen-Bornemisza N.V. in Curaçao that formally owned the shares. Thyssen-Bornemisza N.V. paid dividends to HAIC S.A., which paid them to Hans Heinrich Thyssen-Bornemisza. The company Thyssen-Bornemisza N.V. was regularly taxed in Curaçao (at 3%) but the profits were taxed again in Luxembourg, when HAIC transferred them to the "beneficial owner" (*taxe d'abonnement*).[52]

47 N.N. (1974; 1975).

48 Restructuring of Thyssen-Bornemisza Group, 24.12.1974, SIT TB 02313.

49 "Thyssen to move from Netherlands to Monaco in Fall", in: The New York Times, 2.6.1975, 39.

50 From a certain perspective, it is paradigmatic that "beneficial ownership" was initially a legal term in the Trading with the Enemy Acts in the USA and GB, but since the 1930s has turned into a term of international tax law to identify the "real" taxable person.

51 HAIC-Favorita Transaktion, 1978, SIT TB 02339, 2–3.

52 Ibid.

This tax rate could have been reduced in Luxembourg, if the HAIC had raised its capital from 25 million hfl. to 67 million hfl., but this solution had two disadvantages. First, the TBG would have had to make a one-off payment of 420,000 hfl. for the capital increase. Second, and more importantly, the system was inflexible. In years with lower dividend payments, tax savings would not have been that impressive.[53] The legal advisor of Hans Heinrich Thyssen-Bornemisza from Switzerland, Joseph Groh, a key player in TBG's tax planning, therefore rejected this solution. He reasoned that taxes in Luxembourg were "not compensated by special benefits".[54] In his view, and not only in his view, paying taxes was not a matter of state finance but of cost-benefit calculations.

Thus, the TBG looked for a different solution. It finally renamed its own Favorita Shipping Company Ltd., incorporated in Bermuda, creating the Favorita Holding Company, which henceforth owned the shares of Thyssen-Bornemisza N.V. in Curaçao and de facto replaced HAIC S.A. as the holding company of the family interests.[55] This construction also allowed Hans Heinrich Thyssen-Bornemisza to exercise his property rights through three different companies in three different countries, giving him more flexibility in case of possible political crises and, moreover, ensured the integrity of his property via reciprocal pre-emption rights, so that shares could not easily be sold to third parties.[56] With regard to taxation the TBG achieved its goal as well: after negotiations with the fiscal authorities and the government in Bermuda, the Favorita Holding was exempted from taxes until at least 2006.[57]

However, the underlying transactions were much more complex, as many different companies of the TBG-complex – e.g. from Panama and Liberia – were involved and transfers of shares were internally balanced with receivables from these companies. Therefore, access to specific legal expertise proved an essential precondition. During the whole process, legal experts and business consultants from Switzerland, Luxembourg, Bermuda and the USA were involved in planning – making it a truly transnational project.[58]

Nevertheless, one variable in the "Caribbean puzzle" worried the experts even after the transaction was conducted in 1978: the possible influence of the USA on legal transactions in the Caribbean. As late as 1981, the group's lawyers were still concerned about whether Favorita Holding's contracts with its newly founded subsidiary, Euro-American-Investment Company Ltd., could be considered as sham constructions under American law. The lawyers

53 Interne Notiz, Dr Groh to H.T.B., 13.1.1978, SIT TB/4605.

54 Groh to Genillard, 8.3.1979, SIT TB/5414.

55 HAIC-Favorita Transaktion, 1978, SIT TB 02339, 2–3.

56 Minutes of the Extraordinary General Meeting of Shareholders of Thyssen-Bornemisza N.V., 17.7.1979, 2, SIT TB/5414.

57 HAIC-Favorita Transaktion, 1978, SIT TB 02339, 2–3.

58 E.g. Genillard to Groh, 18.1.1978, SIT TB/5414, Internal Note Groh to Baron Thyssen, 28.3.1978, SIT TB/5413.

did not, however, believe it likely that legal action could be taken in US courts, but that courts in Curaçao would rather have jurisdiction. In their view, if at all, it was only the transfer of shares in Thyssen-Bornemisza N.V. to Hans Heinrich Thyssen-Bornemisza which could be challenged. In such a case, the courts in Curaçao were expected to rule in favour of the TBG.[59] All in all, the TBG's transactions during the 1970s were truly very professional – but not limited to tax avoidance.

13.5 Conclusion

The central question of this chapter focused on the motivations of MNEs and (family) business groups to minimise their taxes beyond a simple desire to reduce costs. It seems clear that the avoidance and optimisation of taxes was neither the only corporate function of the companies examined here nor was it at the core of their tax planning. The chemical MNEs established small subsidiaries in tax havens primarily to facilitate their financing. During their return to the world market in the 1950s and early 1960s, German chemical companies initially turned to foreign capital markets to raise capital for their expansion abroad. In this way, they wanted to avoid financial risks in the form of revaluations and devaluations and were able to use the domestic capital market primarily for investments at home. Thus, the implementation of foreign financial subsidiaries in tax havens and the use of corresponding advantages was a result of the companies' internationalisation strategy. This policy was therefore not accompanied by a transfer of the tax residence of the parent company. Companies continued to tie themselves to their home countries for tax purposes, albeit to a lesser extent – not least in order not to lose access to the home country's resources such as the education system, legal certainty and state subsidies.[60]

In times of rising competition, weakening economic activity and growing profitability awareness, the requirements for tax optimisation increased from the 1970s. With their international financing companies, the chemical MNEs had a flexible instrument for responding to these challenges and for overcoming temporary weaknesses in national capital markets. When the Caribbean subsidiaries lost their function, financing companies in the USA as well as in European financial metropolises took over their tasks. On the one hand, this shows their adaptability to new financial regulations, on the other hand, they contributed heavily to the establishment of global financial flows. As a financial holding, the TBG, however, simply had no home country anymore. The securitisation and flexible management of property rights were the core motivation for the TBG-related relocations during the 1970s. Against the backdrop of negative experiences during World War II,

59 Groenendijk to Groh and Guscetti, 28.4.1981, SIT TB/4606.
60 Marx (2020).

the protection of property was of paramount importance to Hans Heinrich Thyssen-Bornemisza, an example of a more or less global citizen. In this respect, his "tax strategy" primarily consisted of the proactive management of political risk.

These varied motivations – corporate financing versus securing property rights – are the main difference between the production-based and financially based multinationals examined here. It was only with regard to financial matters that they followed the same logic, reducing costs by taking advantage of the opportunities offered by tax havens. It could therefore be said that production, research and development, sales and even financing took different paths in multinationals; only some parts were still tied to the home market and the location of the company headquarters in the 1980s. However, these different paths are ultimately only an expression of the international division of labour and thus typical of MNEs. From the perspective of the companies, tax optimisation was seen as a form of cost reduction, whereas the lost tax revenues of the home country were obviously ignored or did not matter. Multinationals took advantage of the well-developed infrastructure of industrial countries as a matter of course, while at the same time negotiating tax breaks for new settlements or operating in tax havens. As long as there is tax competition between nation states, there will always be legal possibilities, especially for global actors, to optimise, i.e. minimise, their tax payments.[61] However, looking for the best opportunities and the best cost-benefit ratio is at the heart of any business activity. In this respect, all companies are professional tax avoiders.

Archives

BASF Unternehmensarchiv, Ludwigshafen (UA).
Bayer AG: Corporate History and Archives, Leverkusen (BAL).
Stiftung zur Industriegeschichte Thyssen, Duisburg (SIT).

Published Sources and Sources Available Online

BASF. 1971. Geschäftsbericht, https://www.basf.com/global/documents/de/about-us/history/History-in-Figures/1965-1989/1971_BASF_Geschaeftsbericht.pdf., Accessed November 22, 2021.
N.N. 1963. Durch Briefkästen Millionen sparen. *Der Spiegel* 20, May 15, 40–55.
N.N. 1969. Eurodollar. Markt ohne Netz. *Der Spiegel* 44, October 27, 152–157.
N.N. 1974. Dutch may seek Indian Head Inc. *The New York Times*, July 3, 39.
N.N. 1975. Thyssen to move from Netherlands to Monaco in Fall. *The New York Times*, June 2, 39.

61 To address this, the OECD recently proposed a uniform corporate tax rate. OECD 2021.

OECD 2021. International community strikes a ground-breaking tax deal for the digital age https://www.oecd.org/tax/international-community-strikes-a-ground-breaking-tax-deal-for-the-digital-age.htm, Accessed September 21, 2022.

References

Abelshauser, Werner. 2007. Die BASF seit der Neugründung 1952. In *Die BASF. Eine Unternehmensgeschichte*, ed. Werner Abelshauser, 359–637. München: Beck.

Azémar, Céline. 2010. International Corporate Taxation and U.S. Multinationals' Behaviour: An Integrated Approach. *The Canadian Journal of Economics/Revue Canadienne D'Économique* 43 (1): 232–253.

Becker, Johannes, and Clemens Fuest. 2011. The Taxation of Foreign Profits. The Old View, The New View and A Pragmatic View. *Intereconomics* 46: 92–97. https://doi.org/10.1007/s10272-011-0369-4.

Berghoff, Hartmut. 2016. Varieties of Financialization? Evidence from German Industry in the 1990s. *Business History Review* 90 (1): 81–108.

Beurden, Martinus Johannes Cornelis. 2018. *De Curaçaose offshore. Ontstaan, groei en neergang van een belastingparadijs, 1951-2013.* Amsterdam: University of Amsterdam.

Boise, Craig M. and Andrew P. Morriss. 2009. Change, Dependency, and Regime Plasticity in Offshore Financial Intermediation: The Saga of the Netherlands Antilles. *Texas International Law Journal* 45 (2): 377–456.

Brinkmann, Bastian. 2016. Steuerflucht von Konzernen. Wie BASF Steuern drückt. Süddeutsche Zeitung, November 7.

Colpan, Aşli M. and Takashi Hikino. 2018. The Evolutionary Dynamics of Diversified Business Groups in the West: History and Theory. In *Business Groups in the West. Origins, Evolution, and Resilience*, eds. Asli M. Colpan and Takashi Hikino, Oxford: Oxford University Press.

Essers, Peter. 2015. The Radical Changes made to Dutch Tax Regulations during the Second World War. In *Taxing German-Dutch Cross-border Business Activities. A Legal Comparison with Particular Focus on the New Bilateral Tax Treaty*, eds. Heike Jochum, Peter Essers, and Joachim Englisch, 1–50. Osnabrück: Institut für Finanz und Steuerrecht.

Farquet, Christophe. 2012. *The Rise of the Swiss Tax Haven in the Interwar Period: An International Comparison.* EHES Working Papers in Economic History 27, https://5b64f730-5182-4469-99e0-1d7aa15a9563.filesusr.com/ugd/e1c55f_2c2b-c89d42b04982b8e47a9fbdbafea3.pdf, Accessed November 22, 2021.

Farquet, Christophe. 2019. *Quantification and Revolution: An Investigation of German Capital Flight after the First World War.* EHES Working Papers in Economic History 149, https://5b64f730-5182-4469-99e0-1d7aa15a9563.filesusr.com/ugd/e1c55f_9edbd-683809f4e8aa38ef54e25a64bb3.pdf, Accessed November 22, 2021.

Fitzgerald, Robert. 2015. *The Rise of the Global Company. Multinationals and the Making of the Modern World.* Cambridge: Cambridge University Press.

Forbes, Neil, Takafumi Kurosawa, and Ben Wubs. 2019. Introduction. Multinational Enterprise in the Century of Total War and Cold War: Political Risk and Organisational Change. In *Multinational Enterprise, Political Risk and Organisational Change: From Total War to Cold War*, eds. Neil Forbes, Takafumi Kurosawa, and Ben Wubs, 1–20. New York/Abingdon: Routledge.

Gehlen, Boris. 2020. Internationalisierungsfaktor maritime Wirtschaft? Reedereien, Handelsgesellschaften und Werften der Thyssen-Bornemisza-Gruppe 1906/26 bis 1971. *Zeitschrift für Unternehmensgeschichte* 65: 161–195.

Gehlen, Boris. 2021. *Die Thyssen-Bornemisza-Gruppe: Eine transnationale business group in Zeiten des Wirtschaftsnationalismus (1932–1955).* Paderborn: Schöningh.

Gehlen, Boris, Christian Marx, and Alfred Reckendrees. 2020. Ambivalences of Nationality. Economic Nationalism, Nationality of the Company, Nationalism as Strategy: An Introduction. *Journal of Modern European History* 18 (1): 16–27.

Gerten, Andreas, Maximilian Haag, and Daniel Kornack. 2013. Eigen- und Fremdkapital im Steuer- und Gesellschaftsrecht der Vereinigten Staaten von Amerika. In *Eigenkapital und Fremdkapital. Steuerrecht – Gesellschaftsrecht – Rechtsvergleich – Rechtspolitik*, ed. Wolfgang Schön, 775–833. Heidelberg: Springer.

Hampton, Mark P. 1996. *The Offshore Inferface. Tax Havens in the Global Economy, Basingstoke 1996.* Basingstoke: Palgrave Macmillan.

Hay, Richard J. 2001. Information Exchange and the Offshore Financial Centres. *Journal of Financial Regulation and Compliance* 10: 141–161.

Huerlimann, Gisela, W. Elliot Brownlee, and Eisaku Ide (eds.). 2018. *Worlds of Taxation. The Political Economy of Taxing, Spending, and Redistribution since 1945.* Cham: Palgrave Macmillan.

Izawa, Ryo. 2015. The Formation of Companies for Tax Avoidance: The Relationship between UK Multinationals and International Double Taxation in the Interwar Period. *Business and Economic History On-line 13,* http://thebhc.org/sites/default/files/Izawa_BEHO_Final%20Draft.pdf, Accessed November 22, 2021.

Jones, Geoffrey. 2008. Globalization. In *The Oxford Handbook of Business History*, eds. Geoffrey Jones and Jonathan Zeitlin, 141–168. Oxford: Oxford University Press.

Kobrak, Christopher and Jana Wüstenhagen. 2006. International Investment and Nazi Politics: The Cloaking of German Assets Abroad, 1936-1945. *Business History* 48: 399–427.

Krippner, Greta R. 2005. The Financialization of the American Economy. *Socio-Economic Review* 3 (2): 173–208.

Lang, Markus. 2001. *Die Entwicklung des Unternehmensrechts der Niederländischen Antillen.* Münster: Waxmann.

Litchfield, David. 2006. *The Thyssen Art Macabre*. London: Quartet Books.

Lutter, Marcus. 1972. Optionsanleihen ausländischer Tochtergesellschaften. In *Wirtschaftspraxis und Rechtswissenschaft. Festschrift für Walther Kastner zum 70. Geburtstag*, ed. Edwin Loebenstein, 245–268. Wien: Manz'sche Verlags- und Universitätsbuchhandlung.

Marx, Christian. 2019. Between National Governance and the Internationalization of Business. The Case of Four Major West German Producers of Chemicals, Pharmaceuticals and Fibres, 1945-2000. *Business History* 61 (5): 833–862.

Marx, Christian. 2020. Reorganization of Multinational Companies in the Western European Chemical Industry: Transformations in Industrial Management and Labor, 1960s to 1990s. *Enterprise & Society* 21 (1): 38–78.

McKenna, Christopher D. 2006. *The World's Newest Profession. Management Consulting in the Twentieth Century.* Cambridge: Cambridge University Press.

Michie, Ranald C. 2007. *The Global Securities Market. A History.* Oxford: Oxford University Press.

Mollan, Simon and Kevin D. Tennent. 2015. International Taxation and Corporate Strategy. Evidence from British Overseas Business, Circa 1900–1965. *Business History* 57: 1054–1081.

Ogle, Vanessa. 2017. Archipelago Capitalism: Tax Havens, Offshore Money, and the State, 1950s-1970s. *American Historical Review* 122 (5): 1431–1458.

Ogle, Vanessa. 2020. 'Funk Money': The End of Empires, the Expansion of Tax Havens, and Decolonization as an Economic and Financial Event. *Past and Present* 249 (1): 213–249.

Papke, Leslie E. 2000. One-Way Treaty with the World: The U.S. Withholding Tax and the Netherlands Antilles. *International Tax and Public Finance* 7: 295–313.

Picciotto, Sol. 1992. *International Business Taxation. A Study in the Internationalization of Business Regulation*. London: Weidenfeld & Nicolson.

Picciotto, Sol. 1999. Offshore: The State as Legal Fiction. In *Offshore Finance Centres and Tax Havens. The Rise of Global Capital*, eds. Mark P. Hampton and Jason P. Abbott, 43–79. Basingstoke: Palgrave Macmillan.

Piketty, Thomas. 2015. *Capital in the Twenty-First Century*. Cambridge: Harvard University Press.

Reckendrees, Alfred, Boris Gehlen, and Christian Marx. 2022. International Business, Multinational Enterprises and Nationality of the Company: A Constructive Review of Literature. *Business History*, https://doi.org/10.1080/00076791.2022.2118718.

Sævold, Kristine. 2017. *The Formation of a British Tax Haven Policy, 1961-1971: Transit Capitalism in an Era of Decolonization* (Conference Paper. European Business History Association 21st Annual Congress, Vienna).

Saez, Emmanuel and Gabriel Zucman. 2019. *The Triumph of Injustice: How the Rich Dodge Taxes and How to Make Them Pay*. New York: W. W. Norton & Company.

Schoeller, Mark B. 1988. The Termination of the United States-Netherlands Antilles Income Tax Convention: A Failure of U.S. Tax Policy. *Journal of International Business Law* 10 (3): 493–515.

Sklair, Leslie. 2001. *The Transnational Capitalist Class*. Oxford: Blackwell.

Ullmann, Hans-Peter. 2005. *Der deutsche Steuerstaat. Eine Geschichte der öffentlichen Finanzen vom 18. Jahrhundert bis heute*. München: Beck.

Wamser, Georg. 2011. Foreign (in)Direct Investment and Corporate Taxation. *The Canadian Journal of Economics/Revue Canadienne D'Économique* 44 (4): 1497–1524.

Wirsching, Andreas. 2012. *Der Preis der Freiheit. Geschichte Europas in unserer Zeit*. München: Beck.

Zucman, Gabriel. 2015. *The Hidden Wealth of Nations: The Scourge of Tax Havens*. Chicago/London: University of Chicago Press.

14 Tax System Credibility vs. Banking System Reputation?

Tax Evasion from Sweden to Switzerland in the Early 1970s

Thibaud Giddey and Mikael Wendschlag[1]

14.1 Introduction

"How does the money of a rich foreigner get into a secret Swiss account unnoticed?"[2] was the headline used by the German news magazine *Der Spiegel* in March 1973 to cover the trial of Jacques Hentsch. The Swiss banker had been caught red-handed while trying to smuggle cash out of Sweden. He was charged, prosecuted and jailed for a currency export crime that consisted of an attempt to leave Sweden with an unauthorised amount of Swedish currency, regardless of the purposes of the operation. Yet for the vast majority of commentators, the investigation had uncovered an act of tax evasion. While locally handled by the Gothenburg court of justice, the case plainly revealed, as the *Spiegel* report suggested, fraudulent transactions of international tax evasion schemes with Switzerland as the destination.

In this chapter, we analyse how tax evasion cases of the 1970s came to threaten the credibility of the Swedish tax system on the one hand, and the Swiss banking system on the other. In Sweden, which had one of the highest tax rates in the world at the time, the tax evasion cases were seen as threats to the credibility of the tax system. The fact that most of the tax evasion cases involved unreported movements of currency out of the country undermined the Swedish currency control regime as well, and thus the fixed exchange rate regime. In Switzerland, however, these very same cases did not affect taxes or the exchange rate system, but the banking system. By the mid-1970s, the international exposure of the Swiss banking system as potentially facilitating tax evasion, money laundering and white-collar crime with its secretive legal design increased the informal and diplomatic pressure on Swiss politicians to reform the system.

With the international liberalisation of the 1970s and 1980s, the Swedish tax system and currency regime became harder to maintain. Domestically,

1 The authors are grateful to archivist Mira Barkå for her help, Nicolas Chachereau for his precious advice and Gisela Hürlimann, Dorothea Rohde and Korinna Schönhärl for their insightful comments.

2 N. N. (1973a).

DOI: 10.4324/9781003333197-19

the attitude towards tax evasion and avoidance changed as well, further undermining the tax system's credibility. In contrast, the Swiss banking system remained largely unchanged and prospered. The Swedish tax system was reformed by the end of the 1980s. The reform contained, among other things, tax cuts to reduce the incentive for tax evasion.[3] In the meantime, Switzerland had maintained its status as one of the premier financial centres for private wealth management of the world, with thriving banking secrecy regulations up to the late 2000s.

The chapter emphasises one dimension of tax evasion that is not always noticed in the existing literature, namely that tax evasion put a strain on different systems in the countries involved. In Sweden, from where the wealth was transferred, pressure was put on the *tax system* to be reformed (thereby changing the costs and benefits of tax evasion). In Switzerland, to where the wealth was transferred, the *banking system* came under pressure to reform, to make it more transparent to foreign authorities. This disparity reflects very clearly how tax evasion problems are framed in national policy, and it can explain why international cooperation and coordination remained so difficult.

Benefitting from first-hand sources–legal and administrative texts of the time, media reporting, documents from court proceedings as well as archival material–from both the Swedish and Swiss authorities, we are able to account for a case of international tax evasion, framed as illegal currency export, with a high level of detail. The transnational and multifocal perspective, from both the country of origin and the receiving country, provides an innovative approach to tax evasion and its different national legal framings.

The chapter is structured in four parts. In the next part, we outline the development of tax systems, currency regulations and offshore banking after the Second World War with an emphasis on Sweden and Switzerland. In Section 14.3, we present our case study–the 1972–1973 Hentsch affair–and place it within the broader context of Swedish currency crimes. Section 14.4 provides an account of the varying policy responses in Sweden and Switzerland to the Hentsch case. In the conclusion, we discuss our contributions to the research fields of (not) paying taxes through evasion and avoidance.

14.2 International Tax Evasion, Tax Systems and Banking in Sweden and Switzerland, 1945–1980

The history of international tax evasion is closely related to the history of taxation by central governments, and for many countries, it dates back at least to the late nineteenth century. However, mandatory, general and regular taxes on citizens and legal entities were extended and broadened mainly in the course of the twentieth century. In many Western societies, national

3 Henrekson and Stenkula (2015, 13).

wealth, income and property taxes were introduced at the beginning of the century but remained relatively low until after the Second World War.[4] In several developed economies, more and higher taxes were introduced, both to fund a growing public sector and to fulfil social welfare commitments, but also for redistributive purposes–originating in the policy programmes of broad labour movement parties.[5]

In Sweden, where the Social Democratic Party was continuously in power between 1932 and 1976, public support for a progressive tax system to redistribute wealth and resources was relatively strong by the mid-twentieth century.[6] Combined with a golden age of economic growth and development in the 1950s and 1960s, resistance to this system was limited. Despite the absence of aggregated data on the frequency and scale of international tax evasion before the 1960s, several factors suggest that this was a minor problem at the time. For one, emigration (including for tax reasons) was restricted until after the Second World War.[7] Also, the fixed exchange rate regime of the Bretton Woods system in general made international transfers of financial assets difficult.[8] Many countries, including Sweden, had strict currency controls, which in effect made such operations illegal without explicit permission. The Swedish currency act of 1940 put all currency exchanges under the control of the central bank, the Swedish Riksbank. Thus, for anyone in Sweden engaging in international tax evasion, this meant that they not only infringed tax regulations, but also committed a currency crime. After the World Wars, however, the successful internationalisation of several Swedish corporations created more opportunities for Swedish companies and their staff stationed abroad to avoid high Swedish taxes on earnings and wealth. With the collapse of the Bretton Woods regime and the development of the largely unregulated euro-dollar market from the late 1960s onwards, more opportunities arose to store wealth outside the grasp of national tax collectors.[9]

The tremendous post-war growth came to an end in the first half of the 1970s. High inflation, declining production, increasing unemployment and deficits in the balance of payments contributed to a growing discontent with the economic policies of the post-war era. As a result of these deep changes, taxation lost some of its legitimacy and political support in many OECD countries. Furthermore, individual income tax progressivity had declined since the 1970s in countries such as the USA, the UK and France.[10] In contrast, in Sweden, no reforms to reduce the high-income groups' tax burden took place prior to 1990; this delay increased the incentives for moving assets

4 Piketty (2019, chap. 10–13).
5 Steinmo (2003, 206–236).
6 Jansson (2018, 57–78).
7 Lindencrona (1972).
8 Helleiner (1994, 91–95).
9 Buggeln, Daunton and Nützenadel (2017, 1–31); Casey (1972).
10 Piketty and Saez (2007, 3–24).

to other jurisdictions.[11] In 1976, prior to the elections that ended 44 years of social democratic power in government, the famous author and popular figure Astrid Lindgren published an allegory about her absurdly high marginal tax rate of 102%.[12]

The evolution of taxation policy in the 1970s runs parallel to the rise of offshore tax havens, which also shaped the global context relevant to our case study. Vanessa Ogle recently established the deep historical roots of the offshore centres, i.e. locations allowing individuals and corporations to maintain assets while paying low or no taxes and avoiding strict regulations.[13] Between the 1920s and the 1970s, tax havens and offshore financial centres flourished, implementing elements of free-market capitalism such as low taxation and deregulation. Switzerland played a significant part in this expansion of "archipelago capitalism".

The Swiss Confederation became one of the earliest non-colonial tax havens, for several reasons: next to political neutrality and stability, there was a strong culture of secrecy in banking operations that was formalised in the 1934 banking act, which made the disclosure of client information an automatically prosecuted criminal offence.[14] The country's tax system, featuring low tax liabilities and small tax-to-GDP ratio, was another attractiveness factor.[15] It also allowed preferential taxation for distinctive groups of individuals and companies, for example, wealthy foreigners or multinational companies.

The complacency towards tax evaders was also strengthened by Swiss law which differentiated between tax evasion (*Steuerhinterziehung*), i.e. the simple fact of omitting to declare assets, and tax fraud (*Steuerbetrug*), involving an active falsification of documents. Mere tax evasion, although considered a misdemeanour and punished by a fine, was not penalised by criminal law. Until 2009, this subtle distinction allowed the non-cooperative attitude of Swiss authorities towards requests for legal or administrative assistance from third countries, and played a decisive role in the development of Switzerland as a tax haven.[16] This development met with some criticism on the international scene (USA, OECD) as early as the late 1950s. But the Swiss authorities and financial circles successfully fended off the attacks against banking secrecy and offshore services provided by the Swiss financial centre.[17] In 1963, an OECD model convention against double taxation was adopted, which

11 Buggeln, Daunton and Nützenadel (2017, as note 9).

12 Henrekson (2017).

13 Ogle (2017, 1431–1458).

14 Recent research suggests that the Swiss tax haven emerged even before 1914, with significant factors such as the growth of private wealth management, luxury tourism and tax competition between cantons. See Guex (2021).

15 Huerlimann (2018).

16 Emmenegger (2014, 146–164).

17 Farquet (2018b).

included an article on the exchange of tax information, but Swiss representatives refused any restrictions on banking secrecy.[18]

During the 1970s, at a time of the globalisation of offshore financial operations and with the development of the euro-dollar market and the breakdown of the Bretton Woods system, the Swiss tax haven was faced with a resurgence of international criticism.[19] It arose both from multilateral arenas (OECD, Council of Europe, European Commission) and bilateral negotiations. Between 1969 and 1972, the French, German and US governments separately initiated diplomatic pressure on the Swiss tax haven in order to fight tax evasion and capital flight. The only tangible result of the international pressure was the signing of a bilateral treaty introducing—at least nominally—judicial assistance for money laundering issues between Switzerland and the USA in May 1973.[20] However, the scope of the treaty was limited to criminal cases related to organised crime, as well as insider trading, meaning that individual tax fraud by ordinary US citizens could still not trigger an information exchange by Swiss banks or authorities.[21]

Banking confidentiality and low tax regimes were some of the factors, alongside political stability and neutrality, geographical location, a strong and freely convertible currency and qualified multilingual banking staff, which contributed to the attractiveness of Switzerland for international capital. The post-war boom, 1945–1975, is widely considered as the golden age of Swiss banking.[22] The total assets of Swiss banks, inflation-adjusted, increased sixfold between 1945 and 1971.[23] The development of Swiss banking was significantly shaped by the massive influx of international capital flows. The number of foreign deposits increased from 5.6 to 28.6 billion Swiss francs between 1957 and 1968.[24] This internationalisation and the dramatic growth were particularly strong in large commercial banks, but private banks such as Hentsch & Cie, traditionally specialised in cross-border wealth management, also witnessed a rapid development of their international business.[25]

14.3 The Hentsch Case—Tax Evasion and Avoidance from Sweden to Switzerland

On Friday 27 October 1972, Jacques Hentsch was arrested by the Swedish police as he was trying to board a flight from Gothenburg to Copenhagen, carrying a considerable amount of cash—451,200 Swedish crowns and

18 Farquet and Leimgruber (2015).
19 Farquet (2018a).
20 Loepfe (2011, 291–298).
21 Steinlin and Trampusch (2012, 242–259).
22 Mazbouri, Guex and Lopez (2012, 494–499).
23 Giddey (2019, 330–331).
24 Peyer (1971, 101) (not inflation-adjusted).
25 Mazbouri (2020, 93–115).

23,900 Norwegian crowns, a total equivalent to US$98,000 (in today's US$600,000)–in his luggage.[26] Currency and foreign exchange control regulations stated that an individual was only allowed to export a maximal amount of 6,000 Swedish crowns for private purposes. Yet Jaques Hentsch was not just a conventional tourist, he was the 34-year-old son of Robert E. Hentsch, partner of one of the oldest and most reputable private banks in Switzerland, Hentsch & Cie, founded in 1796 in Geneva.

Between 18 and 27 October, Hentsch had been on a business trip to Norway and Sweden, in part with his father, Robert Hentsch. After two days in Oslo meeting with representatives of a Norwegian bank and an insurance company, he flew to Stockholm and was later invited by Swedish friends to an elk hunt. Afterwards, the banker was to fly to Malmö for his final meetings with Swedish clients and banks. According to his statement to the police, however, no flight was available to Malmö that afternoon, and this forced him to fly to Copenhagen.[27]

The police interrogations of Hentsch convey an impression of a poor defence strategy (successive varying versions of the story and retractions) and provide details on the rookie mistakes made in his attempted illegal export of currency. Hentsch stated that the cash in the carry-on belonged to some of the Swiss bank's clients in Sweden and Norway. He would not mention the names of the clients, referring to the 1934 Swiss Banking Act under which a bank employee committed a federal crime if s/he disclosed any information about bank clients to third parties without their consent. But the investigators found a notebook in his luggage containing a coded list of about 50 potential clients. Even carrying a coded list could be considered serious negligence according to Swiss banking practices.

According to Hentsch, the cash he carried was to be deposited on behalf of some Swedish and Norwegian clients in Hentsch & Cie's account at SE-Banken, one of the largest banks in Sweden. The Norwegian and Swedish clients' money was to be invested in shares in major Swedish stock companies that the Swiss bank owned. Hentsch thus denied that the money was being taken to Switzerland. However, the investigation showed that the Swiss bank did not have an account at either the Gothenburg or the Malmö branch of SE-Banken. Furthermore, on the day of Hentsch's planned arrival in Malmö, the banks would be closed, making his statement questionable.[28]

During the first interrogation by the police, Hentsch stated that he had brought in the Swedish currency from Norway, a statement he retracted in later interrogations. Indeed, importing such an amount into Sweden would

26 N. N. (1973a, 118). Exchange rates conversion: OECD National Accounts Statistics: exchange rates.

27 Riksbanken Archive, Valutaavdelningen, Åtalsärenden 70/73, Swedish police report, interrogation of Jacques Hentsch on 28.10.1972.

28 Ibid.

have been a second offence, since both export and import of cash were restricted under the currency act. Hentsch confessed to bringing Norwegian cash out of Norway–and thus also violating the currency laws of Norway. However, he claimed not to have known about the Norwegian and Swedish laws against moving currency out of the country without the permission of the central banks. Regarding the violation of the Swedish currency laws, he argued that his flight arrangements had forced him to commit a technical violation of the rules. Had he been able to fly from Gothenburg to Malmö as intended, no crime would have been committed.[29]

The banker remained in custody for 25 days and was released with a travel ban in late November. On 19 December 1972, the Gothenburg lower court of justice acquitted Hentsch with a very narrow margin. The court accepted the defence that he only committed a technical violation of the currency act by boarding an outbound flight, and that Hentsch had not intended to leave the country. However, the state prosecutor, who had requested a five-month prison sentence, appealed against the acquittal. The travel ban was thus extended and Hentsch remained in Sweden. When the case was brought to the higher court in early 1973, the prosecution could present the testimony of one of the major Swedish clients of the Swiss banker, the business man Arne Lundberg,[30] who admitted that he had given Hentsch the specific task of depositing SEK 300,000 in a Swiss bank account, and not in a Swedish one in Malmö.[31] On 16 February 1973, Hentsch was sentenced to a four-month prison sentence, five-year re-entry ban and the confiscation of the incriminated SEK 451,200. Hentsch appealed to the Supreme Court, but the appeal was dismissed. He served the remainder of his sentence in the state penitentiary of Mariestad. According to a report by a Swiss Embassy representative who visited him, his detention conditions were rather good.[32] Hentsch returned to Switzerland in May 1973.

This case is in many ways just the tip of the iceberg and represents one of many examples of international tax evasion from Sweden to Switzerland–or other lower-tax jurisdictions–that occurred in the early 1970s and escaped detection. It stood out as the largest currency-bust by the Swedish customs, but this does not necessarily mean that larger amounts were not involved in other unreported cases.

29 Riksbanken Archive, Valutaavdelningen, Åtalsärenden 70/73, Swedish police report, interrogation of Jacques Hentsch on 28.10.1972.

30 N. N. (1973b, 5); IngaBritt och Arne Lundbergs forskningsstiftelse (2013, 12).

31 A[ndreas] O[platka] (1973).

32 Hentsch was well-treated, although he was the only foreigner in a prison mainly holding thieves and drug traffickers. He had access to a TV in the canteen and a radio in his cell, was happy with the "military" food and enjoyed the gardening job he had been assigned. See: Swiss Federal Archives (hereinafter SFA), CH-BAR#E2001E-01#1987/78#5042*, Letter from Faessler to Thalmann, 17.05.1973.

Table 14.1 Number of currency crimes reported and cleared from 1967 to 1979 by the Swedish authorities

	1967	1968	1969	1970	1971	1972	1973	1974	1975	1976	1977	1978	1979
Reported cases by the Riksbank*	2	1	44	27	35	29	65	72	120	114	n.i	n.i	n.i
Reported cases to the police, total	n.i	10	68	48	69	97	100	137	233	150	484	202	389
Cleared cases by the police, total	n.i.	8	41	29	44	31	43	64	39	57	42	61	49

Sources: *Sveriges Riksbank 1901-1998, serie A3A Valutastyrelsens protokoll, volymerna A3A:4 – A3A:27 (collected by Mira Barkå, archivist at Sveriges Riksbank); Kriminalstatistik, Del 1 Polisstatistik, Statistiska centralbyrån, 1967-1973; Rättsstatistik årsbok 1975-1980. N.i. = no information.

Table 14.1 shows the number of currency crime cases reported to and cleared by the Swedish police from 1967 to 1979, with some data gaps. As mentioned, the currency crimes are connected to–or an expression of–tax evasion at this time. While some breaches of the currency act were possibly not committed for the purpose of tax evasion, in the legal sense this was still the outcome, since currency exchanges without permission implied shirking taxation.

The data show an increase in the number of reported cases from the early 1970s with a peak of 484 cases in 1977. The number of cleared cases, either by closing the investigation or after a court verdict, did not increase to the same degree, suggesting that many cases took several years to process. It is also possible that cases were dropped if the evidence was deemed too weak. It is furthermore possible that the data underestimate the actual number of currency crimes, since the Riksbank's Board for Currency Affairs (*valutastyrelsen*) had some discretion in deciding which cases it would hand over to the police. The basis of the Board's powers to grant and reject applications for currency exchange as well as to report cases to the police was at times criticised for being in conflict with the basic laws of Sweden (*regeringsformen*). Most importantly, the Riksbank's institutional and legal independence made the accountability of the Board difficult to exercise.[33]

While currency exports as exemplified by the Hentsch case were illegal forms of tax evasion, alternative forms of legal tax avoidance co-existed at the same time, and gained momentum. Between 1965 and 1989, around 30,000 Swedes emigrated from Sweden for tax-related reasons.[34] Many high-profile Swedish businessmen moved to Switzerland during this time, in part for

33 Sundberg (1970, 288).
34 Lindkvist (1990).

tax reasons. Among them were Ruben Rausing, founder of Tetra Pak, who moved to Lausanne in 1969, and Ingvar Kamprad, founder of IKEA, who settled there in 1976.

14.4 Swedish and Swiss Policy Responses to Hentsch and Other Tax Evasion Cases in the Early 1970s

14.4.1 Policy Reforms in Sweden

The Hentsch case made the headlines of most newspapers in Sweden at the time of his arrest, exemplifying the strong media interest in tax evasion cases from the early 1970s. While we cannot determine the causal drivers for certain, we find that policymakers also reacted in their responses to tax evasion problems starting in the mid-1960s and intensifying in the 1970s.

In 1963, a government committee presented a proposal for legal reforms to handle tax evasion.[35] The committee rejected the idea of a general tax avoidance law on the grounds that it would be difficult to formulate without allowing unconstitutionally wide room for court discretion. Instead, the committee argued for the legislature–rather than the courts–to spearhead the fight against tax avoidance–by swiftly processing prescriptive laws to stop tax-avoidance schemes upon detection. The committee's proposed strategy was followed, but, as Gustaf Lindencrona put it, "as soon as one [tax evasion] variety was outlawed it was immediately replaced by two new ones".[36] Nevertheless, rather than considering a redesign of the tax system and its strong emphasis on redistribution and progressiveness, policy responses continued to focus on intensifying the pursuit of tax evaders. The overall objective, or fairness, of the tax system was not challenged.

Following a high-profile case of tax evasion by currency crime in 1969 (concerning Victor Hasselblad, the founder of the camera company of the same name), the government created a new commission that investigated the case as well as the related actions of the central bank. As a result, the Swedish Riksbank, in a bid to pass on some of the critique it received for its actions, launched an advertising campaign for a commission to investigate commercial banks' participation in currency crimes and tax evasion.[37] The call did not lead to such a commission being formed.

In 1974, the government appointed a commission to analyse the Swedes' attitudes to paying taxes and to tax evasion. The commission conducted a survey that found that close to a third of all Swedish taxpayers had evaded taxes at some point.[38] The two main motivations identified were an awareness of

35 Statens offentliga utredningar (1963, 52).
36 Lindencrona (1993, 160).
37 N. N. (1969, 13).
38 Vogel (1974, 499–513).

opportunities and the economic burden of the high taxes. The survey further confirmed that high-income groups had a generally more negative attitude to the tax system and a less negative one to tax evasion.[39] At the time, the marginal tax rate on labour income for the top 1% was over 70%.[40]

In 1974, the government also created the Swedish National Council for Crime Prevention (*Brottsförebyggande rådet*), which among other things was tasked to survey economic crimes and propose regulatory reforms in the area.[41] Yet, the government did not initiate a reform of the tax system but rather intensified investigatory and disciplinary actions. In addition to the Riksbank's and the prosecutor's pursuit of currency criminals, in 1975, the national tax agency (*Riksskatteverket*) conducted a nationwide tax raid focusing on share and bond trades in 1973 and 1974. The raid was reported as a success, revealing many cases where shareowners had omitted to declare share dividend payments as well as other share transactions.[42] Many thousands of self-employed taxpayers (e.g. doctors, accountants, owners of restaurants, transport and construction companies, etc.) were investigated for tax evasion.[43]

In 1980, a new act gave more discretion to the tax courts to assess what tax avoidance constituted and what "just" tax planning was, in an attempt to reverse the strategy of prohibiting schemes once detected. However, the reform, combined with the overall deregulation of the financial markets in the 1980s, may have led to less interest among prosecutors, the Riksbank and the courts to take tax evasion cases to trial. By the middle of the 1980s, important constraints in financial regulation were removed.[44] As a result, the "tax reform of the century" in 1990/1991 was in part designed to "combat tax avoidance by removing the incentives for circumventing tax", as Lindencrona put it.[45] In contrast to the earlier situation, the reforms would not rely on new tax-avoidance measures or administrative controls over the taxpayer. Instead, the less complex tax system sought to eliminate many of the pre-1990 tax system's loopholes.

14.4.2 Swiss Diplomatic Involvement and Political Debate

The Hentsch case–among other such occurrences–also affected the diplomatic level and contributed to the political debate on banking secrecy in Switzerland. Swiss diplomats and state representatives were heavily involved in the immediate handling of the Hentsch case. The Swiss embassy in

39 Henrekson (2017); Bastani and Waldenström (2019).
40 Roine and Waldenström (2005, figure 7.9, 83).
41 Kring (2016, 17–28).
42 Lundqvist (1975, 12).
43 N. N. (1974).
44 Larsson (1998).
45 Lindencrona, (1993, 157); see also Englund (2019).

Stockholm as well as the financial and economic services of the federal department of foreign affairs in Bern were rapidly and intensively mobilised to provide some support to Jacques Hentsch, as archival evidence reveals. In December 1972, the Swiss ambassador in Stockholm regretted that the Swedish press had been informed about the affair, "causing a great stir", which was all the more regrettable because Swiss banking secrecy had already from time to time been attacked in the Swedish media.[46] In early January 1973, the Swiss diplomatic service received the news that Hentsch & Cie had sent a former director to Gothenburg to ask Hentsch to resign, threatening dismissal.[47] The collaboration of the Swiss diplomatic service with the suspected criminal went as far as making the ambassador in Stockholm wonder if Hentsch should not be allowed to use diplomatic mail to beg his father and uncle (partners of the bank) to delay his forced resignation. The use of diplomatic mail for such a private matter, involving a man subjected to a travel ban, would have been a violation of the Vienna Convention on Diplomatic Relations, and was finally rejected. In spite of the negative media attention to the case, the Swiss diplomats continued to provide services to their incarcerated fellow citizen.

Although the Hentsch case was quite exceptional because it involved a family member of one of the oldest private banks in Switzerland and because it led to his conviction and prison sentence, this was not the only instance of a Swiss financier being threatened by foreign justice for violating currency regulations and exporting undeclared assets to Switzerland. In 1958–1959, Georges Rivara, a representative of the Swiss Bank Corporation, had been arrested and detained by Spanish police for helping top-level Spanish dignitaries to hide their assets in Geneva.[48] Just as in the Hentsch case, the Swiss embassy in Madrid was very active in defending the interests of the bank involved. A similar pattern occurred in December 1981, when Swiss nationals, representatives from two Swiss banks (Leu Bank and Banca del Gottardo), were arrested by the Guardia di Finanza in Rome for illegal capital export.[49] In early 1982, the two bankers were given a 14- and a 24-month suspended prison sentence.

Rather than being overly concerned with the fate of the prosecuted bankers, Swiss banking officials and diplomatic representatives were anxious about the negative impact that such affairs could have on the reputation of the Swiss banking system, or the country itself. According to a worldwide survey conducted by Swiss officials in 1973, Swedish people had a worse image of Switzerland than people from other countries and the most cited negative

46 SFA, CH-BAR#E2001E-01#1987/78#5042*, Letter from Faessler to Thalmann, 07.12.1972.

47 SFA, CH-BAR#E2001E-01#1987/78#5042*, Memo by Ramseyer, 17.01.1973.

48 Steiner (2010, 59–68).

49 Luksic (1981).

criterion was "the country of banking secrecy and business".[50] It remains hard to tell if the Hentsch case had any influence on the opinions expressed in the survey. Still, it is striking that the bad public image of Switzerland mainly relied on the reputation of its financial centre, which was perceived to be successful at the expense of others.

From the Swiss perspective, the Hentsch case should be understood as part of the larger trends of international and domestic pressure on banking secrecy and the tax evasion transactions thus enabled. As mentioned, the Swiss tax haven was faced with a resurgence of international criticism both from multilateral arenas (OECD, Council of Europe, European Commission) and bilateral negotiations.[51]

On the Swiss domestic scene, criticism of banking secrecy and tax evading practices remained low until the emergence of a "new left" during the 1970s, more aware of international and Third-World issues.[52] Following the success of the Social Democratic Party in the 1975 federal election, in 1976, Jean Ziegler, a member of the Swiss Parliament, professor of sociology and a critical voice of capitalism, published a widely discussed essay which controversially uncovered some of the tax evasion and money laundering operations facilitated by Swiss banks.[53] Ziegler also tabled several parliamentary motions on related matters: one of them explicitly mentioned the arrest of Hentsch in Sweden.[54] Ziegler requested more active cooperation from the Swiss authorities against currency trafficking, but his motion was dismissed by the government. The Federal Council replied that, while regretting that Swiss citizens broke foreign laws, no measures should be taken to punish foreign currency regulation violations, which were not considered as crimes by Swiss law.

Yet the domestic criticism of banking secrecy started to spread beyond the ranks of the political left.[55] During the mid-1970s, both budget deficits due to the economic crisis and the rise of the Swiss franc on the exchange market led federal authorities and central bankers to marginally reconsider their fundamental support of banking secrecy. The most notable expression of the growing domestic criticism of banking secrecy was an initiative introduced by the Social Democrats in 1978, calling for a lifting of banking secrecy and an extension of cooperation with other countries. It had been launched in the immediate aftermath of one of the largest scandals in Swiss banking, the

50 SFA, CH-BAR#E2001E-01#1987/78#437*, Survey about the image of Switzerland abroad, 25.10.1973, p. 13.

51 Farquet (2018a, 258–270).

52 Farquet (2017, 126–148).

53 Ziegler (1978).

54 *Amtliches Bulletin der Bundesversammlung,* 1973, Petite question Jean Ziegler du 11 décembre 1972, modifiée en petite question du 14 mars 1973. Jean Ziegler also later mentioned the case in his 1978 book, 51.

55 Farquet (2017).

Chiasso scandal in spring 1977.[56] This affair involved a branch of the Credit Suisse bank, which had specialised in hoarding Italian assets but suffered significant losses, causing the whole tax evasion scheme to collapse. However, the initiative was widely rejected (73% of the electorate) in a referendum in 1984. On the international and multilateral scene (OECD, Council of Europe), the discussions of the 1980s did not bring significant progress in the fight against tax havens either.[57] The window of opportunity for a more effective grasp of tax evasion, opened by the scandals and crises of the mid-1970s, was closed by the late 1980s. Switzerland's outstanding position in offshore markets–and its strict banking confidentiality–was maintained.

14.5 Conclusion

The international trend of financial and economic liberalisation and deregulation that marked the last decades of the twentieth century affected most countries, but not all in the same way, and not all policy areas alike. In this chapter, we have looked at how tax evasion from Sweden to Switzerland developed in the early 1970s and how it affected the tax and banking systems, respectively. In the country from which taxable wealth and income are transferred, it is the national tax system that risks losing credibility in terms of fulfilling its purposes and being applicable to all tax entities. However, in the country to which the wealth is transferred for tax evasion reasons, it is the banking system and its reputation that are put on the line under international pressure. The fact that countries in a tax evasion transaction are affected differently may be an impediment to international cooperation and coordination. Of course, the cases of Sweden and Switzerland, being opposite extremes with, at one end of the spectrum, high and progressive tax rates and, at the other end, a secretive banking system, may not be representative enough to make generalisations. More importantly, our research also highlights how the respective efforts of the Swedish authorities, on one hand, and the Swiss bank and state representatives, on the other hand, led to contrasting outcomes. The Swedish government largely failed to restore the credibility of the tax and currency regime system and ultimately adapted its regime in the 1990s and 2000s, in part due to a perceived failure to discourage tax evasion. The Swiss banks and diplomats, however, successfully pushed back international and domestic criticism on banking secrecy and maintained a non-cooperative approach until the 2008 global financial crisis, which generated a significant influx of capital.

While we could not determine the scale and scope of actual tax evasion from Sweden to Switzerland during the 1970s, we found that public and political concern with the issue increased substantially during the period. It

56 Jung (2000, 245–257).
57 Farquet (2017).

seems that the Riksbank and other actors pursued court convictions, of currency crime and tax evasion, to a higher degree from the 1970s until the mid-1980s. The policy actions taken in Sweden during the 1970s were intended to maintain the tax system's character of high tax rates and strong focus on progressiveness, by intensifying the pursuit and punishment of individual tax evaders and so discouraging tax evasion and currency crime. In Switzerland, these very same cases did not put pressure on the tax or exchange rate system, but on the banking system. By the 1970s, the international exposure of the Swiss banking system as potentially facilitating tax evasion, money laundering, white-collar crime, etc., with its secretive legal design put pressure on Swiss politicians to reform the system. However, with Swiss banks as the destination of the capital transfers, the cases were seen rather as unfortunate manifestations of quite lucrative business practices that benefited the banking system. Swiss authorities, while dissatisfied with the negative publicity of the jail sentencing, worked hand-in-hand with bank representatives to limit the consequences of the case and stick to business-as-usual.

Taking a broader perspective, the Hentsch case is also symptomatic of the rise of offshore financial centres during the 1970s. The offshore world and tax havens in particular saw significant growth between 1945 and 1970, when the "avoidance industry", including the legal architecture of offshoring practices, grew into a profession.[58] This period was followed by a boom of tax havens in the 1970s, with the end of the Bretton Woods system of fixed exchange rates and removal of capital controls, the decline of industry in the North and the related rise of services and finance. Switzerland rose into a major safe haven for capital in the post-war era. An estimate assessed that the share of European household wealth kept in Swiss banks grew from 2% in 1950 to 4.5% in 1970.[59] Those developments of offshore practices were in large part tolerated and even encouraged by governments in the Western world.[60]

The last few years seem to have witnessed a reversal of some of the historical trends we examined in this chapter. In the wake of the tax reforms of the 2000s, featuring the repeal of inheritance (2005) and wealth tax (2007), Sweden now has one of the highest rates of billionaires per capita (one for every 250,000 people).[61] In Switzerland, on the other hand, increasing international pressure following the 2008 global financial crisis has led to significant changes. Over a period spanning from 2008 to 2017, the Swiss authorities gradually accepted the principle of an automatic exchange of information with tax authorities in the account holders' country of residence, thus ending banking secrecy for foreign clients.[62] Ironically, Ingvar Kamprad, as an

58 Ogle (2017).
59 Zucman (2015, 24).
60 Ogle (2017).
61 N. N. (2019).
62 Straumann (2018, 106–125).

individual taxpayer, decided to leave his Swiss tax shelter in 2013 to spend his final years in southern Sweden, while his IKEA Empire is still organised in a deliberately complex nest of entities, with home jurisdictions in tax havens such as Luxembourg and Liechtenstein.

Archives

Riksbanken Archive, Stockholm.
Swiss Federal Archives (SFA).

Published Sources

Amtliches Bulletin der Schweizerischen Bundesversammlung, 1973.

N. N. 1969. Riksbanken startar annonskampanj idag mot privatbankerna. *Aftonbladet*, August 10, 13.

N. N. 1973a. Wie's gemacht wird. *Der Spiegel*, March 12, 118.

N. N. 1973b. *Göteborgs handels- och sjöfarts-tidning, Åtal för valutabrott*, March 14.

N. N. 1974. Riksrazzian mot läkarna är snart avslutad Jättekap gav 95 milj. *Arbetet*. Västsvenska editionen, January 25.

N. N. 2019. Wealth inequality in Sweden. In the rich man's world. *The Economist*, November 30.

Luksic, Vanja. 1981. "Italie. Banquiers suisses arrêtés : un trafic important", *Journal de Genève*, December 16.

Lundqvist, Lars. 1975. "Råd från "skattefusk-expert": Slopa alla småavdrag", *Arbetet* Västsvenska editionen, September 13, 12.

O[platka], A[ndreas]. 1973. Wende im Verfahren gegen einen Genfer Bankier in Schweden. *Neue Zürcher Zeitung*, January 1.

References

Bastani, Spencer and Daniel Waldenström. 2019. Salience of Inherited Wealth and the Support for Inheritance Taxation. *SSRN Scholarly Paper*. Rochester, NY: Social Science Research Network, https://papers.ssrn.com/sol3/papers.cfm?abstract_id=3338837. Accessed November 22 2021.

Buggeln, Marc, Martin Daunton, and Alexander Nützenadel. 2017. 'The Political Economy of Public Finance since the 1970s: Questioning the Leviathan'. In *The Political Economy of Public Finance: Taxation, State Spending and Debt since the 1970s*, eds. Marc Buggeln, Martin Daunton, and Alexander Nützenadel, 1–31. Cambridge: Cambridge University Press.

Casey, William. 1972. 'Internationalization of the Capital Markets'. Speech at the First International Meeting on Stock Exchanges, Milan, Italy, March 15th, Securities and Exchange Commission, https://www.sec.gov/news/speech/1972/031572casey.pdf. Accessed November 22 2021.

Emmenegger, Patrick. 2014. 'The Politics of Financial Intransparency: The Case of Swiss Banking Secrecy'. *Swiss Political Science Review* 20: 146–64.

Englund, Peter. 2019. Skattereformen 1991 – Hur lyckad blev den? *Ekonomisk Debatt* 47: 18–29.

Farquet, Christophe. 2017. 'The Swiss Tax Haven, the Bretton Woods System Crisis and the Globalisation of Offshore Finance'. In *The Political Economy of Public Finance: Taxation, State Spending and Debt since the 1970s*, eds. Marc Buggeln, Martin Daunton, and Alexander Nützenadel, 126–48. Cambridge: Cambridge University Press.

Farquet, Christophe. 2018a. *Histoire du paradis fiscal suisse : expansion et relations internationales du centre offshore suisse au XXe siècle*. Paris: Sciences Po.

Farquet, Christophe. 2018b. 'Les banques suisses et la libération financière. Essor et protection du marché de l'évasion fiscale, 1958–1963'. *Revue suisse d'histoire* 68(2): 298–328.

Farquet, Christophe and Matthieu Leimgruber. 2015. 'Catch Me If You Can! Tax Havens, the Market for Tax Evasion and Fiscal Diplomacy from the League of Nations to the OECD, 1920-1990'. Archive ouvert UNIGE, https://archive-ouverte.unige.ch/unige:115676. Accessed November 22 2021.

Giddey, Thibaud. 2019. *Histoire de la régulation des banques en Suisse (1914-1972)*. Publications d'histoire économique et sociale internationale 41. Genève: Librairie Droz.

Guex, Sébastien. 2021. 'The Emergence of the Swiss Tax Haven, 1816–1914', *Business History Review*, 1–20.

Helleiner, Eric. 1994. *States and the Reemergence of Global Finance: From Bretton Woods to the 1990s*. Ithaca, New York: Cornell University Press.

Henrekson, Magnus. 2017. 'Taxation of Swedish Firm Owners: The Great Reversal from the 1970s to the 2010s'. *SSRN Scholarly Paper*. Rochester, NY: Social Science Research Network, https://papers.ssrn.com/sol3/papers.cfm?abstract_id=2949277. Accessed November 22 2021.

Henrekson, Magnus and Mikael Stenkula (eds.). 2015. *Swedish Taxation: Developments since 1862*. New York: Palgrave Macmillan US.

Huerlimann, Gisela. 2018. 'Swiss Worlds of Taxation: The Political Economy of Fiscal Federalism and Tax Competition'. In *The Political Economy of Public Finance: Taxation, State Spending and Debt since the 1970s*, eds. Marc Buggeln, Martin Daunton, and Alexander Nützenadel, 83–104. Cambridge: Cambridge University Press.

IngaBritt och Arne Lundbergs forskningsstiftelse. 2013. *IngaBritt och Arne Lundbergs forskningsstiftelse*. Göteborg: IngaBritt och Arne Lundbergs forskningsstiftelse.

Jansson, Jenny. 2018. 'Creating Tax-Compliant Citizens in Sweden: The Role of Social Democracy'. In *The Leap of Faith: The Fiscal Foundations of Successful Government in Europe and America*, ed. Sven H. Steinmo, 57–78. Oxford: Oxford University Press.

Jung, Joseph. 2000. *Von der Schweizerischen Kreditanstalt zur Credit Suisse Group. Eine Bankengeschichte*. Zürich: NZZ libro.

Kring, Claes. 2016. 'En Strategi För Samhällets Samlade Åtgärder Mot Ekonomisk Brottslighet'. In *Nitton Röster Om Tjugo Års Ekobrottsbekämpning. Från 1995 Års Samlade Åtgärder till Dagens Samverkan. En Antologi*, eds. Lars Korsell and Björn Blomqvist, 17–28. Stockholm: Brå, Stockholm.

Larsson, Mats. 1998. *Staten och kapitalet: det svenska finansiella systemet under 1900-talet*. Stockholm: SNS förlag.

Lindencrona, Gustaf. 1972. *Skatter och kapitalflykt: Beskattningens Inverkan på det finansiella kapitalets och dess ägares rörlighet över Sveriges gränser mot bakgrund av den pågående ekonomiska integration i Västeuropa*. Stockholm: Jurist- och samhällsvetareförbundets Förlag.

Lindencrona, Gustaf. 1993. 'The Taxation of Financial Capital and the Prevention of Tax Avoidance'. In *Tax Reforms in the Nordic Countries, 1973–1993 Jubilee Publication*, ed. by Nordiska skattevetenskapliga forskningsrådet, 157–71. Uppsala: Iustus Förlag.

Lindkvist, Hans. 1990. *Kapitalemigration*. Stockholm: Ekonomiska forskningsinstitutet vid Handelshögsk.

Loepfe, Willi. 2011. *Der Aufstieg des schweizerischen Finanzplatzes in der Nachkriegszeit. 1945 bis 1975.* Weinfelden: Wolfau-Druck.

Mazbouri, Malik. 2020. 'La banque privée comme métaphore : "vieille banque" et "banque nouvelle" en Suisse (1800-1930): (première partie)'. *Revue suisse d'histoire* 70: 93–115.

Mazbouri, Malik, Sébastien Guex, and Rodrigo Lopez. 2012. 'Finanzplatz Schweiz'. In *Wirtschaftsgeschichte der Schweiz im 20. Jahrhundert*, eds. Patrick Halbeisen, Margrit Müller, and Béatrice Veyrassat, 467–518. Basel: Schwabe.

Ogle, Vanessa. 2017. 'Archipelago Capitalism: Tax Havens, Offshore Money, and the State, 1950s–1970s'. *The American Historical Review* 122: 1431–58.

Peyer, Kurt. 1971. *Ausmass und Bedeutung des Auslandskapitals in der Schweiz.* Zürich: Juris.

Piketty, Thomas. 2019. *Capital and Ideology.* Cambridge, London: The Belknap Press.

Piketty, Thomas, and Emmanuel Saez. 2007. 'How Progressive Is the U.S. Federal Tax System? A Historical and International Perspective'. *Journal of Economic Perspectives* 21: 3–24.

Roine, Jesper and Waldenström, Daniel. 2005. Top incomes in Sweden over the twentieth century, SSE/EFI Working Paper Series in Economics and Finance, No. 602.

Statens offentliga utredningar.1963. *Om Åtgärder Mot Skatteflykt: Betänkande Av 1953 Års Skatteflyktskommitté.* Stockholm: Esselte.

Steiner, Yves. 2010. 'Des banques suisses pincées la main dans le sac dans l'Espagne franquiste'. *L'Economie politique* 46: 59–68.

Steinlin, Simon and Christine Trampusch. 2012. 'Institutional Shrinkage: The Deviant Case of Swiss Banking Secrecy'. *Regulation & Governance* 6: 242–59.

Steinmo, Sven. 2003. 'The Evolution of Policy Ideas: Tax Policy in the 20th Century'. *The British Journal of Politics & International Relations* 5: 206–36.

Straumann, Tobias. 2018. 'Zurich and Geneva: The End of the Golden Age'. In *International Financial Centres after the Global Financial Crisis and Brexit*, eds. Youssef Cassis and Dariusz Wójcik, 106–25. Oxford: Oxford University Press.

Sundberg, Halvar. 1970. 'Riksbanken, Valutastyrelsen Och Ämbetsansvaret'. *Förvaltningsrättslig Tidskrift*: 281–302.

Vogel, Joachim. 1974. 'Taxation and Public Opinion in Sweden: An Interpretation of Recent Survey Data'. *National Tax Journal* 27: 499–513.

Ziegler, Jean. 1978. *Switzerland Exposed.* London: Allison & Busby. (Original French edition1976).

Zucman, Gabriel. 2015. *The Hidden Wealth of Nations: The Scourge of Tax Havens.* Chicago, London: The University of Chicago Press.

Personal Names Index

Subject Index